Introduction to Sport Law

John O. Spengler, JD, PhD · University of Florida

Paul M. Anderson, JD · Marquette University Law School

Daniel P. Connaughton, EdD · University of Florida

Thomas A. Baker III, JD, PhD · University of Georgia

Human Kinetics

Library of Congress Cataloging-in-Publication Data

Introduction to sport law / John O. Spengler ... [et al.].
    p. cm.
    Includes bibliographical references and index.
    ISBN-13: 978-0-7360-6532-0 (hard cover)
    ISBN-10: 0-7360-6532-6 (hard cover)
    1. Sports--Law and legislation--United States. I. Spengler, John O. (John Otto), 1962-
    KF3989.I58 2009
    344.73'099--dc22

                                2008042664

ISBN-10: 0-7360-6532-6 (print)   ISBN-10: 0-7360-8540-8 (Adobe PDF)
ISBN-13: 978-0-7360-6532-0 (print)   ISBN-13: 978-0-7360-8540-3 (Adobe PDF)

The Web addresses cited in this text were current as of October 2008, unless otherwise noted.

Acquisitions Editor: Myles Schrag; **Developmental Editor:** Amanda S. Ewing; **Assistant Editors:** Melissa J. Zavala and Christine Bryant Cohen; **Copyeditor:** Julie Anderson; **Proofreader:** Joanna Hatzopoulos Portman; **Indexer:** Betty Frizzéll; **Permission Manager:** Dalene Reeder; **Graphic Designer:** Nancy Rasmus; **Graphic Artist:** Denise Lowry; **Cover Designer:** Bob Reuther; **Photo Asset Manager:** Laura Fitch; **Photo Production Manager:** Jason Allen; **Art Manager:** Kelly Hendren; **Associate Art Manager:** Alan L. Wilborn; **Illustrator:** Denise Lowry; **Printer:** Thomson-Shore, Inc.

Printed in the United States of America   10   9

The paper in this book is certified under a sustainable forestry program.

Human Kinetics
Web site: www.HumanKinetics.com

United States: Human Kinetics, P.O. Box 5076, Champaign, IL 61825-5076
800-747-4457
email: humank@hkusa.com

Canada: Human Kinetics, 475 Devonshire Road Unit 100, Windsor, ON N8Y 2L5
800-465-7301 (in Canada only)
email: info@hkcanada.com

Europe: Human Kinetics, 107 Bradford Road, Stanningley, Leeds LS28 6 AT, United Kingdom
+44 (0) 113 255 5665
email: hk@hkeurope.com

Australia: Human Kinetics, 57A Price Avenue, Lower Mitcham, South Australia 5062
08 8372 0999
e-mail: info@hkaustralia.com

New Zealand: Human Kinetics, P.O. Box 80, Torrens Park, South Australia 5062
0800 222 062
e-mail: info@hknewzealand.com

CONTENTS

PREFACE

G iven the importance of law in our society and the increasing amount of litigation encountered in sports, the study of law in sport management programs has become a standard part of required coursework. This book is intended to serve as the text for undergraduate students in an introductory sport law class. Prior legal knowledge or experience is not required of students who use this book.

Introduction to Sport Law provides undergraduate sport management students with information in a way that is both approachable and interesting. The purpose of this text is to help undergraduate students learn the common legal concepts taught in sport management curricula. This book was developed because of a common feeling among sport management students and faculty that available sport law texts were too lengthy, contained too much legalese, were more suited for law students than undergraduate students, lacked relevance for sport management professionals, or failed to cover the topics of most interest to undergraduate sport management students. *Introduction to Sport Law* was written to address these issues and provide a book well suited for undergraduate students interested in the study of sport law.

The legal topics presented in the text are covered in most sport law courses and are intended to introduce students to the legal issues that are most critical to the management of sport. The authors' approach to this text is to begin with topics that are most fundamental to faculty and students, as well as those subjects that are most practical and relevant, and to follow with subjects that are commonly taught in sport law courses but that might have greater theoretical value than practical application.

Chapter 1 presents an overview of the U.S. legal system, including different types of law and the U.S. court system. Chapter 2 looks at tort law and product liability, while chapter 3 focuses on risk management. Chapter 4 looks at agency law, and chapter 5 covers contract law. Chapter 6 looks at employment law, including types of employment discrimination. Chapter 7 introduces the reader to constitutional law, and chapter 8 covers gender equity issues. Chapter 9 looks at intellectual property law, including trademarks, patents, and copyrights. Finally, chapter 10 focuses on antitrust law.

The chapters are organized to provide the student with unique perspectives on the topic, the importance of the topic from the perspective of both sport managers and lawyers, a clear and concise description of the law related to this topic, and legal cases and real-world examples designed to tie concepts together and provide a clear picture and understanding of how the material is applied. The organization of the chapters is designed to enhance learning. Each chapter begins with chapter objectives and a short introduction to the topic, in order to place the topic into context for the reader. The topic is addressed from a legal perspective, and each chapter is written with enough technical language to accurately and clearly state the legal concepts, while staying away from too much legalese. Once the legal topics have been described, the legal concepts are brought to life. This is done through myriad case law examples. Unique case law examples are highlighted in the In the Courtroom sidebars. Next, important points and topics are summarized, and discussion questions provide opportunities to engage students in in-class discussions. Finally, chapters 2 through 10 include moot court cases, which are hypothetical sport law scenarios that students can use as the basis for a classroom mock trial where hypothetical witnesses are called and students form teams to argue different sides of a case.

This book contains a full array of ancillaries. The Presentation Package contains slides that present the content of the chapters in convenient PowerPoint form, making it easier for instructors to prepare for and present lectures. The Test Package has multiple choice and short answer questions, making it easy for the instructor to prepare tests and quizzes based on the book's content. The Instructor Guide contains an introduction, sample syllabus, suggestions for activities, and a complete explanation of how to use the moot court cases in class. The ancillaries are available at www. HumanKinetics.com/IntroductionToSportLaw.

This book will challenge the sport law undergraduate student to think about sport law concepts and apply them to the practical world of sport management. This book will serve the needs of undergraduate sport management students in terms of both learning and practice.

INTRODUCTION

All sport management students and practitioners need a basic under standing of the law, although for different reasons. Some students may wish to study law after completing undergraduate studies, and an introduction to legal issues is the first step in a long journey of learning. For the majority of students, however, this area of study applies to their careers in sport.

Sport law affects sport at every level, from Little League teams to the highest levels of professional sport. If you plan to work in the sport industry at any of these levels, you must understand sport law. This book addresses major legal issues that you might face as a sport manager. It also introduces you to legal concepts and applications to prepare you for further study and on-the-job learning. In this introduction, you will see how different areas of law are applicable to specific levels of sport.

Tort law applies to situations where a civil wrong has been committed. Tort law does not involve criminal conduct but rather addresses conduct that is either careless or intentional that results in harm or injury to a person or property. Unlike criminal law cases, where a penalty or jail time might be imposed, a tort law case might result in an award of money (damages) from the person or organization (the defendant) that caused harm or injury. Types of torts include negligence and intentional torts, which are highly relevant to sport managers given the frequency with which these torts occur.

For those who work in recreational sports, tort law might be at issue when a counselor, coach, or supervisor fails to adequately instruct or supervise players under his or her care. Another situation giving rise to tort law claims is player and participant violence. Player-to-player incidents might involve negligence (such as negligent conduct in a pick-up basketball game) or intentional torts such as battery (e.g., an angry parent hits a volunteer coach). Tort law cases at the high school level often involve students injured in a physical education class or athletes injured in games or practices. In sport law cases in the high school setting, supervision is often at issue. Also, high schools commonly transport student athletes, coaches, and fans in connection with their athletic programs. Transportation is a liability exposure for any institution or school district and creates unique risk management issues that administrators must address.

For those who work in universities, tort law cases (negligence and intentional torts) often center on the provision of safe programs and facilities for students and a safe environment for spectators attending collegiate athletic events. Also in the university setting, students often take sport and fitness courses for credit as part of their curriculum. When injury in a sport and fitness class results in a tort claim, supervision is often the issue. Another issue that universities must address is the provision of emergency care for athletes who are injured in practices or games and the duty owed to intercollegiate athletes by institutions for which they play.

In professional sports, tort law cases often involve alleged negligent or intentional conduct that harms another person. The parties involved on either side (plaintiff or defendant) may include managers, coaches, players, or spectators. Allegations of negligent conduct on the part of management may result from conditions or situations at arenas or stadiums. Lawsuits have been brought, for example, when a spectator is hit by a foul ball at a baseball game while being distracted by a mascot. Another example in professional sport is when management is alleged to be negligent attributable to a lack of adequate security at a game (we are all familiar with recent, well-publicized incidents of players engaging in violent behavior with fans). Examples are becoming quite numerous; from incidents in professional basketball (e.g., the aggressive acts of players who entered the stands at an Indiana Pacers game) to professional baseball (e.g., professional baseball players throwing objects into the stands). Incidents of fan violence or misconduct (e.g., storming the field after a victory) also may give rise to negligence claims against management for failing to take proper security measures.

Risk management is a process or course of action that is designed to reduce the risk (probability or likelihood) of injury and loss to sport participants, spectators, employees, management, and organizations. The key terms in this definition are *reduction of risk* and *injury and loss*. Risk management often emphasizes risk reduction given that the prevention or elimination of all risk is often not feasible. Sports often involve some element of physical risk, from competitive sports such as football and ice hockey to recreational sports such as swimming and jogging.

Some students may wish to become risk managers for sport organizations, managing risk, improving safety, and striving to limit the liability of their organization. Others will be motivated to reduce the organization's risk of liability through their roles as managers and leaders in various organizations. Think about the possibilities. There are many examples of risk in sport:

- A basketball player hits his head on an unpadded wall.
- A racquetball player injures her ankle on a slick floor.
- A tennis player is injured after tripping on a defect in the court surface.
- A golf spectator is struck by lightning.
- A baseball spectator is struck by a foul ball after being distracted by a mascot.
- A swimmer is paralyzed after diving into shallow water.
- A baseball player is injured after sliding into an immovable base.

A risk manager would be responsible for safety in a multitude of situations and for the prevention or reduction of loss through potential litigation.

Contract law is relevant to everyone who wishes to work in sport management, and sport agents and upper-level managers of sport organizations must have in-depth knowledge of contract law. A contract is an agreement between people that is enforceable by law if certain conditions are met. Contracts are common in sports. For example, an arena or stadium might have contracts with food and beverage providers, security companies, and employees. Player contracts (agreements to play for a particular team), scholarships, and coaching contracts (employment contracts) are common types of agreements. Additionally, sport managers will be involved in drafting (for review and approval by legal counsel and management) and administering waivers (a type of contract).

Agency law often brings up images of sport agents who represent a big-time athlete and enjoy all the perceived perks of the profession. The 1990s film *Jerry McGuire* continues to intrigue people and romanticize this profession. Agency, however, deals with more than just sport agents. Employees within a sport organization are considered agents and act on behalf of the organization in executing contracts and performing other essential tasks. Therefore, the law of agency applies to the sport manager in numerous situations and in everyday business matters, such as when employees execute contracts on behalf of a sport business. Agency law affects all areas of sport management because the agency relationship is a key part of business operations in sport.

Employment law applies to all sport managers who are involved in personnel issues, and it encompasses an extremely wide range of issues. Issues of employment are issues about people, and people are different. We differ in age, race and ethnic background, gender, the way we look, our physical abilities, our minds and emotions, and our beliefs, opinions, and outlooks on life. This very uniqueness, and the interaction of personnel with management, can result in an efficient, effective work environment or something quite the opposite. When employee relations fall apart, the legal issues involved are quite diverse, often overlap, and sometimes become complex. Common situations in which lawsuits arise in the employment context include these:

- A qualified female personal trainer is not hired for a job.
- A qualified minority assistant athletic director is not promoted.
- A coach leaves his job before his contract expires.
- A woman's work situation is so uncomfortable that she must quit.
- A maintenance worker is injured on the job.

Therefore, employment law is a critical area for sport managers because it has relevance to management positions in sports.

Constitutional law is directly applicable to sports. Sports are an integral part of a free society where athletes and participants can learn, grow, and compete in a manner that is best suited to their lifestyles. The Preamble of the Constitution of the United States provides the citizens with a means to establish justice, ensure domestic tranquility, promote general welfare, and secure the blessings of liberty. It is by understanding the words found in the Preamble that we start to understand the purpose of sports in a democratic society. There are four broad rights relevant to sports that all citizens enjoy: personal freedom, civil rights, due process, and privacy. Constitutional rights are relevant in high school, university, and professional sport settings and address such issues as school prayer (personal freedom), discrimination (civil rights), student-athlete drug testing (privacy), and employee rights (due process).

Gender equity is a legal issue of critical importance for sport managers, particularly those who work in schools. The primary focus of case law dealing with gender discrimination in athletics is whether educational institutions have complied with Title IX. The key compliance issues are whether institutions or organizations fall within the court's recommended proportionality range of percentage of opportunities versus percentage of total population for a given gender. An understanding of gender equity issues is essential to coaches and school officials in selecting which sports will be made available.

Intellectual property law encompasses copyright, trademark, the right of publicity, and patent issues. The purpose of this area of law is to protect the creative endeavors of individuals and organizations. Copyright laws provide protection to authors of written works, musical works and performances, movies, and other audiovisual works. Television and radio broadcasts of live sporting events are also covered under copyright law. Intellectual property law is applicable to many who work in the sport industry, including such areas as university and professional sports, sport media, marketing, and sport equipment manufacturing and sales.

Antitrust law centers on the issue of competitive markets. Although this is a complex area of law, the premise is easy to comprehend: Markets should be competitive and free of restraints. To this end, state and federal laws have been enacted to protect markets from unlawful restraints on trade and from activities such as price fixing and the formation of monopolies (where there is only one provider of a product or service). The primary federal laws that govern antitrust issues are the Sherman Antitrust Act, Clayton Act, Sports Broadcasting Act, and the Curt Flood Act. Antitrust issues are more common than you might suspect and have been at the forefront of several highly publicized media events involving player salaries, the movement of professional teams to new cities, draft and eligibility issues, broadcasting rights, and sponsorships. Thus, those who work in professional and collegiate sports, sports media and broadcasting, and a variety of other areas need to understand antitrust law.

The implications and importance of law to sport management are clear. If you are involved directly with a lawsuit, an understanding of legal issues and implications may help you handle the legal process and the subsequent stresses. More important, an understanding of law might help you to avoid liability in the first place by knowing how to properly plan and prepare for potential problems.

U.S. Legal System

CHAPTER OBJECTIVES

After reading this chapter, you will know the following:

- The primary sources of law in the U.S. legal system
- The function and process of the federal and state court systems
- The key types of law in the United States
- Common legal resources

© Purestock/age fotostock

An understanding of the U.S. legal system is important for all sport managers. In today's litigious society, sport managers can benefit from understanding and operating within the law. Sport managers also should know how to obtain legal and risk management information, such as statutes, case law, and published standards and guidelines, that can be used to demonstrate the standard of care owed to clients, athletes, and participants. This chapter introduces the U.S. legal system, discussing sources of law, the court system, common legal resources, and types of law.

Sources of U.S. Law

A primary source of U.S. law is the common law tradition that began in medieval England. Another important source is constitutional law, which incorporates the U.S. Constitution and all of the 50 state constitutions. Statutory law includes statutes enacted by Congress and state legislatures as well as ordinances passed by city and county governments. Administrative law is another source of U.S. law and is created by the many administrative agencies (such as the Federal Trade Commission, National Labor Relations Board, and Food and Drug Administration). These important sources of law are briefly described in the following sections.

Common Law

stare decisis—The practice of the courts in following case precedent (prior legal case law decisions) in rendering opinions.

The English common law system forms the basis of many countries' legal systems, including the U.S. legal system. This system of laws was derived from centuries of general rules, customs, and experience. Courts developed common law rules based on decisions of actual legal disputes. In an effort to be consistent, judges based their decisions on the principles of previously decided cases. Using former cases, or precedents, to assist in deciding new cases is the basis of the American and English judicial systems. This practice is known as **stare decisis**. Under this doctrine, judges often follow the precedents established through prior legal case decisions.

Today, this source of law is referred to as common law, judge-made law, or case law.

Constitutional Law

constitutional law—The law relevant to the constitution of the United States and to state constitutions.

The U.S. federal government and every state have separate written constitutions that set forth the organization, powers, and limits of their respective governments. **Constitutional law** is the law expressed in these constitutions. State constitutions often vary; some are modeled closely after the U.S. Constitution, and others provide even greater rights to their citizens. The U.S. Constitution, the supreme law of the United States, was adopted in 1787 by representatives of the 13 newly formed states. Initially, people expressed fear that the federal government might abuse its power. To alleviate such concerns, the first Congress approved 10 amendments to the U.S. Constitution, commonly known as the Bill of Rights, which were adopted in 1791. The Bill of Rights limits the powers and authority of the federal government and guarantees many civil (individual) rights and protections.

Although the Bill of Rights does not directly apply to the states, the U.S. Supreme Court has held that the Fourteenth Amendment includes many of the principal guarantees of the Bill of Rights, thereby making them applicable to the individual states. So, neither the federal government nor state governments can deprive individuals of those rights and protections. However, the rights provided by the Bill of Rights are not absolute. Many of the rights guaranteed by the Bill of Rights are described in very broad terms. For instance, the Fourth Amendment prohibits unreasonable search and seizure but does not define what this entails. Ultimately, the U.S. Supreme Court interprets the Constitution, thereby defining our rights and the government's boundaries. More information about how Constitutional law affects the field of sport management is provided in chapter 7.

Statutory Law

State and federal legislators enact laws termed *statutes.* Local governments, such as cities and counties, create laws termed *ordinances.* Together, these statutes and ordinances are known as statutory law. **Statutory law** covers a myriad of subjects, such as crime, civil rights, housing, and all matters that the legislative branch has constitutional power to legislate. Statutory law is limited to matters of jurisdiction. For example, federal statutory law is limited to matters of federal jurisdiction; similar limitations hold for local and state ordinances and statutes. When jurisdictions overlap (e.g., when two levels of governments have jurisdiction), conflicts may arise. When this happens, the **doctrine of supremacy** applies; federal law will prevail over state law, and state law will prevail over local law (Carper, Mietus, & West, 2000). Statutory law also cannot violate the U.S. Constitution or the relevant state constitution.

Several federal statutes apply to sport management, including the Americans with Disabilities Act (ADA) and the Volunteer Immunity Act. State statutes vary from state to state and include laws that involve the use of automated external defibrillators as well as various immunity provisions such as Good Samaritan and Recreational User Statutes.

Administrative Law

Thousands of local, state, and federal **administrative agencies,** which are specialized bodies created by legislation at all three (local, state, and federal) governmental levels, are granted lawmaking authority to regulate certain activities. These agencies investigate problems within their own jurisdictions, create laws termed **rules and regulations,** and conduct hearings, very similar to court trials, to decide whether their rules have been violated and, if so, what sanctions should be levied. Federal administrative agencies including the National Labor Relations Board (NLRB), Internal

statutory law—Laws (legislation or codes) created by legislators at the state and federal levels.

doctrine of supremacy—A doctrine based on the supremacy clause in the U.S. Constitution stating that the U.S. and state constitutions and federal legislation are superior to common law and state legislation.

administrative agencies—Governmental agencies that have the authority to create laws, rules, and regulations to carry out the responsibilities of government.

rules and regulations—Policies or principles that are publicly agreed upon and that govern an activity or organization.

Revenue Service (IRS), and Occupational Health and Safety Administration (OSHA), as well as a number of local and state agencies, enact and enforce numerous laws every year that affect sport management.

Types of U.S. Law

U.S. law may be classified into criminal and civil law. Both criminal and civil law attempt to persuade citizens to act in ways that are not harmful to others. Nevertheless, these types of law vary in their means of doing so.

criminal law—The body of law that identifies what behavior is criminal and stipulates penalties for violations.

Criminal Law

Criminal law is the body of law that identifies what behavior is criminal and stipulates penalties for violations. The majority of criminal laws are statutes, enacted by the U.S. Congress or a state legislature. The statutory law of individual states regarding criminal law is found in books typically termed *penal codes*.

In a criminal court, which hears only cases involving the alleged commission of misdemeanors and felonies, the people (general public) are represented by a governmental representative (district attorney). To convict a criminal, the district attorney must show beyond a reasonable doubt that the accused person committed the crime. A convicted criminal may be punished by fines, community service, probation, imprisonment, or any combination of these. Although the courts have the power to order restitution to a victim of a crime, the victim usually leaves the courtroom empty handed. Athletes and sport managers may face criminal charges if they violate criminal statutes on theft, stalking, robbery, or assault and battery.

AP Photo/Mary Altaffer

When Marion Jones plead guilty to lying to investigators about her use of performance-enhancing drugs, she was sentenced in federal court under criminal law.

Civil Law

Civil law is the body of state and federal law that pertains to civil, or private, rights that are enforced by civil actions. The vast majority of lawsuits involving sport management involve civil law. Civil courts hear noncriminal matters between individuals, organizations, businesses, and governmental units and agencies. The two parties involved in a civil lawsuit are the plaintiff, which is the person, group, or organization bringing the lawsuit (e.g., a participant injured in a sport event), and the defendant, which is the person, group, or organization being sued (e.g., the coaches and athletic director). It is common for several defendants to be named in a civil suit. In a civil trial, a plaintiff only has to show by a preponderance (a greater amount) of evidence that the defendant is liable. The burden of proof in a criminal trial requires that a court find the criminal guilty beyond a reasonable doubt, whereas the civil standard only requires finding the defendant 51% responsible (preponderance of the evidence). Unlike in a criminal trial, the plaintiff may leave the courtroom with a verdict that will require the defendant to provide financial compensation to the plaintiff. The overwhelming majority of lawsuits involving sport managers and programs focus on civil law and claims.

civil law—A category of law in which monetary damages are often claimed as a result of an act or failure to act by another that results in harm to persons or property.

Anatomy of a Civil Lawsuit

When an individual decides to seek compensation through the civil court system, his or her attorney typically will file a **complaint.** This document, which begins a lawsuit, details the facts that the plaintiff believes justifies the claim and requests damages that the plaintiff is seeking from the defendant. The complaint is often served via a **summons,** typically delivered by a court officer, which notifies the defendant that a lawsuit has been filed against him and provides a certain amount of time for him to respond to the complaint.

On receiving a complaint, a defendant typically will hire an attorney who will represent the defendant's interests. The defendant's attorney usually files an **answer,** which normally denies some or all of the allegations listed in the complaint. In lieu of an answer, the defendant's attorney may seek a dismissal of the complaint. This is referred to as a motion to dismiss and is used when a complaint is legally insufficient to justify an answer. The complaint and answer combined are known as **pleadings.**

After these initial pleadings, the case enters what is commonly known as the **discovery** phase. The discovery phase begins with the filing of the answer and ceases at the beginning of the trial. This pretrial time is when both parties obtain facts and information regarding the case, including information from the other parties, to assist in preparing for trial. Common discovery procedures include requests to produce physical evidence and the use of interrogatories and depositions. A request to produce evidence occurs when one party asks the other to produce, and provide for the inspection of, any designated physical evidence that the second party

complaint—A formal accusation of wrongdoing brought by a plaintiff against a defendant in a legal case.

summons—Official notification to a defendant that he or she must respond to a complaint.

answer—The response of a defendant to a complaint (accusation of wrongdoing).

pleadings—Formal statements in legal documents prepared by attorneys that provide details about a case and may include an answer, a complaint, or both.

discovery—The part of the legal process that involves gathering information verified by oath in preparation for trial.

controls or possesses and that the first party believes to be relevant to the case. For example, attorneys may request to inspect equipment or facilities (e.g., bleachers, gymnasium, softball field) that were used by a plaintiff at the time of injury. Furthermore, documents such as preseason medical records, staff training records, parental permission forms, accident report forms, facility and equipment maintenance records, and waivers can also be requested. **Interrogatories** are written questions sent by an attorney from one party in the lawsuit to another party named in the suit. These questions must be answered within a specified amount of time, and they can be used as evidence in a trial. A **deposition** is a pretrial questioning of a witness. Attorneys representing both parties are typically present at depositions, where a witness answers questions, under oath, which are recorded by a court stenographer. Like interrogatories, deposition transcripts can be used as evidence at a trial.

If there are no disputes over the facts of a case, the case may be decided without going to trial. In a motion for **summary judgment,** the moving party (the one making the request) argues that there is no question of fact (the facts are agreed upon) and that the relevant law requires that he or she be awarded judgment. This motion can be requested at any time but typically is sought after discovery, when a party believes discovery demonstrates that there are no real factual disputes. If the motion is awarded, no trial will take place.

Either party or the court can request a pretrial conference or hearing, which usually takes place after the discovery phase is complete. The main purpose of such informal conferences is to identify the matters in dispute and to plan the course of the trial. At such hearings, a judge may encourage the parties to reach an out-of-court settlement. If a settlement cannot be achieved, the case typically proceeds to trial. Most cases result in settlements.

In a civil trial, the plaintiff usually has to decide whether she wants the case to be heard by a jury. The plaintiff gives the opening statement, which may be followed by the defendant's opening statements and is designed to inform the triers of fact (the judge or the jury) about the matter and the types of evidence that will be presented during the case. Following opening statements, the plaintiff presents her case. The plaintiff then calls and examines her witnesses. Usually, witnesses are then cross-examined by the defendant, redirected by the plaintiff, and then recrossed by the defendant. The defendant then repeats the process with her witnesses.

During trial, two types of witnesses may be called. Fact witnesses are used because they have specific facts (perhaps something they saw or heard) regarding the matter. **Expert witnesses** (also referred to as forensic experts) are used to help educate the judge and jury by sharing their expertise and knowledge. Expert witnesses are typically asked to provide testimony regarding the professional standards that apply to the incident and to the degree that the defendant met, or did not meet, those standards.

Once both parties have completed their questioning, final closing statements are made. After these final statements, the judge in a jury trial pro-

interrogatories—A type of discovery where written information is gathered in preparation for trial.

deposition—A type of discovery where verbal information is provided by a witness in preparation for trial.

summary judgment—A written document (motion) produced by attorneys and brought before the court claiming that a case should be decided based on the applicable law, given that there are no remaining facts in dispute.

expert witnesses—A person who, through skill, training, background, education, or experience, renders opinions on matters relevant to legal cases.

vides the jury instructions regarding the options the jury has in reaching a decision based upon the applicable laws. After deliberating, the jury renders a verdict. In a trial without a jury, a judge can either recess the court while making a decision or render a decision shortly after closing statements.

After the trial court's decision, verdicts can be appealed. The party that lost the case can make a request (an appeal) to have the court proceedings reviewed by a higher court in hope that the lower court's decision will be reversed. The appellate court can agree with (affirm) the lower court's decision, disagree with (reverse) it, send the case back to the lower court (remand) with instructions for a new trial, or modify the lower court's judgment.

U.S. Court System

The U.S. court system is hierarchical in nature (see figure 1.1) and consists of a variety of courts at both the state and federal levels as well as some specialized administrative courts. There are also specific courts designed to hear only certain types of legal disputes, for example, bankruptcy and small claims courts. The vast majority of legal disputes are resolved prior to trial. If they do proceed to trial, federal and state judges preside in these courts to settle cases brought before them. The different types and levels of courts are described in the following sections.

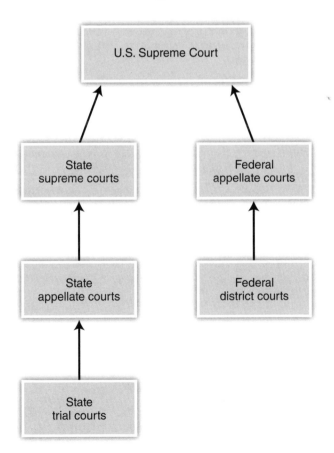

Figure 1.1
Hierarchy of the U.S. court system.

Trial Courts

The U.S. court system is hierarchical in nature. The lowest level, or entry-level court, typically termed a *trial court* or *district court,* is followed by an intermediate appellate court; the highest court typically is a supreme court. Trial courts carry out the initial proceedings (trials) in lawsuits. These trials have three distinct purposes (Carper et al., 2000):

1. To determine the facts of the dispute (What happened between the parties?)
2. To decide what rules of law should be applied to the facts
3. To administer those rules

At the end of every trial, the court renders judgment in favor of one of the parties. Usually, when well-established existing law is applied, these disputes are resolved at the trial court level and most are not appealed.

Appellate Courts

Within a certain amount of time following a trial court's final decision, the losing party can appeal the decision. An appeal is a formal request to a higher court to review the lower court's decision. These review courts are known as appellate courts. Having three or more judges, these courts review lower court decisions for substantive and procedural correctness. In other words, they attempt to determine whether the proper law was correctly applied to the issue at hand.

Appellate courts must work from a court transcript of what was said and what evidence was used in the lower court, such as contracts, photographs, business records, waivers, and leases. State appellate courts do not review new evidence, listen to witnesses, make different or new determinations of fact, or use a jury. Instead, these courts review written briefs prepared by attorneys that include legal arguments about how the law was incorrectly stated or applied to the facts that were presented to the lower court. The appellate court determines whether the lower court correctly applied the law.

remand—The act of sending an appealed legal case back to the trial court to determine an issue of fact.

If an appellate court determines that a lower court incorrectly applied or interpreted the law, it will modify or reverse the lower court's decision and either provide a new revised judgment or **remand** (send back) the case to the trial court for a new trial to be conducted using the appellate court's instructions. Even if it is determined that an error occurred at the trial court, it may not be sufficient to overturn the trial court's decision. A slight or insignificant error, or one that is not prejudicial to the interests of the appellant, is unlikely to affect the original ruling of a case.

If an appeals court decides a case, the judges typically write and publish a written opinion. In such an opinion, the appellate court will state the rules of law applied as well as the rationale for reaching its decision. When reaching decisions, appellate courts interpret and apply relevant statutory law along with appropriate common law derived from precedent. On occasion, when there is no controlling statute or precedent that applies to a case, an appellate court may create a new rule or extend an existing principle to the case at hand. Thus, new law is created and is termed **judge-made law** or **case law**.

judge-made law— Legal decisions made in a court of law by a judge.

case law—Published legal decisions decided in a court of law by a judge or jury.

U.S. Federal Court System

The federal court system is a three-level model consisting of (1) trial courts known as district courts, (2) intermediate courts of appeal, and (3) the U.S. Supreme Court. The federal court system also includes some special courts such as maritime, military, and bankruptcy courts. The federal court system conducts trials involving federal matters, such as the enforcement of federal laws. Therefore, where a federal question arises (a federal law is at issue in a case), the case will likely be held in federal court. Even where a federal law is at issue, however, the damages (i.e., money sought) in a case must be at least $75,000 for the case to go to federal court. Another way for a case to be brought to federal court, as opposed to state court, is if there is diversity jurisdiction. **Diversity jurisdiction** occurs where parties (individuals or organizations) to the lawsuit are from different states. For example, a fan from Tennessee might be injured at a stadium in Alabama. A subsequent lawsuit might be held in federal court given that a person and an organization (stadium management) are from different states.

diversity jurisdiction—The jurisdiction of a federal court to hear a case brought by people and organizations from different states.

The United States is divided into 96 federal judicial districts, and there is at least one U.S. district court in each state and territory. The number of district courts per state varies depending on population changes and caseloads. The U.S. courts of appeal consist of 13 federal judicial circuits, which hear cases appealed from the U.S. district courts (see figure 1.2). The highest level of the federal court system is the U.S. Supreme Court. Nine justices, appointed by the U.S. president for lifetime appointments, sit on the U.S. Supreme Court. The Court acts as the final appeal for the federal courts of appeals. Further information on U.S. federal courts may be found at www.uscourts.gov.

State Court System

The state court system parallels the federal system, although the states may give their courts different names than the federal system. All states have entry-level (trial) courts, but they may be named a circuit court in one state, a supreme court in another, and something else in another. Trial court decisions are made by judges or juries. These decisions, made at the local level, are not published. Therefore, the full case decisions that you are able to read and that are publicly available only come from the upper level state courts (courts of appeal and supreme courts), not the trial courts. Every state also has some form of an appellate system and specialized courts

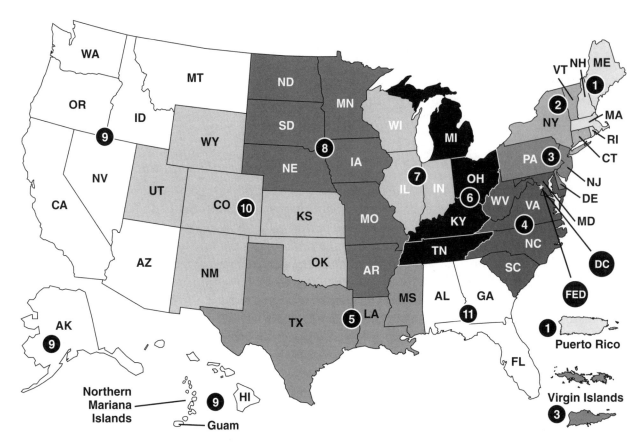

Figure 1.2 Federal judicial circuits.

for specific legal matters. The typical hierarchy of the state court system is the trial court, the court of appeals, and the state supreme court. Further information about state court systems can be found at the National Center for State Courts Web site at http://ncsconline.org.

Legal Resources

primary sources— Sources of law derived from original sources such as published court decisions or statutes.

secondary sources— Sources of law derived from sources secondary to an original source such as articles that interpret or analyze case law decisions or statutes.

Sport managers and practitioners should study aspects of the law that relate to the field, although at times they may have to obtain specific legal information. Legal resources can be grouped into primary and secondary sources. **Primary sources** consist of court decisions (case law), U.S. and state constitutions, statutes, and administrative agency regulations. Primary sources are the actual law and, therefore, are the primary legal sources relied upon in determining what the law requires. In contrast, **secondary sources** examine, inform, or review various legal topics and issues. Examples of secondary sources include law review articles and legal encyclopedias, textbooks, dictionaries, and journals (e.g., *The Sport & Recreation Law Reporter, Journal of Legal Aspects of Sport*). Although secondary sources should never be relied on as legal authority, they can be very useful to the sport manager by providing information about a specific legal issue.

Case law (also referred to as court opinions) is published in a series of books known as reporters. At the federal level, all reported U.S. district court cases are published in the reporter known as the *Federal Supplement.* U.S. circuit court cases (courts of appeal) are reported in the *Federal Reporter.* U.S. Supreme Court cases are typically reported in three major sets of reporters: the *Supreme Court Reporter,* the *United States Reports,* and the *United States Supreme Court Reports Lawyers' Edition.*

Most state court opinions are published by the West Publishing Company in a set of reporters referred to as regional reporters. Every regional reporter prints opinions from courts based on a specific geographical region. A total of seven regional reporters each print decisions for a number of states (e.g., Southern [So.], Southeastern [S.E.], Southwestern [S.W.], Northeastern [N.E.], Northwestern [N.W.], Pacific [P.], or Atlantic [A.] reporters). California and New York have their own official reporters for publishing decisions from their courts. Additionally, reporters are grouped according to series, starting with a first series and moving to additional series designated as "2d," "3d," etc.

Although reports and the cases they contain are typically found in law libraries, case decisions can also be obtained from the Internet. Although certain legal search engines and databases, such as *Lexis* and *Westlaw,* may only be accessed for a fee and therefore are primarily only used by members of the legal profession, the *Lexis/Nexis Academic Universe* database is available through many academic institutions. This database permits students and researchers to obtain primary and secondary sources and offers keyword search engines for law reviews, legal news, statutes (i.e., codes), and case law. Contact your local or institutional library to see whether you have access to *Lexis/Nexis Academic Universe.*

Summary

A challenge for sport managers is to recognize and understand legal issues, effectively manage such issues, and reduce the possibility that legal problems will result. A sport manager can best manage such issues by understanding the sources of law, the U.S. court system, types of legal resources, and the steps in a lawsuit. By being familiar with these legal topics, as well as the relevant laws and legal issues that affect the sport industry, a sport manager can reduce or eliminate many legal problems.

Knowledge and understanding of key aspects of the law have become increasingly important for sport managers in today's litigious environment. It is useful for sport managers to know how to obtain legal information, such as statutes, case law, and published standards and guidelines. Likewise, it is important to understand when it is best to obtain legal assistance. Because the law is constantly changing, a wise professional will stay abreast by attending relevant conferences, reading the professional literature, and seeking advice from legal professionals.

DISCUSSION QUESTIONS

1. Identify and describe the major sources of U.S. law.
2. Explain the primary differences between criminal and civil law.
3. Describe the names and structure of your state's court system.
4. Identify and explain the steps in a civil trial.
5. Identify which reporter publishes your state's court opinions.
6. Obtain and read a sport management–related case opinion from a reporter or via the Internet.

Tort Law and Product Liability

CHAPTER OBJECTIVES

After reading this chapter, you will know the following:

- The elements of negligence liability and how it applies to sport
- The defenses to the tort of negligence and the application to sport management
- Intentional torts and their application to sport settings
- Product liability and its application to sport management

Lisa Blumenfeld/Getty Images

tort—A civil wrong or injury that often results in monetary damages.

damages—Money that is sought for a wrong committed by another in tort or contract.

negligence—An unintentional tort that results in personal injury.

This chapter addresses a topic with important practical implications for sport managers: tort law. A **tort** is a category of law that encompasses situations where a civil wrong has been committed. A tort does not involve criminal conduct but rather conduct that is either careless or intentional that results in harm or injury to a person or property. Unlike criminal law, where a penalty or jail time might be imposed, a tort might result in an award of money **(damages)** from the person or organization (the defendant) that caused injury or harm. Types of torts include negligence and intentional torts, which are discussed in this chapter and are of critical importance to sport managers given the frequency in which they occur. This chapter discusses negligence, intentional torts, and product liability as they apply to sport management.

Negligence

Negligence occurs when someone sustains personal injury but there is no intent to cause injury. The injured person (the plaintiff) may initiate a negligence lawsuit in which she seeks money for the injury. Examples of negligence include lawsuits against fast food chains for claims that fast food made an individual overweight or obese and the famous case of the woman who sued McDonald's after she spilled hot coffee in her lap. Most negligence cases never go to trial, because the cases are settled by the attorneys and their clients.

Examples of negligence occur in the sport world. Within the broad category of torts, negligence is the most likely type of lawsuit a sport manager will face. We know about many of these negligence cases from either the media or published legal decisions. Thousands of published cases involve negligence in sport. An example of a negligence case in the sport setting is *Green v. Konawa Independent School District* (2005). After participating in an elementary school track and field competition at the Konawa track and field facilities, Green, a fourth-grade student, was instructed by a teacher to sit on one of the stands outside the facility to wait until the event was completed. Four students, including Green, climbed to the top level of the stands. One of the students, who weighed more than 200 pounds (more than 91 kilograms), leaned over the top rail, causing the stands to collapse. Green was hurt in the fall, and his father sued the school district, alleging that the school was negligent for failing to secure the stands and adequately supervise the students.

In this section, we look at the elements of negligence, gross negligence, and defenses to negligence.

Elements of Negligence

The plaintiff (injured person) has the burden of proving her case when negligence is alleged. When lawsuits are brought, the plaintiff goes on the offensive and attempts to provide reasons for why she should prevail in a lawsuit; however, the plaintiff must follow rules set forth by the legal system. The rules, or parts of the case, that must be proved are often called *elements.* With negligence, four key elements must be proved:

- Standard of care
- Breach of duty
- Causation
- Injury (damages)

Each element must be found to exist before a plaintiff may recover (be awarded money) in a negligence case. Figure 2.1 illustrates the elements of negligence.

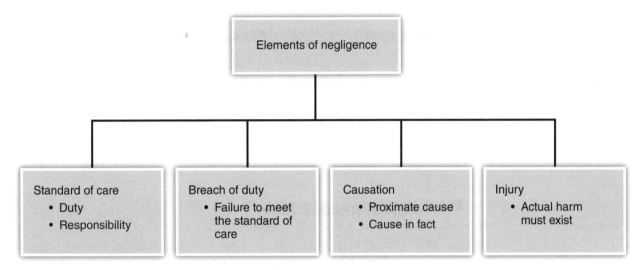

Figure 2.1
Elements of negligence.

✂ *Standard of Care*

Negligent conduct occurs when a defendant fails to meet his duty or responsibility (standard of care) for the protection of others and, as a result, causes another to be injured or harmed. Establishing the standard of care is critical to whether a case is won or lost. The **standard of care** is the duty or responsibility owed by a defendant (this could be a person or an organization) to another. The responsibility of the sport practitioner is often viewed in the context of providing a reasonably safe sport environment for those under her care. The following list provides factors that a court might consider when determining the standard of care. Often, a combination of these factors influences the final determination of the standard of care, or responsibility, owed by a sport manager.

- *Case precedent.* Courts refer to the outcomes and facts of prior cases to determine the standard of care (the duty or responsibility of the plaintiff). The practice of using prior legal decisions with similar facts to determine the outcome of later cases is referred to as stare decisis. This doctrine, which provides stability and predictability in the law, is also flexible because some courts may overrule prior decisions in cases where public policy or other relevant legal matters dictate the need for change.

standard of care— The duty, or responsibility, of persons to act in a reasonable manner to provide for the safety of others.

- *Rules and regulations.* The standard of care might be written in a rule put forth by a regulatory agency. For example, there are rules governing sliding in high school baseball games, the number of lifeguards required for a pool of a certain size, slide tackling in soccer, and contact in university football. Certain sport-specific rules might help determine the standard of care in a sport negligence lawsuit.

- *State and federal laws.* Legislation may mandate a certain act. For example, in some states, fitness centers and high school athletic departments are required to have automated external defibrillators (AEDs) on the premises. State law dictates the standard of care for these facilities, mandating a duty to have these devices on the premises and specifying the circumstances in which they should be used.

- *Community practice or industry standard.* The standard of care might be influenced by what others in the industry (i.e., **industry standard**) or community are doing. For example, do other softball complexes in the city or state adhere to certain safety practices or have similar safety features at their facilities? If the majority of facility supervisors in the region have lightning safety plans in place to protect players from injury, for example, a lightning safety plan for softball complexes in that region might be considered the standard of care. Therefore, the sport manager should know what others in the community and industry are doing with regard to safety.

- *Federal regulatory agencies.* Certain federal agencies may have guidelines and recommendations relevant to sport safety with bearing on the standard of care in sport negligence cases. For example, the **Consumer Product Safety Commission (CPSC)** has guidelines regarding the safety of moveable soccer goals; these guidelines may be used by courts in determining whether the standard of care was met. The CPSC recommends that moveable soccer goals provide warnings, be anchored on level ground, and be constructed according to certain guidelines. These recommendations might be used by a court in determining the standard of care if a person is injured when a soccer goal tips over on him.

- *Professional associations.* **Position statements** are often published by organizations such as the National Collegiate Athletic Association (NCAA), the American College of Sports Medicine (ACSM), and the National Athletic Trainer's Association (NATA) that provide guidelines on subjects as diverse as lightning safety and equipment safety. Guidelines contained in association position statements might be used by the courts in determining the standard of care.

- *Agency and organization manuals.* An agency's own policies and procedures manual might be used in determining whether it met its own standards. Lawyers in negligence cases often seek out the agency policy as evidence in determining the standard of care. For example, if language in an agency policy manual states that staff members must call 911 in the event of a head injury, this might be construed as the standard of care as it pertains to the emergency action plan.

industry standard—Standard practice within an industry or profession.

Consumer Product Safety Commission (CPSC)—A federal regulatory agency that provides safety guidelines and recommendations for consumer products.

position statement—A professional association's stance on a matter of public importance. Position statements often provide recommendations on safety matters.

- *Expert opinion.* The opinions of **forensic experts** from various fields might be used to help a court determine the standard of care. In sport, experts come from a wide variety of disciplines: sport management, engineering, medicine, psychology, economics, and others. Engineers might be called to consult on a sport negligence case where structural or equipment design defects are at issue. Economists might provide testimony as to lost future earnings when a young victim loses the ability to work for the remainder of his life as he had anticipated. Sport safety experts might provide testimony on supervision, instruction, emergency planning, or other issues specific to the sport setting.

A person or organization's duty (standard of care) is triggered by the relationship with the injured person (the plaintiff). Certain relationships automatically give rise to a duty to protect another person from an unreasonable risk of harm. For example, although a swimming pool patron is under no legal obligation to rescue a fellow swimmer in distress, the lifeguard is responsible because of the nature of his relationship to the patron (e.g., it is the lifeguard's job to render assistance). The same idea holds true for coaches and players, sport instructors and students, and others who provide a service with an associated obligation. Consider the In the Courtroom case on page 18 where the court recognized a duty owed by the school and coach to an injured student-athlete.

The duty might also arise in another context, even where the types of relationships described previously don't exist. For example, even though a person has no general duty to come to someone's aid, once someone voluntarily begins to render assistance, she must proceed with reasonable care. For example, a coach attending a game as a spectator sees a player collapse on the field and decides to render aid. If the player has a neck injury and the off-duty coach (spectator) moves the player and aggravates the injury, the coach may be liable for negligence even though he did not have a duty to render aid based on a player–coach relationship. Thus, he assumed a duty that normally he would not possess.

The final way in which a duty may be found is if it is set forth by statute. For example, state law prohibits the sale of alcohol to minors. Suppose that a 17-year-old high school student becomes intoxicated after drinking beer that was sold to him illegally by arena concessions staff. While driving home from the game, this intoxicated person runs into a pedestrian; the arena and concessionaire have likely breached a duty owed to the pedestrian. As such, the arena and concessionaire may be deemed negligent per se for selling alcohol to a minor, resulting in injury to the pedestrian. If a defendant violates a statutory duty and is deemed **negligent per se,** then the defendant is negligent as a matter of law (*Restatement [Third] of Torts* § 324, 2005). In such a case, the plaintiff need only prove the elements of causation and actual harm to prevail in court. Thus, the statute sets up both the legal duty and the standard of care for the plaintiff. Determining whether there is a duty owed and the applicable standard of care is a key element of a negligence case. Once the duty, or standard of care, is established, the next step for the plaintiff is to prove that the defendant failed to meet the standard of care.

forensic expert—An expert who, through skill, training, background, education, or experience, renders opinions on matters relevant to legal cases.

negligent per se—Situation where a plaintiff only needs to prove causation and injury to prevail on a negligence claim.

In the Courtroom

Avila v. Citrus Community College District (2003)

Jose Luis Avila was a 19-year-old student at Rio Hondo Community College and played on the school's baseball team. During a game against Citrus College, Avila was hit in the head with a pitch that was thrown with such force it cracked his helmet. He alleged that the pitch was deliberately thrown to retaliate for a Rio Honda pitch that hit a Citrus College batter.

After being hit by the pitch, Avila staggered, felt dizzy, and was in pain. The Citrus College coaching staff did not check him, provide any aid, or summon medical care. His coach told him to go to first base. After going to first base, he complained to the first-base coach but was told to stay in the game. Once at second base, he still felt dizzy and in pain. An opposing player yelled to Rio Honda's dugout that they needed a different runner. Avila walked to his bench but his injuries were not tended to.

Avila alleged, among other things, that Citrus College was negligent for not providing or calling for medical aid when it was obvious that he needed medical attention. He also claimed that Citrus College was negligent for failing to supervise and control the pitcher and the game, provide umpires or other supervisors to control the game and prevent retaliatory or reckless pitching, and provide an adequate helmet to protect him from serious head injury. Finally, Avila alleged that Citrus College was negligent for failing to reasonably train and supervise coaches, managers, trainers, and employees in providing medical care to injured players and for holding an illegal preseason practice game in violation of community college baseball rules. Citrus College contended that it was immune under government code (section 831.7) on recreational immunity and that it had no duty to supervise Avila. The trial court dismissed the case in favor of the defendants.

On appeal, the court ruled that extending immunity to this case based on section 831.7 was not appropriate. The court stated that "coaches and instructors owe a duty of due care to persons in their charge" and section 831.7 "was not intended to affect the relationship between schools and their students" (p. 818). Regarding the duty allegation, the court stated, "It is surely foreseeable that a student might be injured if supervision is lax (or non-existent) at a school-sponsored sports event, and if medical care is not summoned when an injury occurs" (p. 819). The trial court's decision was reversed (*Avila v. Citrus Community College District,* 2003).

breach of duty—A failure to act in a reasonable manner for the safety of others; a failure to meet the standard of care.

Breach of Duty

The second element of negligence, **breach of duty,** requires the plaintiff to prove that the defendant breached the duty of care. The plaintiff must establish that the defendant failed to conform to the duty of care owed to the plaintiff (*Restatement [Second] of Torts* § 282, 1965). To show that the duty of care was breached, the plaintiff must prove that the defendant's conduct, viewed as of the time it occurred, imposed an unreasonable risk of harm (Keeton, 1984).

By establishing the existence of an unreasonable risk of harm, the plaintiff shows that the defendant breached the standard of care that was owed under the circumstances. A good way to conceptualize breach of duty is to first think about the standard of care and where it comes from and then think about situations where the standard of care is not met. The following example should help you understand the concept of breach.

- *Case precedent as basis for breach.* During a baseball game, a batted ball passes through a hole in the netting that was designed to protect spectators behind home plate and strikes an elderly spectator in the face, fracturing her jaw. Suppose that case precedent has determined that fans only assume the risk of being struck by foul balls when sitting outside of protected areas but that stadiums have a duty to provide a safe environment behind netted areas. Based on the duty identified through case precedent, a breach of the standard of care has occurred.

- *Violation of rules and regulations as basis for breach.* A county municipal health code regulation states that pools in the county must have a minimum of six lifeguards on duty at all times for a pool of a certain size. There are four lifeguards on duty at a time when a child drowns in the pool. If the municipal rules regulating the number of lifeguards is determined to be the standard of care, then the pool management has breached its duty (not met the standard of care) in guarding the pool.

- *Violation of state or federal law as basis for breach.* You operate a fitness facility in a state that requires all health and fitness centers in the state to have at least two AEDs on the premises. Suppose that the statute also requires staff to be trained in the use of the AED. If someone suffers sudden cardiac arrest and dies, and you had neither an AED nor anyone trained in its use, you would have violated your duty as required by state law, also possibly invoking the doctrine of negligence per se.

- *Violation of federal regulatory agency guidelines as basis for breach.* A court determines that the CPSC guidelines for moveable soccer goals are the standard of care in a negligence case. The guidelines state that goals must be constructed properly, placed on level ground, and anchored. If an injury and subsequent negligence lawsuit arose after a goal tipped over on a child, and the goal in question was top-heavy and not anchored, the standard of care would have been breached.

- *Professional association position statements.* Safety guidelines relevant to lightning safety contained in a position statement from a well-recognized professional association require that sport participants wait at least 30 minutes after a lightning storm has passed to return to the field of play, and these guidelines are determined to represent the standard of care. If a coach or sport supervisor returns the team to the field 15 minutes after the storm has passed and a player is struck and killed, in a negligence (wrongful death) lawsuit, the supervisor would have breached the duty of care.

• *Violation of agency policy as breach.* An organization has a policy that requires all staff to call 911 immediately in the event of a suspected head injury. If a staff member fails to call 911 at all, or fails to call in a timely manner, and further injury results, the staff member has breached the standard of care as contained in her organization's policy.

In all of these hypothetical cases, the issue will turn on whether the defendant's actions posed an unreasonable risk of harm to the plaintiff. Consider the In the Courtroom case on page 21 and whether the defendants posed an unreasonable risk of harm to the student athlete.

Causation

causation—The connection between an act (or failure to act) and harm.

Causation is the third element that must be proved in a negligence case. Causation refers to the claim in a negligence case that the acts or inaction of the defendant brought about injury to the plaintiff. Proof of causation is often a key part of a negligence case, with the outcome hinging on its resolution. There are two types of causation that a court might consider, depending on the jurisdiction (state where the case is brought), when rendering decisions in negligence cases: cause in fact and proximate cause.

Consider this case in the context of causation. John Lowe (plaintiff) was seriously injured when struck on the left side of his face by a foul ball at a professional baseball game. The Quakes, at their home games, feature a mascot who goes by the name of Tremor. He is a caricature of a dinosaur, standing 7 feet (2.1 meters) tall with a tail that protrudes from the costume. Tremor was performing his antics in the stands just along the left field foul line. Tremor's tail touched the plaintiff, who was standing in front of Tremor. The plaintiff was distracted and turned toward Tremor. In the next moment, just as the plaintiff returned his attention to the playing field, he was struck by a foul ball before he could react to it. Very serious injuries resulted from the impact. As a result, the underlying action was commenced against the California League of Professional Baseball and Valley Baseball Club, Inc., which does business as the Quakes (defendants) (*Lowe v. California League of Professional Baseball,* 1997).

Did the stadium cause the injury to the spectator? Should it be liable? Consider this case in light of the types of causation described next.

cause in fact—But for the act (or failure to act), the injury would not have occurred.

cause of action—Circumstances that give rise to a lawsuit; often used interchangeably with the term *lawsuit.*

Cause in Fact   Even if there is a breach of the duty of care owed to another, it still remains to be proved that the defendant's breach was the factual cause **(cause in fact)** of the plaintiff's harm. In other words, there must be some reasonable, direct connection between the plaintiff's **cause of action** for negligence and the defendant's action or omission (Keeton, 1984). An act or omission is not a cause of an event if the event would have occurred without it. This maxim has been used by courts to establish a "but for" or "sin qua non" rule. Simply put, causation in fact requires a finding that but for the defendant's conduct, the plaintiff would not have been hurt.

Day v. Ouachita Parish School Board et al. (2002)

As a member of the freshman football team at West Monroe High School (WMHS), Morgan Day was required to participate in a weight training class held during school hours. The class was supervised by WMHS' strength coach and three other coaches. Sixty football players were divided into five groups and were supervised by one of the coaches. Several senior students on the team helped the coaches supervise and instruct the class participants.

During one of the classes, Morgan injured his back while lifting weights. The next day, he played in a freshman football game even though his back was bothering him. Shortly thereafter, Morgan sought medical treatment. After an examination, the treating orthopedic surgeon provided Morgan with a written medical excuse which stated, "(1) No football for 1 week (2) No weightlifting, squats or power cleans. Diagnosis—lumbar strain and injured L-5 disc" (p. 1040).

Morgan presented the note to the freshman coach and the note was posted in the office. The coaches testified that they believed the physician's note meant that Morgan could not participate in football or weightlifting for 1 week. Morgan and his mother claimed that they interpreted the note to mean that Morgan could not play football for 1 week and could not lift weights for an indefinite amount of time.

One day after the medical excuse was posted, Morgan was observing the class but not lifting weights when an assistant coach instructed him to perform a dumbbell power clean push press. Morgan reminded the coach that he was medically excused; however, the coach insisted that the exercise would not affect his low back. After performing a few repetitions of the exercise, Morgan experienced severe pain and needed to lie down.

Morgan again saw the orthopedic surgeon complaining of back pain. Magnetic resonance imaging revealed a disc protrusion between the fourth and fifth vertebrae. The physician wrote another medical excuse that prohibited Morgan from all weightlifting and football activities until further notice. Morgan was referred to another specialist. He also went to other orthopedic surgeons and a neurosurgeon.

After the disc injury, Morgan was unable to play high school football or baseball. He lost interest in school and failed his classes because of excessive absences. He withdrew from WMHS and enrolled in an alternative school. Morgan's mother sued the school board and the coach who instructed Morgan to perform the lift after the medical excuse had been delivered. The trial court found the defendants liable for Morgan's back injury (Day v. Ouachita Parish School Board et al., 2002).

In some jurisdictions, causation may be found to not have occurred if it can be shown that something else caused the plaintiff's harm. However, the law recognizes that there can be more than one cause for a plaintiff's harm. Accordingly, if a plaintiff can prove that any of two or more causes would have brought about the harm, then the plaintiff may recover against any or all of the actors. The substantial factor test is used to determine whether multiple causes each resulted in the plaintiff's harm (Keeton, 1984). If the defendant's conduct played a substantial factor in causing the plaintiff's harm, then the defendant's conduct factually caused the plaintiff's harm. Thus, if the actions or omissions of multiple defendants each played a substantial factor in bringing about the plaintiff's harm, then all of the defendants would be deemed liable and the plaintiff may recover against any single defendant, or all of the defendants, for compensation (*Restatement [Second] of Torts* § 432, 1965).

proximate cause— Requirement that the act (or failure to act) and the injury be strongly or directly linked.

foreseeability—The ability to foresee or anticipate whether a certain event will happen.

Proximate Causation   The cause in fact requirement is another type of causation used in courts in various jurisdictions. Under this type of causation, the plaintiff must establish that the defendant's negligence was the proximate cause of the injuries (Wong, 2002). The concept of **proximate cause** stems from policy considerations that place manageable limits on liability caused by negligent conduct (57A American Jurisprudence 2nd § 427, 2003). The proximate cause requirement is based on the premise that defendants should not be liable for all the consequences of their actions, especially far-reaching consequences. There are two conflicting applications of the policy. The first is termed the *direct causation* view. It holds that defendants are liable for all consequences of their negligent acts if there are no superseding intervening causes. The second application, which is more popular and is widely used, is termed the *foreseeability* or *scope of risk* view (Keeton, 1984). Jurisdictions that incorporate **foreseeability** into their proximate cause determination require plaintiffs to prove that the injury was foreseen by the defendant, or reasonably should have been foreseen, and was the natural and probable result of the negligence (57A American Jurisprudence 2nd § 429, 2005). Accordingly, the foreseeability component of proximate cause is satisfied if a person of ordinary caution and prudence could have foreseen the likelihood of injury (*Regions Bank & Trust v. Stone County Skilled Nursing Facility, Inc.*, 2001).

Injury

actual harm—Clear and convincing proof of physical or emotional injury to a person.

For any cause of action based on negligence, some **actual harm** or injury must exist (*Restatement [Second] of Torts* § 907, Comment a, 1965; Wong, 2002). Proof of damage is an essential part of the plaintiff's case in negligence because negligent conduct in and of itself does not rise to the type of interference with the interests of society as a whole to warrant a complaint (Keeton, 1984). For example, many of us experience negligent acts committed by others every day. We have all likely experienced a near miss by a car running a red light. This upsets us because the other driver breached the standard of care (broke the traffic law) and this caused us distress. The act of the driver was careless, if not negligent, but there is no cause of action for negligence because we suffered no physical harm and the emotional distress was minimal and of a degree that is common to most throughout a normal day. For negligence to be found, in addition to the previously mentioned elements, there must exist some real (actual) physical or emotional harm.

Once actual harm or injury is established, many types of damages may be recovered to compensate the plaintiff. The types of damages available depend on the circumstances but may include compensation **(compensatory damages)** for physical pain and suffering, mental distress, direct economic loss, **loss of consortium,** and wrongful death (van der Smissen, 2003). In some jurisdictions, there is the possibility that a plaintiff may recover **punitive damages** against the defendant. Punitive damages differ from compensatory damages because punitive damages are awarded to punish the defendant rather than compensate the victim (Keeton, 1984). However, punitive damages are only awarded to punish outrageous, reckless, willful, or wanton conduct (Wong, 2002). For example, punitive damages may be sought against a stadium concessionaire who sells alcohol to a visibly intoxicated patron who injures another in a car wreck or against a hockey player who uses his stick to hit another player, resulting in serious injury.

Gross Negligence

Thus far, this chapter has focused on what is required for ordinary negligence. However, the common law recognizes that tortuous conduct may be so great that it amounts to more than just negligence, even though it falls short of being intentional (Keeton, 1984). For these situations, courts have distinguished between ordinary negligence and situations where the defendant acts with a heightened degree of carelessness, or gross negligence (*Fidelity Leasing Corp. v. Dun & Bradstreet, Inc.,* 1980). In **gross negligence,** the defendant's responsibility is magnified so that it is at a higher degree than that found in ordinary negligence (57A American Jurisprudence § 227, 2005). Some courts have stated that gross negligence amounts to a failure to exercise even the care that a careless person would use (*Whitley v. Com.,* 2000). However, other courts have interpreted gross negligence to require a showing of willful, wanton, or reckless misconduct (Keeton, 1984). The majority of jurisdictions distinguish between acts that are willful, wanton, or reckless and those that involve gross negligence (Keeton, 1984). Regardless of which type, the determination is subjective.

A good case example to consider when thinking about the concept of gross negligence is one involving a professional football player who died of heat stroke, resulting in a wrongful death claim for improper medical care. After reading the In the Courtroom case on page 24, think about whether the acts of the coaching staff were grossly negligent.

As previously stated, some jurisdictions distinguish between gross negligence and willful, wanton, and reckless conduct. These jurisdictions recognize situations in which a defendant may act with intentional indifference to the point that her actions exceed the culpability required for

compensatory damages—Damages (money) intended to compensate a defendant for the actual value of injuries or damages that he or she experiences.

loss of consortium—Loss of the services or involvement of a family member brought about by the wrongful actions of another.

punitive damages—Damages (money) designed to punish a defendant for a wrongful act that results in pain and suffering by a plaintiff.

gross negligence—A high level of negligence (subjectively determined), where a defendant has demonstrated a high degree of carelessness.

Stringer v. Minnesota Vikings Football Club, LLC (2005)

In the case of *Stringer v. Minnesota Vikings Football Club, LLC* (2005), a professional football player, Korey Stringer, died from heat stroke after the second day of practice at the 2001 Minnesota Vikings training camp. In the 2 days of training camp and prior to his death, Stringer vomited several times and fell to his knees or the ground several times but stood up by himself. Because of these events, Stringer was treated by the Vikings' medical service coordinator and by an assistant trainer. Both of these practice days were very hot and humid, and 11 players were treated for heat-related illness on the second day of practice.

During the morning practice of the second day, Stringer became sick and vomited again but continued to practice. Shortly after that practice ended, Stringer dropped to his knees, fell on his right side, and then lay down on his back. The assistant trainer, who thought that Stringer was doing fine, took him to an air-conditioned trailer as a preventive measure. While in the trailer, Stringer relaxed for several minutes and was given water to drink and an iced-down towel for his forehead. After the trainer removed his socks and shoes, Stringer lay on the table and began humming and moving his head back and forth for 10 minutes or more. The assistant trainer eventually called the training room to request a golf cart to transport Stringer, but when the cart arrived, Stringer was unresponsive. This was the first time anyone checked any of Stringer's vital signs, including his pulse, which was steady and slow. At this point no one had called for an ambulance. A few minutes later, the medical coordinator arrived and, believing that Stringer was hyperventilating, treated him for such. Soon thereafter, those present attempted to reach a physician who provided medical services for the Vikings. A few minutes later, the physician telephoned and a decision was made to call an ambulance. An ambulance arrived 8 minutes after it was dispatched and transported Stringer to a hospital. Hospital staff reported that Stringer's body temperature was 108.8 °F. Despite attempts to cool and treat Stringer, his condition worsened and he died from heat stroke less than 2 hours after arriving at the hospital. Stringer's wife filed suit, alleging that the coordinator of medical services and the assistant trainer had a personal duty to protect and care for Stringer's health and that they were grossly negligent in performing such duty. By alleging that the medical coordinator and assistant trainer were grossly negligent, the plaintiffs were basically saying that the actions, and inaction, taken by these people amounted to extremely careless conduct. Whether actions amount to gross negligence is a subjective determination based on the facts of a case. A key issue here was whether the time delay in getting emergency medical services on site amounted to gross negligence.

gross negligence (Keeton, 1984). Even though a defendant acts with intentional indifference, the defendant's actions remain negligent rather than intentional because the defendant did not intend to bring about the harm. In these situations, the risk of harm is so great that the defendant probably knows that the harm will follow (*Restatement [Second] of Torts* § 500, 1965). Some courts have tried to distinguish among willful, wanton, and reckless conduct (*Neary v. Northern Pacific Railway,* 1910). For most jurisdictions, however, these terms can be used collectively or interchangeably (*Mania v. Kaminski,* 1980). A defendant who is found liable for willful, wanton, and reckless conduct may incur civil sanction through punitive damages (*Hackbart v. Cincinnati Bengals, Inc.,* 1979).

In *Hackbart v. Cincinnati Bengals,* a professional football player was struck in the head by an opposing player after a play had ended. The plaintiff (Hackbart) was seriously injured as a result. The reckless nature of the act was considered in light of the fact that it was committed after a play had ended and in light of the manner in which the incident occurred. Also, consider the case of *Nabozny v. Barnhill* (1975), in which a soccer player was seriously injured after being kicked in the head by an opposing player. The plaintiff (Nabozny) was kicked during a game after he had dropped to one knee, caught the soccer ball, and held it to his chest while in the penalty area. The defendant (Barnhill) continued to run in the plaintiff's direction and kicked the side of his head in the penalty area. The court held that a player is liable for an injury in tort if the conduct of the defendant was either deliberate, willful, or with a reckless disregard for the safety of another. The case was remanded to the trial court for a factual determination of this issue.

Negligence Defenses

Sport managers can use several defenses when defending against negligence claims. Most of these defenses focus on the plaintiff's conduct. Plaintiffs must show all the elements of negligence to prevail in court. Sport managers who are defendants in negligence actions can prevail against a plaintiff's negligence suit if they show that all of the required elements have not been met. If a plaintiff has established each of the required negligence elements, then the defendant's case will rest on whether one of the following defenses to negligence exists.

Assumption of Risk

Assumption of risk is a legal defense by which plaintiffs may not recover for injuries in negligence when they have voluntarily exposed themselves to known and appreciated dangers (Keeton, 1984). Three elements to assumption of risk must be established (*Leakas v. Columbia Country Club,* 1993):

- The risk must be inherent to the sport.
- The participant must voluntarily consent to be exposed to the risk.
- The participant must know, understand, and appreciate the inherent risks of the activity.

assumption of risk—A defense to negligence recognized by some jurisdictions when three elements are met: (1) the risk entered into is inherent to the activity, (2) the plaintiff voluntarily consented to participate in the activity, and (3) the plaintiff had knowledge, understanding, or appreciation of the risks involved in the activity.

inherent risks—Risks that are a necessary part of an activity (e.g., trees on ski slopes; legal tackles in football).

Inherent Risks   **Inherent risks** are those that cannot be removed from an activity without fundamentally altering the nature of the activity. For example, there are risks associated with tackling in football. Football would be a much safer activity if players simply pulled flags off other players to stop their progress rather than hit them with their bodies in a manner that causes them to fall to the ground. However, removing the skill of tackling, and all the risks associated with tackling, would fundamentally alter the game of football. Thus, risks associated with tackling are inherent to the sport.

voluntary consent—An agreement (express or implied) to participate in an activity in a manner, time, and place of one's own choosing.

Voluntary Consent   Certain aspects of a sport, such as physical contact, are accepted (consented to) as part of the sport. Obvious examples of situations in which there is **voluntary consent** to contact and potential injury are legal tackles in football and legal checking in hockey. Even some sports that are technically considered noncontact, such as basketball, involve physical contact that is a known and accepted part of the game (e.g., setting picks). When physical contact resulting in injury goes outside the rules of the game (e.g., helmet-to-helmet contact in football), or when unnecessary physical contact resulting in injury occurs between plays or outside of game time, consent fails to be a valid defense. The participant must voluntarily consent to be exposed to the risk for a successful defense to be raised.

Knowledge, Understanding, and Appreciation   After the defendant establishes that the risk leading to injury was inherent and voluntary, it must be shown that the plaintiff knew, understood, and appreciated the risk. The knowledge aspect of assumption of risk requires the defendant to show that the plaintiff knew the nature of the activity and the risks associated with that activity. Continuing with the football example, let's say a child wishes to play football in a youth sport league but has no knowledge of the game or how it is played. If the child is thrown into a scrimmage game on the first day of practice and is injured when tackled for the first time, it would be difficult for the league to establish that the child had knowledge of the risks associated with tackling in football.

© Human Kinetics

Young athletes may not be able to fully grasp all of the inherent risks associated with a sport.

Similarly, defendants must show that plaintiffs understood the activity in terms of their own condition and skill. To show that a plaintiff legally volunteered to risk exposure, the defendant must show that the plaintiff understood his own abilities and physical condition in relation to the risks associated with the activity. If someone knows that he has a specific health condition that should prevent him from playing tackle football, but that person does so anyway, it could be shown that he had the requisite understanding of the risks associated with the activity.

Finally, it must be shown that the plaintiff appreciated the type of injuries that are associated with the activity. Sport activity leaders have a legal duty to warn participants of the dangers inherent in the activities and the types of injuries that participants could sustain. Someone might know of risks associated with an activity and have a general understanding of her own condition and skill in relation to those risks, but if she does not appreciate the injuries associated with that activity, then there is no assumption of risk. How can it be shown that a person has made an informed decision to voluntarily expose herself to risks associated with an activity when she doesn't even appreciate the injuries she could possibly incur through participation? The common theme running through the knowledge, understanding, and appreciation requirements of assumption of risk is information. For someone to assume a risk, she must make an informed decision to expose herself to that risk.

Express and Implied Assumption of Risk There are two types of assumption of risk, express and implied. Express assumption of risk occurs when the participant uses language to evidence that he has assumed the risks of an activity (Keeton, 1984). The language used by the participant can be either oral or written. For example, after a sport activity leader informs a participant of risks associated with an activity, the participant may verbally inform the sport activity leader that he knows, understands, and appreciates the risks of the activity but would like to participate anyway. An example of a written expression of assumption of risk is a participation agreement, a document that sport managers often require sport participants to sign prior to participation. If the participant is a minor, parental signatures are also required. These participation agreements contain language expressing the dangers of associated with an activity and state that the participant assumes the risks associated with the activity.

Implied assumption of risk exists when the participant's conduct or actions show that he voluntarily assumed the risks by taking part of the activity (Keeton, 1984). For example, Paul played organized football throughout childhood and high school, and now he decides to play in a recreational adult football league. Simply by playing in the league, Paul assumes risks that he has known, understood, and appreciated for many years.

Typically, the courts have found that spectators assume the risk of injuries that might be caused by implements flying into the spectators' seats (e.g., foul balls being hit into the stands along the first or third baselines) when the person is sitting outside of a protected area, as the In the Courtroom case on page 28 illustrates.

Costa v. Boston Red Sox Baseball (2004)

In *Costa v. Boston Red Sox Baseball* (2004), the plaintiff was struck in the face by a batted ball while attending a baseball game at the defendant's stadium. She filed suit and claimed that the defendant owed her a duty to warn her of the danger of being hit by the batted ball.

After arriving late to the game, the plaintiff and three companions took their seats in an unscreened area in Fenway Park. Their seats were on the first base line behind the Red Sox dugout. A player hit a line drive foul ball that struck the plaintiff's face, causing severe and permanent injuries. She had been at the game no more than 10 minutes before being injured.

The plaintiff claimed marked ignorance of the sport of baseball. Besides one time when she was 8 years old, she had not been to a baseball game. She had also not seen baseball on television except when she had changed channels. Prior to the injury, she had no subjective understanding of the risks posed by a foul ball.

The plaintiff claimed that she was entitled to a reasonable warning of the dangers of sitting in an unprotected area so that she could have made an informed decision whether to remain sitting there. She acknowledged that a disclaimer existed on her admission ticket but claimed that she did not look at the ticket. Furthermore, she claimed that the disclaimer was inadequate to relieve the defendant's duty to warn, especially because the print was very small. After her injury, signage was installed that stated, "Be Alert. Foul Balls and Bats Hurt" (p. 301). The plaintiff claimed that the signage was necessary prior to the accident, and that if she had been adequately informed of the danger, she would not have accepted the risk posed by her seat.

The trial court granted the defendant's motion for summary judgment and the appellate court affirmed, stating, "Even someone of limited personal experience with the sport of baseball reasonably may be assumed to know that a central feature of the game is that batters will forcefully hit balls that may go astray from their intended direction. We therefore hold that the defendant had no duty to warn the plaintiff of the obvious danger of a foul ball hit into the stands. The result we reach is consistent with the vast majority of reported decisions involving injuries to spectators at baseball games" (p. 303).

Contributory Negligence and Comparative Fault

theory—A legal concept or model on which the outcome of a case may hinge.

Contributory negligence is a defense to negligence that focuses on the negligent conduct of the plaintiff. Contributory negligence is also an absolute defense in that it precludes recovery for the plaintiff if contributory negligence is established. The **theory** provides that plaintiffs may not recover if they are negligent and their negligence contributes proximately to their injuries. Thus, the defense is a complete one. It shifts the loss totally from the defendant to the plaintiff, even if the plaintiff's failure to exercise reasonable care is much less marked than that of the defendant. Because of the harsh results for plaintiffs, only a few states have retained contributory negligence as a defense.

Most jurisdictions have adopted **comparative negligence,** a system that apportions damages according to the degree to which each party (plaintiff and defendant) is at fault. In comparing fault, jurisdictions either go with a pure comparative fault system or modify the concept. A pure comparative fault system is one where plaintiffs recover no matter how negligent they are. For example, if a plaintiff is 90% at fault, the plaintiff still recovers 10% of the financial award for damages incurred. Some jurisdictions require the defendant to be more at fault than the plaintiff before financial recovery is available to the plaintiff. These states are called modified rule jurisdictions because they have modified the concept of comparative fault to prevent plaintiffs from recovering if they are more at fault than the defendant. For example, if it is determined that the plaintiff is 51% responsible for the harm, the plaintiff is barred from recovering for damages incurred.

comparative negligence—A defense to negligence whereby some degree of fault and subsequent monetary damages are shifted away from the defendant. In a pure comparative negligence jurisdiction, the defendant is only liable for the proportion of fault attributed to himself.

Intentional Torts

Unlike the tort of negligence, where a careless act is committed, an **intentional tort** is what its name implies, a tort (civil wrong resulting in harm to person or property) that is committed with intent. When a person commits an intentional tort, it does not mean that she meant harm or had an evil motivation. Instead, intent means that a person (the defendant) intended the consequences of the act or knew with substantial certainty that a particular consequence (specific outcome) would result from the act. In sports, sometimes intentional acts are committed that result in harm to officials, athletes, and sport spectators. The business of sport places unique stressors on individuals working in the profession. Arena, stadium, and event managers, for example, often work extremely long hours. Sport participants (and parents of youth sport participants) can get especially abusive and hostile toward coaches and referees. Physical and emotional fatigue can take a toll on even the most well-intentioned people. Therefore, some types of intentional torts may affect the sport profession. The types of situations that might result in or be construed as intentional torts include making verbal threats, touching someone without his or her permission, spreading rumors, dealing with abusive patrons inappropriately, holding someone against his will, and entering the land or taking the property of another without their permission. Intentional torts are broken into two main categories: harm to persons and harm to property. Figure 2.2 shows the categories of intentional torts that these acts encompass.

intentional tort—An act that is both wrongful and knowingly committed.

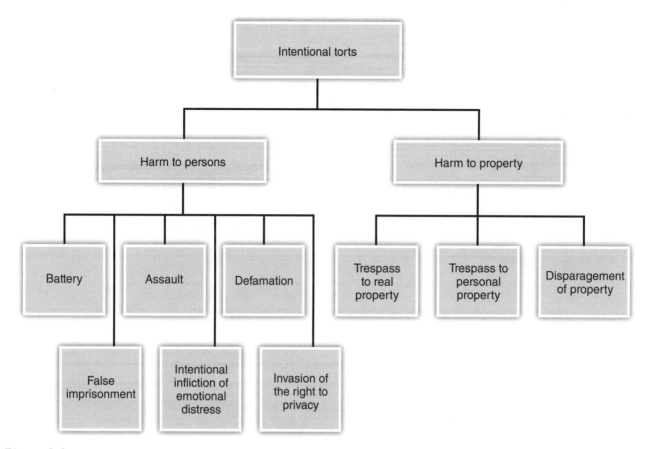

Figure 2.2
Categories of intentional torts.

Harm to Persons

In the realm of sport, certain intentional acts result in personal harm to others. The harm can be in the form or physical injury, emotional injury, or damage to a person's reputation. The following text describes certain types of intentional torts that address this type of harm. The lawsuits dealing with personal harm are battery, assault, defamation, false imprisonment, intentional infliction of emotional distress, and invasion of the right to privacy.

Battery and Assault

Civil law often makes a technical distinction between assault and battery that differs from the common perceptions of these acts. The distinction is that battery involves touching someone, whereas assault is the threat to touch someone.

battery—An intentional tort involving the harmful or offensive touching of another.

Battery is generally defined as the intentional, harmful, or offensive touching of another that is unprivileged and unpermitted. Intent comes into play in terms of the person's intent to make contact with another, either directly or indirectly (e.g., throwing a baseball at a group of spectators). The touch can be either harmful or offensive, offensive meaning that you don't have to bruise someone or physically hurt them to commit a battery. Offensive touching may arise in conjunction with a sexual harassment claim. Harmful touching is common in sport, but often there is no liability because it is permitted (or consented to) as a part of the game. Situations that might involve battery include those in which aggressive spectators hit referees, a sport instructor or coach touches a student or player inappropriately, or a professional athlete rushes into the stands and strikes a heckler. Organizations often put rules in place to avoid situations that might lead to battery and subsequent lawsuits against the organization; such rules might apply to touching, discipline, hazing, and ways that referees should handle conflicts.

Assault is closely associated with battery but differs in that assault is the threat of a battery (the threat of harmful or offensive touching). The importance of assault is that an organization might be held liable for the acts of an employee who threatens to touch another in a harmful or offensive way. Employees should be instructed to not take matters into their own hands, not only by not hitting or touching another but also by not threatening another. Waiting for the proper authority to handle a heated situation is usually the best measure.

AP Photo/Ted S. Warren

Battery can occur in many sporting situations regardless of the age of the athletes or the level of play. Here, former Kansas City Royals first base coach Tom Gamboa is attacked by two fans who rushed the field.

Defamation

Most people have heard about the intentional tort of **defamation**. Gossip in the workplace, untrue and harmful media reports that are made to increase sales, untrue negative remarks that are made without knowing that they were overheard, and negative untrue evaluations of work performance can all lead to defamation under the right circumstances. There are two specific types of defamation: libel and slander. **Slander** is the verbal form of defamation, whereas **libel** is the written form. A defamation lawsuit proposes that someone has been injured as a result of something written or spoken about her that was untrue or false, harmful, and made known to another person. The law uses certain terms to describe that which is harmful and made public. The term used for harm is *defamatory;* therefore, one element of defamation is making a statement that is defamatory. The term used to describe a statement that is made public is *published to a third party*. This means that a third person, someone other than the person making the statement and the person affected by the statement, hears what is said. The rules for defamation differ by whether the affected person is a public figure or an ordinary citizen. Public figures generally have less protection for untrue and negative statements made about them. For public figures, actual malice or a reckless disregard for the truth must be shown. Also, some categories of defamatory statements are potentially more libelous than others. These include statements about someone's moral character (e.g., falsely calling

assault—An intentional tort involving the believable threat of a harmful or offensive touching of another.

defamation—A false and defamatory statement made in the presence of a third party; may be either spoken (slander) or written (libel).

slander—The verbal form of defamation.

libel—The written form of defamation.

someone a child molester), statements about a person's chastity (e.g., sexual promiscuity), statements that a person has a "loathsome disease," and statements that affect a person's occupation and profession. Sport managers should discourage gossip in the workplace, back up performance evaluations with facts, and instruct staff and employees to avoid saying harmful things about others and to say nothing at all about a matter if they are unsure of the truth regarding that matter.

False Imprisonment

false imprisonment—
The intentional, wrongful, and unreasonable confinement of another.

Another type of intentional tort is the tort of **false imprisonment.** Although the word *imprisonment* brings to mind being locked in a prison or elsewhere, in the eyes of the law confinement does not necessarily have to occur to prove false imprisonment. It may be interpreted, depending on the court and jurisdiction, that a person is "imprisoned" merely if he believes that he cannot leave a certain location (e.g., a child is told by an adult to stay in one place for an unreasonable amount of time, or someone believes she cannot leave an area without being harmed). False imprisonment may arise from seemingly innocent situations. A child might be held against her will as punishment, without the coach or supervisor realizing his error in keeping that child from leaving a certain area for an unreasonable amount of time. An innocent person might be held against her will because a store manager falsely but innocently believed that the person had stolen an item from the store. Because of the potential for false imprisonment claims, the sport manager should be extremely careful in holding someone against his will. Some issues for sport managers to consider involve the reasonableness of their actions. For example, did the sport manager have reasonable suspicion to detain the person? Was the person detained for a reasonable amount of time? Were the use and amount of force reasonable? Was the person brought back from a reasonable distance outside the business after leaving the premises? The sport manager should consider and discuss such issues with legal counsel prior to acting.

Intentional Infliction of Emotional Distress

intentional infliction of emotional distress—Extreme and outrageous conduct that results in severe emotional distress to another.

Intentional infliction of emotional distress is a type of tort that arises when someone intentionally commits an act that represents extreme and outrageous conduct and results in severe emotional distress to another person. The person (the defendant in a lawsuit) intended to commit the outrageous act, and the injury is severe and emotional, not physical. A type of act considered extreme and outrageous enough to result in severe emotional harm to another person is sexual harassment, which sometimes includes claims for intentional infliction of emotional distress. A woman, for example, might be called, text-messaged, or e-mailed repeatedly with language that is sexual in nature and highly offensive, enough so to be considered extreme and outrageous. Additionally, the messages or the manner in which the messages are sent might be so offensive as to result in severe emotional distress or trauma to the victim.

Intentional infliction of emotional distress might also arise when someone intends to play a practical joke on another that goes well beyond the bounds of decency. Suppose that someone calls another and tells him (falsely) that a member of his family has been involved in a life-threatening accident. Upon hearing this, the person receiving the call would likely become severely emotionally distressed. Additionally, the message would likely be considered extreme and outrageous. In this situation, there is no battery (touching) or assault (threat). The tort of intentional infliction of emotional distress therefore covers situations where injury arises from acts that are not covered under other types of tort causes of action.

In the sport context, it is possible that a coach might be sued for intentional infliction of emotional distress under certain circumstances. Suppose that a football coach tells his player, a 225-pound senior linebacker, to go out and intentionally injure by spearing (using the helmet as a weapon) a 140-pound freshman quarterback who is playing for the first time on an opposing team. The mother of the freshman player sees her son become seriously injured as a result of an illegal spearing by the senior player. A suit for intentional infliction of emotional distress might be brought by the mother due to the extreme and outrageous acts of the opposing coach and the resulting severe emotional injury this caused her. Consider the In the Courtroom case (below) and ask yourself whether you think the actions of the coach were extreme and outrageous, and more important, what a coach would need to do before his actions would rise to this level.

In the Courtroom

Kavanagh v. Trustees of Boston University, 795 N.E.2d 1170 (Mass. 2003)

In *Kavanagh v. Trustees of Boston University* (2003), Kevin Kavanagh, a member of the Manhattan College basketball team, was punched in the nose by an opposing Boston University (BU) player during an intercollegiate basketball game. The punch resulted in a broken nose, but Kavanagh returned to play later that game. The player who threw the punch was immediately ejected from the game. Kavanagh brought suit against the trustees of BU and BU's basketball coach, alleging that the university was vicariously liable for the actions of its scholarship athlete and that the university and coach were negligent since they did not take any steps to prevent the act. Additionally, he alleged that the BU coach intentionally inflicted emotional distress on him as a result of the actions of the player whom he coached. Kavanagh claimed that the coach incited the team's aggressiveness by shouting encouragement from the sideline, not taking players who were allegedly elbowing opposing players out of the game, and praising his players, including ones who were committing fouls. The court concluded that neither BU nor its coach had any reason to foresee that its student athlete would engage in violent behavior, and Kavanagh failed to show that BU's coach engaged in reckless or intentional conduct rather than aggressive coaching. The appellate court affirmed the decision.

Invasion of the Right to Privacy

invasion of the right to privacy—Interference with a private citizen's right to privacy in his or her personal life.

The **invasion of the right to privacy** concept encompasses several types of intentional torts, all of which are relevant to sport. The United States Supreme Court has interpreted various amendments of the U.S. Constitution to find that U.S. citizens have a fundamental right to privacy. Some states have taken this a step further by enacting legislation that specifically provides for rights to privacy. The intentional tort of the invasion of the right to privacy provides further recourse for those who have been harmed in any of the following four ways.

appropriation—The use, without permission and for one's own benefit, of the name, likeness, or other identifying characteristics of another person.

Appropriation   The first category of intentional tort involving privacy is **appropriation.** Appropriation occurs when someone uses, without permission and for their own benefit, the name, likeness, or other identifying characteristic of another person. There are many examples that could be placed in the sport context. For example, suppose that someone puts the image of a professional football player on T-shirts and sells these to the public. This is an example of appropriation if the player did not give his permission and the sale was for the benefit of the seller. Suppose that you run a youth sport league and take photos of children playing softball. You post the photos on the Internet and distribute brochures containing the photos in order to promote your league. This is an example of appropriation if the identities of the children were made known in the pictures, and the pictures were taken and made public for the benefit of the league sponsors without the permission of the children, parents, or legal guardians. It is therefore important that, when the likeness of someone is recorded (even if for innocent purposes), permission be obtained before making the image public.

intrusion—The invasion of a person's home or personal belongings without permission.

Intrusion   A second type of intentional tort with privacy implications is **intrusion** (also called intrusion on seclusion). This tort may arise where someone invades a person's home or searches personal belongings without permission. An example might be a coach who searches the backpack of a player on an opposing team with the hope of finding performance-enhancing drugs or something else that might embarrass or incriminate the opposing player or team. Where this is done without permission, the tort of intrusion might apply. Intrusion might also be relevant where offices, lockers, bags, or other personal belongings of players, coaches, or staff are searched without permission. Even in situations where wrongdoing on the part of another might be suspected, one must never invade the privacy of another by searching their personal belongings without permission. In the scenario addressed here, it would be best to alert the proper authorities to handle a matter of suspected wrongdoing rather than take matters into one's own hands and be sued for invasion of privacy (intrusion).

false light—The publishing of false ideas or information attributed to a person.

False Light   The third type of intentional tort relevant to privacy is called **false light.** False light is similar to defamation and may actually be brought in tandem with a defamation lawsuit. This tort puts a person in the public spotlight over ideas or information attributed to them that is untrue. Suppose that a newspaper publishes a story about a college soccer player, and the article wrongly claims that the player is a strong supporter of a racist organization. This story would place the player in a false light by making the public think that the player held racist views when he did not. The story would also require the player to face the public to rebut the claims made in the story, thus interfering with his right to privacy.

Public Disclosure of Private Facts   The fourth type of intentional tort with privacy implications is **public disclosure of private facts.** This tort would arise when facts about a person's private life, which an ordinary person would find objectionable, are made public. The public is often fascinated with the personal lives of athletes. Therefore, media outlets sometimes push the limits in terms of providing information about athletes that goes beyond their performance on the field and court. If a newspaper, for example, published a story about a star high school athlete that dealt with the athlete's sex life or finances, this might give rise to the tort of public disclosure of private facts. Public disclosure of private facts and the other privacy torts provide legal recourse for private citizens when someone violates their right to privacy.

Harm to Property

The intentional torts discussed to this point have all dealt with harm to people, either emotional or physical. Intentional torts, however, also involve harm committed on (or interference with) a person's property, either real or personal. **Personal property** consists of those things that can be moved, such as sport equipment like soccer goals or smaller items like bats, helmets, and gloves. **Real property** is both land and objects that are permanently attached to the land, such as fields, courts, and swimming pools.

Trespass to Real Property

Trespass occurs when a person intentionally enters the land of another, or causes another person or object to enter the land of another, without permission or **necessity.** Several key points are important to your understanding of trespass. First, for the intentional tort of trespass to be found, actual physical harm to the property does not have to occur. Suppose there are posted "no trespassing" signs around a college football stadium and field to protect the turf between games during the season. Some people decide to disregard the signs and play a game of ultimate Frisbee on the field. Even if they don't harm the field in any way, they could still be found liable for the intentional tort of trespass.

The intent of this tort is not just to prevent harm to property but also to prevent people from interfering with the exclusive possessions of a person or organization's property, in this case the university. It is important for a sport organization to post "no trespassing" signs on their property to give notice that entry to the land is not allowed. If the trespasser has entered the property with criminal intent, however, the intruder is understood to be a trespasser even without posted signs. Conversely, there are times when

public disclosure of private facts—Making factual information public about a person's private life, which an ordinary person would find objectionable.

personal property—Movable property such as sport equipment.

real property—Fixed property such as sport stadiums, fields, courts, or unmovable goals.

necessity—A defense to trespass in which an innocent person enters the land of another to avoid imminent and serious injury to the body or property of oneself or another person.

trespass to land is acceptable. It may be necessary, for example, to enter the land of another to protect oneself or another person from harm. Suppose that a serious thunderstorm with lightning has arisen and a person must enter a stadium with posted "no trespassing" signs to protect himself or his family from the weather. This might be considered a necessity where liability for trespass would not occur.

Trespass to Personal Property

trespass to personal property—The initial nonpermitted taking of another person's personal property.

Trespass to personal property occurs when someone takes the personal (movable) property of another without the permission of that person. For example a person drags a movable soccer goal off the property of a sport complex and places it in her backyard. She has committed the intentional tort of trespass to personal property. The initial taking of the property constitutes trespass to personal property. If she keeps the property in her possession, then she has committed the intentional tort of **conversion.** She has deprived the owner of the possession of his personal property without a valid reason. Damages or harm might occur to the sport organization if, by virtue of not having possession of their property, they lose business. A sport organization running youth soccer leagues might lose money if they cannot effectively run their programs without necessary equipment that has been wrongfully taken from them. A catering company, for example, might lose business and profits if someone takes their delivery van and they are not able to deliver their food and provide services. Trespass to personal property and conversion mirror concepts in criminal law such as larceny and theft. Remember, however, that the discussion here centers on civil law where the harmed person can seek to recover monetary damages from the wrongdoer where an intentional tort of trespass or conversion has occurred.

conversion—Taking and depriving another of his or her right to the exclusive possession of personal property.

Disparagement of Property

disparagement of property—Untrue statements about personal property that result in financial hardship to a business; types consist of slander of quality and slander of title.

The final type of intentional tort discussed in this chapter is **disparagement of property.** This tort arises when someone makes a comment about the property of another that is untrue and results in harm to the person in possession of the property. There are two types of disparagement of property: slander of title and slander of quality. **Slander of title** occurs when someone makes false statements about the ownership or title of someone's property. This basically amounts to a statement that someone else is in possession of stolen property and does not have a valid title to the property. Suppose that someone makes public a false accusation that a certain business is selling stolen baseball trading cards. It would be unlikely that anyone would then want to buy trading cards from this business if they believe that the cards have been stolen. This would obviously result in a loss of business and potential profits to the store, with potential subsequent financial hardship for the store owner.

slander of title—Untrue statements about the ownership (title) of personal property that result in financial hardship to a business.

slander of quality—Untrue statements about the quality of personal property that result in financial hardship to a business.

A second type of disparagement of property is **slander of quality.** This type of tort arises when someone makes false statements about the quality of someone's product or merchandise. Suppose that a business sells championship rings studded with diamonds. If a person falsely accuses the business of selling rings with fake diamonds, and this is believed, then it is unlikely that any schools or sport franchises would purchase rings from this business, and subsequent financial loss and hardship would be placed on the business. Slander of quality and slander of title are similar to defamation but should not be confused with this tort. The distinction is that defamation deals with untrue statements about a person, whereas disparagement of property deals with untrue statements about personal property.

Product Liability

Product liability is liability for harm caused by a consumer product. At one time, consumers who were harmed by products could only recover against those who sold them the product. Thus, manufacturers would be shielded from liability if the consumer purchased the harmful product from a distributor rather than directly from the manufacturer. Laws now extend liability down the chain of manufacture. The chain of manufacture includes any person or entity that made or distributed the good before it reached the end user. Thus, coaches and sport organizations who sell or provide equipment to athletes may be susceptible to product liability claims.

> **product liability—**
> Liability attached to the manufacture or distribution of a product.

For example, Phil's parents agree to let him play youth football and purchase his helmet and pads directly from the youth sport organization. Unfortunately, the helmet sold to Phil is unreasonably designed and Phil is severely injured as a result. Phil's parents can bring a claim on his behalf against any or all of the following parties: (a) the company that made the helmet, (b) the company that distributed the helmet to the youth sport organization, and (c) the youth sport organization that sold the helmet to Phil. Plaintiffs can use three theories when suing manufacturers under product liability: negligence, strict liability, and breach of warranty (Kiely & Ottily, 2006). The first two theories (negligence and strict liability) are found in tort law, whereas the third (breach of warranty) is a contractual remedy. Also, defenses are available to manufacturers who are sued for harm caused by their product. Most of these defenses focus on the plaintiff's actions. Defenses include (a) improper equipment installation, (b) improper modification, (c) use of the product for unforeseeable purposes, and (d) failure to use the product in accordance with instructions (Owen & Madden, 2000).

Negligence

The first theory that plaintiffs can use to recover is negligence. Plaintiffs using negligence as a theory in their product liability claim must establish each of the four elements of negligence (duty, breach, causation, and injury [damages]) to prevail in court. Negligence is a theory of liability that can be used in all product liability cases no matter what the type of defect. However, negligence is not always easily established because it is often difficult for plaintiffs to show that manufacturers, distributors, or other parties in the chain of manufacture acted unreasonably in the creation or sale of the product.

The case of *Sanchez v. Hillerich & Bradsby Co.* (1992) provides a sport-related example of a product liability claim. On April 2, 1999, Andrew Sanchez, a baseball player for California State University, Northridge, was pitching against the University of Southern California (USC). During the game, he was struck on the head by a ball that was hit by Dominic Correa, a player for USC. The ball was traveling extremely fast. The bat used by Correa when the injury occurred was an aluminum bat called the Air Attack 2, which was designed and manufactured by Hillerich & Bradsby Co. (H&B). Prior to the 1999 season, the National Collegiate Athletic Association (NCAA) notified all athletic conferences under its umbrella, including the Pac-10, of which USC is a member, that certain new aluminum bats like the Air Attack 2 were dangerous. The hazardous nature of the bats stemmed from the fact that the bats increased the speed of batted balls, thus reducing the reaction time of players in the field who could be struck by the balls. In its notice to the conferences, the NCAA stated that it had implemented new rules to decrease the speed of batted balls and that these rules would be effective August 1, 1999. In 2000, Sanchez filed a lawsuit against H&B and the NCAA asserting causes of action for product liability and negligence. The trial court granted summary judgment motions for H&B, USC, and Pac-10, finding that Sanchez would be unable to establish causation. Sanchez argued that the design of the bat increased his risk of injury. However, the trial court held that Sanchez had to prove that the bat's design actually caused his injuries. On appeal, the case was remanded back to the trial court to determine whether the type of bat was the cause of the injury.

Strict Liability

strict liability—Legal concept where liability results regardless of fault; often used in product liability cases.

The second theory used in product liability is called **strict liability.** Strict liability is a concept of liability regardless of fault. Thus, plaintiffs using this theory are not burdened with the task of showing that a party in the chain of manufacture acted unreasonably. Instead, plaintiffs using strict liability need only show that the product was defective when it left the defendant's hands, and the defect caused the plaintiff's injuries.

The policy behind allowing strict liability to be used in product liability cases is that between the product manufacturer and the consumer or user, the manufacturer is in the better position to anticipate hazards associated with the product and take measures to guard against said hazards. The problem with strict liability is that unlike negligence, it cannot be used in all cases. The Third **Restatement of Torts** (*Restatement [Third] of Torts*, 2005) provides that there is no strict liability for used goods. This is based on the idea that buyers expect a somewhat greater risk of defect when the product they are buying is not new. However, special circumstances may require the use of strict liability even though the goods were used. This rule is not applicable when the goods are considered "nearly new."

Restatement of Torts—A comprehensive document that provides a uniform set of rules relevant to the law of torts.

For example, cars are often provided to representatives of sport organizations for use during major sporting events like the Super Bowl and the

World Series. These cars are lent to league representatives and other sport dignitaries a short time before the event so that the representatives and dignitaries can travel about the community that hosts the event. When the event is completed, the cars are often sold at discounted prices to the car distributors who lent the cars for league use. These cars are not new but have not experienced a lot of use. Thus, these cars may be labeled "nearly new," and some jurisdictions may be willing to allow strict liability to apply to harm caused by these cars.

Breach of Warranty

The third theory that can be used by plaintiffs is **breach of warranty. This theory is not a tort theory of liability but instead a contractual remedy.** Breach of warranty is a remedy most commonly used by those who are simply dissatisfied with their product and wish to have it repaired or replaced. This theory is used every time a product breaks or fails to work properly and the consumer returns it to the store or distributor. The theory is a contractual theory because of the contractual relationship that exists between manufacturers or distributors and those who purchase their products. These contracts are found in the purchase agreements and are called warranties.

Contractual remedies typically are not used to compensate for personal injuries. However, tort theories usually must be brought within very short amounts of time after the injury is known or should have been known, otherwise the plaintiffs are precluded from bringing a lawsuit. Conversely, plaintiffs with contract claims have much longer amounts of time to bring their claims before they are barred. Most jurisdictions give plaintiffs 10 years to assert a breach of contract claim. Thus, plaintiffs who are harmed by their product may be barred from bringing tort actions but may still have cause to sue under breach of warranty.

There are two types of warranties: express and implied. An **express warranty** arises through advertising, sales literature, product labeling, and oral statements in which the seller asserts a fact or makes a promise that relates to the quality of goods and induces the buyer to purchase the goods. Accordingly, consumers can claim a breach of an express warranty if an affirmation or promise is not satisfied. For example, if the manufacturer of a basketball shoe advertises that the shoe will improve the vertical leap of consumer athletes by 1 inch (2.5 centimeters) and a consumer establishes that this is not the case, the consumer might have a claim against the manufacturer for breach of an express warranty.

Implied warranties are those that exist as a matter of law whenever consumer goods are sold. These warranties can be found in article 2 of the **Uniform Commercial Code (UCC).** The UCC is a set of laws governing the sale of consumer goods that has been adopted by every U.S. state but Louisiana. Two types of implied warranties flow with every sale of a consumer good: the implied warranty of fitness for a particular purpose and the implied warranty of merchantability.

breach of warranty— The failure to uphold an express or implied promise to abide by certain terms and conditions relevant to the sale or lease of goods.

contractual remedies—Ways in which contract law can be applied to resolve a wrong done to a plaintiff.

express warranty— An express agreement (spoken or in writing) that the product will be of a certain quality and type, as well as other agreed upon provisions.

Uniform Commercial Code (UCC)—A lengthy document, adopted in 49 U.S. states, that provides a uniform set of rules relevant to the sale of goods (contracts).

implied warranty of fitness—An implied promise by the seller that the product is appropriate for the particular purpose for which it was sold.

The **implied warranty of fitness** exists when the retailer, distributor, or manufacturer knows of a certain purpose for which the goods are required and, further, that the buyer is relying on the skill and judgment of the seller to select and furnish suitable goods. When this situation occurs, then there is an implied warranty that the goods are fit for the purpose. For example, if a consumer walks into a store looking for a golf club that improves distance but is also allowed on all courses, and the golf pro who sells the club to the consumer knows of the consumer's desires and sells the consumer a club that is not legal on Professional Golf Association–regulated courses, then the consumer may have a claim for breach of the implied warranty of fitness for a particular purposes.

implied warranty of merchantability—An implied promise by the seller that the product is reasonably appropriate for the general purpose for which it was sold.

The **implied warranty of merchantability** is satisfied when the consumer goods (a) pass without objection in the trade under the contract description; (b) are fit for the ordinary purposes for which such goods are used; (c) are adequately contained, packaged, and labeled; and (d) conform to the promises or affirmations of fact made on the container or label (UCC § 2-313). In other words, the implied warranty of merchantability states that the goods will do what they are generally supposed to do. This is the most commonly used implied warranty because it is relied on when products do not work.

Note that the warranty is called the warranty of merchantability rather than consumerability. It is called the warranty of merchantability because it is a derivative warranty, meaning that it derives from the warranty that manufacturers have with distributors. Accordingly, the warranty is that the product will be merchantable, meaning it can be sold. Merchants typically buy in bulk from manufacturers and because of this they cannot expect perfection from all of the products sold to them. Similarly, consumers claiming breach of the warranty of merchantability cannot expect perfection from their products; consumers can only expect that the products are good enough to be sold.

Because warranties are based in contract they can be modified or disclaimed like any other contract provision if the parties agree to the modification or disclaimer warranty (Kiely & Ottily, 2006). This means that manufacturers can limit the application of warranties or do away with them all together. An example of a limitation would be where a manufacturer limits the warranty of merchantability to only 1 year. Most manufacturers do limit the warranty of merchantability to 1 year, and this limitation can be found in the warranty given to the consumer. By law, the warranty of merchantability cannot be done away with completely; however, all other warranties can be disclaimed.

Types of Defects

manufacturing defect—A defect that occurs during, or is associated with, the manufacture of a product.

Three types of defects can result in legal liability. The first, called a **manufacturing defect,** exists when a product is manufactured incorrectly. Manufacturing defects do not affect the entire product line. In fact, manufacturing defects are established by comparing the harmful product with other products off the same line.

The second type of defect is called a **design defect.** These defects exist when a product is unreasonably designed. Design defects exist before the product is manufactured, and thus the entire product line is defective. The Third Restatement (*Restatement [Third] of Torts Restatement,* 2005) does not impose strict liability at all for design defects but instead requires a risk-utility approach, under which a product is defective in design when the foreseeable risks of harm posed by the product could have been reduced or avoided by the adoption of a reasonable alternative design warranty (Kiely & Ottily, 2006). The omission of this alternative design is what makes the product unreasonably safe.

For example, a company designs a new football helmet so that it is lighter than all other helmets while affording the same level of protection. However, the lightweight design also causes the helmet to fly off users' heads when hit from a certain angle. Using the risk-utility approach, a court will have to determine whether the risk is greater than the utility (meaning benefits or usefulness). In doing so, a court will ask whether the new lightweight design is so useful that it justifies the increased danger of having the helmet fly off. Furthermore, the court will examine whether an alternative design could have been used that would manage the risk while maintaining the utility. Ultimately, the court will find that the helmet line is defective if the risk associated with the new design outweighs the utility of the new design.

Last, manufacturers have a duty to warn their consumers of the dangers that are inherent in the reasonable use of a product. But the duty does not stop there; manufacturers must also warn customers of dangers resulting from foreseeable misuses of the product. The policy behind this rule is that manufacturers have superior knowledge of the limitations of the product because they made the product. Thus, manufacturers know more about the product than does the consumer. Manufacturers also have a responsibility to warn of defects discovered after a product has been marketed. So the duty to warn continues throughout the sales life of the product.

Warnings must be reasonable. For this reason, strict liability is generally not available in failure to warn defect cases. After all, strict liability occurs regardless of fault, meaning that plaintiffs do not have to establish that the manufacturer acted unreasonably. However, if no warning exists, then strict liability may be used. In determining whether a warning is reasonable, courts will examine whether the warning is conspicuous (i.e., easy to locate on the product). Furthermore, a warning must be easy to read and comprehend to be considered reasonable. A warning may be unreasonable if it uses complicated language that confuses the consumer.

design defect—A product that is designed in a faulty manner which ultimately results in injury to consumers.

Summary

Tort law has practical implications for the day-to-day management of sport facilities and programs. A sport manager will likely encounter a tort lawsuit at some time during her career; she may be involved directly in the lawsuit, or her organization may be involved in a tort lawsuit in which she is not personally involved. Although negligence is the most likely type of lawsuit a sport manager will encounter, intentional torts and product liability lawsuits also occur in the sport setting. Knowledge about these areas of law will help the sport manager handle the emotional strain that accompanies a lawsuit as well as help her prepare for the litigation process. This important area of law is also an interesting one. You should keep this text as a resource in addition to reading tort law articles and cases to keep you abreast of current issues in tort law.

DISCUSSION QUESTIONS

1. Explain why an understanding of tort law is important to sport professionals.
2. Describe the concept of negligence and its relevance to sport management.
3. Describe how and why intentional torts might occur when managing sport programs and services.
4. Explain why the doctrine of assumption of risk is important to the sport profession.
5. Explain the importance of product liability to both (a) the manufacturers of sports equipment and (b) those who buy and distribute equipment to players under their care.
6. Describe the types of warranties and their relevance to the sport industry.

MOOT COURT CASE

In October 2006, Harry Heckler and his wife Harriett Heckler attended a minor league baseball game between the Raleigh River Rats and the Jacksonville Windjammers at the River Rat Stadium in North Carolina. It was a perfect day with mild temperatures and clear skies. Harry and Harriett are big fans of the River Rats and attend every home game. They have season tickets along the third base line on the first row so they can be near the players and heckle the opposing players near their dugout. On the day in question, Harry and Harriett were having a great time drinking beer, eating peanuts, and heckling the players. The stadium had a policy of only serving one beer at a time to customers (and ending all sales after the seventh inning), but Harry was a regular and was well known by the beer vendors. Harry also had befriended one of the servers, Sally Slosh, who regularly would slip him an extra beer or two. Harry would assure her that he was not drunk and that the other beers were for his wife and friends. In reality, he might bring one beer back to his wife but he would drink the rest. He would later testify that he could not remember exactly how many beers he had on this particular day, but it may have been more than five. He also said that he could "hold his beer" quite well. During the seventh inning stretch, after the song "Take Me Out to the Ball Game," Harry spotted one of the opposing pitchers from the Windjammers, Carlos Curveballer. Carlos was a strong family man whose one weakness was an occasional hot temper. This was exhibited in some brushback pitches (the players called it "chin music") when he became angered on the mound. Harry and Harriett knew about his temper and decided they would try to help their team by amping up the heckling. Harry yelled out, "Hey Carlos, your mother wears Army boots." Harriett, not to be outdone, yelled, "And she's ugly too." Carlos ran toward Harry and started shaking his fist at him while cursing in Spanish. Harry stood up and shook his fists back at him while cursing in English and making racial slurs. The conflict had escalated. Carlos then did something unexpected; he threw a ball toward Harry. Harry ducked and the ball hit Harriett in the face. Harriett fell to the ground, unconscious. The ball had hit her jaw, breaking her teeth and the bones on the right side of her face. She was injured further when she fell to the ground, breaking her left arm and cracking three ribs. Stadium security personnel were summoned, and 911 was called. Emergency medical personnel took Harriett to the nearest hospital. Harry and Harriett sued the stadium, Carlos Curveballer, and the Windjammers baseball organization for Harriett's injuries.

3

Risk Management

CHAPTER OBJECTIVES

After reading this chapter, you will know the following:

- The foundations of risk management and key elements of the decision-making process
- The essential components of an emergency action plan and a crisis management plan
- The key elements of a lightning safety plan
- Management issues for sport facilities and those with disabilities

AP Photo/Tom Uhlman

risk—The likelihood or probability of harm.

risk management—The process of reducing or eliminating the risk of harm to participants and loss to an organization through injury and subsequent lawsuits.

Sport law is about managing **risk** in sport. When you apply legal principles to the facts in sport law cases, practical implications for management (e.g., facility and program safety for sport participants, staff, employees, and spectators; employee relations; gender equity in sport) become evident. **Risk management** is a course of action designed to reduce the risk (probability or likelihood) of injury and loss to sport participants, spectators, employees, management, and organizations.

Risk management often centers on reducing the risk of harm given that the elimination of all risk is often not feasible. The very nature of sport involves some degree of risk: The only practical way to eliminate all risk is to close a facility, remove a risky piece of equipment, or eliminate the provision of a sport or service. To remove the risk completely from sport would have a potentially negative consequence to sport providers in that the sport activity likely would lose its appeal to the vast majority of participants. For example, it would not be reasonable to completely remove the risk of injury from hockey by eliminating contact through checking. This would destroy the very nature of the sport. It is more reasonable to provide rules regarding contact and use of protective equipment, require coaches to teach those rules, and require referees to enforce the rules.

The types of risk that managers should consider include personnel issues, such as the risk of sexual harassment and discrimination, and issues concerning harm, such as the risk of physical injury to spectators, players, coaches, supervisors, and other employees. The potential physical risks in sport that might affect management through litigation are numerous. The possibilities are extensive and well covered in various texts (Appenzeller, 1998; Clement, 2003; Dougherty, 2002; Spengler, 2006).

Broad categories of risk, particularly in university and professional sport, include fan and player violence, terrorism (foreign and domestic), fan celebrations and storming the field, natural weather events such as lightning, food and beverage concessions, and health emergencies among players, coaches, and fans. For managers, additional general risk categories include blood-borne pathogens (e.g., the risk of disease transmitted through contact with blood or bodily fluid, as occurs in boxing, basketball, and fitness), sudden cardiac arrest (which gives rise to the need to purchase and install automated external defibrillators), child protection issues (protecting children from sexual predators through background checks and on-site safety procedures), fire, heat-related illness (including hydration issues and emergency action plans), lightning and severe weather, security (protection from violence), sport-related trauma (commonly head and neck injuries), and vehicular accidents and injuries (harm resulting from incidents, usually involving vehicles transporting players and participants).

This chapter addresses perspectives on approaching risk management and the risk management process and illustrates risk management applications.

Perspectives on Approaching Risk Management

As a person who is ultimately responsible for the safety and welfare of your employees, participants, and spectators, you can approach risk management from several perspectives. Put yourself in the shoes of the following people or organizations when you think about safety in sport venues.

Manager

This person often has a great deal of latitude in decision making. Each of us has unique personal experiences that affect our decisions, such as sport injuries or near misses; education and training through sport law and risk management courses, such as the one you are currently taking; exposure to media influence, such as hearing of sport-related lawsuits in the news; on-the-job experiences with sport-related injuries and possibly even lawsuits; and other factors, such as hearing stories relayed by friends and colleagues. When making decisions, a manager must sort through this information to determine what is relevant and reliable. This requires self-evaluation. Suppose, for example, that your nephew was seriously injured in youth football because his volunteer coach did not provide him with a properly fitting helmet. This may have instilled in you the importance of providing proper safety equipment for young athletes in your program.

In addition to thinking about factors that might influence individual perceptions, the manager has practical matters to consider. For example, how much will it cost to implement safety procedures and buy safety devices and equipment (e.g., lightning monitors, automated external defibrillators, wall padding for gyms)? Other practical considerations include the availability of information necessary to develop a comprehensive safety plan, support from upper management in implementing a new safety measure, and the cost of insurance. These issues are discussed later in this chapter.

Risk Manager or Director of Loss Prevention

A risk manager or loss prevention director has primary responsibility for the safety of a sport facility. This person might be responsible for alcohol service training, safety inspections, fire prevention, blood-borne pathogen protection, weather-related risk management, food service and equipment, and emergency services, including medical services planning, emergency action plans, and crisis management. If you have a risk manager on staff, that person would handle the details and day-to-day operations of managing risk, but you as a manager, the person with ultimate responsibility, would still need to understand the important safety issues at your facility and the policy and procedures for managing specific risks. If a loss prevention expert is not on your staff, you will need an even greater understanding of safety policy and procedures and risk management.

Outside Auditor

When we live in the same environment for some time, we often filter out many of the details of our surroundings. An outside auditor would conduct a comprehensive examination of your facility or some component of your facility, taking a fresh look at the surroundings. This person is often better able to identify **hazards** given that she is looking for them and seeing the facility with a different perspective. When you manage day-to-day operations of a facility, take a step back occasionally to view your surroundings as if for the first time. Make it a habit to look for actual and potential hazards. In other words, think like an outside auditor.

hazard—Something that holds the potential to cause harm.

Insurance Company

The insurance company is interested in limiting financial loss. This type of loss often flows from damage to property or personal injury to employees, guests, or participants. The cost is often measured in terms of repair or expenses associated with litigation (this can be either settlements or trial expenses). An insurance company will consider the probability and severity of harm that might result from the program or service offered and the conditions surrounding the provision of this program or service. For example, the likelihood (probability) and severity of injury associated with having a diving board in an unguarded pool might raise the risk of financial loss to a level where the insurance company is not willing to insure the risk. Sometimes the potential severity of risk is great but the likelihood is relatively low (e.g., a severe weather event). The precautions that you might take in this instance are more difficult to justify. If the risk is great enough that it might result in the death of a single person, however, you must make an ethical decision (with potential legal consequences) as to whether implementing a safety plan is simply the right thing to do.

Lawyer

Good lawyers think about winning cases. Personal injury cases are often won on the facts and a determination of the standard of care. The standard of care in a negligence (personal injury) case, as you learned in the previous chapter, may be determined by a number of factors. These might include (1) community or industry standard (what sort of safety measures similar organizations are putting into practice and whether these measures have themselves become accepted community or industry standards), (2) rules and regulations (whether the law requires that certain actions be taken), (3) organizational policy and procedures (your own rules), (4) prior case law, and (5) expert opinion. Therefore, you should think about your reasons for having safety plans, policies, and procedures. For example, are you keeping up with the standards that other sport organizations are meeting? Are you meeting the requirements of city codes and regulations? Are you making the same mistakes that others have made regarding safety that resulted in lawsuits and published case decisions that you have read? Thinking like a lawyer can help you avoid loss to your organization through litigation.

Jury of Your Peers

A key determination in the outcome of many legal decisions is whether a certain action was reasonable. Juries and judges in a court of law determine what is reasonable. When you are deciding whether your actions, the conditions of the facility, or other matters that might have legal consequences are legal, ask yourself what is reasonable. Ask someone you trust who has good common sense whether something that holds potential risk is unreasonably dangerous. If you ask a lawyer, you will probably get a very conservative answer. If you ask an extreme sport enthusiast, you might get an answer at the other end of the spectrum. Ask a jury of your peers, however, and you will get a good idea of what is reasonable.

A diligent and thorough assessment that incorporates some combination of the preceding ways of thinking will be a good start when you consider managing your risk and that of your sport organization.

Loss Prevention and Risk Management

Ultimately, risk management is about loss prevention. It is about providing for the safety of those to whom you owe a duty or responsibility and protecting your organization from liability through the implementation of reasonable safety measures. Losses to a sport organization as a result of litigation can be substantial. The following are categories of loss, some easily measured and others not.

- Money: Easily measured in terms of loss, money is a key concern for insurance companies. Organizations are affected if insurance rates increase or a policy is dropped after a successful lawsuit or large settlement against the sport organization. Organizations that are self-insured will also suffer financial loss.

- Time and effort: Lawsuits take time, some more than 10 years, to make it through the appeal process. Even with lawsuits that are settled relatively quickly, the affected parties must provide answers in the discovery process through written interrogatories and oral depositions. Preparing for depositions, traveling, and fulfilling other requirements of the discovery process can cost personnel a great deal of time and effort.

- Stress: The pretrial, trial, and appeals process can be very stressful to both management and the affected parties. Depositions, in which a defendant can be questioned under oath and on the record for many hours, can create a great deal of stress. Picture yourself sitting across the table from an accomplished trial attorney who is questioning you about the facts surrounding an incident that holds implications for liability on the part of your organization or you personally. The goal of the questioning is to gather information from you that can potentially be used against you in court. Imagine that this attorney is very aggressive in her approach toward obtaining information that supports her side of the case. This would likely be a very stressful situation.

- Image and good will: An organization stands to lose its good image nationally and in the community if misdeeds and negligent acts are brought to light through media attention to the lawsuit. This might influence everything from ticket sales to the monetary value of an organization.

Risk Management Process

Managing risk in sport is a process. This process has three primary components with multiple influences to each. Figure 3.1 will help you conceptualize the process and will familiarize you with the following components of a risk management process:

- Recognition
- Analysis
- Action

Each component has unique influences designated by the arrows in the model. The first step in the risk management process is the recognition by management of the importance of reducing or eliminating certain risks. This recognition results in a decision by management to act on either a specific risk or identified risk category. Once recognized, risks are then analyzed through identification and evaluation, and appropriate action (performance tasks and implementation of policies and procedures) is taken. Each part of the process is discussed next.

Recognition

Recognition of risk involves thinking about both the general categories of hazards to address and the specific hazards within those categories. Managers may not always recognize the importance of addressing certain risks and the subsequent liability that might result from a failure to do so. Influences on the recognition of risks and the decision whether to address potential risks include certain practical management issues and a manager's attitudes and perceptions (self-evaluation). One important management concern is cost.

Many decisions are based on the amount of money available to an organization. It may be costly to implement new risk management plans and procedures because of personnel or equipment costs. For example, whether the organization is able to provide automated external defibrillators (AEDs) (portable lifesaving devices that a bystander can use to revive a victim of sudden cardiac arrest, including administering an electric shock to the chest when appropriate) is dependent, in part, on whether it can afford to purchase AEDs. When negligence lawsuits are brought against sport providers

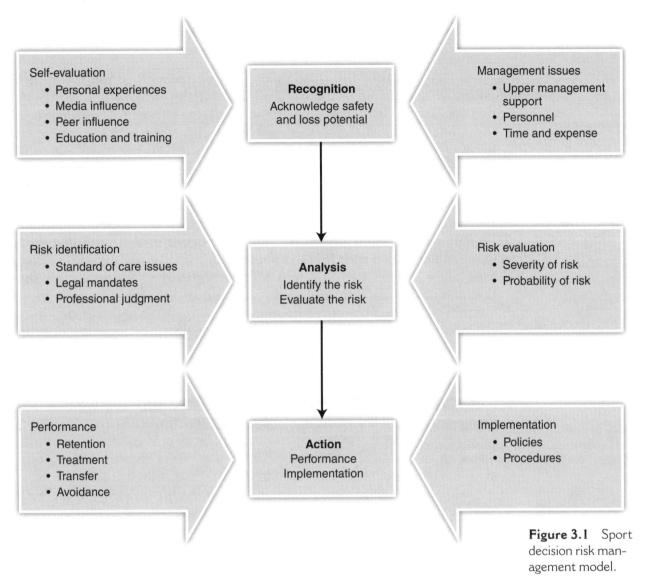

Figure 3.1 Sport decision risk management model.

for failure to provide a safe environment, cost and financial burden to the provider are often factors in the case. Before a sport organization decides to not provide safety equipment based on cost, however, it is important to exhaust all potential funding options. Depending on the nature of the sport organization, grant or subsidy programs might be available that reduce or eliminate the cost of implementing safety standards. Some examples of alternative funding sources include local civic organizations or local businesses, government and private grants, public charities, and traditional fundraising events. Additionally, as certain technologies such as AEDs evolve, their cost is often reduced.

Other management issues shape decisions as to whether a potential specific hazard or general hazard category warrants recognition and action, such as time, effort, and human resources; information and support; and necessity. When an organization has limited personnel, decisions must be made as to the best use of employees' time, skills, and energy. In some cases, management may decide that certain safety procedures are not practical given limited human resources. One factor may be the perception that it would take too much time, effort, or expense to develop a comprehensive safety policy or procedure. This perception, however, might be inaccurate given the wealth of information regarding safety procedures available online from professional associations (often in the form of published position statements written by experts and standard-setting organizations, e.g., the American Society for Testing and Materials). Much of this information is easy to access and is available in a format that can be transferred to fit specific organizational needs with minimal time and effort. Additionally, guidance is available from sport safety consultants and published texts.

Another management concern might be that the implementation of a sport-specific safety plan is too problematic. The perceived problems might lie with training time and costs. When an organization has limited staff, management may decide that it is not feasible to pull employees away from their daily functions and responsibilities to attend training sessions and then later to practice safety procedures on a regular basis. Despite these concerns, however, both the importance of saving lives and reducing injuries and the ever-present potential for liability in sport activities warrant attention to safety.

In an organization with layers of authority, action on identified risks often cannot be taken at the ground level without upper-management support. Those working with day-to-day operations might need to convince managers about the liability and harm that an identified hazard might pose. Limits on liability insurance coverage might be important factors for upper management; however, the importance of safety from an ethical standpoint should also be a prime consideration.

Consider this: "It is also wise for those responsible for safety to examine their personal motivations and consider the source of these motivations. For example, your decision regarding whether to implement a risk management plan for a particular risk category (e.g., lightning safety) might be influenced by your perception of risk. Be aware of factors that might influence this perception" (Spengler, Connaughton, & Pittman, 2006, p. 5). For example, a coach who must decide whether to implement lightning safety procedures might be influenced by past experiences. Perhaps he or a friend or relative was struck or nearly struck by lightening, or maybe a young player on his team was struck by lightning and the coach administered CPR to save the player's life. Another influence might be the media; perhaps the coach has read news stories describing the dangers of lightning in outdoor sport programs. The coach might be influenced by professional training experiences, such as a course or panel discussion on lightning safety in sport conducted by a professional association. Friends and colleagues may have told the coach stories about near misses with lightning and the importance of having lightning safety plans and procedures.

In addition to these concerns, "you likewise have an ethical responsibility to provide for the safety and well being of participants and spectators. When determining whether to implement safety measures, emphasis is often placed on the bottom line—the impact that safety measures would have on financial resources. Yet, the cost of potential injury or death to participants in the absence of safety plans is obviously of great concern as well. Even in situations in which a plan would cost an organization more to implement than it would save in terms of protection from lawsuits, there remains an ethical responsibility to provide for the safety and well-being of patrons" (Spengler et al., 2006, p. 5).

Analysis

Once the manager recognizes the need to address risk, she should analyze specific risks or general categories of risk. The analysis should consist of two parts, which often overlap and work together: risk identification and risk evaluation.

Risk Identification

Risk identification involves finding hazards and determining the potential liability that might result if a hazard is not properly addressed. For example, a common area for hazards is indoor and outdoor play areas and facilities. Some hazards include uneven turf on playing fields, glass doors or windows in gyms, slippery surfaces, baseball and softball fixed bases, low fences, and inadequate protective equipment. As a risk manager, how will you identify risks? One method is to review the facility's incident and accident report forms. Is there a pattern or a common cause for past incidents? If you have access to injury statistics or evidence of prior incidents for a particular sport or activity, you should investigate this area further. A record of prior incidents, however, will only be available if management has developed an emergency plan that includes maintaining proper records.

© Walter Bibikow/age fotostock

What potential risk factors can you identify in this facility? Identifying potential risk is part of developing a sound risk management plan.

Identification, therefore, ties directly to the development of good risk management plans. A complete discussion of emergency action plans and other risk management issues relevant to sport can be found in *Risk Management in Sport and Recreation* (Spengler et al., 2006). In risk identification, an element of common sense or professional judgment often is involved. Common sense, in this context, refers to the natural ability of a person, absent study, investigation, or research, to recognize a hazard. The hazards identified through common sense likely are obvious and should be addressed first. Other hazards, however, might not be so obvious. For these, we would look to the origins of the standard of care. These might include industry or community standards, published guidelines, standards and recommendations from professional associations, case precedent, statutory mandates, and applicable rules and regulations. Statutory mandates (e.g., state laws that require a certain organization to take certain actions) often apply to sports. For example, "in some states, it is required by law that sport and recreation organizations implement safety measures or comply with certain safety standards. For example, it may be that the case that high schools, park districts, and even health clubs must have automated external defibrillators (AEDs) at their facilities. If required by state law, and compliance is mandatory, the decision regarding whether to implement a particular safety measure has been made for you. It is therefore important to be familiar with—or seek counsel from someone familiar with—laws relevant to your organization and program" (Spengler et al., 2006, p. 3). The manager's background, education, and training, in combination with the previously addressed issues, are key factors in her ability to identify hazards and risks to the sport organization. University classes, continuing education, and on-the-job training are vital in helping the manager understand legal and safety issues in sport.

Risk Evaluation

The second component of analysis is the evaluation of risks. A risk may appear to be hazardous, but more analysis is necessary to determine the extent of risk that the hazard poses. This part of the analysis involves an evaluation by the sport manager of both the frequency and the severity of the identified risk. This procedure enables sport managers to prioritize their risks and attend to them in a timely manner. Not all hazards or risks are worthy of attention. The possibility of injury from a potential hazard might be so remote that it would only happen through a freak accident. Thus, managers should focus on hazards that are serious enough and likely enough to result in appreciable injury to someone. How do we evaluate the likelihood of injury? This evaluation is tied to risk identification: When you identify risks, you should also evaluate them. When we consider the likelihood that an event (e.g., injury from slipping on a wet floor) will occur, we are applying the legal concept of foreseeability. When it is reasonably foreseeable that a hazard (the wet floor) might injure a participant, the potential for liability on the part of the sport organization is increased. A risk might be considered foreseeable if it occurs in places or situations where injuries have occurred in the past (e.g., there is a high likelihood of risk), places of high inherent risk or danger, and situations in which participants do not understand or appreciate a particular risk given a lack of education, training, skill, or maturity (this often refers to children).

In addition to evaluating the likelihood of injury, a manager must assess how serious a potential injury might be. You can probably guess the types of sport activities, facilities, and programs that hold the greatest prospect for serious injury. Swimming and diving, gymnastics, cheer stunts, certain contact sports, exercise in extreme weather conditions (e.g., hot and humid climates), and competitive cycling all carry a high degree of risk for personal injury. Risk can be evaluated either subjectively or objectively, with both the severity and probability of risk viewed in combination. If an objective approach is taken, the severity and probability of risk can be ranked, with action to reduce the risk becoming more necessary as the severity and likelihood of the risk increase (figure 3.2).

Where the severity of a potential injury is high and the likelihood of injury is high, the organization clearly must reduce or, if possible, eliminate the risk of injury or death. A more difficult situation arises, however, when the likelihood is moderate to high and the severity is low (e.g., the potential injury is quite minor—a scrape or bruise), or there is some combination of middle-ground ranges in severity and frequency. There is no rule for when to take action to reduce the risk, or attempt to eliminate the risk, through the closure of a facility or elimination of a program or service, for example. Management must make a judgment call about whether to take action and, if so, what action to take. This takes us to the third step of the process: action.

Figure 3.2 Sport risk evaluation model.

Action

Once a risk has been recognized and analyzed, the manager must decide whether to act on the perceived risk and, if so, the type of action to take. Four options (potential actions to take) are provided by this model:

- **Retention** (keeping the situation as is)
- **Treatment** (taking action to reduce the risk such as covering an exposed sprinkler head on a playing field)
- **Transfer** (using ways to place the risk of liability on another, often through leases and contracts)
- **Avoidance** (eliminating the risk by eliminating the program, facility, or service that gives rise to the potential risk)

To understand the actions that each option calls for, consider the security operations of a university or professional sport stadium before and after the terrorist attacks of September 11, 2001. The potential severity of harm from such an attack is obviously quite high at any time. The perceived likelihood or probability of harm, however, changed before and after September 11. Before the terrorist events, the perceived risk of a terrorist attack at a sport stadium was moderate to low. Therefore, standard security operations in place at that time were often deemed adequate and were *retained*. The threat to the security of public places was elevated after September 11. Therefore, security measures were developed in an effort to *treat* (reduce) the risk of a

retention—The response to an evaluation of risks where no action is taken. The situation is kept as is.

treatment—The response to an evaluation of risks where some action is taken to reduce the risk.

transfer—The response to an evaluation of risks where methods are devised to place the risk of liability on another (e.g., through contractual agreements).

avoidance—The response to an evaluation of risks where action is taken to eliminate the risk (e.g., eliminating a program, facility, or service).

terrorist attack on sport stadium facilities. Treatment options at some stadiums included the prohibition of certain items from entering the stadium premises, physical barriers at entrance points to keep vehicles a safe distance from the facility, heightened security and searches of game patrons, and no-fly zones around the stadium. In addition to treating the risk through tangible risk reduction measures, stadiums also sought ways to *transfer* the risk of financial loss to their organization. The primary method was through insurance, with increased premiums becoming a substantial additional cost for stadiums. In other contexts, some organizations will attempt to transfer their liability through leases and contracts. The manner in which a contract is written is critical to whether an organization will be protected from liability. Another option for organizations with large financial assets is self-insurance. This involves setting a large sum of money aside to deal with financial losses that result from risk (e.g., litigation costs). The final option, and most dramatic, is to *avoid* the risk. Some sport events were cancelled immediately after September 11, both to show support for the victims, their families, and the United States and to plan for and implement additional security measures.

To formalize the specific actions that are chosen, the manager will produce and implement policies and procedures. A policy is a written rule governing the conduct of the agency's activities and programs, whereas a procedure is a written statement regarding employee actions in given circumstances. Information relevant to forming risk management policies and procedures is often available from professional associations and regulatory agencies as well as online. Thus, the Internet has had a great impact on the availability of risk management procedures. Table 3.1 provides examples of information relevant to risk implementation given various categories of risk (Spengler et al., 2006). A good example of how the Internet has influenced the availability and accessibility of sport safety information is in procedures for lightning safety. Easily accessible sources from a variety of organizations (e.g., National Oceanographic and Atmospheric Association [NOAA], professional sport organizations) provide lightning safety procedures that are applicable to sport organizations and venues. It is relatively easy for sport managers to access this information and develop their own procedures from these sources.

Traditionally, policies and procedures were printed and bound into books or pamphlets, whereas now this information is usually available in electronic form. The challenge for organizations with bound copies of policies and procedures was to see that they were read by employees and did not just sit on a bookshelf and gather dust. In our electronic age, managers face the same dilemma without the dust. In whatever form, safety policies and procedures must be available to employees and others (e.g., volunteers) in sport programs and facilities, and these people must read and follow the policies and procedures. If a policy or procedure exists that has not been properly communicated or followed and an injury and subsequent lawsuit arise because of this, the potential for liability is great. The plaintiff's lawyers can build their case using the sport organization's own policies and procedures, which will be reproduced and enlarged for use in court. An expert witness may even base

Table 3.1 Safety Issue and Risk Implementation Sources

Safety Issue	Organization	Abbreviation	Home page
Sports equipment	American Academy of Orthopaedic Surgeons	AAOS	www.aaos.org
Child-protective equipment	American Academy of Pediatrics	AAP	www.aap.org
Aquatics	American Red Cross	ARC	www.redcross.org
Emergency policy for health and fitness	American College of Sports Medicine	ACSM	www.acsm.org
Sports equipment and facilities	American Society for Testing and Materials	ASTM	www.astm.org
Soccer goals	Consumer Product Safety Commission	CPSC	www.cpsc.gov
Lightning	National Athletic Trainers' Association	NATA	www.nata.org
College athletics	National Collegiate Athletic Association	NCAA	www.ncaa.org
Crisis planning for schools	U.S. Department of Education	USDOE	www.ed.gov

Adapted, by permission, from J. Spengler, 2006, *Risk management in sport and recreation* (Champaign, IL: Human Kinetics), 2.

her opinion regarding the standard of care on these policies and procedures. Therefore, the sport manager must ensure that safety policies and procedures are communicated, implemented, and documented.

One common procedure for sport organizations is routine maintenance and inspection of facilities. Inspections may occur frequently and often occur on a set schedule. For example, bleachers may be inspected weekly for structural defects or weakness. If the schedule is provided as part of a formal safety inspection procedure, the sport manager responsible for oversight of maintenance and inspection must ensure that the schedule is adhered to. It is not difficult to imagine what an expert witness and lawyer for a plaintiff would say if the bleachers failed and someone was injured because the schedule was not followed and a problem was missed. In addition to observing regular maintenance and inspection, sport facilities sometimes bring in outside experts to conduct facility audits. These are detailed examinations of facilities or certain facility components. Audits are conducted less frequently (maybe only once or twice a year) than inspections and are much more detailed, including detailed checklists for many different items. As with inspections, however, once a problem has been found, the sport manager must determine whether that item represents a safety hazard that warrants attention. If the manager decides that the problem poses a threat to safety (through an evaluation of the risk), measures must be taken to either reduce or eliminate the risk of harm.

The following In the Courtroom case is from the published decision (later settled for an undisclosed amount) in the appellate court case of *Verni v. Aramark et al.* (2006). The case raises the issue of managing the risk of alcohol service in sport stadiums and arenas.

Verni v. Aramark et al., 903 A. 2d 475 (N.J. App. 2006)

At approximately 11 a.m. on October 24, 1999, (Defendant) Lanzaro and Michael Holder arrived at Giants Stadium and attended a football game. Lanzaro admitted that he did not clearly remember all of the events of the day but recalled that while tailgating before the game, he had consumed two or three of the eight 12-ounce beers he had in his truck. He described himself as a binge drinker. The men entered the stadium at approximately 12:30 p.m. for the 1 p.m. kickoff. Lanzaro, who had purchased his ticket from a scalper, did not sit with Holder but rather sat in the third or upper tier in section 310. Lanzaro admitted that during the first half of the game he purchased two or more 16-ounce light beers from an unidentified individual operating a concession stand in the upper tier. Lanzaro "guzzl[ed]" the beer, drinking approximately one beer every 10 minutes, and "never had an . . . empty hand," claiming he was drunk by the end of the first quarter. Just before halftime, at approximately 2:30 p.m., Lanzaro left his seat and walked down the "spirals," the ramps leading to the different stadium levels, to meet Holder. En route, Lanzaro, purchased "four or more" 16-ounce light beers from an unidentified individual operating a portable beer cart in the lower level spiral. Lanzaro claimed he told the server how many beers he wanted and then "duked" or tipped the server an extra $10 to bypass the stadium's two-beer limit. Although Lanzaro could not recall his conversation, he said he had not been abusive, vulgar, or disrespectful because he wanted to be served, explaining that "if you're a happy drunk, people give you beer. If you're a disrespectful drunk, they cut you off."

Lanzaro walked approximately 50 to 75 feet (15-23 m) to meet George Lanzaro, his brother, Lisa Lanzaro, his sister-in-law, and Holder in the spiral by Gate D. George and Lisa, who had been sitting with Holder, confirmed that Lanzaro walked toward them carrying six 16-ounce beers. George claimed that Lanzaro appeared to be intoxicated because he had "a blank sta[re] look," was animated and loud, and had "a very slight sway." Lisa confirmed that Lanzaro appeared intoxicated because he was slurring his words, he was using rapid hand movements while talking, "his eyes were drunk . . . like floating eyeballs," and he "cupped" his cigarette. Lisa said she gave Lanzaro a sandwich because she "thought he was drunk." Neither Lisa nor George Lanzaro observed Lanzaro purchase the beer. Holder testified at trial that he could not recall whether Lanzaro had appeared intoxicated but admitted that at depositions he had testified that Lanzaro had not seemed drunk. In any event, Lanzaro maintained that he drank only one or two of the beers he bought in the spiral and offered the rest to his family. Lanzaro then left and purchased marijuana in the spirals from an unidentified individual but claimed he only had a "couple of hits" because he "was too drunk." He admitted, however, that he likes to smoke marijuana because it makes him "feel a little bit more drunk."

Lanzaro and Holder left the stadium sometime around the beginning of the third quarter. Lanzaro drank a beer in the parking lot before driving to Shakers, a go-go bar. While there, Lanzaro ordered a light beer but claimed he had only "a couple sips" because he was "done," meaning intoxicated, and then he and Holder left. Lanzaro drove to a liquor store where Holder bought a six-pack of beer and a bottle of champagne, which they brought to The Gallery, another go-go bar. The Gallery did not have a liquor license but allowed its patrons to bring alcohol. It provided cups, ice, and service. Lanzaro and Holder remained at The Gallery for approximately 40 minutes, during which time Lanzaro admitted he may have consumed a beer but said that he and Holder did not drink the champagne because it was for the dancers. Gunther Bilali, the owner of The Gallery, set forth in deposition testimony read to the jury that he was not present at the time but that the hosts at his establishment would not allow a visibly intoxicated patron to enter. After leaving The Gallery, Lanzaro drove to a fast-food restaurant where he and Holder ate.

At approximately 5:47 p.m., shortly after leaving the restaurant, Lanzaro swerved across the lane of traffic and struck a 1999 Toyota Corolla driven by Ronald Verni. The parties stipulated that "Lanzaro's driving was the cause of the accident." On arrival at the scene, Officer Lange and Patrolman Thomas Barnett of the East Rutherford Police Department observed that Fazila Verni was in the back seat "wedged behind the driver" and that Antonia Verni, age 2, who was also in the back seat, was unconscious. A test taken at 6:25 p.m. confirmed that Lanzaro had a blood-alcohol concentration of .266%. Lanzaro was arrested, subsequently convicted of vehicular assault, and sentenced to a 5-year term. The Verni family sued Lanzaro and multiple other parties, including Aramark, the concessionaire responsible for the beer vendors at the game.

Risk Management Applications

The applications of risk management to sport are numerous. Several issues that are important to sport managers are discussed here: emergency action planning, crisis management, and lightning safety. Given that risk management issues often arise in the context of managing facilities, a discussion would not be complete without addressing the issue of disabled participants and application of the Americans with Disabilities Act.

Emergency Action Planning

An important issue at all levels of sport is the provision of emergency care for athletes who are injured in practices or games. The outcome of a lawsuit may hinge on the degree of care that was provided to an injured person after an initial injury. If improper care is provided, or too much time is taken in rendering aid, an injury can substantially worsen. For example, improperly moving an athlete with a suspected neck or head injury can result in permanent, devastating injury. Additionally, waiting too long to perform CPR can result in brain damage or death. Therefore, an essential risk management function is to prepare, communicate, and practice an **emergency action plan** (EAP) specific to one's sport program or facility.

emergency action plan—A comprehensive, proactive plan that addresses potential medical emergencies occurring in a sport setting.

A properly planned and rehearsed EAP can help an organization reduce the amount of time it takes to respond to a medical emergency, and respond in a manner that results in the best possible provision of care to an injured person. Some factors in emergency planning might include knowing the distance of local EMS from your facility and an estimated response time to your facility, purchasing and locating emergency medical equipment (e.g., automated external defibrillators [AEDs]), having staff properly trained and certified in CPR and first aid, having athletic trainers on staff where feasible, and having proper communication devices and phone numbers available to call for emergency assistance. Once emergency medical plans have been developed, it is imperative that they be communicated to staff and rehearsed on a regular basis. The rehearsal of EAPs helps reduce apprehension and potential panic should an actual medical emergency occur. The case of *Kleinknecht v. Gettysburg College* (1993) (see the In the Courtroom case below) addressed the duty of emergency care owed to university athletes by institutions for which they play.

In the Courtroom

Kleinknecht v. Gettysburg College, 989 F.2d 1360 (3rd Cir. 1993)

In September 1988, Drew Kleinknecht was a 20-year-old sophomore student at the college, which had recruited him for its Division III intercollegiate lacrosse team. Lacrosse is a contact sport. In terms of sport-related injuries at the college, it ranked at least fourth behind football, basketball, and wrestling, respectively. Lacrosse players can suffer a variety of injuries and incidents, including unconsciousness, wooziness, and concussions. Before Drew died, however, no athlete at the college had experienced cardiac arrest while playing lacrosse or any other sport.

In September 1988, the college employed two full-time athletic trainers, Joseph Donolli and Gareth Biser. Both men were certified by the National Athletic Trainers' Association, which requires, inter alia, current certification in both cardiopulmonary resuscitation (CPR) and standard first aid. In addition, 12 student trainers participated in the college's sport program. The trainers were stationed in the two training room facilities at Musselman Stadium and Plank Gymnasium.

Drew participated in a fall lacrosse practice on the softball fields outside Musselman Stadium on the afternoon of September 16, 1988. Coaches

Janczyk and Anderson attended and supervised this practice. No trainers or student trainers were present. Neither coach had certification in CPR. Neither coach had a radio on the practice field. The nearest telephone was inside the training room at Musselman Stadium, roughly 200 to 250 yards away. The shortest route to this telephone required scaling an eight-foot-high cyclone fence surrounding the stadium. According to Coach Janczyk, he and Coach Anderson had never discussed how they would handle an emergency during fall lacrosse practice.

The September 16, 1988, practice began at about 3:15 p.m. with jogging and stretching, some drills, and finally a six-on-six drill in which the team split into two groups at opposite ends of the field. Drew was a defenseman and was participating in one of the drills when he suffered a cardiac arrest. According to a teammate observing from the sidelines, Drew simply stepped away from the play and dropped to the ground. Another teammate on the sidelines stated that no person or object struck Drew before his collapse.

After Drew fell, his teammates and Coach Janczyk ran to his side. Coach Janczyk and some of the players noticed that Drew was lying so that his head appeared to be in an awkward position. No one knew precisely what had happened at that time, and at least some of those present suspected a spinal injury. Team captain Daniel Polizzotti testified that he heard a continuous funny gurgling noise coming from Drew, and knew from what he observed that something major was wrong. Other teammates testified that Drew's skin began quickly to change colors. One team member testified that by the time the coaches had arrived, "Drew was really blue."

According to the college, Coach Janczyk acted in accordance with the school's emergency plan by first assessing Drew's condition, then dispatching players to get a trainer and call for an ambulance. Coach Janczyk himself then began to run toward Musselman Stadium to summon help. The Kleinknechts dispute the college's version of the facts. They note that although Coach Janczyk claims to have told two players to run to Apple Hall, a nearby dormitory, for help, Coach Anderson did not recall Coach Janczyk's sending anyone for help. Even if Coach Janczyk did send the two players to Apple Hall, the Kleinknechts maintain, his action was inappropriate because Apple Hall was not the location of the nearest telephone. It is undisputed that two other team members ran for help, but the Kleinknechts contend that the team members did this on their own accord, without instruction from either coach.

The parties do not dispute that Polizzotti, the team captain, ran toward the stadium, where he knew a training room was located and a student trainer could be found. In doing so, Polizzotti scaled a chain-link fence that surrounded the stadium and ran across the field, encountering student trainer Traci Moore outside the door to the training room. He told her that a lacrosse player was down and needed help. She ran toward the football stadium's main gate, managed to squeeze through a gap between one side of the locked gate and the brick pillar forming its support, and continued on to the practice field by foot until flagging a ride from a passing car. In

» continued

» continued

the meantime, Polizzotti continued into the training room where he told the student trainers there what had happened. One of them phoned Plank Gymnasium and told head trainer Donolli about the emergency.

At the time of Polizzotti's dash to the stadium, Dave Kerney, another team member, ran toward the stadium for assistance. Upon seeing that Polizzotti was going to beat him there, Kerney concluded that it was pointless for both of them to arrive at the same destination and changed his course toward the College Union Building. He told the student at the front desk about the emergency on the practice field. The student called his supervisor on duty in the building, and she immediately telephoned for an ambulance. Student trainer Moore was first to reach Drew. She saw Drew's breathing was labored, and the color of his complexion changed as she watched. Because Drew was breathing, she did not attempt CPR or any other first aid technique, but only monitored his condition, observing no visible bruises or lacerations.

By this time, Coach Janczyk had entered the stadium training room and learned that Donolli had been notified and an ambulance called. Coach Janczyk returned to the practice field at the same time Donolli arrived in a golf cart. Donolli saw that Drew was not breathing, and turned him on his back to begin CPR with the help of a student band member who was certified as an emergency medical technician and had by chance arrived on the scene. The two of them performed CPR until two ambulances arrived at approximately 4:15 p.m. Drew was defibrillated and drugs were administered to strengthen his heart. He was placed in an ambulance and taken to the hospital, but despite repeated resuscitation efforts, Drew could not be revived. He was pronounced dead at 4:58 p.m.

Prior to his collapse on September 16, 1988, Drew had no medical history of heart problems. The Kleinknechts themselves describe him as "a healthy, physically active and vigorous young man" with no unusual medical history until his death. In January 1988, a college physician had examined Drew to determine his fitness to participate in sports and found him to be in excellent health. The Kleinknechts' family physician had also examined Drew in August 1987 and found him healthy and able to participate in physical activity.

Medical evidence indicated Drew died of cardiac arrest after a fatal attack of cardiac arrhythmia. A postmortem examination could not detect the cause of Drew's fatal cardiac arrhythmia. An autopsy conducted the day after his death revealed no bruises or contusions on his body. This corroborated the statements by Drew's teammates that he was not in play when he suffered his cardiac arrest and dispelled the idea that contact with a ball or stick during the practice might have caused the arrhythmia. The National Institutes of Health examined Drew's heart as part of the autopsy but found no pathology. A later examination of the autopsy records by a different pathologist, and still further study by yet another physician after Drew's body was exhumed, also failed to reveal any heart abnormality that could have explained Drew's fatal heart attack.

Crisis Management

In addition to the potential for medical emergencies to occur in the sport setting, there is the potential for greater harm to a sport organization. This broad category of harm is termed a **crisis**. Crises are large in scope, negative, and disruptive, and they can threaten an organization's mission and reputation. During a crisis, the mission of the organization is usually placed on hold until the crisis is resolved. Examples of crises are catastrophic weather events, fires, and terrorist events. When crises occur, the goal of the organization should be to react quickly and effectively to stabilize the situation and then to act in a positive manner to return the situation back to normal. Since most crises catch people and organizations by surprise, placing them in a reactive mode, it is important for the sport manager to develop a sound plan before the onset of a crisis. This plan is called a **crisis management plan** (CMP). This is similar to an emergency action plan (EAP) but is specific to emergency situations that are greater in scope and generally more damaging to more people. A comprehensive CMP should cover a wide range of potential crises.

The primary goal of crisis management planning is to develop comprehensive written contingency plans based on existing resources and operational capabilities that will enable sport managers to effectively deal with crises. CMPs must be specifically developed for every sport program. Every program has unique factors that must be considered, including the nature and location of the program, the participants, the staff, the response time of local emergency medical services (EMS), and the facility and equipment involved. Despite the uniqueness of each program, several components should form the foundation of all CMPs.

Create a Planning Team

The first component is the planning stage in developing the CMP. This requires the formation of a planning team who will begin the process. The team's primary task is to identify the possible risks and crises that may arise in their organization. Several methods of identifying potential risks and crises exist, including consultation with outside experts, reviewing industry trends, and studying accident and injury report forms. Locations where past incidents have occurred and the nature of the incidents and how they were handled will be valuable to the sport manager in developing a CMP.

Develop an Action Plan

The second component is the development of an action plan for crisis response for each major category of hazard that may confront the organization. The action plan should include several key considerations for the sport manager. The first planning issue for the sport manager to consider is personnel: those who will be critical to crisis response. The action plan should identify, by job title, those employees who will handle the crisis. Specific duties and responsibilities of each responder must be carefully outlined in a simple and clear format. It is recommended and often required that certain employees be certified in CPR and first aid. The second

crisis—An emergency or significant critical event that must be planned for proactively and can often be dealt with by the affected organization.

crisis management plan—A comprehensive, proactive plan designed to lessen the negative impact on an organization in the event of a crisis.

planning issue to consider is the sport facility. The location of emergency exits and shelters; gas, power, and water shutoff valves; alarm systems; backup power systems; main electrical panels; and fire hoses and extinguishers should be clearly identified. Locations for meeting EMS should also be identified and evacuation procedures developed. A third planning issue, in addition to the facility, is an evaluation of emergency equipment. The plan should identify and catalog the type of equipment available (e.g., public address and communication equipment, firefighting equipment, first aid kits, automated external defibrillators, and backboards), where it is stored, and who will have access to it.

Establish Emergency Communication Rules

A third issue of importance in developing the CMP is communication. Before a crisis occurs, the sport organization should identify outside experts who will work side by side with the organization in a crisis. Internally, the sport organization should designate who will be responsible for emergency communications. All staff should be trained regarding where and how to make emergency communications. For example, all staff should know the exact location of telephones or other communication devices and know the procedures for making emergency phone calls. Specifically, staff should be trained on dialing the correct emergency number. This may be as simple as informing staff that they must dial a 9 or other number to reach an outside line before dialing 9-1-1 or other emergency number. Staff should be trained to stay calm and provide accurate information to emergency responders. It is also important that staff know, in the event of a crisis situation, to not hang up the phone until the operator or dispatcher states that they have all of the necessary information.

Establish Postcrisis Communication Rules

The fourth component of importance to the CMP is postcrisis communication. The organization should determine who will meet with staff for debriefing and who will meet with the media. Preparations for a timely, accurate, and appropriate response must begin soon after a crisis has occurred. News media will expect and demand an immediate response. A decision on whether a news conference or release would be an appropriate means of conveying information to the news media and public must be made. The means of internal communication to be used if the crisis affects employees and participants must also be determined. The main switchboard or operator must be informed about where to refer phone calls pertaining to the crisis. At the earliest possible stage, staff members must be advised of the crisis situation. Clear instructions on handling the media and telephone calls concerning the situation should be communicated, and staff should be told that that they may be called on to perform special duties related to the incident. The organization should address alternative or additional means of conveying information. This might include such items as letters to parents or fans, letters to newspaper editors, and consultation with boards or other entities.

Create Postcrisis Reports

The fifth component of importance to the CMP is postcrisis reports. In response to a crisis, the sport organization should determine who completes reports and when. All crises should be carefully documented with the use of an appropriate incident or injury report form approved by the organization's legal counsel. Staff members should be very familiar with these forms and the policies and procedures surrounding their use. For example, it is typically required that these forms be brought to the administration's attention within 24 hours of the incident. They must be retained for at least the length of the respective states' statutes of limitations. Assigned personnel should know how to complete them and to whom they should be sent. Policies should be established for filing and retaining reports. Additionally, postcrisis responses should adhere to certain follow-up procedures. For example, it should be determined who (e.g., injured participants, parents, EMS, law enforcement, risk management, insurance companies) is contacted and when. The organization should also determine how contacts are to be made and by whom (e.g., phone calls, visits to those injured). Finally, a preassigned spokesperson who will speak to the media should be selected. All personnel should be informed that only the media contact person speaks to the media.

Test the Plan

The final component of importance to the CMP is testing the plan. Once a CMP has been developed, it must be tested. A crisis manager or committee designated by the sport organization should discuss the plan, event by event, situation by situation, and develop schematics of how the plan works. The CMP should then be tested in conditions as close to real life as possible and adjusted accordingly. A final CMP draft should then be developed and circulated to all affected parties (Connaughton, Spengler, & Bennett, 2001).

Once all components of the CMP have been addressed, all employees should be provided with a written copy, or access to a copy, of the organization's CMP. Additionally, all employees should be trained in the CMP at the beginning of their employment and periodically thereafter. Students and certain program participants can also be trained to assist in the event of a crisis. Depending on the program, its location, and the participant's age, they may be able to do things such as ensure that EMS or certain administrators have been notified, retrieve first aid supplies, or, at the very least, behave in a manner that does not impede the CMP. CMPs must be regularly practiced, evaluated, and updated. Practicing CMPs will assist in working out any flaws. Announced and unannounced practice of the CMPs should be conducted at least on a yearly basis (Appenzeller & Seidler, 1998). Sport and recreation managers, physical educators, coaches, fitness instructors, and others involved in providing physical activities should establish a plan if a crisis occurs. Developing a CMP with the advice of appropriate counsel is an important proactive measure that might lessen the negative consequences of a crisis.

Lightning Safety

Another risk for sport managers involves injuries and fatalities to players or participants from lightning strikes. For outdoor sports, particularly those that are supervised, lightning safety is a major concern. Fortunately, there is accessible guidance on managing the risk of lightning in sport programs and facilities. This guidance comes in the form of position statements from professional associations. Sport managers should be aware of professional associations that have lightning safety recommendations or guidelines that are relevant to their programs. If they wish to follow the recommendations, they would ultimately need to develop a risk management plan that addresses lightning safety and identifies policies and procedures that reduce the risk of injury and death from lightning.

Professional associations in the field of sport and recreation management that have published and adopted lightning safety recommendations include the National Athletic Trainers' Association (NATA) and the National Collegiate Athletic Association (NCAA). The NATA has published a position statement on lightning safety for athletics and recreation (Walsh et al., 2000), which other associations have adopted in some form. The recommendations are also similar to those set forth by the American Meteorological Society (Holle & Lopez, 1999).

The National Athletic Trainers' Association has been instrumental in formulating lightning safety recommendations that are focused on both sports and recreation. The NATA recommends the formulation and implementation of a "comprehensive, proactive lightning safety policy or emergency action plan specific to lightning safety" (Walsh et al., 2000, p. 472). The NATA identified six essential components of a lightning safety policy or emergency action plan:

1. Organizations should designate a person with the authority to remove participants from sport and recreational activities in the event of lightning. That person would undergo formal training in lightning safety identification and emergency procedures.

2. A weather watcher should be appointed who looks for indications of threatening weather and notifies the person with authority to cancel or suspend play if severe weather becomes dangerous.

3. A method for monitoring lightning associated with approaching storms should be identified. It is recommended that monitoring consist of both watching the sky and implementing another form of monitoring through electronic means.

4. It is recommended that safe structures for seeking shelter from lightning be built, properly identified, and placed in areas where they can be quickly accessed if needed. Dugouts and other buildings that are not grounded should be discouraged for use in lightning storms.

5. Specific criteria for suspending and resuming sport and recreational activities should be implemented. It is recommended that a flash-to-bang count be used to determine when play should be suspended. The

flash-to-bang count is the time between when a flash of lightning is seen and the associated thunder is heard. If there is an interval lasting 30 seconds or less between the flash of lightning and the sound of thunder, the immediate evacuation of participants from the outdoors to a safe shelter is recommended (Cooper, Holle, & Lopez, 1999). For resuming play, it is recommended to wait at least 30 minutes after the last lightning strike is seen or thunder is heard.

6. It is recommended that lightning safety strategies be implemented, such as requiring staff members to maintain current cardiopulmonary resuscitation (CPR) and first aid certification. Knowledge of CPR and first aid is critical for first responders who might attempt to resuscitate and provide care to a lightning strike victim (Walsh et al., 2000).

In conjunction with the National Severe Storms Laboratory, the NCAA has also developed lightning safety guidelines for collegiate athletic programs (NCAA, 2001):

1. The NCAA suggests that a chain of command be designated to determine who will monitor for threatening weather and who will make the decision to remove athletes from a site or event. This should include the development of an emergency plan that indicates instructions for participants as well as spectators.

2. A weather report should be reviewed each day to determine the potential risk of threatening weather.

3. During events, the National Weather Service should be monitored for severe weather or lightning watches or warnings.

4. Coaches and athletes should know the closest safe structure or location to the field or playing area and how long it takes to get there.

5. Athletic officials and coaches should be aware of how close lightning is to the field or playing area. This may be determined by several measures, including the flash-to-bang count and lightning predictors or detectors.

It is important for sport managers to understand the scope and nature of lightning safety policies and procedures in sport programs. The NATA, NCAA, NOAA, and other organizations provide excellent reference and guidance on lightning safety policies and procedures. By following these recommendations, facilities and programs can be designed and managed to minimize the risk from lightning strikes. If the risks associated with lightning are understood, and measures are implemented to reduce the risk of lightning-related injury, sport managers can provide better protection to participants.

Facilities and the Americans with Disabilities Act

When managing risk for sport facilities, safety measures should be implemented with concern for everyone, including both able-bodied people and those with disabilities. The Americans with Disabilities Act of 1990

(ADA) was passed in order to provide a national mandate furthering the elimination of discrimination against individuals with disabilities (42 U.S.C. §12101(b)(1), 2008). The ADA enhances the protections provided by the Rehabilitation Act of 1973, which prohibits discrimination against people with disabilities by government agencies who receive federal funds (Pub.L.No. 93-112, 1973).

To understand whether the ADA applies to a particular individual, that individual must first be classified as disabled as defined in the statute. This is really the most important inquiry because it is possible for an individual to be disabled in some way as understood in normal parlance, and yet not under the definition of disabled found in the statute. The ADA provides that a person is disabled if he or she has a physical or mental impairment that substantially limits one or more of the major life activities, has a record of such impairment, or is regarded as having such an impairment (42 U.S.C. § 12102(2)). For purposes of the statute, a physical or mental impairment involves any of the following:

- Any physiological disorder or condition, cosmetic disfigurement, or anatomical loss affecting one or more of the following body systems: neurological; musculoskeletal; special sense organs; respiratory, including speech organs; cardiovascular; reproductive; digestive; genitourinary; hemic and lymphatic; skin; and endocrine

- Any mental or psychological disorder such as mental retardation, organic brain syndrome, emotional or mental illness, and specific learning disabilities

- Contagious and noncontagious diseases and conditions such as ortho-pedic, visual, speech, and hearing impairments; cerebral palsy; epilepsy; muscular dystrophy; multiple sclerosis; cancer; heart disease; diabetes; mental retardation; emotional illness; specific learning disabilities; HIV disease (whether symptomatic or asymptomatic); tuberculosis; drug addic-tion; and alcoholism (28 C.F.R. § 36.104(1), 2008)

Perhaps most important for many situations that develop in the high school and college setting is that learning disabilities are specifically men-tioned as impairments that qualify someone as disabled under the statute. In addition, a major life activity is defined as "functions such as caring for oneself, performing manual tasks, walking, seeing, hearing, speaking, breathing, learning, and working" (28 C.F.R. § 36.104(2), 2008). As a result, the ADA can have an impact on a person's participation in sports because it may involve the major life activities of seeing, hearing, walking, or other aspects of this definition.

After a determination that a person is disabled under these definitions, the analysis then shifts to the part of the ADA that may apply to the particular situation. Title III applies to the sport context, perhaps most important in regard to accessing sport facilities. Title III bars discrimination against dis-abled individuals "in the full and equal enjoyment of the goods, services, facilities, privileges, advantages, or accommodations of any place of public accommodation by any person who owns, leases (or leases to), or operates a place of public accommodation" (42 U.S.C. §12182(a), 2008). The statute specifically includes gymnasiums, golf courses, and other places of exercise and recreation as places of accommodation covered under this part.

Many forms of discrimination are banned under Title III. Perhaps most important in connection to sport and recreational activities is when individuals with disabilities are barred from enjoying the goods and services of the place of public accommodation; when there is a failure to make reasonable modifications, unless such modifications would fundamentally alter the nature of the goods and services of the place of public accommodation; and when there is a failure to remove structural and other facility barriers to disabled individuals. Many lawsuits have been brought within the sport context with regard to access to sport and recreational facilities themselves. Many cases have been brought against the architects, designers, and owners of these facilities in order to force them to comply with the ADA's regulations. Facilities constructed before January 26, 1993, are considered existing facilities that must remove architectural barriers only where such removal is readily achievable in relation to the effectiveness, practicality, and cost of such removal.

Facilities designed and constructed for first occupancy after January 26, 1993, are viewed as new construction and must comply with the ADA's more strict accessibility standards (28 C.F.R. subpart A, 2006). These regulations, the Americans with Disabilities Act Accessibility Guidelines (ADAAG), put forth minimum technical requirements for new construction and alterations of existing facilities so that both accommodate people with disabilities. These guidelines are especially important in the sport and recreation industry because they can affect every stage of the design and building process. At every stage of this process, the builder, owner, tenants, and all others involved must make sure that the facility being built will accommodate disabled patrons in very specific technical ways. For instance, facilities must remove architectural barriers by installing ramps; making curb cuts in sidewalks and entrances; rearranging tables, chairs, vending machines, display racks, and other furniture; repositioning telephones; widening doors; and eliminating turnstiles or providing alternative accessible paths (28 C.F.R. §36.304(b)).

Edward Resnick, a quadriplegic man who uses a wheelchair, sued the owners of Pro Player Stadium, home of the Miami Dolphins and Florida Marlins, when he was unable to purchase accessible seating for football and baseball games (*Access Now et al. v. South Florida Stadium Corp. et al.*, 2001). Pro Player Stadium was constructed in 1987, before the enactment of the ADA. Therefore, the stadium had to comply with the ADA's "readily achievable" standard applicable to existing facilities and remove barriers only when such measures are effective, practical, and fiscally manageable. Although Resnick demonstrated several ways in which access to the stadium could be improved for people with disabilities, he was unable to show that the facility was not in accord with the ADA and its architectural guidelines. Therefore, the court found that Pro Player Stadium was not in violation of the ADA, and the stadium owner had no legal obligation to make the facility modifications that he suggested.

Summary

Decisions pertaining to safety are the most important decisions that sport managers will make. These decisions often result in the formation of risk management policies and procedures. Risk management is a process that begins with the recognition by management of the importance of reducing or eliminating certain risks. This recognition results in a decision by management to act on either a specific risk or an identified risk category. Once recognized, risks are analyzed, with appropriate action taken and safety measures implemented as deemed necessary. An effective risk management plan that is communicated to employees and staff, and one that is properly carried out, can help an organization reduce the probability of injury to its patrons and the subsequent liability that often results.

DISCUSSION QUESTIONS

1. Suppose you manage a stadium that serves alcohol to patrons at sport events. Explain the key factors that would influence your decision making relevant to the components of risk management:
   - Recognition
   - Analysis
   - Action

2. Is it worth the time and effort for a sport organization to implement procedures to manage the risk of an incident such as a lightning strike where the likelihood of death or injury is low but the potential severity of injury is high? Why?

3. Provide a brief hypothetical example of situations in which each of the following courses of action would be justified:
   - Retention
   - Treatment
   - Transfer
   - Avoidance

4. Discuss the components of a crisis management plan relevant to a potential terrorist attack on a sport stadium.

5. Do you believe that a lightning safety plan for supervised sport activities is necessary? Explain.

MOOT COURT CASE

Doug was the supervisor of an after-school sport program (run by ASP, Inc.). Doug was also an avid fan of dodgeball, having played the sport since childhood, and enjoyed the adrenaline rush and competitive nature of the game. Dodgeball was just one sport in a series of activities provided by the after-school sport program that included kickball, basketball, soccer, volleyball, and various other games. On a particularly hot day in early August, Doug was supervising a group of eight 6th graders in an outdoor basketball game. The children were complaining about the heat and several looked as though the heat was taking a toll on them. Doug, mindful of the dangers of heat illness, believed that it was best to take his group inside. It was getting late in the day anyway, with only an hour left until activities ended for the day. Doug brought the children inside into a multipurpose play area that was set up for volleyball. Christie, a counselor with the program, was with her group of 8th graders playing volleyball. She also had eight in her group. Doug suggested that they play dodgeball because Christie's group was tired of playing volleyball and putting both groups together on one volleyball court didn't seem like a good idea. Doug suggested that they take down the net. They would leave the posts up and just warn the players to stay away from them because it was too much work to take them down. Doug and Christie split the groups so that each had four 6th graders and four 8th graders on a team. They also warned the children about the volleyball posts. The children began play and seemed to enjoy it. To make the game more interesting, players who were hit with the ball would only sit out for a few minutes and could then return to the game. They were instructed to sit behind the volleyball posts near the center line when hit by a ball.

Suzie was one of the 6th graders in Doug's group. Despite her age, she was one of the best players on the court. While throwing a ball, she was struck in the waist by a ball thrown by an opposing team member. Suzie was disappointed but ran to the sidelines to sit out. As she was running, a ball thrown by an 8th grader on the other team struck her ankle and she lost her balance. Suzie fell forward and struck one of the volleyball posts with the side of her head. Both counselors immediately came to her aid and asked her how she felt. She said that her head hurt somewhat but that she was OK and wanted to keep playing. Doug and Suzie looked for swelling but saw none. Even though they knew she had struck the post with a lot of force, they decided that she could keep playing. Thirty minutes later, the game ended and Suzie told Doug that her head was hurting worse. It was only 10 minutes until the end of class and the parents were already arriving to pick up their children. Doug wasn't sure of the policy or standards relevant to head injuries but asked Christie to call 911, and she went to make the call. She returned 10 minutes later and said that she was delayed because she kept trying to make the call but didn't know that she needed to dial out first by dialing 9. She finally figured this out on her own. By this time Suzie was nauseous and incoherent and could not stand up. Her mother had just arrived and was holding Suzie. The ambulance arrived 10 minutes later and took Suzie to the hospital. It was determined later that she had suffered a serious head injury. Suzie's mother sued Doug and ASP, Inc., for negligence.

4

Agency Law

CHAPTER OBJECTIVES

After reading this chapter, you will know the following:

- How agency relationships work and the authority that agents have
- The function of a sport agent
- The duties of agents and principals within the agency relationship
- The many ways in which athlete agents are regulated

© Icon SMI

Sport managers work with many types of agents in the sport industry. The focus in sport is often on athlete or player agents; however, many other types of agents are involved in the industry, from marketing, sponsor, and endorser agents to representatives of coaches and team and facility owners. When one individual represents a second individual or entity in negotiations with a third individual or entity, that initial individual is acting as an agent of the second party.

This chapter focuses on the law related to agents. We begin with a discussion of the history of sport agents and the role they serve. We then focus on principals of **agency law,** including establishment of the agency relationship, authority of agents, and the duties agents must uphold. We then move to an analysis of agency contracts, followed by an in-depth look at the regulation of player agents. Next, the focus shifts to an analysis of contract law, criminal law, and tort law disputes involving agents. The chapter ends with a discussion of the future of sport agency.

agency law—The law that applies to and explains the relationship between principal and agent. Agency law specifically defines the rights and responsibilities of both principals and agents, the authority of the agent as he or she works for the principal, and the creation of the agency relationship itself.

Although agents are involved at virtually every level of the sport industry, player agents are the focus of regulations, disputes, litigation, and most of the analysis within the industry. Therefore, although this chapter discusses principals of agency that apply to all agents, the examples provided frequently involve player agents. This does not change the analysis; it merely reflects the fact that player agents are the most regulated professionals within the U.S. sport industry, to the point where specific state and federal laws apply only to player agents.

Sport Agents

agency relationship— The relationship between the principal and the agent.

Determining when the first individual in the sport industry entered into an **agency relationship** is impossible. A clearer historical record can be established related to player agents. The first well-known player to hire an agent to represent him in contract negotiations was early football star Red Grange. In 1925, Grange hired an agent to negotiate his contract with the NFL's Chicago Bears. Still, the profession did not truly expand until the 1960s, when attorney Mark McCormack began to work with legendary golfer Arnold Palmer. As Palmer began to make more money from sponsorship and endorsement deals, athletes from other sports began to seek the representation of player agents.

At the time, not all teams were excited about working with player agents. In the early 1960s, NFL Hall of Fame center Jim Ringo of the Green Bay Packers hired an agent to renegotiate his contract with legendary Packers coach Vince Lombardi. When Lombardi saw the agent, he left the room for a short time and returned to tell Ringo that the negotiations were done because he had been traded to the Washington Redskins.

The player agent profession did not see explosive growth until the 1970s. Until then, most athletes in professional team sports were bound by reserve clauses (discussed further in chapter 10) in their contracts stipulating that if the player did not automatically sign a new contract with the team for the next season, all of the provisions of his present contract would be automatically renewed. Therefore, players had no freedom to move from team to team seeking higher salaries. In the 1970s, the professional sports leagues adopted free agency, and players were free to offer their services to other teams and often relied on agents to help them in these negotiations.

There has been continuous growth in the field of sport agency. Each of the four major professional sports leagues in the United States currently has hundreds of registered player agents, although many individual agents represent multiple players (see table 4.1). For instance, notorious baseball player agent Scott Boras represents an estimated 65 baseball players (Scott Boras, n.d.), whereas football player agent Drew Rosenhaus represents 109 football players (Clients, n.d.).

Table 4.1 Number of Player Agents in Professional Team Sports

League	No. of agents	No. of players*
Major League Baseball	>300	3,632
National Basketball Association	350	438
National Football League	850	2,568
National Hockey League	150	804

*The information for the number of players is taken from the complete list of players provided on each league's Web site.

Sport agents assume many roles for the player, team, coach, or owner for whom they work. These roles include the following:

- Negotiating employment contracts
- Negotiating concession agreements with concessionaires
- Representing an organization in negotiations with sponsors, advertisers, and media outlets
- Representing an organization, athlete, or coach in negotiations with endorsers
- Entering the team or organization into events
- Entering into contracts with security, ushers, merchandisers, and others associated with games and other events
- Managing the relationship with outside entities including community organizations, facility boards, and charitable foundations
- Conducting estate, tax, and financial planning for athlete, coach, and organization clients
- Securing investment and appearance opportunities for the athlete or coach
- Working as the conduit between an athlete, coach, or organization in developing an Internet presence or marketing campaign

Agents act in countless ways for their clients. To understand the nature of this relationship, we next look at the principles of agency law.

Concepts in Agency Law

The law of agency is often understood by reference to the *Restatements of the Law*. Written by legal scholars who are members of the American Law Institute, the Restatements explain what the law is in a certain area and how it is changing. Courts often rely on the Restatements to provide consistent explanations of certain areas of law. One of the most widely used Restatements is the *Restatement of Agency*.

The Restatement defines an agency as "the fiduciary relationship that arises when one person (a 'principal') manifests assent to another person (an 'agent') that the agent shall act on the principal's behalf and subject to the principal's control, and the agent manifests assent or otherwise consents so to act" (*Restatement [Third] of Agency* § 1.01, 2008). In simpler terms, *agency* refers to the relationship between two parties in which one party, known as the agent, agrees to act as the representative of the other party, known as the principal. Of particular note, the agent should act for the benefit of the principal and subject to the control of the principal. In sport, these relationships are everywhere:

- Students who sell their university's merchandise at a game are acting as agents of their school (the principal).
- Ticket sellers selling tickets for games or other events are acting as agents of the team (the principal) they work for.
- Sport managers promoting a facility as a possible location for playoff or other games and events are acting as agents of the facility (the principal).
- Health club workers trying to draw in clients for the club are acting as agents of that club (the principal).

There are many types of agency relationships in sport, particularly informal agency relationships, such as this one between the fan and the concession staff.

© Human Kinetics

Agency law refers to the law that applies to and explains these situations and specifically defines the rights and responsibilities of both principals and agents, the authority of the agent as he or she works for the principal, and the creation of the agency relationship itself. This relationship between the agent and the principal is governed by law and bears further examination.

Agency Relationship

An agency relationship is the relationship between the principal and agent. Such relationships are consensual, meaning both parties must agree to become part of the relationship. In addition, although agency relationships often are described by contracts between the principal and agent (such as a student employment agreement providing that the student will work in a merchandise store for the school), agency relationships also can be created simply by oral agreement. However, for any agency relationship to be established by an agreement, both parties must have the legal capacity to enter into the agreement (as discussed in chapter 5).

Generally, no formality is required to create an agency relationship. All that is necessary is that the parties agree to enter into an agency relationship. This lack of formality can lead to problems when one party disputes the existence of the agency relationship. In evaluating whether an agency relationship has been created, courts look objectively at the situation to determine whether an agency relationship was established rather than focus on what the parties say they intended. The court typically will focus on whether the principal did or said something that the agent could have reasonably interpreted as the principal's intent to allow the agent to act on the principal's behalf. Consider the following hypothetical example.

Al is an agent for the Greater Milwaukee Open (GMO), a professional golf tournament. As part of his job, Al attends charity functions and industry mixers to meet golfers, sponsors, and others in the industry. At one event, he happens to stand next to Tiger Woods and so introduces himself. Al tells Tiger about the GMO and describes how wonderful the tournament is. Tiger says, "That sounds great. I would love it if you could help me play at that event this year." Tiger is then pulled aside quickly by the media before Al can respond. Al is excited and tells his employers at the GMO that Tiger Woods has agreed to let Al help Tiger play in the GMO. The GMO then leaks a story that Tiger will play in the tournament next year. Ticket and sponsorship sales climb as a result of the announcement. In reality, Tiger never intended to play in the GMO because it conflicts with another tournament. Three weeks after the story is leaked, Tiger's player agent contacts Al to tell him that Tiger has not committed to play in the GMO. Al disputes that, claiming that he and Tiger had a verbal agreement that Al would act as an agent on his behalf and help him play in the GMO. Eventually, the GMO sues Tiger Woods for lost revenue associated with the loss of sponsorships and returned tickets when the media learn that he will not play in the GMO. Although Al has a good argument that he relied on Tiger's statement that he wanted Al's help to allow him to play, the court also looks closely at what Tiger said and finds that no agency relationship was created.

Beyond these simple misunderstandings, in order to understand what an agent can do you need to understand the different levels of authority that an agent may possess. These different levels of authority are discussed next.

Authority

The scope of the agent's authority to act on behalf of the principal is vitally important. If the agent does not have the authority to act on behalf of the principal or exceeds the authority she was given by the principal, the agent's actions cannot bind the principal and the principal cannot be held liable for the acts of the agent.

A typical example could involve a university coach. The coach in question is a highly sought-after men's basketball coach and enters into a written agreement with an agent who will help him negotiate with schools to attain the best salary. However, the agreement does not include any reference to the agent's seeking marketing and endorsement opportunities for the coach, because the coach typically talks to marketers himself. If the agent starts to negotiate with Nike, Adidas, or other apparel companies without the coach's knowledge or approval, the agent may have acted without the authority of the coach and any apparel contract entered into would not be binding on the coach. This could be especially problematic because many schools enter into their own apparel contracts with apparel companies. Therefore, the coach would merely be an agent of the school in regard to these apparel contracts and so not able to negotiate his own deal.

The level of an agent's authority can best be understood by analyzing the legal concepts of actual authority (including express and implied authority), apparent authority, and ratification (see figure 4.1). Each of these concepts creates and defines the particular agency relationship.

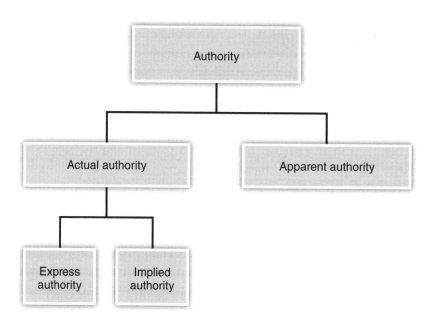

Figure 4.1 Levels of authority.

Actual Authority

actual authority—
Authority under which the agent reasonably believes that his or her actions are within the scope of authority given to them by the principal.

An agent acts with **actual authority** when the agent reasonably believes that his actions are within the scope of authority given to him by the principal. Scope of authority refers to the limits on the agent's authority and typically includes the amount of authority needed to accomplish the goals of the agency relationship. There are two types of actual authority: express and implied.

Express Authority   An express agency relationship is created when the agent and principal enter into a written or oral agreement. Any written or oral communication that grants the agent authority to perform an act is considered **express authority.** Any standard agency contract can establish an express agency that provides the agent with express authority. Many professional team sports unions mandate that player agents must enter into standard representation agreements with union members (the players in the particular sport) before representing any players within the sport. These standard agreements create an express agency relationship between the player and agent that clearly defines the exact amount of authority that the agent will have in acting on behalf of the player. Such an agreement might contain language similar to that found in figure 4.2. Under this agreement, the agent's express job is to "represent, advise, counsel, and assist Player in the negotiation, execution, and enforcement of his playing contract" (NFL Players Association, 2007).

Implied Authority   **Implied authority** refers to the agent's authority and ability to perform incidental acts that are reasonably necessary to accomplish the agent's express responsibilities as provided in the **agency agreement** (either oral or written). Implied authority must be consistent with the express authority granted within the agency agreement, but implied authority will not be specified within the agreement, because unforeseen situations often arise that force the agent to take action for the benefit of the principal.

In the NFL Players Association **Standard Representation Agreement** shown in figure 4.2, the player agent is expressly authorized to "represent, advise, counsel, and assist Player in the negotiation, execution, and enforcement of his playing contract." Nothing within this language specifies that the agent has the authority to meet with a particular team or representatives of a team or to determine the exact manner in which the player will receive his salary. However, any player would want the agent to do this. Therefore, the agent must have the implied authority to be able to act in this way for the benefit of the player.

The focal point for determining whether an agent acted with implied authority is the agent's reasonable understanding at the time the agent took action. If a court finds that the agent's interpretation of the agency relationship was unreasonable and that the agent lacked authority to perform an act, then the improper act falls outside the scope of the agent's authority. Actions that fall outside the scope of an agent's authority are considered *ultra vires.* From a risk management standpoint, agents and principals alike should try to limit the potential for ultra vires acts. The easiest way to avoid these acts is to include detailed written language within the agency agreement that describes all of the ways in which the agent may act.

Apparent Authority

In situations where it is unclear whether the agent has actual authority, the agent may have what is termed **apparent authority.** In these situations, because of the behavior of the principal, a third party may believe that the agent is acting with actual authority. As a result, if the principal allows a situation to exist that may mislead others about the actual authority of the

express authority— Any written or oral communication that grants the agent authority to perform an act.

implied authority— The agent's authority and ability, not expressly provided in the agreement, to perform incidental acts that are reasonably necessary to accomplish the agent's express responsibilities as provided in the agency agreement (either oral or written).

agency agreement— The verbal or written agreement that formalizes the relationship between an agent and a principal.

Standard Representation Agreement—Document that many professional player unions require agents to enter into with any players that they represent. Agents who do not use the standard representation agreement cannot represent players in the particular league.

apparent authority— A situation where the principal allows a situation to exist that may mislead others about the agent's actual authority. In these situations, a third party may be able to rely on the agent's actions to hold the principal accountable.

In consideration of the mutual promises hereinafter made by each to the other, Player and Contract Advisor agree as follows:

1. General Principals

This Agreement is entered into pursuant to and in accordance with the National Football League Players Association (hereinafter "NFLPA") Regulations Governing Contract Advisors (hereinafter "the Regulations") effective December 1, 1994, and as amended thereafter from time to time.

2. Representations

Contract Advisor represents that in advance of executing this Agreement, he/she has been duly certified as a Contract Advisor by the NFLPA. Player acknowledges that the NFLPA certification of the Contract Advisor is neither a recommendation of the Contract Advisor, nor a warranty by NFLPA of the Contract Advisor's competence, honesty, skills or qualifications.

Contract Advisor hereby discloses that he/she (check one): [ ] represents or has represented; [ ] does not represent and has not represented NFL management personnel in matters pertaining to their employment by or association with any NFL club. (If Contract Advisor responds in the affirmative, Contract Advisor must attach a written addendum to this Agreement listing names and positions of those NFL Personnel represented).

3. Contract Services

Player hereby retains Contract Advisor to represent, advise, counsel, and assist Player in the negotiation, execution, and enforcement of his playing contract(s) in the National Football League.

In performing these services, Contract Advisor acknowledges that he/she is acting in a fiduciary capacity on behalf of Player and agrees to act in such manner as to protect the best interests of Player and assure effective representation of Player in individual contract negotiations with NFL Clubs. Contract Advisor shall be the exclusive representative for the purpose of negotiating player contracts for Player. However, Contract Advisor shall not have the authority to bind or commit Player to enter into any contract without actual execution thereof by Player. Once Player agrees to and executes his player contract, Contract Advisor agrees to also sign the player contract and send a copy (by facsimile or overnight mail) to the NFLPA and the NFL Club within 48 hours of execution by Player. If Player and Contract Advisor have entered into any other agreements or contracts relating to services other than the individual negotiating services described in this Section, describe the nature of the other services covered by the separate agreements (NFL Players Association, 2007, appendix D).

Figure 4.2 Language from the NFL Players Association Standard Representation Agreement.

Reprinted, by permission, from National Football Players Association. Available: www.nflplayers.com/images/pdfs/Agents/NFLPA_Regulations_Contract_Advisors.pdf.

agent, apparent authority may exist and a third party may be able to rely on the agent's actions to hold the principal accountable.

The power found in apparent authority is based on a third party's reasonable belief that the agent has the authority to act on behalf of the principal based on the action or inaction of the principal. Simply put, the principal created an appearance of authority through conduct or behavior that misled the third party into reasonably believing that the agent had the authority to act on behalf of the principal.

For an example of apparent authority, consider Patty, a professional billiards player who was very marketable after winning six professional tournaments in a row. Patty attended a party with her friend and manager, Anton. Anton was not Patty's agent but had assisted her in some billiard-related sponsorship contracts. While at the party Patty was approached by Tom, a representative of a major motion picture studio who wanted to make a movie about Patty's life and career. Patty dismissed Tom's conversation about making the film and said, "Talk to Anton, he handles my business."

Patty had no intention of ever making a movie and believed that Anton knew that she was just blowing off the idea by leaving him to discuss the matter with Tom. However, Anton decided that a movie would be good for Patty and set up a meeting with studio representatives for the next day. At that meeting Anton reached an agreement to have Patty's story made into a film. After finding out what Anton had done, Patty contacted the studio and bailed out of the project. The studio had already purchased the rights to the story from Anton and decided to enforce its rights to Patty's story through a lawsuit. A reviewing court might find that when Patty told Anton to speak to Tom, she gave Anton the apparent authority to act on her behalf. If the court found that Tom's reliance on Patty's statements was reasonable, then Patty might be bound to honor the agreement or pay the studio damages. The rationale behind apparent authority is based on the idea that the third party is innocent and has reasonably been misled by the principal into believing that the agent has authority to act.

Ratification

When an agent acts without authority and the doctrine of apparent authority does not apply, then the principal is generally not legally bound by the agent's acts. However, if a principal affirms acts performed by an agent who lacked authority, then those acts are as legally binding for the principal as if the agent acted with actual authority in the first place. This is known as **ratification.**

In order to be ratified, an agent's actions must be those that the principal can delegate and the agent can perform. For example, testifying in court and voting are not delegable acts. Ratification does not apply when third parties intend to deal with the agent in the agent's individual capacity and do not intend to deal with the principal. If no agency relationship exists at all, then there can be no ratification. A principal also cannot ratify something that had no legal effect in the first place. For instance, a principal cannot ratify a contract if no consideration was provided in the first place so that no contract exists because the contractual element of consideration is not present.

Although not commonly used in the sports world, the principle of ratification can be very beneficial for the principal. This is most evident in the world of player agents. Some players allow their agents to negotiate on their behalf, without the players' being present or taking any part in the negotiations.

ratification—The principal's affirmation of an agent's actions, even though the agent lacked authority to act on behalf of the principal at the time of those actions.

This is common with successful players who are in high demand. The agent can negotiate on the player's behalf with the team that offers the best salary. Imagine that NBA star Dwyane Wade leaves all dealings with teams to his Chicago-based agent Henry Thomas, with the instruction that Thomas find Wade the best salary. Thomas talks to several teams and eventually gets the highest salary offer from the New York Knicks. Thomas comes to a tentative agreement with the Knicks on Wade's behalf because they will pay Wade $3 million more per year than any other team. It would not be surprising for Wade to ratify the contract with the best salary offer that Thomas developed for him.

A player will not always wish to ratify an agent's actions. During game 4 of the 2007 Major League Baseball World Series, Alex Rodriguez' agent Scott Boras announced that Rodriguez would opt out of his contract with the New York Yankees. This was important because the Yankees had stated publicly that they would not negotiate a new contract with Rodriguez if he opted out of his current contract. Almost immediately, Rodriguez refused to ratify his agent's move and contacted the Yankees to negotiate directly. He eventually signed a 10-year, $275 million deal without Boras' direct involvement (Feinsand & Madden, 2007).

Duties

fiduciary duty—Any duty to act for the benefit of someone else while subordinating one's own personal interests.

An agency relationship is considered to be a fiduciary relationship. This means that the agent has the **fiduciary duty** to act primarily for the benefit of the principal in all matters connected to the agency relationship. In addition, this fiduciary relationship establishes several duties that the agent and the principal must uphold within the relationship. Often the agency agreement will specify the duties that each party has within the agency relationship. However, there are some general duties that each party owes to the other.

Agent Duties to Principal

The agent owes several duties to the principal, including the duty to exercise reasonable care and skill within her work as an agent and to provide information related to the agency relationship if the principal requests it. Beyond these duties, the duty of loyalty and the duty of obedience must be analyzed in further detail.

duty of loyalty—Duty under which the agent must act solely and completely for the benefit of the principal.

Duty of Loyalty   The agent's primary duty is the **duty of loyalty.** This means that the agent must act solely and completely for the benefit of the principal. An agent is prohibited from competing with the principal in anything related to the subject matter of the agency unless the principal has expressly agreed to allow the agent to compete (*Restatement [Third] of Agency* § 8.04, 2006). Furthermore, the agent may not, without the principal's consent, act on behalf of one with interests adverse to those of the principal in matters in which the agent is employed (*Restatement [Third] of Agency*, § 8.03). If an agent's interests become adverse to those of the principal, the agent must put the principal's interests first.

Agency law also prevents agents from using their status as agent to enter the principal into agreements that benefit the agent personally without first telling the principal of the agent's interest in the agreement. Even with the principal's consent, such a self-dealing transaction will only be enforced by the courts if the transaction is fair and reasonable.

For example, Anne represents Parker, a swimmer who has won two Olympic gold medals. Anne knows that now is the time to capitalize on Parker's success to maximize her income potential. In addition to representing swimmers, Anne also co-owns a company that manufactures swimwear. It would be beneficial to Anne if Parker would agree to be sponsored by Anne's swimwear company. The fiduciary duty of loyalty prevents Anne from negotiating a deal with the company without first telling Parker about her interest in the company. If Anne neglects to tell Parker about her interest in the company and enters into a transaction with the company on behalf of Parker, then the transaction may be nullified by Parker. Furthermore, even if Anne informs Parker about the interest she holds in the company, the transaction could still be nullified if a court finds that the deal is not fair and reasonable for Parker.

In addition, during the agency relationship, an agent might have access to the principal's personal property or private information. The fiduciary duty of loyalty prevents the agent from using certain things—the principal's property, the agent's position, or nonpublic information acquired by the agent while acting within the scope of employment—for the agent's own purposes or for the benefit of another without first seeking the principal's agreement (*Restatement [Third] Of Agency*, § 8.05, 2006). This duty holds true even after termination of the agency relationship. Therefore, agents cannot use information obtained during the agency for personal gain after the termination of the agency relationship.

Duty of Obedience   The agent is under a duty to follow all reasonable instructions given by the principal, but this duty is not absolute. For example, consider a situation where an agent represents a motocross athlete. The agency relationship covers all sponsorship and appearance contracts. If the agent and athlete decide to pool their funds to create a separate company that will design, manufacture, and sell motorcycles, the agent's **duty of obedience** does not extend to dealings with the athlete within the new company. Because the agent has a legal interest in the company as a part owner, this interest supersedes the duty of loyalty in this situation.

If the principal provides instructions to the agent to do something that might harm only the principal's interests, then the duty of obedience requires the agent to perform the task as ordered. The agent should inform the principal that the desired actions could be harmful, but if the principal still desires the course of action, the agent should do as the principal instructs. This can be problematic because principals often have short memories and might blame the agent for any harm incurred as a result of the agent's actions. A good way for an agent to manage this risk is to document the communication that informs the principal of the harmful potential. Such communication

duty of obedience—The agent's duty to follow all reasonable instructions given by the principal.

should make it clear to the principal that the agent has advised against the course of action but will act according to the principal's wishes.

Conflicts of Interest

Many potential conflicts of interest can occur in the athlete–agent business. For example, what if a sport agent represents two shortstops that compete in Major League Baseball and both players are up for the same job opening? The interests of these two players are adverse but they have the same agent. How can an agent represent both players in order to fulfill his fiduciary duties of obedience and loyalty to them? This is especially problematic in leagues that contain salary caps (discussed in chapter 10) that restrict the amount of money the team can pay out in player salaries. Even after informing his clients of the situation and potential conflict, the agent may decide that he cannot responsibly represent both players and may terminate one of the relationships so that he can focus on one client. If the agent does not terminate one of the representations, he must exercise caution and represent both clients with the same degree of competence and vigor.

Principal Duties to Agent

Principals owe agents a duty to compensate them fairly for the work performed and to reimburse them for all expenses they incur on behalf of the principal. Principals also owe agents a duty to compensate them for any losses suffered and to cooperate with agents by not working counter to or interfering with their efforts. The principal also has a duty of good conduct, which means that the principal should not do anything that would demean the agent or damage her reputation (Gregory, 2001).

Contract Liability

Under contract law, lawsuits often arise in which a court must determine who is liable for the performance of a contract: the principal, the agent, or both parties. Sometimes contracts are breached because the goods are damaged, because they don't conform to certain expectations (express and implied warranties), or for various other reasons. If an agent has acted within the scope of her authority in executing a contract, the issue becomes who should be held liable for a breach of the contract (the principal or the agent). The key issue in cases where an agent contracts with a third party is whether the identity of the principal was known to the third party at the time the contract was made. There are three situations that might arise when a contract is made and three possible outcomes regarding liability for performance of a contract.

disclosed principal— A principal who is known to a third party with whom an agent of the principal has formed a contract.

• In the first situation, an agent contracts with a third party and the third party knows the identity of the principal and knows that the agent is acting on behalf of the principal when the contract is made (executed). In this type of scenario, we have a **disclosed principal**, and the principal is liable for the performance of the contract. The agent is not liable.

• In the second situation, an agent contracts with a third party and the third party knows that the agent is acting for someone (a principal); however, the third party doesn't know the identify of the principal. In this case, we have a **partially disclosed principal,** and the principal is liable for the performance of the contract. In most states, the agent is also liable for performance of the contract.

• In the third situation, the agent contracts with a third party, who has no knowledge that the agent is acting in the capacity of an agent; that is, the third party does not know about the existence of the principal. In this case, we have an **undisclosed principal,** and both the principal and agent are liable for performance of the contract. The agent may, however, be given the opportunity to seek compensation from the principal if the agent is forced to pay the third party for damages.

To avoid the time and trouble of legal entanglements, the agent who is acting on behalf of another (the principal) should inform the third party of the existence and identity of the principal.

Tort Liability

Under tort law, the principal may be liable when torts are committed during the **scope of employment** or scope of agency. This type of liability extends to employers (the principal) under the doctrine of **respondeat superior.** Under this doctrine, the employer (as principal) potentially can be held liable for the acts of an employee (agent) committed while the agent is acting on behalf of the principal during the course of the agent's job. Under the doctrine of respondeat superior, direct (personal) fault of the principal is not required. If an agent or employee injures another, a court will look to a number of factors in determining whether a principal will be liable under the doctrine of respondeat superior. The key issue is whether the agent acted within the scope of employment when someone was injured because of an act committed by the agent. A court would consider the following factors:

• Whether the agent committed an act (resulting in injury to another) that was authorized by the principal

• The time, place, and purpose of the act

• Whether the act was commonly performed by employees on behalf of their employers

• Whether the employer's interest was enhanced by the act

• The extent of involvement of the employee's private interests

• Whether the employer furnished the means by which the injury was inflicted

• Whether the employer had reason to know that the employee would perform the act in question (whether the agent had done it before)

• Whether the act involved the commission of a serious crime

partially disclosed principal—A principal whose exact identity is unknown; a third party contracting with an agent knows that the agent is working on behalf of some principal, but the third party doesn't know who the principal is.

undisclosed principal—A principal whose identity and existence are unknown to a third party with whom an agent of the principal has formed a contract.

scope of employment—The realm of activities engaged in by an agent when acting on behalf of a principal.

respondeat superior—A legal doctrine that holds people and organizations high in the chain of command (principals) liable for the negligent acts of those lower in the chain of command (agents).

When determining liability, a court would not need to find that all eight factors weighed in favor of liability, only that liability could be inferred from an analysis of some combination of these eight factors. The In The Courtroom case below illustrates a court determining liability.

Averill, Jr v. Luttrell, 311 S.W.2d 812 (Tenn. App. 1957)

According to the undisputed proof, the assault occurred during the 6th inning of the game while the plaintiff, who played the position of short-stop for the Chattanooga Lookouts, was batting for his team. Pitching for the Nashville Vols was Gerry Lane, a resident of Chattanooga, and catching was the defendant Averill. The contest between the teams was keen and the players as well as the fans were tense with excitement, some of which was probably attributable to Lane's pitching against his hometown team. Lane had made three pitches known as curves or sliders, called by the umpire as "balls," and on each Luttrell had stepped forward to meet the ball before the break or curve started. These balls barely missed Luttrell, who had to dodge, and his teammates and the crowd had the impression that he was being, in baseball parlance, dusted off by Lane, who on his fourth pitch hit Luttrell on the seat of his pants.

It appears that immediately after Luttrell threw his bat in the direction of the pitcher's mound, Averill, without any warning whatsoever, stepped up behind Luttrell and struck him a hard blow on the side or back of the head with his fist. The force of the blow rendered Luttrell unconscious, and on falling face first to the ground he sustained a fractured jaw. Thereafter, the players and the fans who rushed out onto the field engaged in what was described as a free-for-all until the police arrived in sufficient force to restore order, after which the game continued. Meantime, Luttrell was removed by ambulance to the hospital, and Averill, who was put out of the game by the umpire, was arrested. It was undisputed that there was no previous animosity or malice between Averill and Luttrell, who testified that when they spoke it was on friendly terms. Nor was there any proof showing that Averill had ever committed a similar act or that his employer should have anticipated his unwarranted assault.

It was conceded that the assault made by Averill was no part of the ordinary risks expected to be encountered in sportsmanlike play. Nor was there any proof showing that the assault was other than a willful independent act on Averill's part, entirely outside the scope of his duties. The assault was neither incident to nor in the furtherance of his employer's business, and under the circumstances we think that the Nashville Baseball Club would not be liable under the doctrine of respondeat superior and that the learned trial judge should have sustained the defendant's motion for a directed verdict made at the conclusion of the plaintiff's proof.

It seems to be the rule generally that a master (principal) is not liable for the willful acts of his servant (agent) who steps aside from his master's business and commits an act wholly independent and foreign to the scope of his employment.

Regulation of Athlete Agents

The most scrutinized career for an agent is representation of athletes. The highest-profile athlete agents represent athletes in the NFL, NBA, NHL, and MLB. Some agents also represent athletes within virtually all other sports as well, including boxing, motor sports, tennis, soccer, volleyball, and swimming. Athlete agents might work alone and represent a stable of clients, like well-known agents Scott Boras in baseball or Drew Rosenhaus in football, but athlete agents also work for larger companies like Octagon and IMG, where groups of agents, lawyers, marketing representatives, and others jointly represent multiple athletes.

Athlete agents generally focus on helping their clients find teams to play for or events to play at. Some agents also represent athletes in dealing with the media, advertisers, sponsors, event organizers, and authorities. An agent must be a jack of all trades, understanding more than merely how to get the athlete a position with a team. Because of the extensive knowledge base needed, many agents have advanced degrees in law or business, and many professional sports unions require certification of skills and registration for any agent who wants to represent their players.

The competition is intense. An agent's livelihood often depends on the success of the players who he represents. As a result, many agents act in unscrupulous ways, which has led to several types of regulations, from state and federal laws to professional union regulations.

These regulations only affect and regulate agents who represent professional athletes. Other types of agents within the sport industry, for example, an agent representing a television station in negotiations with a sports league or an agent representing an event in negotiations with a television station, are not subject to these regulations.

It is interesting to focus on the regulation of athlete agents, because it is an example of the way in which the government and private organizations can impose regulations on individuals in sports. In addition, one reason for extensive regulation of athlete agents is because their actions can negatively affect the young athletes involved and, as a result, the universities and high schools where these athletes participate in sports.

Impact on Athletes

Recent high-profile examples of agent abuse show that agents continue to try to influence athletes as well as their families and friends in order to convince an athlete to sign with an agent. In September 2005, allegations surfaced that former USC running back Reggie Bush and his family accepted benefits worth more than $100,000 from marketing agents while Bush was still a student. These benefits were supplied by two groups that were attempting to sign Bush as a client. Bush's current agents, Mike Ornstein, Michael Michaels, and Lloyd Lake, who attempted to launch an agency called New Era Sports & Entertainment, pursued Bush as their first client. Bush himself received two hotel stays, one in Las Vegas and another in San Diego, and $13,000 to purchase and modify a car. Bush's family received airfare to the 2005 Heisman Trophy ceremony, hotel stays, suits for Bush's stepfather and brother to wear during the ceremony, a makeover for his mother for the event, and limousine transportation. In addition, Bush's family was allowed to live in a house in Spring Valley, California, that was owned by Michaels, without paying rent. Amid ongoing investigations, Bush has asserted that he and his family have done nothing wrong. Ornstein has denied giving Bush or his family any benefits while Bush was still at USC and describes any travel arrangements for the Bush family made by his employee as loans that were paid back (Robinson & Cole, 2006).

In a similar situation, former USC basketball player O.J. Mayo allegedly received thousands of dollars in cash, clothes, and other benefits during the 2007-2008 academic year from Rodney Guillory, a 43-year-old Los Angeles event promoter. While Mayo was in high school, Guillory received monthly payments from Bill Duffy Associates (BDA), a Northern California sport agency. BDA provided Guillory with around $200,000 before Mayo even arrived at USC. In exchange for payments and gifts from Guillory, Mayo entered a verbal agreement to allow BDA to represent him when he became a professional athlete. Mayo insists not only that he was a struggling university student and did not receive any money but that Guillory was a positive influence and a strong African-American male presence in his life (Katz, 2008).

In both these situations, the athlete involved most likely will not suffer any negative consequences. Instead, the university may face serious sanctions under NCAA rules. Figure 4.3 shows that NCAA bylaws relate specifically to athlete ineligibility attributable to contact with an agent. For each bylaw, the specific part related to conduct causing the athlete to become ineligible is emphasized.

Because of these rules, an eligible university student-athlete cannot receive benefits from or enter into a verbal or written agreement with an agent even if the agreement is related to working with the athlete after his eligibility to participate has expired. This practice is known as postdating an agreement and has been a typical ploy of unscrupulous agents who have tried to convince athletes that they will not become ineligible because the relationship will not begin until after their playing career has ended.

For the student-athlete, the result of violating these rules is that she becomes ineligible to participate in athletics for her university. For some high-level athletes, this is not a problem because they have already decided that they are ready to try their hand at a career in professional sports. However, the school where the athlete played may not be so lucky. Article 19 of the NCAA bylaws provides for the enforcement process that schools must

12.1.1 Amateur Status. An individual loses amateur status and thus shall not be eligible for intercollegiate competition in a particular sport if the individual . . . (g) *enters into an agreement with an agent.*

12.3.1 General Rule. An individual shall be ineligible for participation in an intercollegiate sport if *he or she ever has agreed (orally or in writing) to be represented by an agent for the purpose of marketing his or her athletics ability or reputation in that sport.* Further, an agency contract not specifically limited in writing to a sport or particular sports shall be deemed applicable to all sports, and the individual shall be ineligible to participate in any sport.

12.3.1.1 Representation for Future Negotiations. An individual shall be ineligible per Bylaw 12.3.1 if *he or she enters into a verbal or written agreement with an agent for representation in future professional sports negotiations that are to take place after the individual has completed his or her eligibility in that sport.*

12.3.1.2 Benefits from Prospective Agents. An individual shall be ineligible per Bylaw 12.3.1 if he or she (or his or her relatives or friends) *accepts transportation or other benefits from*

(a) Any person who represents any individual in the marketing of his or her athletics ability. The receipt of such expenses constitutes compensation based on athletics skill and is an extra benefit not available to the student body in general; or

(b) *An agent,* even if the agent has indicated that he or she has no interest in representing the student-athlete in the marketing of his or her athletics ability or reputation and does not represent individuals in the student-athlete's sport (NCAA, 2007).

Figure 4.3 NCAA bylaws relating to amateur status and agents.

Reprinted, by permission, from NCAA, 2008, *2008-2009 NCAA division I manual* (Indianapolis, IN: National Collegiate Athletic Association).

face when rule infractions occur on their campus. If an athlete signs with an agent, she has broken the rules listed previously and her school may face serious sanctions.

The sanctions that USC might face as a result of O.J. Mayo's actions remain to be seen. One university that has faced numerous sanctions related to violations of the NCAA bylaws related to athlete agents is California State University, Fresno. In 2002, a *Fresno Bee* report revealed that basketball player Tito Maddox had accepted illegal benefits from an athlete agent. As a result, the school put itself on 2 years of probation and lost three scholarships within the basketball program (Pugmire, 2008). However, this was not the end of the story. In 2003, the NCAA Committee on Infractions found that a representative of an agent had provided several members of the team with $20 to $100 cash after home games and wired $200 to $250 cash to players at other times (CSU, Fresno Public Infractions Report, 2003). The agent also sent money to some players' relatives to cover the cost of their lodging and transportation to the Western Athletic Conference tournament. Although the infractions review also involved allegations of fraud, improper recruiting, and improper distribution of financial aid, the sanctions imposed on the university are most telling because they evidence what can happen when a university violates NCAA rules, even if it has no direct control of the situation that caused the violation. It is incredibly difficult for an athletic department to monitor a student-athlete at all times, and these problematic contacts with agents often happen on the student's own time. In the situation just described, the university faced numerous sanctions:

- The university was placed on probation for 4 years.
- The men's basketball team was barred from participating in postseason competition for 1 year.
- The university was forced to reduce the scholarships available to the program by three for 2 years.
- The university forfeited all wins in games in which the players involved participated.
- The university had to return 90% of the money it received from participating in the 2000 NCAA tournament (CSU, Fresno Public Infractions Report, 2003).

Obviously, the financial impact on a university can be huge when athlete agents are involved. Perhaps even more harmful is the severe negative publicity that the university will face within its community, among other schools, and with future recruits.

Because of these and other problems with unscrupulous athlete agents, various entities have tried to regulate the conduct of these agents. The main focus of these regulations has been on state and federal laws and regulations by professional players unions.

State Law and the Uniform Athlete Agents Act

Until 2000, the focus of the regulation of athlete agents was at the state level. Many states had laws that regulated the way in which athlete agents could interact with athletes, often focusing on specific regulations for registering as an athlete agent with the state, certain ways in which an agent could communicate with an athlete, and payment of fees to a state body to be able to work as an agent in that state. The problem was that these state laws were not consistent, and so an agent often had to act in very different ways depending on where she was doing business or where the athlete lived or worked.

Consider an agent who represents an NBA player who is with the Milwaukee Bucks. The agent lives and has his office in San Francisco, California. The player lives in Miami, Florida, in the off-season. As an NBA player, the player plays in 30 different cities during the year (not to mention possible foreign locations in certain years), and each city may have a different tax structure that affects any salary the player makes for playing in that city. Before 2000, the agent had to determine whether he would need to be licensed as an athlete agent in each different location, possibly paying multiple fees, and also had to determine what procedures the particular players union had in place (these are discussed in the next section). This became a cumbersome process, and many agents often avoided registration requirements altogether.

In 2000, this landscape changed. The National Conference of Commissioners on Uniform State Laws (NCCUSL) is a group of lawyers and law professors who put together uniform laws that states can incorporate into their statutes so that multiple states will follow the same basic law. An example of a uniform law created by the commissioners is the Uniform Commercial Code (UCC, 2008). In the late 1990s, working with the NCAA, the professional sports leagues, and others, the commissioners developed the **Uniform Athlete Agents Act** (NCCUSL, 2000). The main purpose of this act was to provide for uniformity in registration and certification of athlete agents among the states. The act defines a student-athlete as "an individual who engages in, is eligible to engage in, or may be eligible in the future to engage in, any intercollegiate sport" (NCCUSL, § 2(12)). The act thus focuses on an agent's interaction with student-athletes, which could include high school or university athletes. The act also provides that athlete agents who sign contracts with student-athletes must provide notice to the particular university and must make clear to the student-athletes that the agency agreement may affect their eligibility to participate in athletics while in university. In addition, the act provides civil remedies for institutions when agents and athletes sign these contracts and the school eventually suffers NCAA sanctions.

The easiest way to understand the Uniform Athlete Agents Act is by looking at a state statute from a state that has adopted the act. The Wisconsin Uniform Athlete Agents Act is found in section 440.99 of the state statutes. As with other states' versions of this act, the Wisconsin statute begins with agent registration. Under the statute an agent must register by filing a seven-page application with the Wisconsin Department of Regulation and Licensing and paying a $312 initial credential fee (Wisconsin Statue §§ 440.991-440.9915, 2008). The registration must be renewed each year and can be used to register in any other state that also has adopted the act.

The act also focuses specifically on the agency agreement that an agent would sign with an athlete. It requires that an agent must specifically disclose the amount and method that will be used to determine how much he or she will be paid, the exact expenses that the athlete will reimburse the agent for, and the exact services the agent will provide to the athlete. In addition, any agency agreement must include the following language:

Warning: If you sign this contract

1. you may lose your eligibility to compete as a student-athlete in your sport;

2. if you have an athletic director, within 72 hours after entering into this contract, both you and your athlete agent must notify your athletic director; and

3. you may cancel this contract within 14 days after signing it. Cancellation of this contract may not reinstate your eligibility. (Wisconsin Statute § 440.994, 2008)

Uniform Athlete Agents Act—A standard act created by the National Conference of Commissioners on Uniform State Laws, the main purpose of which is to provide for uniformity in registration and certification of athlete agents among the states. The act becomes an enforceable law if a particular state enacts it within its state statutes.

This provision is intended to notify any student-athlete of the risk of signing an agreement with an athlete agent. It also places a responsibility on the agent to notify the athletic director at the particular school. Perhaps most interesting, a student-athlete can cancel the agreement within 2 weeks after it is signed. If this happens, the agent cannot sue under the contract to have the athlete return any sort of gifts or other compensation the agent may have provided and cannot sue the athlete for breach of contract.

Finally, the act also defines certain types of conduct that an agent cannot engage in. An agent cannot make false promises or provide misleading information about her services in order to induce the athlete to sign with the agent (Wisconsin Statute § 440.996, 2008). This is an especially slippery slope for new agents who want to sell their services and convince athletes

Table 4.2 State Regulations of Athlete Agents

State	Regulation (unless otherwise noted, each is known as the particular state's Uniform Athlete Agents Act)
Alabama	Code of Ala. §§ 8-26A-1-18 (2008)
Alaska	No regulation
Arizona	Ariz. Rev. Stat. §§ 15-1761-1776 (2008)
Arkansas	Ark. Code Ann. §§ 17-16-101-119 (2008)
California	Miller-Ayala Athlete Agents Act, Cal Bus & Prof Code §§ 18895-18897.97 (2007)
Colorado	House Bill 1058 (enacted)
Connecticut	Conn. Gen. Stat. §§ 20-553-569 (2008)
Delaware	24 Del. Code §§ 5401-5420 (2008)
District of Columbia	D.C. Code §§ 47-2887.01-2997.18 (2008)
Florida	Fla. Stat. §§ 468.451-457 (2008)
Georgia	Ga. Code Ann. §§ 43-4A-1-20 (2008)
Hawaii	Act 248, House Bill No. 275 (2008) (enacted)
Idaho	Idaho Code §§ 54-4801-4820 (2008)
Illinois	No regulation
Indiana	Burns Ind. Code Ann. §§ 25-5.2-1-1-25-5.2-2-16 (2008)
Iowa	Registration of Athlete Agents, Iowa Code §§ 9A.1-12 (2008)
Kansas	Kans. Stat. Ann. §§ 44-1516-1536 (2006)
Kentucky	Ky. Rev. Stat. §§ 164.6901-164.6935 (2008
Louisiana	La. Rev. Stat. §§ 4:420-433 (2008)
Maine	No regulation
Maryland	Md. Business Regulation Code Ann. §§ 4-401-4-426 (2008)
Massachusetts	No regulation
Michigan	Senate Bill 581 (2007) (not yet passed)
Minnesota	Minn. Stat. §§ 81A.01-.21 (2007)
Mississippi	Miss. Code Ann. §§ 73-42-1-42-35 (2008)

to work with them but must be careful not to exaggerate their skills in a way that might be misleading. An agent also cannot contact student-athletes unless she is already registered under the statute and must always include the required language within any agency agreement signed. In effect, any athlete agents representing athletes in states like Wisconsin that have adopted the Uniform Athlete Agents Act must create an express agreement with the athlete that contains all of these conditions in writing.

As of May 2008, 35 states plus Washington, DC, had adopted the Uniform Athlete Agents Act into their state statutes (see table 4.2), and three states are reviewing the act in the bill stage (Uniform Law Commissioners, n.d.). Three states (California, Iowa, and Ohio) have alternative statutes that regulate athlete agents, and eight other states (Alaska, Illinois, Maine,

State	Regulation (unless otherwise noted, each is known as the particular state's Uniform Athlete Agents Act)
Missouri	Mo. Ann. Stat. §§ 436.215-272 (2008)
Montana	Statute repealed in 2007 because of lack of licensed agents
Nebraska	No regulation
Nevada	Nev. Rev. Stat. Ann. §§ 398.400-620 (2007)
New Hampshire	N.H. Rev. Stat Ann. §§ 332-J:1-J:14 (2008)
New Jersey	Assembly Bill 1624 (2008) (not yet passed)
New Mexico	No regulation
New York	N.Y. Gen. Bus. Law §§ 899-899-p (Consol. 2008)
North Carolina	N.C. Gen. Stat. §§ 78C-85-105 (2008)
North Dakota	N.D. Cent. Code, §§ 9-15.1-01-1-16 (2008)
Ohio	Athlete Agents, ORC Ann. §§ 4771.01-99 (2008)
Oklahoma	70 Okl. Stat. §§ 821.81-88 (2008)
Oregon	Or. Rev. Stat. §§ 702.005-994 (2007)
Pennsylvania	5 Pa. Cons. Stat. §§ 3101-3320 (2007)
Rhode Island	House Bill 7337 (2007) (not yet passed)
South Carolina	S.C. Code Ann. §§ 59-102-10-102-180 (2007)
South Dakota	S.D. Codified Laws §§ 59-10-1-10-20 (2008)
Tennessee	Tenn. Code Ann. §§ 49-7-2122-7-2141 (2008)
Texas	Tex. Occ. Code §§ 2051.001-553 (2007)
Utah	Utah Code Ann. §§ 15-9-101-119 (2008)
Vermont	No regulation
Virginia	No regulation
Washington	Wash. Rev. Code §§ 19.225.010-225.903 (2008)
West Virginia	W. Va. Code § 30-39-1-39.21 (2008)
Wisconsin	Wis. Stat. §§ 440.99-999 (2007)
Wyoming	Wyo. Stat. §§ 33-44-101-44-114 (2007)

Massachusetts, Nebraska, New Mexico, Vermont, and Virginia) have no statutes that regulate athlete agents.

Federal Law

There have been several attempts in Congress to pass legislation regulating sport agents. None of these attempts were successful until 2004 with the passage of the Sports Agent Responsibility and Trust Act (SPARTA) (15 U.S.C. §§ 7801-7807, 2008). The goal of the act is to protect student-athletes and universities from unscrupulous sport agents by prohibiting agents from making false or misleading promises or providing gifts, cash, or anything of monetary value to student-athletes and those associated with student-athletes. Similar to the Uniform Athlete Agents Act, SPARTA requires agents to give students written disclosures informing them that they could lose their eligibility to play university sports if they sign an agency contract. Agents and student-athletes are required to notify, within 72 hours, the student's athletic director of any agency agreement reached by the student and the agent. If an agent fails to make a timely report, the agent can be fined as much as $11,000 per day. Additionally, the act allows schools to bring civil actions against violating agents if their residents have been adversely affected by an agent's actions.

Interestingly, SPARTA does not provide for any federal registration for agents. Therefore, although SPARTA mirrors the Uniform Athlete Agents Act adopted by many states, its actual impact is unclear. The Federal Trade Commission is the government agency that is named to enforce SPARTA, but without any sort of registration procedure it is unclear how the commission would find agents in order to regulate their behavior. Instead, SPARTA seems to be a redundant version of the Uniform Act that does not add much to the overall regulatory scheme.

Union Regulations

The final level of athlete agent regulation is with the players unions in the four major professional sports leagues: the National Football League Players Association, the National Basketball Players Association, the National Hockey League Players Association, and the Major League Baseball Players Association (see table 4.3). Only the unions in these four professional sports leagues regulate athlete agents who represent the unions' players. Agents who represent athletes in individual performer sports such as swimming and tennis, or in team sports like Major League Soccer, are not regulated to the

Table 4.3   Internet Information on Players Association Agent Regulations

Players association	Agent regulations' Internet address
MLB Players Association	Limited information at www.mlb.com/pa/info/faq.jsp#agent
NBA Players Association	www.nbpa.com/agentapp.php
NFL Players Association	www.nflplayers.com/user/template.aspx?fmid=181&lmid=233&pid=0&type=c
NHL Players Association	www.nhlpa.com/Agents/

same extent. The reason for the regulation in team sports is that the players in these leagues have long histories of strong representation by their players unions and because athletes in these leagues make the highest average salaries of any athletes. In addition, each union requires that its members only hire agents who are certified under the union's rules and that teams also agree to only negotiate with certified agents.

A good example of an agent certification program is the NFL Players Association Regulations Governing Contract Advisors (2007). Under these regulations, an agent must do the following in order to represent NFL players:

- Submit an application fee of $1,650
- Have an undergraduate and postgraduate degree (master's or law degree) from an accredited university
- Submit to a background investigation
- Attend an NFL Players Association educational seminar each year
- Complete a written exam that covers the collective bargaining agreement, salary cap, player benefits, NFL Players Association regulations, and other issues related to player representation (Players, n.d.)

In addition to meeting these requirements, any NFL player agent must uphold a code of conduct mandating that the agent sign only the standard representation agreement with the player, submit all contracts between the player and team to the union, submit itemized statements of all fees charged by the agent, allow for an audit of any dealings with NFL players, and fully comply with applicable state and federal laws (e.g., the state athlete agents laws and SPARTA), among other responsibilities (NFL Players Association, 2007). The regulations include the Standard Representation Agreement that all agents must sign with their players in order to establish the agency relationship. Perhaps most important, the regulations set out the exact fee that an NFL agent can charge. "The maximum fee which may be charged or collected by a Contract Advisor shall be three percent (3%) of the 'compensation' . . . received by the player in each playing season covered by the contract negotiated by the Contract Advisor" (p. 12). Each of the other professional team sports leagues has similar rules.

As described in the disputes that are discussed later in this chapter, agents can violate these rules in many ways. The examples describe several agents who breached contracts and were convicted of crimes. Such agents are quickly decertified by the appropriate players union and can no longer represent athletes within that sport. However, litigation is not always necessary. If an agent engages in any of the prohibited conduct barred by the union's regulations, she will lose the ability to represent athletes in that sport but may not face litigation. For instance, the NFL Players Association Regulations Governing Contract Advisors include 31 different prohibited activities that could cause an agent to be decertified, such as representing a player when the player has not entered into a Standard Representation Agreement with the agent or failing to comply with the maximum fee provisions contained in the regulations (NFL Players Association, 2007, section 3(B)).

Consolidation

The future of sport agency seems to be a focus on consolidation. Since the 1990s, many large sport agencies such as IMG, Octagon, and SFX have expanded their businesses by purchasing the businesses of smaller sport agents. This expansion is often an effort to allow the larger agency to provide more services to a wider variety of clients. Consolidation can allow smaller agents or agencies to increase their fees by providing them with an ability to increase the range of services they offer. These consolidations can benefit athletes, who will have access to larger agencies that can offer financial planning, investment, and marketing services and may even help the athletes enter other areas in the entertainment business, including movies and television.

A famous example of consolidation involves agent Arn Tellem. In 1999, Tellem sold his athlete agent business to SFX only to reacquire it in 2000. In 2006, he then sold his business to the Wasserman Media Group (www.wmgllc.com), which at the time represented about 50 action sports athletes. Adding Tellem's and other agents' business gave Wasserman about 100 NBA and MLB players, making the group one of the largest player agencies (Davis, 2007).

Disputes

Given the extensive regulation of agents by states, the federal government, and professional sports players unions, it might be surprising to some that agents still run into many problems and end up in court. One of the most famous disputes involved agents Norby Walters and Lloyd Bloom. These agents offered athletes cash, loans, clothing, insurance policies, limousines, and other benefits to entice the athletes to sign with the agents. When some of the athletes tried to get out of their agency agreements with Walters and Bloom, these agents "reminded them that they needed their legs to carry their bodies on the field and threatened to involve their organized crime associates to carry out the threats" (Greenberg & Gray, 1998, p. 1026). To enable the athletes, many of whom were still participating in university athletics, to sign with Walters and Bloom, the agents would have the athletes lie to their universities and sign postdated contracts that would become effective when the athletes' eligibility was up. Walters and Bloom were eventually charged by federal prosecutors with allegations of mail fraud, conspiracy, and racketeering (*United States v. Walters & Bloom,* 1990). In 1992, Walters was sentenced to 1 1/2 half years in prison, fined $25,000, and ordered to complete 250 hours of community service. Bloom was sentenced to 5 years of probation and 500 hours of community service (Greenberg & Gray, 1998, p. 1032).

The behavior of Walters and Bloom may be the extreme for unscrupulous sport agents, but they are not alone. Agents also often find themselves in disputes involving other areas of law.

Breach of Contract

The basics of a breach of contract claim are discussed in chapter 5. A recent high-profile case focusing on breach of contract involved famous sport agents Leigh Steinberg and David Dunn. Steinberg claimed that Dunn breached his contract with their firm Steinberg, Moorad, and Dunn by removing trade secrets and confidential client information and using this information to divert high-profile athletes (including NFL stars Reggie White and Drew Bledsoe) to Dunn's new agency, Athletes First (*Steinberg, Moorad & Dunn v. Dunn,* 2002). The trial court found that Dunn breached his contract with Steinberg, Moorad, and Dunn, a 5-year agreement worth $7 million, because the contract included a clause that prohibited Dunn from competing with Steinberg, Moorad, and Dunn. Steinberg was awarded $44 million in damages, and soon after the NFL Players Association suspended Dunn for 2 years for violating the NFL Players Association's agent regulations (Wolohan, 2007).

Tort Law

Other disputes often focus on allegations that the agent made misrepresentations to the athlete or mishandled the agent's funds. In addition to breach of contract claims, these lawsuits include tort claims of fraud and misrepresentation (further discussion of tort law can be found in chapter 2).

A highly publicized case involved William "Tank" Black, the former chairman and CEO of Professional Management, Inc. Black involved his player clients in major financial scams. For example, as president of Black Americans of Achievement (BAOA), a company that produced a board game regarding the accomplishments of African Americans, Black arranged for the athletes to promote the board game in exchange for free stock in the company. The players were not informed of this arrangement and did not agree to it. Regardless, Black told BAOA that his players had promoted the game and were entitled to the stock. As a result, BAOA issued two million shares of free stock in the names of the players and sent the stock certificates to Black, who then sold the stock to the players for $1,240,000, far above the stock's market value. The payments went to a shell company that Black had created, and he then transferred the money to his personal account.

The players eventually sued Black, alleging breach of fiduciary duty, negligence, and breach of contract (*Hillard & Taylor v. Black,* 2000). Black was sentenced to 60 months in prison and ordered to pay $12 million in restitution to his athlete clients. He also was decertified as an NFL Players Association agent (Sharp, Moorman, & Claussen, 2007).

Summary

Many relationships in sport can be understood as a relationship between a principal and an agent. Although the most prominent sport agents represent athletes, sport agents also work with sponsors, facilities, events, equipment manufacturers, merchandisers, ticket sellers, and any other number of entities. An agency relationship can exist any time that one person or entity (the principal) agrees to have another person or entity (the agent) work on his or her behalf.

The agency law principles discussed in this chapter apply to any agency relationship within sport. A formal contract is not needed to establish these types of relationships; any agreement reached verbally or in writing can establish an agency relationship. The important issues involve the type of authority the agent has as she works for the principal. In addition, both agents and principals have fiduciary duties that they must uphold as they work with each other. Agents must work for the benefit of the principal, and the principal must then do whatever he can to make sure the agent has the ability to perform her duties.

Athlete agents are unique because they are so highly regulated. The majority of states have adopted the Uniform Athlete Agents Act, which, along with the federal law and SPARTA, requires athlete agents to follow strict registration requirements and include standard language in their agreements with players. In addition, athlete agents who represent players in the four major professional team sports must follow strict union regulation.

Many agents have engaged in unscrupulous activities when they have avoided their fiduciary duties and acted in their own self-interest or attempted to coerce players to sign with them. With the money involved in sport today, there is no sign that agents will stop engaging in this type of conduct.

DISCUSSION QUESTIONS

1. What type of agent is most prominent in the sport industry and why?
2. What functions can an agent perform?
3. How is an agency relationship established?
4. What different types of authority to act may an agent possess?
5. Why are athlete agents subject to extensive regulations?
6. What types of agreements do athlete agents typically sign in order to set up their relationships with players?
7. What types of duties do agents have to the principal during the agency relationship?

MOOT COURT CASE

Tommy was a new employee of Big Glove Sports, a manufacturer of sporting goods and sports equipment. A key product for Big Glove was its line of baseball gloves. They were sold by Big Glove's agents and employees throughout the United States and Canada. The products were recognizable by the letters *BGS* emblazoned on the side of each glove produced by the company. After his mandatory training, Tommy was provided with a list of 20 local retailers to contact during his first month as a salesperson for BGS. Tommy visited most of the retailers in that first month, but none were interested in buying BGS gloves or other products. Tommy, fearing that he might lose his job if he returned without a sale, decided to visit his second cousin, Jake, who owned a successful sporting goods store. Tommy believed that with his family connections, he might be able to make a sale.

Tommy explained to Jake that he was selling baseball gloves and asked Jake whether he was interested in buying. Jake said that he was in good shape with his line of gloves but would buy extra from Tommy because he was a family member. Tommy didn't have a company contract written up for Jake, so he used a generic contract that Jake had on hand. Tommy signed the contract and left several boxes of gloves with Jake. Tommy was so excited about the sale that he forgot to mention that he worked for BGS and made no reference to BGS in the contract. They shook hands on the deal and Tommy headed for his next appointment, happily daydreaming about a grand reception on his return and his possible future promotion. While preoccupied with these thoughts, Tommy failed to see a red stop light and a Good Samaritan (GS) helping a little old lady (LOL) across the street. Tommy collided with them, seriously injuring the GS and LOL. To make matters worse, back at the store Jake opened the box to see that the gloves had been damaged and could not be used or sold. The GS and LOL sued Tommy (as an agent of BGS) and BGS (the principal) for negligence. Jake sued Tommy (as an agent of BGS) and BGS (the principal) for breach of contract.

5

Contract Law

CHAPTER OBJECTIVES

After reading this chapter, you will know the following:

- The elements of a valid contract
- Common provisions within sport contracts
- The many types of contracts that are found in the sport industry
- The issues that arise when a sport contract is breached

AP Photo/The Indianapolis Star, Mike Fender

From employment agreements to player contracts, from ticket sales to seat licenses, sport managers will encounter many forms of contracts every day. This chapter covers contract law and provides examples of the many types of contracts that sport managers may encounter:

- University and professional coaching contracts
- Player contracts
- Endorsement agreements
- Agent representation agreements
- Collective bargaining agreements
- Scholarships and letters of intent
- Ticket agreements
- Sponsorship agreements
- Concession agreements
- Lease agreements
- Seat license agreements

Contracts are involved at every level of the sport industry. This chapter focuses on the issues that can develop concerning breach of contract issues and damages and remedies for breach.

After reading this chapter, you will better understand the agreements that you might make with organizations and individuals within the sport industry so you can protect yourself and the organization that you work for.

Basics of Contract Law

To understand the principles that apply to a sport contract, you must understand how the law defines a contract, the elements of a contract, and some typical provisions that can be found in all contracts.

Definition

Contract law is often understood by reference to the *Restatements of the Law.* Written by legal scholars who are members of the American Law Institute, the *Restatements* explain what the law is in a certain area and how it is changing. Courts often rely on the *Restatements* to provide consistent explanations of certain areas of law. According to the *Restatement on Contracts,* a contract is "a promise, or set of promises, for breach of which the law gives a remedy, or the performance of which the law in some way recognizes a duty" (*Restatement [Second] of Contracts* § 2, 1990). By entering into a contractual agreement, one party promises to do something in exchange for something that the other party promises to do. As shown later in this chapter, if one party does not live up to these obligations, a court may intervene to provide a remedy.

Contracts are either bilateral or unilateral. **Bilateral contracts** contain two promises. The first promise is in the **offer,** which is always a promise, and the second promise is in the **acceptance.** Any time an offeree accepts an offer via a promise to perform, the contract is bilateral. For example, in May 2008, MLB National League's 2007 Rookie of the Year Ryan Braun agreed to a new contract with the Milwaukee Brewers. This is a bilateral contract because according to the agreement, the Brewers will pay Braun approximately $45 million over the next 7 years, for which Braun has promised to play for the Brewers during the term of the agreement.

In a **unilateral contract** only one party makes a promise. The other party makes no promise but instead performs some act in exchange for the first party's promise. An insurance contract for an athlete is a unilateral contract because the athlete promises to pay a premium, and in return, the insurance company agrees to pay out premiums (i.e., perform) if something should happen to make the insurance policy come into play.

Elements

To be enforceable, a contract must contain several elements. The three required elements are an offer, acceptance, and consideration. The absence of just one of these elements may prevent the formation of a contract.

The Offer

An offer is a conditional promise to do or refrain from doing something in the future (*Restatement [Second] of Contracts* § 24, 1990). An offer is made by one party called the offeror to another party called the offeree. The most important aspect of an offer is that it creates a power of acceptance in the offeree. The term *power of acceptance* means that the party to whom the offer was made has the power to bind the offeror to the contract. A statement may appear to be an offer, but if it does not create a power of acceptance, it is probably not an offer. Such statements are common in negotiations and are often used to determine whether another party is willing to either entertain an offer or make an offer. For example, Jill may ask Frank whether he would like to purchase a Super Bowl ticket. Frank may answer in the affirmative, but did that conversation result in a contract? Specifically, did Jill create a power of acceptance in Frank's favor so that Frank could bind Jill to a contract through his acceptance? Given these limited facts, we have no way of answering the question. Jill's statements to Frank could have been more detailed if she truly wanted to sell her ticket to Frank.

The more detailed the statement, the more likely that it results in an offer because statements that include details like price, quantity, and time for acceptance are more likely to create a power of acceptance. An offer should include the parties and subject matter involved, the way in which the subject matter will be performed, and the consideration (a term that will be defined in more detail further on in this chapter). The more detailed

bilateral contract— Contract that contains two promises: the offer and the acceptance.

offer—A conditional promise to do or refrain from doing something in the future.

acceptance—The act of agreeing to an offer by words or conduct. Acceptance must be communicated to the person making the offer.

unilateral contract— A contract in which the offeree accepts by performance rather than by promise.

the purported offer, the more likely that a reviewing court will find the existence of an offer.

Going back to the Super Bowl hypothetical, what if the statement was more specific? Let's say that Jill asked Frank whether he would purchase a Super Bowl ticket that she owned for $2,000. In this hypothetical we have a statement that lists a particular thing (the Super Bowl ticket) that is to be purchased and a price for that thing ($2,000). The statement is not asking whether Frank would like to purchase the ticket but, instead, whether Frank will purchase the ticket. This second hypothetical statement is more detailed and, as such, is more likely to be deemed an offer.

Acceptance

Once an offer is made by one party, a contract can only be created if another party accepts the offer. Acceptance of an offer must be made in some positive manner, whether by words or by conduct. Notice of acceptance must be communicated to the offeror, and courts generally will not infer acceptance from silent parties.

An interesting example occurred in the NBA in 2004. Carlos Boozer left the Cleveland Cavaliers and signed a 6-year, $68 million contract with the Utah Jazz. The Cavaliers claimed that Boozer had already accepted their contract offer to remain a Cavalier. Boozer answered that he had never agreed to remain a Cavalier; in other words, he had never accepted their contract offer. Instead, he accepted the Jazz' contract offer and has been a successful member of the Jazz ever since.

The offer may also provide the method in which acceptance must be communicated. If so, then acceptance must be communicated in the manner directed by the offer. If the offer is silent as to the method in which acceptance must be communicated, then any reasonable method of communication will suffice.

Relatively recent technological advances have changed the way people communicate. Instant message services, text message services, listservs, and e-mail have become common methods of communication in both personal and professional settings. For the purpose of acceptance, the reasonableness of the communication method selected to communicate the acceptance will depend on the circumstances. For important transactions, it is advisable to select a means that will provide the offeree with proof (i.e., a copy or receipt) that the offeror received notice of the acceptance.

Consideration

consideration—The exchange of value or benefit that each party agrees to give up as a result of the contractual agreement.

Once there is an offer and an acceptance, in order for a contract to be legally enforceable there also needs to be consideration. **Consideration** is the exchange of value or benefit that each party agrees to give up as a result of the contractual agreement. Simply put, consideration is what each party gets in return for the contractual performance.

The best way to understand the concept of consideration is to focus on the requirement that each party must get something in exchange for his or her performance. Thus, gifts cannot serve as valid consideration because a giving party does not receive anything in exchange for the given service or item. Similarly, items or services given for past performance cannot serve as a basis for consideration. The reason past performance is not consideration is because the party that rewards the performance does not receive anything in exchange. After all, that party already received the performance. Had payment been made at the time of performance, that payment would serve as consideration.

For example, Chris is a general manager for a professional baseball organization. At Chris' retirement ceremony, he is given a gold watch by the organization for 20 years of loyal service. However, the watch breaks and Chris wants the organization to provide a new watch, but the organization refuses. Chris sues the organization, claiming that the watch was given in consideration for 20 years of loyal service. Unfortunately for Chris, his contractual claim for a new watch may fail because the watch was given in consideration for services that were already rendered. Therefore, the watch resembles a gift more than consideration. After all, the baseball organization had already received the services and was not getting anything in exchange for the watch. Furthermore, Chris was paid a salary for his services during the 20 years he served as manager for the organization, and that payment was consideration.

Illegal acts cannot serve as consideration. If a party agrees to pay another for an illegal service, that agreement is not enforceable by the courts because it lacks consideration. However, if one party agrees to do or refrain from doing something that causes him or her harm, that service can be deemed consideration as long as it does not violate the law. For example, one person could pay another not to try out for the football team. By not trying out for the team, the accepting party suffers a detriment for which compensation could be provided.

Legality and Legal Capacity

Even if there is a valid offer, acceptance, and consideration, in order for a contract to be formed the underlying transaction must be legal. Courts will not enforce contracts that are based on an illegal promise or transaction. If a player enters into a contract with a bookie to drop a pass in the end zone, thereby causing the point spread that the bookie wants to remain in place, but the bookie does not pay the player for this service, the player cannot ask a court to help him get his money from the bookie because the transaction itself, gambling, is illegal in the majority of jurisdictions in the United States.

In addition, certain classes of people lack the ability, competence, or capacity to enter into binding contracts. Therefore, individuals who are mentally incompetent and those under the legal age for adulthood, which is 18 in most jurisdictions, cannot enter into valid contracts.

Oftentimes in sports, minors are involved in contracts. A contract between a minor and an adult usually is voidable by the minor but binding on the adult. The term *voidable* in this context means that the minor, unlike the adult, has the power to walk away from the contract. However, some exceptions to this rule exist. For example, contracts that provide necessities for the minor may be enforced by adults against minors. Also, adults usually can enter into binding contracts with minors if the minor's parents or legal guardians have authorized the agreement.

For example, National Letters of Intent (NLIs) are contracts signed by high school athletes in which they agree to attend a university on an athletic scholarship. The standard language from the NLI states, on behalf of the student, that

> At the time I sign this NLI, I must receive a written offer of athletics financial aid applicable for the entire 2008-2009 academic year from the institution named in this document. The offer shall list the terms and conditions of the award, including the amount and duration of the financial aid. . . . In order for this NLI to be valid, my parent/legal guardian and I must sign the NLI and the offer of athletics aid prior to submission to the institution named in this document, and any other stated conditions must also be met. If the conditions stated on the financial aid offer are not met, this NLI shall be declared null and void. An institution submitting an improper offer of athletics aid may be in violation of the NLI program and subject to sanctions. (NLI, n.d.)

As is clear from the language of the NLI, a large number of athletes are minors and so their parents or legal guardians are also required to sign these contracts before they can be enforced against the minor.

Typical Provisions

Contracts do not need to be written in order to be valid. Oral contracts can be legally enforceable if there is a valid offer, acceptance, and consideration. Specific considerations dealing with oral contracts are discussed in the section titled Contract Law Issues on p. 131. Regardless of the validity of an oral contract, you are best advised to enter into written contracts to ensure that you protect your own rights and the rights of your employer.

Written contracts in sport come in many different varieties, which are discussed in the next section. However, some general provisions are common to many different types of sport contracts:

- Party designations
- Term
- Warranties and representations
- Obligations and duties
- Termination

These provisions are found in the majority of sport contracts, so we discuss them in detail next.

Party Designation

A written contract must clearly identify the parties, typically by the full name of the individual or organization involved. For example, the NBA Uniform Player Contract starts by listing the team and player by name:

> THIS AGREEMENT made this _____ day of _____,
> 20_____ by and between _____ (hereinafter
> called the "Club"), a member of the National Basketball Association
> (hereinafter called the "Association") and _____
> whose address is shown below (hereinafter called the "Player").
> (NBA, 2005, exhibit A)

Terms of the Agreement

Another basic provision of any sport contract is a clause providing the term of the agreement. The term is the defined amount of time that the contract will exist. The language setting the term of the contract could be as basic as "This Agreement shall commence upon execution and remain in full force and effect through _____" or more detailed as provided in the license agreement between the Atlanta Falcons and the Georgia Dome: "This Agreement shall expire upon the later of (a) June 30 of the License year in which occurs the Maturity Date of the Revenue Bonds issued by the Authority, or (b) June 30 of the twentieth (20th) License Year" (Miller & Anderson, 2001, p. 48). As this example shows, a contract does not have to specify the exact term of the agreement as long as the contract includes methods that can be used to calculate the exact term.

Warranties and Representations

A typical sport contract includes a section of warranties or representations by the parties. Warranties or representations are legal promises that certain facts are true. In most professional sports team lease agreements, the team must warrant that it is a valid member of the particular league. For example, within the team's lease agreement for Ralph Wilson Stadium, the Buffalo Bills warrant that the team will

> (i) keep and maintain the Team as a member in good standing of the NFL;
>
> (ii) keep and maintain the Franchise in good standing with the NFL . . .;
>
> (iii) keep and maintain the Stadium as the facility designated to and by the NFL as the home facility for the Team; and
>
> (iv) continuously operate the Team at the Stadium in accordance with NFL Rules and Regulations. (Miller & Anderson, 2001, p. 25)

Obligations and Duties

A sport contract typically includes a section that describes the duties and obligations of the parties involved. This section should specifically set out all of the duties that each party has agreed to assume and the time at which the parties will undertake the actions necessary to fulfill these duties. The following contractual language provides a boxing promoter's duties within an agreement with a sponsor.

1. THE FIGHTS: At Promoter's expense, Promoter agrees to perform all acts necessary for the holding of at least *(enter number of fights)* boxing Fight cards on the dates and at the locations to be mutually determined by the parties. Each Fight card will include at least *(enter number of bouts)* preliminary professional boxing bouts. Promoter warrants that it will produce the Fights in accordance with the following specifications:

(a) The Fights will be televised on *(enter television channel)* in *(enter city, state)*. (Promoter will use its best efforts to televise the Fights on other network and cable channels in addition to Channel *(enter channel number)*.

(b) The starting time of each Fight card shall be communicated to a Miller representative at least *forty-five (45)* days prior to the Fight card.

(c) All Fights will be produced in a first class manner in accordance with prevailing professional, ethical and business standards, with the utmost regard for the safety of all persons, property, the environment and Miller's goodwill, will be contested in good faith, and will be sanctioned by all required state regulatory bodies.

(d) All Fights will be planned, designed and executed in compliance with *California* alcoholic beverage laws and regulations and in accordance with any conditions imposed by the *California Alcoholic Beverage Control Board.*

(e) In that all arrangements for the Fights and related Promoter organized activities (and any financial loss relating thereto) shall be solely Promoter's responsibility, Miller shall have no obligation to pay any amounts to Promoter or others as a result of the Fights or related Promoter organized activity, except the amounts payable to Promoter which are specified in Clause 7 below.

(f) All payments for boxers, judges, ring officials, ring girls, announcers, medical personnel, site rentals, a.v. equipment, electricians, stage hands, special security and police, clean-up personnel, ushers, tickets, ticker sellers, ticket takers, box office employees, truck loaders and unloaders, licenses, taxes, advertising and publicity services of every type required, lights, microphones and prop equipment and all other expenses of the Fights shall be the responsibility of Promoter. By way of specification (and not limitation), a Promoter shall perform all obligations imposed under worker's compensation, unemployment compensation insurance, disability benefits, boxing licensing, social security, withholding tax laws and union contracts.

Termination Provision

The final part to any sport contract is the termination provision. This clause sets forth each party's right to terminate the contract under certain circumstances. Termination usually occurs either at the expiration of the contract term or when a party breaches the agreement in some way that causes the contract to be terminated. For example, in a standard licensing agreement between an apparel company and a professional football player, the termination clause provides the following:

9. Termination and Post Termination Right

a. Licensor shall have the right to terminate this Agreement upon thirty (30) days written notice in the event Licensee defaults on any of its obligations hereunder, including without limitation the obligation to pay royalties in a timely manner as set out herein, provided Licensee does not cure its default 'Within the thirty (30) day notice period.'

b. Licensor shall have the right to immediately terminate this Agreement in the event that Licensee:

(i) files a petition in bankruptcy or is adjudicated a bankrupt or insolvent, or makes an assignment or arrangement for the benefit of creditors, or discontinues its business, or has a receiver appointed.

(ii) breaches the provisions of this Agreement relating to unauthorized use of, or assertion of rights in, the Smith Attributes, or challenges the validity or ownership of the Smith Attributes.

Sport Contracts

Various types of contracts are used within the sport industry. The next section discusses employment agreements, contracts with professional and student-athletes, and agreements connected to sport facilities.

Student-Athletes

As mentioned earlier, a student-athlete who signs the National Letter of Intent enters into a contract with the school that also signs the letter. The NLI will be void and no longer a contract if the school does not admit the student or the student does not meet NCAA initial eligibility requirements.

The student-athlete must also receive a scholarship offer from the school that represents the financial aid portion of the agreement. The NLI and the financial aid scholarship make up the contractual agreement between the student-athlete and the school that binds the school to provide the student-athlete with financial aid and a chance to participate in athletics, in exchange for the student-athlete's commitment to attend the school and remain eligible to participate in athletics. The contract lasts 1 year, and the scholarship must be renewed by the parties each year. A hypothetical scholarship offer is shown in figure 5.1.

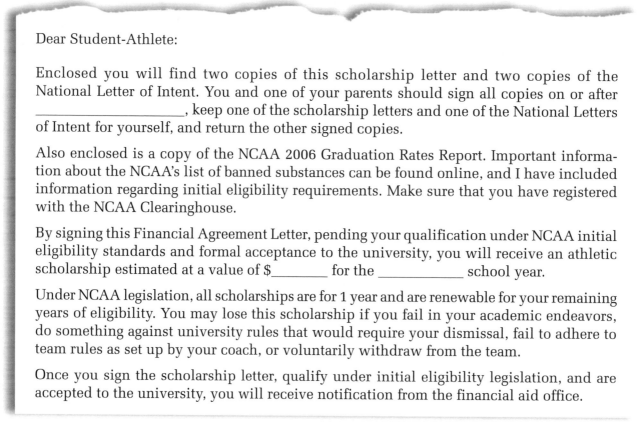

Dear Student-Athlete:

Enclosed you will find two copies of this scholarship letter and two copies of the National Letter of Intent. You and one of your parents should sign all copies on or after _____, keep one of the scholarship letters and one of the National Letters of Intent for yourself, and return the other signed copies.

Also enclosed is a copy of the NCAA 2006 Graduation Rates Report. Important information about the NCAA's list of banned substances can be found online, and I have included information regarding initial eligibility requirements. Make sure that you have registered with the NCAA Clearinghouse.

By signing this Financial Agreement Letter, pending your qualification under NCAA initial eligibility standards and formal acceptance to the university, you will receive an athletic scholarship estimated at a value of $_____ for the _____ school year.

Under NCAA legislation, all scholarships are for 1 year and are renewable for your remaining years of eligibility. You may lose this scholarship if you fail in your academic endeavors, do something against university rules that would require your dismissal, fail to adhere to team rules as set up by your coach, or voluntarily withdraw from the team.

Once you sign the scholarship letter, qualify under initial eligibility legislation, and are accepted to the university, you will receive notification from the financial aid office.

Figure 5.1   A hypothetical scholarship offer to a student-athlete.

Several cases have agreed that the NLI and scholarship constitute a legal and binding contract, starting with *Taylor v. Wake Forest University* (1972). In this case, Taylor entered into a scholarship to play football at Wake Forest University. After participating in football for one semester and performing badly academically, he decided to stop participating in football. As a result the school terminated his scholarship. He then sued the school, claiming that it owed him for the money he had to pay to continue to go to school once the scholarship was terminated. The court agreed that there was a contract between Taylor and the school but also found that under the scholarship contract, he had agreed to maintain his athletic eligibility, physically and academically. Although his improved academic performance met the appropriate standards, when he refused to meet the physical requirements of the scholarship by refusing to participate in football, in the absence of any injury or excuse other than to devote more time to studies, he was not upholding his part of the contract.

The NCAA manual lays out the specific details of the grant-in-aid offered to student-athletes within the scholarship. A school can only give a student financial aid that does not "exceed the cost of attendance that is normally incurred by students enrolled in a comparable program at that institution" (NCAA, 2007, p. 176). The cost of attendance includes the "total cost of tuition and fees, room and board, books and supplies, transportation, and other expenses related to attendance at the institution" (p. 176). These scholarships can only be granted for 1 year and cannot be terminated on the basis of skill or performance on the field of play. As long as the student-athlete remains eligible to participate in athletics at the university, the university must provide that student-athlete with financial aid for the year in question.

Employment

A sport manager will come across many different types of employment contracts. Two of the most interesting types of sport contracts involve athletes and coaches.

Athletes

The contract that is the foundation for the legal relationship between players and management within any team sport is the **collective bargaining agreement (CBA).** The CBA is the contract negotiated between the union (known as players associations in professional sports) and management (team owners) in major professional team sports. CBAs are typically hundreds of pages long, because they include all of the terms and conditions of employment for players, such as salaries, codes of conduct, drug testing provisions, amateur draft rules, and grievance procedures.

collective bargaining agreement (CBA)—A written agreement between employers and employees that provides the exact terms and conditions of the employment relationship between the parties.

Most leagues' CBAs are available on the Internet on either the players association or league Web site. For example, the current NBA Collective Bargaining Agreement can be found on the NBA Players Association's Web site: www.nbpa.com/cba.php. As with all sport CBAs, the NBA's CBA contains a Uniform Players Contract that all players must sign. Some of the most interesting provisions of the NBA Uniform Player Contract (which are common to other Uniform Player Contracts) are provided in figure 5.2.

Perhaps most interesting to some are the assignment, other athletic activities, and termination clauses. Under paragraph 10, the team is allowed to assign the player's contract to another team. This provision allows for teams to trade players under contract. Under paragraph 12, players are restricted from engaging in many other activities that could harm their ability to perform as an NBA basketball player, including hang gliding, bungee jumping, and driving a motorcycle. Finally, the contract contains a detailed section on termination that allows the team to terminate the player for many reasons,

Exhibit A

National Basketball Association Uniform Player Contract

THIS AGREEMENT made this day of ___ is by and between ___ (hereinafter called the "Team"), a member of the National Basketball Association (hereinafter called the "NBA" or "League"), and ___, an individual whose address is shown below (hereinafter called the "Player"). In consideration of the mutual promises hereinafter contained, the parties hereto promise and agree as follows:

. . .

2. SERVICES

The services to be rendered by the Player pursuant to this Contract shall include: (a) training camp, (b) practices, meetings, workouts, and skill or conditioning sessions conducted by the Team during the Season, (c) games scheduled for the Team during any Regular Season, (d) Exhibition games scheduled by the Team or the League during and prior to any Regular Season, (e) if the Player is invited to participate, the NBA's All-Star Game (including the Rookie-Sophomore Game) and every event conducted in association with such All-Star Game, but only in accordance with Article XXI of the Collective Bargaining Agreement currently in effect between the NBA and the National Basketball Players Association (hereinafter the "CBA"), (f) Playoff games scheduled by the League subsequent to any Regular Season, (g) promotional and commercial activities of the Team and the League as set forth in this Contract and the CBA, and (h) any NBADL Work Assignment in accordance with Article XLII of the CBA.

3. COMPENSATION

(a) Subject to paragraph 3(b) below, the Team agrees to pay the Player for rendering the services and performing the obligations described herein the Compensation described in Exhibit 1 or Exhibit 1A hereto (less all amounts required to be withheld by any governmental authority, and exclusive of any amount(s) which the Player shall be entitled to receive from the Player Playoff Pool). Unless otherwise provided in Exhibit 1, such Compensation shall be paid in twelve (12) equal semi-monthly payments beginning with the first of said payments on November 15th of each year covered by the Contract and continuing with such payments on the first and fifteenth of each month until said Compensation is paid in full.

. . .

9. UNIQUE SKILLS

The Player represents and agrees that he has extraordinary and unique skill and ability as a basketball player, that the services to be rendered by him hereunder cannot be replaced or the loss thereof adequately compensated for in money damages, and that any breach by the Player of this Contract will cause irreparable injury to the Team, and to its assignees.

Figure 5.2 Sample of provisions of the NBA Uniform Player Contract. These types of provisions are common to player contracts in other sports as well.

Reprinted, by permission, from National Baseball Players Association, *Collective bargaining agreement 2005-2011* (New York: NBPLA).

Therefore, it is agreed that in the event it is alleged by the Team that the Player is playing, attempting or threatening to play, or negotiating for the purpose of playing, during the term of this Contract, for any other person, firm, entity, or organization, the Team and its assignees (in addition to any other remedies that may be available to them judicially or by way of arbitration) shall have the right to obtain from any court or arbitrator having jurisdiction such equitable relief as may be appropriate, including a decree enjoining the Player from any further such breach of this Contract, and enjoining the Player from playing basketball for any other person, firm, entity, or organization during the term of this Contract. The Player agrees that this right may be enforced by the Team or the NBA. In any suit, action, or arbitration proceeding brought to obtain such equitable relief, the Player does hereby waive his right, if any, to trial by jury, and does hereby waive his right, if any, to interpose any counterclaim or set-off for any cause whatever.

10. ASSIGNMENT

(a) The Team shall have the right to assign this Contract to any other NBA team and the Player agrees to accept such assignment and to faithfully perform and carry out this Contract with the same force and effect as if it had been entered into by the Player with the assignee team instead of with the Team.

. . .

12. OTHER ATHLETIC ACTIVITIES

The Player and the Team acknowledge and agree that the Player's participation in certain other activities may impair or destroy his ability and skill as a basketball player, and the Player's participation in any game or exhibition of basketball other than at the request of the Team may result in injury to him. Accordingly, the Player agrees that he will not, without the written consent of the Team, engage in any activity that a reasonable person would recognize as involving or exposing the participant to a substantial risk of bodily injury including, but not limited to: (i) sky-diving, hang gliding, snow skiing, rock or mountain climbing (as distinguished from hiking), rappelling, and bungee jumping; (ii) any fighting, boxing, or wrestling; (iii) driving or riding on a motorcycle or moped; (iv) riding in or on any motorized vehicle in any kind of race or racing contest; (v) operating an aircraft of any kind; (vi) engaging in any other activity excluded or prohibited by or under any insurance policy which the Team procures against the injury, illness or disability to or of the Player, or death of the Player, for which the Player has received written notice from the Team prior to the execution of this Contract; or (vii) participating in any game or exhibition of basketball, football, baseball, hockey, lacrosse, or other team sport or competition. If the Player violates this Paragraph 12, he shall be subject to discipline imposed by the Team and/or the Commissioner of the NBA. Nothing contained herein shall be intended to require the Player to obtain the written consent of the Team in order to enable the Player to participate in, as an amateur, the sports of golf, tennis, handball, swimming, hiking, softball, volleyball, and other similar sports that a reasonable person would not recognize as involving or exposing the participant to a substantial risk of bodily injury.

Figure 5.2 *(continued)*

» continued

» continued

13. PROMOTIONAL ACTIVITIES

(a) The Player agrees to allow the Team, the NBA, or a League-related entity to take pictures of the Player, alone or together with others, for still photographs, motion pictures, or television, at such reasonable times as the Team, the NBA or the League-related entity may designate. No matter by whom taken, such pictures may be used in any manner desired by either the Team, the NBA, or the League-related entity for publicity or promotional purposes. The rights in any such pictures taken by the Team, the NBA, or the League-related entity shall belong to the Team, the NBA, or the League-related entity, as their interests may appear.

. . .

16. TERMINATION

(a) The Team may terminate this Contract upon written notice to the Player if the Player shall:

(i) at any time, fail, refuse, or neglect to conform his personal conduct to standards of good citizenship, good moral character (defined here to mean not engaging in acts of moral turpitude, whether or not such acts would constitute a crime), and good sportsmanship, to keep himself in first class physical condition, or to obey the Team's training rules;

(ii) at any time commit a significant and inexcusable physical attack against any official or employee of the Team or the NBA (other than another player), or any person in attendance at any NBA game or event, considering the totality of the circumstances, including (but not limited to) the degree of provocation (if any) that may have led to the attack, the nature and scope of the attack, the Player's state of mind at the time of the attack, and the extent of any injury resulting from the attack;

(iii) at any time, fail, in the sole opinion of the Team's management, to exhibit sufficient skill or competitive ability to qualify to continue as a member of the Team; provided, however, (A) that if this Contract is terminated by the Team, in accordance with the provisions of this subparagraph, prior to January 10 of any Season, and the Player, at the time of such termination, is unfit to play skilled basketball as the result of an injury resulting directly from his playing for the Team, the Player shall (subject to the provisions set forth in Exhibit 3) continue to receive his full Base Compensation, less all workers' compensation benefits (which, to the extent permitted by law, and if not deducted from the Player's Compensation by the Team, the Player hereby assigns to the Team) and any insurance provided for by the Team paid or payable to the Player by reason of said injury, until such time as the Player is fit to play skilled basketball, but not beyond the Season during which such termination occurred; and provided, further, (B) that if this Contract is terminated by the Team, in accordance with the provisions of this subparagraph, during the period from the January 10 of any Season through the end of such Season, the Player shall be entitled to receive his full Base Compensation for said Season; or

(iv) at any time, fail, refuse, or neglect to render his services hereunder or in any other manner materially breach this Contract.

Figure 5.2 *(continued)*

including the player's failure to conform his personal conduct to standards of citizenship and good sporting behavior.

Because players in professional team sports must sign these Uniform Player Contracts, the players are only able to negotiate over their salary and, in most leagues, salaries are subject to both a rookie scale and a **salary cap.** The NBA's rookie salary scale is set in article VIII of the collective bargaining agreement (NBA, 2005). The salary cap for nonrookie contract players is found in article VII. The salary cap is provided as a percentage of basketball-related income (BRI), which includes gate receipts (from regular season, exhibition, and playoff games), broadcasting revenues, novelty and concession sales, proceeds from in-arena signage and luxury suite sales, naming rights proceeds, and proceeds from premium seat licenses (NBA, 2005, Art. VII, § 1(a)). The current NBA CBA runs from 2005 until 2011, and for those years the salary cap will be an escalating percentage of BRI from 49.5% in 2005-2006 to 51% into the 2010-2011 season (NBA). Although the exact cap cannot be calculated into the future beyond the percentage given, these percentages equated to $49.5 million in 2005-2006, $53.135 million in 2006-2007, and $55.63 in 2007-2008.

salary cap—An agreed upon amount of money that teams must pay out in player salaries for any particular year. The amount is agreed to in negotiations between players and teams and is included in the league's collective bargaining agreement.

Endorsement

Professional athletes in all sports enter into agreements with endorsers and sponsors. These contracts allow the athletes to receive compensation above and beyond their salary from the team itself (see table 5.1).

Table 5.1 Highest Compensated Athletes

Rank	Player	Sport	Salary	Endorsements	Total
1	Tiger Woods	Golf	$22,902,706	$105,000,000	$127,902,706
2	Phil Mickelson	Golf	$9,372,685	$53,000,000	$62,372,685
3	LeBron James	Basketball	$12,455,000	$28,000,000	$40,455,000
4	Floyd Mayweather, Jr.	Boxing	$20,000,000	$20,250,000	$40,250,000
5	Kobe Bryant	Basketball	$19,490,625	$16,000,000	$35,490,625
6	Shaquille O'Neal	Basketball	$20,000,000	$15,000,000	$35,000,000
7	Alex Rodriguez	Baseball	$29,000,000	$6,000,000	$35,000,000
8	Kevin Garnett	Basketball	$22,000,000	$9,000,000	$31,000,000
9	Peyton Manning	Football	$17,500,000	$13,000,000	$30,500,000
10	Derek Jeter	Baseball	$22,000,000	$8,000,000	$30,000,000

Adapted from Smith and Street's *SportsBusiness Daily*, June 5, 2008, "Tiger Woods tops SI's list of top earners for fifth straight year."

Endorsement contracts grant a sponsor or endorser the right to use the athlete's name, image, or likeness in connection with advertising the sponsor's or endorser's product. Many athletes in individual performer sports like golf and tennis enter into endorsement deals with equipment and apparel manufacturers that make products for their sport. Team sports athletes often enter into agreements to sponsor shoes, gloves, or other equipment and apparel.

The provisions and amounts of money involved in an endorsement agreement vary with the popularity of the athlete and the resources of the sponsor. Of course, if an athlete is nationally or internationally known, like Tiger Woods, he will be able to command more money in endorsements, and endorsers will line up to get him to advertise their products.

Figure 5.3 provides sample language from a shoe endorsement agreement for a professional basketball player. Under the agreement, the athlete grants the company the exclusive right to use his name and likeness in the marketing of the company's products. The athlete also agrees that he will not endorse any competitor's products and agrees to use the company's products during events.

THIS AGREEMENT is made as of _____ by and between _____ ("Company"), and _____ ("Athlete").

Recitals: Athlete is a well-known professional athlete whose endorsement has commercial value. Company desires to obtain the worldwide right to use Athlete's endorsement and services in connection with its products and services, and Athlete desires to grant such rights to Company.

NOW, THEREFORE, in consideration of the foregoing and the mutual promises set forth in this Agreement, Company and Athlete agree as follows:

1. DEFINITIONS. When used in this Agreement, the following terms will have the meaning set forth below unless the context requires otherwise:

. . .

1.5 Endorsement: "Endorsement" includes the following or any part thereof. (a) Athlete's name, nickname, likeness, voice, live or recorded performance, photograph, signature or facsimile thereof, and biographical materials; (b) any and all trademarks, service marks, trade names, domain names, rights of publicity, copyrights and designs owned by or on behalf of Athlete; and (c) all other materials or indicia relating to or identifying Athlete.

. . .

1.10 Products: "Products" means all (a) footwear; (b) athletic, athletically-inspired and casual apparel, headwear and accessories; (c) eyewear, watches and performance measurement devices; (d) sports and fitness equipment; (e) posters; and (f) inflatables.

1.11 Territory: "Territory" means the entire world.

. . .

Figure 5.3 Sample wording for an endorsement contract.

3. LICENSE TO COMPANY: Subject to and in accordance with the terms and conditions of this Agreement:

3.1 Exclusive License: Athlete grants to Company the exclusive right and license during the Term and throughout the Territory to use the Endorsement in connection with: (a) the production, distribution, marketing, advertising, promotion and sale of Products; and (b) the design, development, creation, manufacture, production, distribution, marketing, advertising, promotion and sale of Licensed Products.

3.2 Exclusivity of Endorsement: Athlete agrees that during the Term he will not participate in any activity for the purpose of advertising or promoting a Competitor. Athlete specifically agrees that he will not permit the use of the Endorsement either in connection with any Product other than a Company Product or by or for the benefit of a Competitor. Athlete warrants and represents that he has disclosed to Company the details of any and all conflicts, potential conflicts, and disputes of which he is or reasonably should be aware which might compromise or restrict Company's ability to utilize the Endorsement or produce Licensed Products as intended by this Agreement.

. . .

6. ATHLETE SERVICES:

6.1 Use of Company Products: Athlete warrants that he uses Company Products and agrees to use Company Products exclusively during all athletic workouts, practices, tournaments, games, events, exhibitions, media interviews and during all public activities where it is appropriate to wear Products ("Public Activities"). Athlete further agrees to use Company Products in the same condition as received from Company with any Company trademarks visibly displayed and with no other trademarks, trade names, logos or symbols affixed thereto. Athlete acknowledges that he has tested and worn Company Products and that Company Products are satisfactory for his use in professional competition and training. Athlete agrees that he will advise Company in writing if he experiences any difficulty with the fit, durability or comfort of Company Products and acknowledges that his failure to so advise Company will constitute an ongoing affirmation of his satisfaction with Company Products. Company agrees to provide *sufficient* quantities of Company Products for Athlete's professional use at no cost to Athlete.

Figure 5.3 *(continued)*

Athlete Agent

Athletes in many sports enter into contracts with the agents who will represent them in negotiations with teams, endorsers, or events. Many professional leagues have developed standard representation agreements or other rules that agents must follow in these situations. Further details on athlete agents and the agreements they sign with players can be found in chapter 4.

Coaches

The contracts that coaches sign are often for incredibly high salaries in both university and professional sports (see table 5.2).

Table 5.2   Highest Paid Coaches in Select University and Professional Sports

Football head coach	School	Annual compensation
Nick Saban	Alabama	$4,000,000
Charlie Weis	Notre Dame	$3,500,000
Bob Stoops	Oklahoma	$3,450,000
Kirk Ferentz	Iowa	$2,840,000
Pete Carroll	USC	$2,782,000
Mack Brown	Texas	$2,664,000
Tommy Tuberville	Auburn	$2,231,000
Philip Fulmer	Tennessee	$2,050,000
Jim Tressel	Ohio St.	$2,012,700
Dennis Franchione	Texas A&M	$2,012,200
Coach	**Professional team**	**Annual salary**
Phil Jackson	Los Angeles Lakers (NBA)	$10,330,000
Mike Holmgren	Seattle Seahawks (NFL)	$8,000,000
Joe Girardi	New York Yankees (MLB)	$7,500,000
Don Nelson	Golden State Warriors (NBA)	$6,000,000
Mike Shanahan	Denver Broncos (NFL)	$6,000,000
Nate McMillan	Portland Trail Blazers (NBA)	$5,500,000
Gregg Popovich	San Antonio Spurs (NBA)	$5,500,000
Jeff Fisher	Tennessee Titans (NFL)	$5,500,000
Lovie Smith	Chicago Bears (NFL)	$5,500,000
Doc Rivers	Boston Celtics (NBA)	$5,000,000
Flip Saunders	Detroit Pistons (NBA)	$5,000,000
Jeff Van Gundy	Houston Rockets (NBA)	$5,000,000
Pat Riley	Miami Heat (NBA)	$5,000,000
Bill Belichick	New England Patriots (NFL)	$5,000,000
Tony Dungy	Indianapolis Colts (NFL)	$5,000,000

Reprinted, by permission, from M.J. Greenberg, 2008, "College athletics - Chasing the big bucks," *For The Record*, April-June 19(2): 6-10.

Drafting a contract for a university coach has become an art form; in addition to earning a base salary, these coaches now receive revenues from speaking engagements, summer camps, endorsement deals, television and radio shows, appearance fees, and many other revenue streams. For example, in head basketball coach Kelvin Sampson's employment agreement with

Indiana University, in addition to earning a base salary of $500,000 per year, Sampson received many other fringe benefits:

- Standard university employee benefits
- Reasonable travel expenses associated with his work as coach
- Two cars
- Eight season tickets to regular home games plus up to 22 single-game tickets
- Reimbursement for moving expenses
- Outside, marketing, and promotional income associated with Sampson's work promoting the basketball program: $600,000 during the first year of the contract and escalating to $1,150,000 in the final year of the contract
- Commercial endorsements
- Pay for summer camps (Indiana University, 2007)

Sampson was also eligible to earn supplemental compensation in the event that his team won the Big Ten regular season conference championship, won the Big Ten Tournament, or played in the NCAA tournament, as follows:

Article V—Supplemental Compensation

5.01. Supplemental Compensation for Big Ten Conference Regular Season Conference Championship, Big Ten Tournament Championship, and NCAA Men's Basketball Tournament Play

A. If the University men's basketball team which is under the direct supervision of the Employee wins "outright" or "ties" the regular season (not post-season tournament) conference men's basketball championship, the Employee will receive an additional amount of Twenty Thousand Dollars ($20,000).

B. If the University men's basketball team which is under the direct supervision of the Employee wins the conference men's post-season tournament basketball championship the Employee will receive an additional amount of Forty Thousand Dollars ($40,000).

C. If the University men's basketball team which is under the direct supervision of the Employee advances to the NCAA Division I Men's Basketball post season Tournament round of sixteen (16) teams, the Employee will receive an additional amount of Twenty Thousand Dollars ($20,000).

D. If the University men's basketball team which is under the direct supervision of the Employee advances to the NCAA Division I Men's post-season Basketball Tournament of four (4) teams, the Employee will receive an additional amount of Twenty Thousand Dollars ($20,000).

E. If the University men's basketball team which is under the direct supervision of the Employee wins the NCAA Division I Men's Basketball post season Tournament Championship (National Champions), the Employee will receive an additional amount of One Hundred Thousand Dollars ($100,000).

F. If Employee is named the NCAA Coach of the Year, the Employee will receive an additional amount of Twenty Five Thousand Dollars ($25,000). (Indiana University, 2007)

When Indiana hired Sampson, he was already on probation for violating NCAA rules related to permissible phone calls to recruited student-athletes. Early in his tenure at Indiana, the school found that he had violated the rules again and took away a potential $500,000 bonus. In February 2008, the NCAA sent a Notice of Allegations to Indiana alleging five major infractions of NCAA rules involving Sampson (NCAA, 2008). Although Sampson's original employment agreement contained strong language allowing the university to terminate him as a result of any "significant, intentional, or repetitive violation of any law, rule, regulation, constitutional provision, bylaw or interpretation of the . . . NCAA" (Indiana University, 2007, p.11), Sampson would not admit to any wrongdoing, and before the NCAA finished its investigation, the university and Sampson agreed to a separation agreement that terminated the employment agreement, and the university paid him a $750,000 settlement and recorded his agreement to resign (Separation Agreement, 2008). As a supplement to this agreement, both the university and Sampson agreed to release all potential legal claims against each other related to his employment at Indiana University.

Because of the strength of his or her employment contract, it is very difficult for a university to fire a coach. Jim O'Brien was hired as the head basketball coach at Ohio State University for the 1997-1998 season. After several amendments, his contract paid him an annual salary of approximately $800,000 running until 2007. According to his contract, he could only be terminated for cause as provided in section 5.1:

Termination for Cause—Ohio State may terminate this agreement at any time for cause, which, for the purposes of this agreement, shall be limited to the occurrence of one or more of the following:

(a) a material breach of this agreement by Coach, which Coach fails to remedy to OSU's reasonable satisfaction, within a reasonable time period, not to exceed thirty (30) days, after receipt of a written notice from Ohio State specifying the act(s), conduct or omission(s) constituting such breach;

(b) a violation by Coach . . . of applicable law, policy, rule or regulation of the NCAA or the Big Ten Conference which leads to a "major" infraction investigation by the NCAA or the Big Ten Conference and which results in a finding by the NCAA or the Big Ten Conference of lack of institutional control over the men's basketball program or which results in Ohio State being sanctioned by the NCAA or the Big Ten Conference. (*O'Brien v. The Ohio State University*, 2007, ¶15)

In June 2004, the university fired O'Brien because it found that he had violated NCAA rules in 1998 by providing a $6,000 loan to a Serbian basketball player. O'Brien argued that he gave the money to the player to help his family and not to recruit him to play for the university. The player, Aleksander Radojevic, is a 7-foot 3-inch (2.2-meter) center who eventually played for the NBA's Utah Jazz. Radojevic was eventually ruled ineligible to participate in university basketball because he had played professionally in Europe.

The university had the option to terminate O'Brien without cause, and if it did so section 5.2 of the contract would come into play and the university would owe O'Brien the majority of his salary for the full term of his contract. In February 2006, O'Brien sued the university, claiming that his termination was in violation of the just cause provision of his contract. The court agreed, finding that O'Brien's conduct was not a material breach of his employment contract and so the school could not terminate him (*O'Brien v. The Ohio State University,* 2006). The court then awarded O'Brien $2.5 million under the termination without cause provision of his contract. The school appealed but lost again (*O'Brien v. The Ohio State University,* 2007).

What can be learned from the Sampson and O'Brien situations? Universities, lawyers, and sport managers must draft coaching contracts carefully and must understand how they apply in every situation. As the Ohio Court of Appeals said in *O'Brien*,

> OSU was the drafting party. OSU is not lacking in sophistication, and has only been prejudiced as a result of being held to its own bargain. OSU entered into this agreement with O'Brien having more-than-adequate knowledge and awareness of the risks and liabilities appurtenant to competing in NCAA Division I university sports. The Radojevic matter was not the first problem to hit the OSU campus. The tradition and legacy of OSU and its sports team, however, has survived, and will continue to do so. (2008, p. 95)

Game and Event Contracts

In planning games and events for sport organizations, sport managers may also come across many contracts related specifically to the event itself.

Game contracts are entered into in order to facilitate an individual game or contest between two sport organizations (i.e., athletes, teams, clubs, associations) (McMillen, 2007). Sport managers who work for sport facilities must take great care in entering into these contracts when scheduling games at a certain facility because such scheduling will affect the ability to host any other events at the facility. Many considerations will come into play when game contracts are developed, including the date and time of the event; ability to use and display the trademarks, names, and logos of the organizations competing; television and radio rights; travel expenses; and security and concessions.

Event-specific contracts, although similar to game contracts, may relate less to hosting a particular game and more to hosting an overall sporting event like the Super Bowl or a combination of events like the NCAA basketball tournament (McMillen, 2007). An event contract may include a game contract along with agreements related to the facility lease, concessions, corporate sponsorships, marketing, and television or other media contracts. Figure 5.4 is a hypothetical contract that includes many of the clauses that would be seen in a typical event contract, such as the host's responsibility for planning the event, printing programs, providing for meeting space, and providing the necessary ticket sellers and vendors and the exact financial arrangement and term for the agreement.

National Association of Athletics

2007 and 2008 NAA Men's and Women's Swimming National Championships

AGREEMENT

The National Association of Athletics (hereinafter referred to as the "NAA") and the Community College District (hereinafter referred to as the "Host") agree to the following conditions relative to the organization, management and administration of the 2007 and 2008 NAA Men's and Women's Swimming National Championships (the "Championships") to be held at the College Natatorium, March 2-5, 2008.

I. APPROVAL AND ACKNOWLEDGEMENTS

A. The NAA hereby approves College as the official host of the Championships. The Championships shall consist of those individuals and relay teams that meet the required qualification standards. The official schedule and time shall be mutually agreed upon by the Host and the NAA.

B. The Championships shall be conducted under the direct control and supervision of NAA, including implementation of policies established by the NAA Swimming Association (the "NSA"). Policies regarding format of the Championships are subject to change by the NAA Council (the "NC") and the NSA. The NAA shall approve the designation of the Host's Championships coordinator, who shall work with the NAA national administrator in organizing and conducting the Championships.

C. Corporations with business interests beyond the local area of the Championships site shall not be solicited for financial support without the prior written approval of the NAA. Further, no business or corporations shall be identified or receive recognition as a title sponsor of the Championships without prior written approval from the NAA.

D. Alcoholic beverages and tobacco products of any form shall not be advertised, sold, disbursed, or brought onto the site of the Championships.

Figure 5.4 Hypothetical event contract.

E. The Host shall honor all NAA credentials issued to authorized player, coaches, officials and media for admittance to the Championships. NAA membership cards presented will be honored for a complimentary ticket to the Championships.

F. The NAA, in consultation with the Host, shall be responsible for any and all negotiations for radio and television broadcast rights. Any internet broadcast or Web site by the Host must be approved in writing by the NAA.

G. The name National Association of Athletics, initials NAA, logo and other NAA symbols and insignia (the "NAA Marks") are the exclusive property of the NAA. The Host is awarded limited rights and privileges in using the NAA Marks to promote, advertise and market the Championships.

II. RESPONSIBILITIES OF THE PARTICIPATING INSTITUTIONS

A. The participating institutions shall pay the established entry fees, which must accompany the official entry form, made payable to the Host. Entry fees shall be $5.00 per individual for each event entered and $20.00 for each relay entry.

B. Participating institutions shall pay or the cost of transportation, housing and meals (with the exception of the Championship banquet) in route to and from, and while at the Championships. All teams must stay at the assigned hotel.

C. Participating teams shall attend and participate in the Championships Banquet and any awards presentations as deemed necessary by the NAA.

III. NAA RESPONSIBILITIES

A. The NIA, in cooperation with the Host, shall coordinate and administer the Championships, including, but not limited to, the qualification of individuals and teams and schedule of events. The NAA Men's and Women's Swimming Rules Committee shall be responsible for hearing protests and enforcing rules of competition.

B. The NAA shall order and ship all approved awards for the Championships, but all costs of the relating to such awards shall be the financial obligation of the Host.

C. The NAA shall print and provide credentials for use by participants, coaches, authorized media and officials.

D. The NAA shall be responsible for the cost of printing and postage of all entry information and related materials.

E. The NAA and the Host shall have final approval of the agenda for the Championship Banquet. The Championship Banquet agenda shall be carefully controlled by the Host and the NAA in regard to time.

IV. HOST RESPONSIBILITIES

A. The Host shall provide the Natatorium for practice and meet competition March 2-5, 2008. This includes use of the pool for practice a day prior to the Championships. Use of the pool complex shall include all facilities and equipment necessary to administer the

» continued

Figure 5.4 *(continued)*

» continued

Championships, including, but not limited to, spectator seating, lights, scoreboards, computerized timing system, computer program for all heating and seeding, public address system, parking lots, restrooms, dressing rooms, meeting rooms, ticket booth, concession/souvenir stands, press room, team benches, signage, water coolers, and all normal preparation and maintenance of such facility.

B. The Host shall provide all Championships personnel necessary to conduct the Championships, including, but not limited to, ticket sellers and taker, adequate security/police, concession vendors, maintenance crew, hospitality workers, public address announcers and computer operators.

C. The Host shall provide travel, housing and meals for the Championship officials and Head Official. Officials' ground travel shall be reimbursed at the rate established by the Internal Revenue Service at the time of the Championships. The NAA in consultation with the Host will select and assign the Head Official. The Host in consultation with the Head Official will select and assign the official starters, meet referees and certified officials necessary for the supervision and conduct of the Championships, including, but not limited to, timers, turn inspectors, stroke/turn judges and diving judges from the local swimming and diving officials association.

D. The Host shall provide a press room and financial support for travel and housing for one (1) media representative. The site shall be equipped with the necessary equipment to meet the standards and approval for the NAA. Specific needs include: three (3) telephone lines, one (1) high speed copier, one (1) on-line work station with internet access and an e-mail account for use by NAA authorized personnel, one (1) laser printer, and one (1) facsimile (fax) machine.

E. The Host shall provide the Championships Vendor with a covered area to market and sell NAA merchandise at the site, hotel headquarters, banquet area and registration area. Each sales area shall be equipped with tables, chairs, electricity and a phone line. The Host shall provide a sales staff (normally two (2) full-time equivalents) to market and sell merchandise at the locations previously listed. In exchange for providing the aforementioned sales areas and staff, the Host shall receive ten percent (10%) of gross sales (total receipts less any applicable taxes) in such areas.

F. The Host shall provide travel, housing, meals and/or meal expenses up to $25.00 per diem for a maximum of two (2) NAA representatives.

G. The Host shall provide a certified trainer to cover all sessions of the Championship including the operation and administration of training room. The trainer must be NAA approved.

H. The Host shall have medical assistance reasonably available for the Championships to include a physician and an ambulance service on-site or on-call throughout the Championships, through volunteers provided by the Sports Foundation. Onsite medical equipment should include, but is not limited to, AEDs (Automated External Defibrillators), backboards, crutches, splints/braces and biohazard containers. The Host shall not be held responsible

Figure 5.4 *(continued)*

for any errors, omissions, or other acts of any personnel supplied pursuant to this section or for any damages resulting from use of the medical equipment (including but not limited to malfunction).

I. The Host shall be responsible for arranging an opening banquet for all players, coaches and Championships officials.

J. The Host shall negotiate the best possible rates for team housing to include a room block of not less than 150. Rooms should be double-double, non smoking. The Host shall provide complimentary hotel rooms for the NAA representatives.

K. The Host shall provide the necessary meeting room space during the course of the event at the event headquarters hotel or on campus. These rooms shall be used for coaches' business meeting, diving coaches meeting, rules committee meeting, executive committee and pre-Championships general coaches meeting. The Host shall provide meeting/hospitality space at the competition venue as deemed necessary by the NAA.

L. The Host shall produce the championships souvenir program in consultation with the NAA and shall be responsible for all expenses related to printing of all programs.

M. The Host shall print and provide an informational press packet for the media covering the event. The NAIA and the Host will work together to discuss what information will need to be provided to the media.

N. The Host shall be responsible for the printing of event tickets and the management of all Championships admissions. NOTE: Approval of the copy for the front and backside of Championships tickets and the cost of admissions must be approved by the NAIA Administrator.

O. The Host shall be responsible for the advance publicity and promotion of the Championships to include any paid advertising, posters, flyers and related expenses.

A. The Host shall be responsible for all expenses related directly to the administration of the Championships, including, but not limited to, printing, postage, telephone calls and supplies.

B. The Host shall provide general commercial liability insurance for the event at a minimum of $1,000,000 per occurrence, naming the NAIA as an additionally insured party. Host shall provide the NAIA with a copy of said coverage thirty (30) days prior to the event.

C. The Host shall provide the official photographer and photography services to include reproduction, sales and distribution covering the banquet, Championships and awards ceremonies.

V. FINANCIAL AGREEMENT

A. The Host shall submit an estimated budget of income and expenses to the NAA at least Sixty (60) days prior to the beginning of the Championships.

B. A financial report of all income and expenses related to the Championships shall be sent to the NAA within sixty (60) days of the conclusion of the Championships.

» continued

Figure 5.4 *(continued)*

» continued

C. The Host shall submit an economic impact, attendance and room pick-up report to the NAA National Office within sixty (60) days of the conclusion of the Championship.

D. The NAA Administrator will invoice the Host immediately following each of the Championships for the expenses incurred by the NAA that are the financial responsibility of the Host under this Agreement.

E. The Host shall be responsible for all authorized Championships expenses and shall have the right to retain all income derived from the Championships. If the event expenses exceed income, the Host shall be responsible for the deficit. If the event income exceeds expenses, the net income shall be divided between the Host and the NAIA on a 50-50 percentage basis.

VI. LENGTH OF AGREEMENT

A. The length of this Agreement shall cover the 2008 NAA Men's and Women's Swimming National Championships.

Figure 5.4 *(continued)*

Waivers

waiver—A contract between the sport organization and the participant; it is signed prior to participation in a sporting event. By signing the waiver, the participant agrees to absolve the sport organization from liability for any injuries that the participant suffers as a result of participation.

Another type of sport contract is a **waiver.** Sport organizations often use waivers to protect themselves and their business from the financial effects of lawsuits that might occur when individuals are injured at an event or facility. A waiver is a contract between the sport organization and the participant; it is signed prior to participation in a sporting event. Waivers are especially important in recreational and club sports and in health and fitness organizations because the organization may not be able to withstand payments for injuries that could occur at its facility.

The waiver must meet the essential elements of a contract in order to be valid. These elements were discussed previously in this chapter but are provided here again in the context of waivers. To have a valid and enforceable contract (waiver), one that will legally bind the parties to an agreement, you need to first have a valid offer and acceptance. As such, a contract represents an exchange. It is an agreement to *offer* a product, service, or experience that requires *acceptance* of the terms of that offer. With a waiver, there is an offer to provide a sport experience (the offer to allow one to participate) in exchange for an acceptance of the terms of the waiver (an agreement to absolve the sport organization from liability for injuries that she suffers as a result of participation). As you recall, the thing of value that is exchanged is called consideration. The consideration in waiver agreements is somewhat different from ordinary contracts for the sale of goods, for example, where tangible objects are exchanged (e.g., money for a car). With waivers, the consideration is intangible: the exchange of a right (to participate) for a promise (to not hold the sport organization liable for injury).

Two overriding concepts form the basis for an enforceable waiver: fairness and the ability of the person or organization to understand the terms of the waiver that they are signing. Factors that influence ability to understand the language of a waiver come from several sources, namely the characteristics of the person agreeing to the terms of the waiver, and the way the waiver is written. What factors might make it difficult for someone to understand the terms of a waiver? One that probably comes first to mind is the age of the person. Waivers signed by a minor (a person under the age of either 18 or 21, depending on the state) are unenforceable. The law uses the term *capacity* to describe the ability of a person to understand the terms of a contract. It is perceived that a person under the state-mandated legal age of majority does not have the capacity to enter into a waiver and therefore should not be held to the contract. Other situations where one might lack the capacity to understand the terms of a waiver are intoxication and disability. Mental status can be influenced by health status and disability, or by being under the influence of alcohol or drugs. Where a person cannot understand the terms of a waiver due to intoxication or disability, the waiver likely will not be enforceable and therefore not offer protection from liability for the sport organization. Therefore, when implementing waivers, it is important for the sport manager to understand the mental state and age of the person signing the waiver.

A second issue that relates to the ability to understand a waiver is the way that the waiver is written. For example, a waiver written in confusing language or with legalese may be difficult for the average person to understand. The size and font of lettering should be easily readable. A waiver is an example of a contract in which the language is very important.

The fairness of the contract is also an overriding principle that governs the enforceability of waivers. The term *equal bargaining power* is often used in determining whether a waiver was fair between the contracting parties. This term basically means that one party should not be overwhelmed or unduly intimidated by the other party given their status and power. Some large organizations and governments, for example, stand in positions where they have far superior bargaining power. Some situations might arise in which one party stands in a position where they have no choice but to accept the terms of a waiver given the power that another party has over them. In these cases unequal bargaining power might be brought up as an argument against the enforceability of a waiver. Another issue of fairness also involves whether a party has voluntarily entered into a waiver agreement. Waivers may be deemed unenforceable if one side is forced or tricked into signing the waiver. We should be free to enter contracts as we choose. Sport managers should be aware of those situations where people feel they have lost their choice in entering a waiver.

Further, fairness may be an issue in which a sport organization attempts to avoid any and all liability in their waiver, even that amounting to acts of gross negligence. Most jurisdictions will not uphold waivers that attempt to relieve the organization from any form of liability. Waivers are generally intended to relieve the sport organization only of liability for ordinary negligence. So, when dealing with waivers, sport managers should be aware of the bargaining power of both parties, the characteristics of the person signing the waiver, and the clarity of the language of the waiver. All of these considerations (those relevant to contracts) should be taken into account and discussed with a competent attorney when waivers are drafted and administered.

A waiver clause for a participant in a swimming meet might look like this:

> In consideration of the acceptance of this entry, I, for myself and for my executors, administrators, and assigns, waive and release any and all claims against United States Swimming, U.S. Masters Swimming, Wisconsin Swimming Inc., the Swim Club, and any of their staffs, officers, officials, volunteers, sponsors, agents, representatives, successors, or assigns and agree to hold them harmless from any claims or losses, including but not limited to claims for negligence for any injuries or expenses that I may incur at this meet or while traveling to and from this meet. I am a bona fide amateur athlete, am registered with United States Swimming and U.S. Masters Swimming, or am swimming and competing independent of any affiliation and am eligible to compete in all events I have entered.

Lease Agreements

A lease agreement is a contract entered into between a facility owner (lessor) and a party that wants to use the facility for a defined amount of time (lessee). Under any sport lease agreement, the party that owns a facility (lessor) promises to allow another party to use the facility (lessee) for some designated amount of time in consideration for some form or payment, whether the lessee makes actual financial payments in the form of rent or whether the lessee promises to use the particular facility and no other facility for the duration of the lease contract.

In professional sports, the lessor often is not simply one entity; instead, it is the community itself and some other organization (usually known as a facility district) created to assist in the funding of the facility. This means that anyone working for the team must understand the exact nature of the lessor in order to understand the rights that the team has under the lease agreement. For example, the Green Bay Packers entered into a lease agreement with the Green Bay–Brown County Professional Football Stadium District and the City of Green Bay (joint owners of Lambeau Field and the property the field stands on) to allow the Packers to lease "the entirety of the Site and the Existing Facility, together with the rights appurtenant to the Site and the Existing Facility, and all of the City's Ownership Interest in and to the Lambeau Field Complex" (Lease Agreement, 2001).

Professional team facility leases have many detailed and unique provisions that define the relationship between the parties. These lease agreements often run hundreds of pages and include many sub-agreements or separate agreements that lay out funding, development schedules, construction agreements, facility management agreements, and other contracts important to understanding the entire lease agreement.

Although the media often focuses on the enormous public investment in sport facilities, from the lowest level of sports to the professional leagues, teams and sport organizations often make commitments under the lease agreement. These commitments are the consideration necessary to create an enforceable contract. Often this is in the form of rental payments. For example, the Milwaukee Brewers Baseball Club agreed to pay rent in the following amounts to the Southeast Wisconsin Professional Baseball Park District during the 30-year term of their lease (*Amended and Restated Lease Agreement,* 2004):

AP Photo/Morry Gash

The Green Bay Packers lease Lambeau Field from the City of Green Bay and the Stadium District.

Lease Year	*Annual Rent*
1-10	$900,000
11-20	$1,200,000
21-30	$1,208,401

Annual rental payments are in addition to most teams' agreements to pay the costs associated with maintenance, operations, security, and facility improvements. As a result, most teams promise to make significant financial commitments within the lease agreement.

One of the most interesting provisions of a modern lease agreement is a direct answer to the franchise relocation issues discussed in the antitrust chapter (chapter 10). City administrators worry that teams will leave their facilities during the term of the lease agreement. As a result, many lease agreements contain clauses that relate to retaining the team in the event that it attempts to break the lease agreement. These provisions are typically called *nonrelocation agreements* because by entering into these contracts, the team agrees that it will not relocate to a different facility during the term of the lease agreement. The *Amended and Restated Lease Agreement By and Among Southeast Wisconsin Professional Baseball Park District, State of Wisconsin, and Milwaukee Brewers Baseball Club, Limited Partnership* (2004) contains a separate agreement (although acknowledged within the full lease agreement) that makes clear that both parties encouraged each other to enter into the nonrelocation agreement:

> E. As an inducement to the Team to continue to cause the Milwaukee Brewers to play their Baseball Home Games in the City, the District, the State and the Team have agreed to cause the "Stadium Project" and "Infrastructure" . . . to be constructed pursuant to that certain Construction Administration Agreement. . . .

> F. As an inducement to the District and the State to assist the Team in causing the Stadium Project and Infrastructure to be constructed, the Team has agreed to enter into this Non-Relocation Agreement. (*Amended and Restated Non-Relocation Agreement*, 2004, p. 1)

Under the nonrelocation agreement, the team agreed to play all of its home games for each season at Miller Park, and if the team breaks this agreement, the state and ballpark district can immediately terminate the lease, go to court to stop the team from leaving the stadium, and can force the team to fulfill its obligations under the lease.

Seat License

Another interesting type of facility contract that has become very important in university and professional sports is a seat license. Often referred to as a personal seat license, permanent seat license, seat deposit, or PSL, a seat license provides a buyer with the option to purchase tickets for a small fee. However, the license does not pay for the tickets or guarantee that certain seats or other options will be available. Instead, by paying the seat license fee, the purchaser is given some level of priority and the ability to buy tickets before other purchasers. Many professional sports teams' season ticket packages now include seat deposits that act in the same way and must be paid above and beyond the normal price for the tickets. Universities also have begun to incorporate seat licenses and deposits within their season ticket selling schemes. Teams and schools create seat licenses to raise funds that often are used for renovations or facility construction. As long as demand for the particular tickets is high, fans have continued to pay these fees. For example, the Green Bay Packers recently added a deposit to their season ticket package to help the team pay for the costs associated with rising player salaries and the renovation of Lambeau Field. In 2001, season-ticket holders had to pay seat user fees of $1,400 (for seven-game packages) and $600 (for three-game packages). There has been little complaint: Packers season tickets have been sold out since 1960, and if fans want to keep their tickets, they have to pay the seat deposit (2008 Green Bay Packers Tickets, n.d.).

Contract Law Issues

With any contract there is the potential for many issues to arise, from the contract being breached by one party to a court having to interpret the contract to assess damages or remedies in a particular situation. This section provides an overview of these issues.

Any time that one party does not meet its obligations under a contract, that party may be found to have breached the contract. The Parole Evidence Rule and the Statute of Frauds are common law rules that assist in understanding the contract when it is breached. In addition, the nonbreaching party can seek several remedies to compensate for its loss.

Parole Evidence Rule

The **Parole Evidence Rule** provides that when contracting parties express their full intentions in writing, no other evidence can be introduced in a court of law that contradicts the terms of the written agreement. If one party breaches a written contract, the Parole Evidence Rule stops either party from looking to prior written or oral statement that might contradict the terms of the written agreement. Simply put, the Parole Evidence Rule prevents litigants from asserting facts that existed before contract formation that are inconsistent with or contradict the existing written contract.

Sport managers should be cautious when material terms or conditions are omitted from a written agreement, because there is the chance that a court may view the written agreement as fully integrated, meaning that the parties intended the written agreement to be final and complete. If the contract is viewed as fully integrated, then a court will not hear any evidence pertaining to any material terms or conditions that are not included in the original written agreement. In contract negotiations, many drafts may be circulated among the parties before a final written contract is completed. It is each party's responsibility to ensure that the final contract represents exactly what the party bargained for.

Statute of Frauds

Common law usually does not require contracts to be in written form. However, when parties enter into an oral contract there may be problems involving ambiguity, mistakes, or even fraud, and the common law allows parties to assume these risks for many types of agreements. In addition, some contracts must be in written form according to the legal principle known as the **Statute of Frauds.** According to this principle, three types of contracts must be in written form, and these are most relevant to sport managers: (1) contracts concerning the sale, mortgage, or lease of an interest in land; (2)

Parole Evidence Rule—Rule under which litigants cannot assert facts that existed before the contract was formed if those facts are inconsistent with or contradict the existing written contract.

Statute of Frauds—Principle stating that three types of contracts must be in written form: (1) contracts concerning the sale, mortgage, or lease of an interest in land; (2) contracts that cannot be performed within 1 year of their making; and (3) contracts for the sale of goods that have a value in excess of $500.

contracts that cannot be performed within 1 year of their making; and (3) contracts for the sale of goods that have a value in excess of $500. Accordingly, lease agreements for stadiums and arenas, long-term coach or player contracts, and contracts for sport apparel that exceed $500 are examples of contracts that require a written document to be enforced.

Remedies

When a party breaches the terms of a legally enforceable contract, the party that suffers from the breach can seek compensation from the courts. The compensation awarded by courts of law for breach of contract is called *damages*. Damages are awarded in contract cases to put the aggrieved party in an economic position identical to that which the party would have been in had the contract been performed.

Compensatory Damages

compensatory damages—Damages provided by a court that are equal to the amount of money necessary to make up for whatever monetary loss a party has suffered.

Compensatory damages consist of money necessary to make up for whatever monetary loss a party has suffered attributable to the breach of contract. For instance, if an athlete has agreed to pay an agent an hourly rate for work that the agent does and then the athlete breaches the agency contract to sign with another agent, the agent could sue and ask for compensation equal to the per-hour rate in the contract for the time of the agent's work.

Consequential Damages

consequential damages—Monetary relief for economic losses that were caused indirectly by the original breach of contract.

Consequential damages are monetary relief for a party's economic losses that were caused indirectly by the original breach of contract. In the example of the athlete who signs with another agent, if this action caused other athletes to leave the original agent, the agent may sue asking for consequential damages relating to this extra loss.

Liquidated Damages

liquidated damages—Specific amounts of damages that the parties agreed to within the contract itself that must be paid by party that breaches the contract.

Liquidated damages are specific amounts of damages that the parties agreed to within the contract itself. When the parties negotiate the details of a contract, they agree to an amount that must be paid by the breaching party. This has become a typical provision within facility lease agreements, because cities want to protect themselves in the event that a team breaches the lease agreement. For example, the former Charlotte Hornets' lease agreement to play in the Charlotte Coliseum included a liquidated damages clause stating that if the team

> fails or refuses to play its Team Home Games in the Coliseum . . . [the team] shall pay to Authority as liquidated damages the sum of $3 million for each Basketball Season or portion thereof in which Team Home Games are not played in the Coliseum as required by this Agreement. (Miller & Anderson, 2001, pp. 363-364)

Similar provisions can be found in many other types of sport contracts. These provisions are important when there is no remedy or other amount of damages that the nonbreaching party will find sufficient to compensate for its loss. Therefore, if you believe that the loss of a team, coach, or high-profile event will cause significant damage above what a court will be able to reimburse you for in a breach of contract action, you should consider including a liquidated damages clause within your contract.

Specific Performance

At times, no amount of monetary damages will be sufficient to compensate the nonbreaching party. In these situations, the nonbreaching party may seek to have the breaching party forced to uphold its obligations under the contract. In these rare situations, courts can issue an injunction to order parties to carry out their contractual duties; this remedy is called **specific performance.** Specific performance provisions are rare and in sports are typically only applied in situations that involve unique items and not in employment contracts involving athletes or coaches. An interesting situation involving specific performance can be found in the In the Courtroom case on page 134.

Duty to Mitigate

A party that is harmed by another party's breach of contract is under a duty to mitigate, or reduce, its damages. The duty to mitigate damages prevents wronged parties from doing nothing while damages accumulate. Courts enforce the duty to mitigate by limiting a party's ability to recover for damages that were caused by a breach of contract if the party that was harmed could have prevented the harm without undue risk, burden, or humiliation (*Restatement [Second] of Contracts* § 350, 1990).

For example, say Marcus is the head groundskeeper for a professional baseball stadium. Marcus hires Billy's company to replace the irrigation system for the stadium. Billy's company does not perform the job as requested in the contract and because of this the sprinklers burst hours before a game, causing the field to collect water. Billy's crew is not on site so they cannot stop the flooding. Marcus' stadium is now under a duty to mitigate the damages. Although the water collection was caused by a breach of contract by Billy's company, because Marcus and his employees did not take steps to prevent the field from flooding, a court will reduce the amount of damages that Marcus' stadium will be able to recover from Billy's company. A court will determine the point at which the stadium could have limited the harm and cap the recoverable amount at that point.

Alternative Dispute Resolution

More and more sport contracts include clauses focusing on alternative dispute resolution (ADR) methods so that the parties involved can attempt to

specific performance—When one party to a contract seeks to have a court force the breaching party to uphold its contractual obligations, the court can issue an injunction to order the breaching party to carry out its contractual duties.

Levert v. University of Illinois (2003)

In *Levert v. University of Illinois* (2003), a group of people ordered tickets through the University of Illinois Athletic Ticket Office for the January 1, 2002, Nokia Sugar Bowl Game in New Orleans, Louisiana. This Sugar Bowl game featured Louisiana State University (LSU) versus the University of Illinois (UI).

Tickets were a very hot commodity for LSU fans because the Sugar Bowl game was the first Bowl Championship Series game for LSU and was going to be played in LSU's home state. Prior to the game, the plaintiffs, who were LSU fans, realized that they might improve their chances of securing tickets for the Sugar Bowl by attempting to purchase some of the 15,000 tickets that had been allotted to the University of Illinois. The Illinois ticket office began selling these tickets during December 2001, and sometime between December 4 and December 10, each plaintiff ordered a number of tickets via a Web site and by calling the ticket office.

For the online transactions, the plaintiffs alleged that the Illinois ticket office charged each purchaser's credit or debit card and then confirmed the ticket purchase by sending a confirmation to the purchaser's e-mail address. The plaintiffs asserted that in at least one telephone transaction, a ticket office representative, after taking the caller's name, address, and credit card information, assured the caller that tickets would be mailed.

Several days later, the Illinois ticket office informed the individual plaintiffs either through an e-mail transmission or by telephone that it would not honor their ticket requests because of the high demand for Sugar Bowl tickets from donors of the Fighting Illini Scholarship Fund and public and student football season-ticket holders. Accordingly, the ticket office cancelled all sales to the plaintiffs and reversed their credit or debit card transactions. The plaintiffs then sued, seeking an injunction for specific performance by asking the court to force the ticket office to give them the tickets they had ordered.

At a December 27, 2001, hearing, the trial court ordered the University of Illinois to provide the plaintiffs with a designated number of Sugar Bowl tickets for purchase within 24 hours. Although a written judgment was not signed until after the game was held, the plaintiffs secured their tickets and were able to attend the game. This case provides an example of how a court may award specific performance in a sport setting. Because the Sugar Bowl game was LSU's first Bowl Championship Series game, an argument was made that there was no way to compensate the LSU fans monetarily for the opportunity to cheer on their Tigers in that particular game. The only way to compensate the plaintiffs was to require performance from the University of Illinois.

solve their disputes without going to court. Parties turn to ADR to reduce the costs, in time and money, of litigation.

There are several forms of ADR. **Arbitration** is a process in which a neutral third party (the arbitrator or panel of arbitrators) renders a decision after a hearing at which both parties are given a chance to be heard and to present evidence. The value of arbitration as a form of ADR is that arbitration decisions are typically final and binding on the parties and can be enforced by a court.

Perhaps the most well-known form of arbitration in sports involves athletes in international competitions. Each international federation has agreed that all disputes involving its sport must be submitted to arbitration before the Court of Arbitration for Sport (CAS), an international arbitral body based in Switzerland. Each national governing body that regulates a sport within a particular country agrees to follow the international federation rules as part of its membership in the Olympic movement. Athletes who participate in international sports for that country agree to follow the rules of the national governing body and therefore must submit any disputes related to their competition to CAS. CAS is not a typical court; it is made up of hundreds of arbitrators who form panels that hear and resolve disputes. Lists of arbitrators, the guidelines for arbitration before CAS, and recent arbitration decisions can all be found at www.tas-cas.org.

According to the contract they sign when they agree to join the national governing body in their particular country, athletes must first submit disputes related to international competitions to arbitration. For example, Floyd Landis lost his Tour de France title after appealing the results of a drug test that found he had violated international doping rules. The CAS panel that heard his dispute found that although there were some discrepancies in the testing used on Landis, he still violated the international doping standards (*USADA v. Landis,* 2007).

Another form of ADR is mediation. **Mediation** (sometimes called facilitation) is a private, informal process where a neutral third party (the mediator) helps the parties in a dispute reach an agreement. Although the mediator can help the parties reach a decision, the mediator's decision is not binding on the parties. Instead, it is up to the parties to uphold the agreement. Mediation provisions are less common in sports, although some sport leases have mediation clauses that allow the parties to submit disputes to mediation, and CAS allows for mediation to be used in limited ways.

Some sport lease agreements contain provisions that allow for mediation and arbitration. For example, the Carolina Hurricanes' lease agreement mandates that the parties must initially attempt to negotiate to settle any dispute. If they are unable to come to a resolution, they must then submit the dispute to mediation. If they are unable to settle the dispute within 60 days using mediation, they must then submit the dispute to arbitration (Miller & Anderson, 2001, pp. 353-354).

arbitration—Process in which a neutral third party (the arbitrator or panel of arbitrators) renders a decision after a hearing at which both parties are given a chance to be heard and to present evidence.

mediation—A private, informal process where a neutral third party (the mediator) helps the parties in a dispute reach an agreement; sometimes called facilitation.

Summary

Sport managers deal with many kinds of contracts during their careers. Understanding employment agreements, collective bargaining agreements, and endorsement and event contracts is essential to protect the sport manager and the sport organization.

All contracts must include a valid offer, acceptance, and consideration. Although oral contracts are legally enforceable, sport managers would be well advised to prepare written contracts that include all of the details of the agreement; this protects the manager and the organization in the event the contract is disputed.

Most sport contracts have common features. Even student-athletes sign contracts in the Letters of Intent and scholarships they enter into with their university. Professional athletes often sign contracts in the form of endorsement deals, uniform player contracts, and agreements with athlete agents. Coaches at the university and professional levels enter into contracts with escalating salaries. Every sporting event involves contracts: the agreement detailing the event itself, the lease agreement for the facility, and the seat license agreement for the tickets that customers purchase. Waivers are also common within sports as event organizers attempt to protect themselves from liability.

Business relationships often go sour and a contract may be breached. In these situations, you may want to seek damages or other remedies including asking the court for specific performance of the breaching party's obligations under the contract. More and more contracts include alternative dispute resolution provisions that call for arbitration or mediation as alternatives to lengthy and expensive litigation.

DISCUSSION QUESTIONS

1. What can be provided as proper consideration in order to create a contract?
2. Who has the legal capacity to enter into a contract?
3. What are some typical provisions that can be found in most sport contracts?
4. Why is the relationship between a student-athlete and a college best understood as a contract?
5. Describe some of the special considerations that make it difficult to terminate a college coach's contract.
6. What does a waiver do?
7. What are some typical issues that can develop when one party breaches a sport contract?

MOOT COURT CASE

Samantha Slowpitch, a sophomore transfer student at Topten University, was a skilled softball player who truly loved the game. The first thing that Samantha did when she arrived at school was to form a coed intramural softball team with people who came highly recommended as good players. The long-awaited first game finally came, and Samantha and her team showed up early to warm up. During warm-ups, an intramural department staff member approached Samantha and told her that she and her teammates needed to sign up. She was handed a double-sided piece of paper with spaces for team names and ID numbers on one side. At the bottom of the page, in 10-point font, it read "Exculpatory agreement on reverse side." Samantha signed her name and glanced at the back side of the paper. At the top, it read "Waiver" followed by what she later recalled as "something that looked like a waiver." She recalled bits and pieces of the document such as "hold harmless," "acts of negligence," "occurring during the game of softball," "in consideration for," and some reference to "turf" and "thrown or batted balls." She did not read the document carefully given that she was excited about playing her first game and didn't want to waste time reading a full page of small print. After signing her name on the roster side of the paper, Samantha handed the roster to the rest of the team for them to sign. No other members of the team read the waiver language on the reverse side of the paper. Samantha and her team then took the field for their first game of the semester. They had the game well in hand, winning 6 to 1, when Samantha ran to catch a routine fly ball. As she was running toward the ball, Samantha stepped into a six-inch-deep depression in the turf and severely injured her ankle. The depression was caused by a utility truck that had parked there earlier in the day to repair a damaged outdoor flood light atop a pole in the outfield. Samantha was carried off the field and taken to the hospital, where it was determined that she would not be able to play softball again for the remainder of the year. Samantha was severely upset and emotionally distraught. In addition, her ankle was broken and there was some ligament damage. Samantha sued Topten University and the intramural department for negligence in failing to maintain the turf in proper condition. The university and intramural department defended their case based solely on the waiver.

6

Employment Law

CHAPTER OBJECTIVES

After reading this chapter, you will know the following:

- Key legal issues in employment for sport managers
- Relevance of the doctrine of employment at will
- Primary issues in employment discrimination
- Key legal issues relevant to sexual harassment
- The main elements of federal employment legislation

© Human Kinetics

Employment law encompasses a wide range of issues concerning people and their relationships at work. The work environment in sport may refer to traditional jobs such as managing staff and facilities or planning events, but it also refers to athletes' jobs. Lawsuits arise over many situations in the employment context: An employee is fired or passed over for promotion, a qualified job applicant is not hired, an employee is sexually harassed while on the job, or an employee injures herself or others while on the job. Employment cases in sport are often the subject of much commentary, debate, and legal action. The issues discussed in this chapter are diverse and useful from a practical standpoint in that they pose the different types of situations where employment related issues may arise. In this chapter, we discuss the employment relationship, discrimination, sexual harassment, and federal employment laws.

Employment Relationship

A good starting point for discussing employment issues in sport is the employment relationship. Parties involved in a legal conflict must be able to prove whether an employment relationship exists. Employees, as agents of an organization, have certain rights and obligations when acting on behalf of the organization. For example, a sport manager employed by a sports team has the authority to enter into a contract with a sports equipment company to buy helmets for the team. An organization might be liable for torts committed by its players, such as situations involving player–player and player–fan violence at sport events, if these actions were committed within the scope of employment. State and federal employment laws provide certain rights to employees and obligations to employers, but an employment relationship must be proven. These laws govern important issues such as Social Security payments, insurance plans, withholding taxes, workers compensation, unemployment compensation, workplace safety, and employment discrimination (e.g., the Civil Rights Act of 1964). For these and other reasons, it is important to determine whether an employment relationship exists. Once this determination is made, the topics discussed later in this chapter become highly relevant.

employment at will—A legal doctrine that holds that the employment relationship can end at any time and for any reason. Important exceptions to this doctrine are public policy, implied contracts, and the application of federal laws such as those governing discrimination.

The employment relationship is usually formed by contract between an employer and an employee. The contract spells out the nature of the employment along with the rights and responsibilities of the parties (e.g., salary, work duties, benefits). Situations arise, however, where there is no express agreement in the form of an employment contract and the employment relationship is not clear. In thinking about the employment relationship, ask yourself whether a university scholarship athlete should be considered an employee of a university (see the In the Courtroom case on page 141). This will stretch your thoughts on the issue of the employment relationship.

The employment relationship is typically governed by the common law doctrine of **employment at will.** According to this doctrine, either the employer or employee may terminate the employment relationship at any time and for any reason. As with all legal doctrines, however, there are exceptions.

Coleman v. Western Michigan University (1983)

Coleman, a football player for Western Michigan University, was injured while playing football for the university. He received his scholarship for the entire year following his injury, but the scholarship was revoked the following fall because of "cutbacks in the university's scholarship program" (p. 36). He sued the school, claiming that he was an employee and, as such, was entitled to the rights and benefits of an employee. He wanted to keep his scholarship. Coleman argued that he was an employee as defined by the Michigan's Worker's Disability Compensation Act, in which an employee is defined as "every person in the service of another, under any contract of hire, express or implied"(p. 37).

The Court applied the "economic reality" test to determine whether an employment relationship existed. Four factors were examined as a part of this test:

(1) the proposed employer's right to control or dictate the activities of the proposed employee;

(2) the proposed employer's right to discipline or fire the proposed employee;

(3) the payment of "wages" and, particularly, the extent to which the proposed employee is dependent upon the payment of wages or other benefits for his daily living expenses; and

(4) whether the task performed by the proposed employee was "an integral part of the proposed employer's business." (p. 38)

These factors would have to be considered together, as a whole, to determine whether an employment relationship was present. The court considered all of these factors and determined that no employment relationship existed.

As for the first factor, although the university could control Coleman's actions on the field, the university had no more control over Coleman than it did over other students. This applied to discipline as well. As to the wages portion of the test, the court agreed that Coleman's scholarship constituted wages. "In return for his services as a football player, plaintiff received certain items of compensation which are measurable in money, including room and board, tuition and books" (p. 40). But as for the fourth factor, the court concluded that Coleman did not perform an integral part of the employer's "business." Playing football, reasoned the Court, was not an integral part of the university's business; rather, the business of the university was education. Taking all of these factors into account, the court determined that no employment relationship existed between the university and Coleman.

One important exception is that if there is an employment contract, the terms of that contract would govern when and why an employee might be terminated. Also, where discrimination is the reason for terminating an employee, something must be available to protect people from this unfair treatment. That *something* is state and federal law (statute). Certain laws, as discussed later in this chapter, prohibit an employer from firing an employee when a state or federal statute has been violated (e.g., when an employee has been fired in a discriminatory manner). Hiring and retention issues and the relevant laws that govern these matters are discussed next.

Discrimination

Common to all sport managers is the job of hiring, promoting (or deciding not to promote), and firing employees, coaches, or players. The work goes beyond difficult and is often unpleasant when people must be told that they didn't get the job, they don't deserve a promotion or a raise, or, worst of all, they are fired. The financial burden and associated stress upon notice of termination can be quite devastating and difficult for individuals and families. Worse yet, some individuals are not hired, are fired, or are not promoted for subjective discriminatory reasons that are unethical and violate state or federal law. With most hiring, retention, and promotion decisions, the potential for actual or perceived discrimination exists. Consider the following hypothetical in the context of making employment decisions.

You own and operate a sport and fitness club. The club boasts a variety of services, from supervised sport instruction to personal fitness training and nutrition counseling. Your business has been in operation for more than a year and membership has expanded rapidly. You have 20 employees on your payroll, several who would be considered independent contractors. An independent contractor is someone who contracts with an employer to do some type of work but is not under the physical control of the employer. An independent contractor is not an employee and may or may not be considered an agent of the employer: The distinction depends on the level of control that the employer has over the contractor and the performance of her work. Although you are enjoying the success of your business, you are also concerned about legal issues relevant to employment, particularly discrimination.

Your full-time employees are a group of excellent people, 3 Hispanic, 4 African American, 2 Asian American, and 11 Caucasian employees (9 are females and 11 are males). All are of the age of majority; possess the requisite certifications, training, and skills; and are highly qualified for their jobs. Your work has increased to the point that you must hire an assistant manager to help with administrative duties and teach some of the sport and fitness classes. You have a diverse applicant pool in terms of age, gender, and race and ethnicity. You also posted a job announcement to hire someone to supervise and referee basketball league play at your facility; this position is now closed, and you only have three applicants. The only applicant who is qualified by way of experience and knowledge of the game uses a wheelchair for mobility. You have heard about federal laws that prohibit discrimination in matters of employment. Federal law recognizes several protected classes to which discrimination laws apply:

- Race, color, and national origin
- Gender
- Religion
- Age
- Disability

We now look at several employment discrimination issues, using this hypothetical example to walk us through the issues.

Title VII of the Civil Rights Act of 1964

The first three categories of protected classes (race, color, and national origin; gender; and religion) are offered protection from discrimination under the Civil Rights Act. **Title VII of the Civil Rights Act** and its amendments apply to governmental agencies, federal government employees, labor unions, and employers with 15 or more employees. Section 2000e defines employers to whom the law applies.

Title VII of the Civil Rights Act— A federal law that prohibits discrimination in employment matters by reason of race, color, national origin, gender, or religion.

> The term "employer" means a person engaged in an industry affecting commerce who has fifteen or more employees for each working day in each of twenty or more calendar weeks in the current or preceding calendar year, and any agent of such a person, but such term does not include (1) the United States, a corporation wholly owned by the Government of the United States, an Indian tribe, or any department or agency of the District of Columbia subject by statute to procedures of the competitive service (as defined in section 2102 of title 5), or (2) a bona fide private membership club (other than a labor organization) which is exempt from taxation under section 501(c) of title 26, except that during the first year after March 24, 1972, persons having fewer than twenty-five employees (and their agents) shall not be considered employers.

This law applies to our sport and fitness club which, as you recall, has 20 employees. This law governs the first three categories listed: race, color, and national origin; gender; and religion. Your hiring decision with regard to applicants therefore must be made with respect to Title VII. As such, you should also know about the **Equal Employment Opportunity Commission (EEOC),** the U.S. governmental agency that monitors compliance with Title VII. If one of your applicants is qualified and believes she has been discriminated against in the hiring process, she would first file a claim with the EEOC. The EEOC would then decide whether to investigate the claim and take action. If not, the individual may bring a lawsuit against you and the organization directly.

Equal Employment Opportunity Commission (EEOC)—A governmental agency that monitors compliance laws relevant to employment discrimination.

**disparate-impact
discrimination**—A
type of discrimina-
tion that is uninten-
tional, where the per-
centage of workers in
a particular business
does not mirror the
percentage of those
in protected classes
in the local labor
market.

When you have a diverse applicant pool, an issue to avoid is a potential discrimination claim based on race, color, or national origin. Discrimination claims can be brought on the basis of either intentional or unintentional acts of the employer. Unintentional discrimination is termed **disparate-impact discrimination.** This is where the employer's workforce does not mirror the percentage of those in protected classes in the local labor market. You know that your policy on employment decisions does not discriminate against applicants on the basis of color, race, or national origin, given that the diversity of your workforce mirrors that in the local job market. In fact, your workforce is more diverse than the local labor market.

Decisions on hiring, promotion, and retention must be based solely on job-related qualifications and cannot reflect discriminatory practices. This is the basic requirement in Title VII and is stated as follows:

Sec. 2000e-2. Unlawful employment practices

(a) Employer practices

It shall be an unlawful employment practice for an employer—

(1) to fail or refuse to hire or to discharge any individual, or otherwise to discriminate against any individual with respect to his compensation, terms, conditions, or privileges of employment, because of such individual's race, color, religion, sex, or national origin; or

(2) to limit, segregate, or classify his employees or applicants for employment in any way which would deprive or tend to deprive any individual of employment opportunities or otherwise adversely affect his status as an employee, because of such individual's race, color, religion, sex, or national origin.

**disparate-treatment
discrimination**—An
intentional form
of discrimination
where a qualified job
applicant in a pro-
tected class is denied
employment.

**bona fide
occupational
qualification
(BFOQ)**—A defense
to claims of discrimi-
nation asserting that
a particular trait of
a job applicant or
employee is neces-
sary for a particular
job even though
excluding others
without this trait is
discriminatory.

Also, your personal ethics dictate that you treat all applicants equally and do not intentionally discriminate against anyone. Suppose, however, that a member of a protected class is not hired and argues that he has been discriminated against. If he believes that he has been intentionally discriminated against, he has to prove three things:

1. He is a member of the protected class (e.g., by race, color, or national origin).
2. He is qualified for the job.
3. The job remained open or was offered to someone not in the protected class.

This type of discrimination (intentional discrimination) is termed **disparate-treatment discrimination.** If a case for disparate-treatment discrimination can be shown, the burden of proof rests on the business, which must defend its actions (i.e., you have to defend your actions). One type of defense is the **bona fide occupational qualification (BFOQ)** defense. This defense arises when a particular trait is necessary for a particular job (e.g., only females are hired for the job of female locker room attendant). Race, however, is not considered a BFOQ. Gender, however, as illustrated might be considered a valid BFOQ.

Title VII also covers discrimination based on religion, another issue you want to know more about in relation to the hiring process. You understand that certain religions observe days of rest or days in which observers are prohibited from working. This could make it difficult to schedule work duties and cover sport and fitness classes. Under Title VII, however, you cannot base your decision to hire solely on these potential time conflicts when they stem from an applicant's sincerely held religious beliefs. The manager must reasonably accommodate the religious practices of the employees. The exception would be when this places an undue hardship on the functioning of the business.

You also have a concern regarding gender discrimination. To this point, you have hired close to equal numbers of males and females. Some of your female hires were made based on a need to hire an instructor for women's-only fitness and conditioning classes held in a private area of the facility. Your facility restricts some fitness classes to women given a high demand for this service. Female participants in these programs were unanimous in their desire to have a female instructor. Gender, in these instances, would be essential to the job. Therefore, it was okay to select only females for this hire. However, the assistant manager's position does not involve teaching the women's-only classes, and there is no other issue that makes a particular gender essential to the job function. Therefore, applicants for this position cannot be discriminated against and selected based on their gender. Your plans are to advertise the position and hire the most qualified person regardless of gender. See chapter 8 for further discusion of gender discrimination.

When hiring a new employee, no matter at what level of sport, you need to understand the many areas of potential employee discrimination including race, color and national origin, gender, religion, age, and disability.

Affirmative Action

In addition to your efforts and intentions to avoid discrimination, you have also heard about affirmative action. **Affirmative action** is a proactive process whereby employers actively seek out, hire, and promote qualified individuals in protected groups. This is designed to reduce or eliminate discriminatory practices in hiring, promotion, and retention of employees, by providing

affirmative action— Actions taken by employers to actively seek out, hire, and promote qualified individuals in protected groups.

increased employment opportunities to people in protected classes, and to ensure equal opportunity in employment. The purpose of affirmative action is to eliminate or remedy the present effects of past discrimination. Although affirmative action is not a requirement under Title VII (and is not recognized in some states), you should consider affirmative action requirements when advertising and writing descriptions and applications for job positions. A sample affirmative action statement is shown in figure 6.1.

Another important issue with regard to affirmative action is the provision of advertisements (job position announcements) in publications, online sources, and venues specific to protected groups.

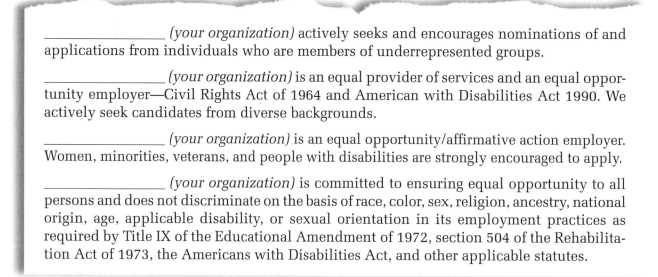

_____ *(your organization)* actively seeks and encourages nominations of and applications from individuals who are members of underrepresented groups.

_____ *(your organization)* is an equal provider of services and an equal opportunity employer—Civil Rights Act of 1964 and American with Disabilities Act 1990. We actively seek candidates from diverse backgrounds.

_____ *(your organization)* is an equal opportunity/affirmative action employer. Women, minorities, veterans, and people with disabilities are strongly encouraged to apply.

_____ *(your organization)* is committed to ensuring equal opportunity to all persons and does not discriminate on the basis of race, color, sex, religion, ancestry, national origin, age, applicable disability, or sexual orientation in its employment practices as required by Title IX of the Educational Amendment of 1972, section 504 of the Rehabilitation Act of 1973, the Americans with Disabilities Act, and other applicable statutes.

Figure 6.1 Sample affirmative action statement.

Age Discrimination in Employment

Most of your employees are young and fit, which is mainly a function of the types of applicants who were interested in working in a sport and fitness club. You are also located in a university town, so most of your potential employees are university age. You should be aware of the federal law governing age discrimination. Enacted in 1967, the applicable law is the **Age Discrimination in Employment Act (ADEA).** This law prohibits employment discrimination on the basis of age for people at least 40 years old. The law applies to businesses with 20 or more employees and whose activities influence interstate commerce. An employer to whom the law applies is defined as follows.

Sec. 630. Definitions

...

(b) The term "employer" means a person engaged in an industry affecting commerce who has twenty or more employees for each

Age Discrimination in Employment Act (ADEA)—A federal law that prohibits discrimination in employment matters by reason of age.

working day in each of twenty or more calendar weeks in the current or preceding calendar year: Provided, that prior to June 30, 1968, employers having fewer than fifty employees shall not be considered employers. The term also means (1) any agent of such a person, and (2) a State or political subdivision of a State and any agency or instrumentality of a State or a political subdivision of a State, and any interstate agency, but such term does not include the United States, or a corporation wholly owned by the Government of the United States.

Commerce is defined as follows:

The term "commerce" means trade, traffic, commerce, transportation, transmission, or communication among the several States; or between a State and any place outside thereof; or within the District of Columbia, or a possession of the United States; or between points in the same State but through a point outside thereof.

The ADEA applies to organizations that are involved in interstate commerce. The fitness center advertises nationally (via the Internet), has members who cross the state line to participate in sport and fitness classes, and is accessible to the state and interstate highway system. As such, it is likely that the fitness center's activities affect interstate commerce. The business also has 20 or more employees. Therefore, if a qualified applicant is 40 years old or more, you must ensure that there is no implication of discrimination in the hiring process. This is true for promotion and termination as well. If a claim was brought by someone who thought that he was being discriminated against, it would come either through the EEOC, as with other types of discrimination, or directly through a private lawsuit against the club. Earlier, we discussed intentional and unintentional discrimination. Suppose that a 75-year-old man applied for the job of weight room supervisor, where he would be required to spot the bench press and other heavy weight activities. A 25-year-old man was selected, and the 75-year-old man sued for discrimination. Suppose the older man accused you of unintentional discrimination (disparate-impact discrimination), claiming that the club hired more young people to work in the weight room than other clubs in the local area. If the club required, as a condition of employment, that applicants be able to bench press at least 200 pounds (91 kilograms), then the club might raise the **business necessity** defense. This defense asserts that a hiring practice with a discriminatory effect is a business necessity. For example, the requirement of being able to bench press 200 pounds has had the effect of having younger people work in the weight room of the club. If the club could prove that a definite connection exists between job performance and the (legitimate) strength requirement, then the club would likely succeed in the business necessity defense.

An example of an age discrimination lawsuit in which the ADEA was at issue is *Moore v. University of Notre Dame* (1998). Moore, a 60-year-old football coach for the University of Notre Dame, was fired. He sued, among

business necessity— A defense to claims of unintentional discrimination asserting that a legitimate hiring practice is a business necessity even though it has a discriminatory effect.

other things, for age discrimination under the ADEA. He found employment after his discharge, coaching at another school, but for less money. He sought certain remedies available under the ADEA. These included reinstatement (getting his job back), back pay (salary lost from Notre Dame while out of the job), and front pay. Front pay is "a lump sum representing the discounted present value of the difference between the earnings an employee would have received in his old employment and the earnings he can be expected to receive in his present and future, and by hypothesis, inferior, employment. Front pay is awarded for a reasonable amount of time, until a date by which the plaintiff, using reasonable diligence, should have found comparable employment" (p. 900). The court denied reinstatement but did award front pay given that the coach used due diligence to find another job, along with the presumption that his chances of finding a job with comparable pay at his age were slim.

Discrimination Based on Disabilities

In addition to having the preceding concerns, you seek fairness in the hiring process for the assistant manager and for the basketball referee. For both jobs, the applicable law is the **Americans with Disabilities Act of 1990 (ADA).** The ADA was passed to prohibit, on a national scope, discrimination against individuals with disabilities (42 U.S. (§ 1201 et seq., 2008)). It is divided into seven parts, called titles, several of which are applicable to employment. The ADA furthers the protections provided by the Rehabilitation Act of 1973, which prohibits discrimination against people with disabilities by government agencies that receive federal funds.

Title I of the ADA applies to employees of sport organizations (with 15 or more employees) who are disabled and can demonstrate that they are otherwise qualified for the job. In other words, if they can show that they have the necessary skills, experience, and education and can perform the essential functions of their job with or without some form of accommodation to their disability, the employer cannot discriminate against them. In your hiring decision, you as an employer are under a legal obligation to make a reasonable effort to accommodate the work-related needs of an employee with disabilities. This accommodation requirement would apply to job applicants as well. The term *reasonable accommodation* means that an employer finds work responsibilities and environments that allow employees with disabilities to be successful in performing their job functions. Title I of the ADA applies to both job applicants and employees of sport organizations who have disabilities and can demonstrate that they are otherwise qualified for the job. If the person with a disability can show that he has the necessary skills, experience, and education and can perform the essential functions of the job with or without some form of accommodation to his disability, the employer cannot discriminate against him. In other words, the applicant must be qualified for the job. The employer must provide certain accommodations to allow him to work as long as those accommodations do not force an undue burden on the employer.

Americans with Disabilities Act of 1990 (ADA)—A federal law that prohibits discrimination in employment matters by reason of disability.

For the manager in the fitness club, it might mean providing access to the basketball courts for the applicant who uses a wheelchair or technological assistance for the assistant manager in her use of computers or other electronic devices. Many types of accommodations are relatively simple and inexpensive to implement. In these situations, making accommodations is of prime importance.

For the basketball referee hire, an issue of concern is safety. A referee who officiates basketball games obviously must be able to move around the court. You are concerned that a person in a wheelchair might pose a safety hazard both to players and to herself. The ADA, however, requires accommodation and prohibits discrimination against people with disabilities. Concerns over the safety of participants (e.g., someone colliding with the wheelchair) must be weighed in light of the employment, participation, and accessibility requirements of the ADA. A person with a disability cannot be dismissed out of hand, and an employer cannot make blanket requirements such as never allowing wheelchairs on a basketball court under any conditions. Decisions must be made case by case. Some guidance is provided from *Anderson v. Little League Baseball Inc.* (see the In the Courtroom case on page 150), although the case involved a volunteer coach rather than an employee.

This case provides a good example of an application of the ADA in sport as well as an example concerning accommodation. In all employment decisions relevant to hiring, promotion, and retention, managers must be aware of and avoid potential discrimination.

There is another context in which the ADA might apply to employment. Professional athletes make their living performing in their respective sports. In essence, their role as a professional athlete is their job. The ADA has been applied to professional sports where athletes have requested and required accommodations based on their disabilities. The claim is that without the accommodation, they are unable to participate, resulting in the loss of their job as a professional athlete.

Title III of the ADA bars discrimination against disabled individuals "in the full and equal enjoyment of the goods, services, facilities, privileges, advantages, or accommodations of any place of public accommodation by any person who owns, leases (or leases to), or operates a place of public accommodation" (42 U.S.C. §12182(a), 2008). The statute specifically includes gymnasiums, golf courses, and other places of exercise and recreation as places of accommodation covered under this part. Many forms of discrimination are banned under Title III. Perhaps most important in connection to sports and recreational activities is when individuals with disabilities are barred from enjoying the goods and services of the place of public accommodation, a failure to make reasonable modifications, unless such modifications would "fundamentally alter the nature" of the goods and services of the place of public accommodation, and failure to remove structural and other facility barriers to disabled individuals.

Perhaps the most well-known and influential professional sport case involved professional golfer Casey Martin. Martin was born with Klippel-Trenaunay-Weber syndrome, a rare disorder that caused a progressively

---

In the
Courtroom   ## *Anderson v. Little League Baseball Inc.*

In *Anderson v. Little League Baseball Inc.* (1992), a father who was paraplegic and used a wheelchair was the coach of his son's Little League baseball team. The father attended games and coached from the third-base coaching box. He had been coaching his son's team for three years without injuries or incidents. He was unexpectedly told by Little League that he could no longer coach his son's team. The league cited safety concerns. Little League created a policy banning wheelchairs from the field because of a perceived threat of injury to the players. The policy was absolute without consideration made to the circumstances of each activity or individual case. The coach sued Little League, claiming discrimination under the ADA. The federal district court found in favor of the plaintiff, struck down the policy disallowing wheelchairs, and determined that cases were to be decided individually. The court also found, contrary to the claims of Little League, that the coach did not pose a direct threat to the health and safety of the players. The court stated, "In determining whether an individual, such as plaintiff, poses a direct threat to the health or safety of others, a public accommodation must make an individualized assessment, based on reasonable judgment that relies on current medical knowledge or on the best available objective evidence, to ascertain: (1) the nature, duration, and severity of the risk; (2) the probability that the potential injury will actually occur; and (3) whether reasonable modifications of policies, practices, or procedures will mitigate the risk (28 C.F.R. § 36.208(c))" (p. 345).

worsening muscle and bone condition in his right leg and resulted in severe pain when he walks. He started playing golf at age six, won junior championships in Oregon, and then went to Stanford University, where he was the captain of the 1994 team that won the NCAA championship. After leaving Stanford, he walked for two years on the Hooters Tour, though he also played on the Tommy Armour Tour because it allowed carts. He then entered the PGA Tour's qualifying school tournament in the hopes of making the PGA or Nike Tour. He made it through the first two stages of the tournament using a cart, as allowed under the rules, but was barred from using a cart in the third stage. He then sued the PGA Tour, claiming that the no-cart rule failed to make tournaments accessible to people with disabilities and was in violation of the ADA (*Martin v. PGA Tour, Inc.*, 1998). The district court granted an injunction allowing Martin to use a cart in the third stage and the PGA lifted the no-cart rule for the third stage. Martin was also allowed to use a cart in two tournaments on the Nike Tour. The PGA then returned to court contending that it was not subject to the ADA.

Initially, the court noted that golf courses are specifically covered under Title III of the ADA. The PGA argued that allowing Martin to use a cart would fundamentally alter the nature of PGA golf by providing him with an unfair advantage over golfers who had to walk. Deeming that walking does not add much to the fatigue of a typical golfer, the court disagreed and held that allowing Martin to use a cart would not fundamentally alter the game. Therefore, in accord with the ADA, the PGA had to provide Martin with the reasonable accommodation of a golf cart when he competed in events.

The immediate backlash was staggering. Commentators, other golfers, and armchair quarterbacks everywhere criticized the decision, most believing that even though Martin was obviously disabled he should be forced to walk a golf course as every other golfer does. No one seemed to recognize that Martin could not compete unless he used the cart, and that, regardless of this accommodation, he would soon lose all use of his leg as a result of his disability.

Of course the PGA appealed the initial decision (*Martin v. PGA Tour, Inc.*, 2000). The appellate court focused on whether Title III of the ADA even applied to the PGA. The PGA argued that although the ADA applies to golf courses in general, the areas roped off for PGA Tour events are not open to the public, so it is not a place of public accommodation under the ADA. The court disagreed because no matter how selective a facility is in giving access (i.e., only allowing the best golfers to play), it still is a place of public accommodation. Therefore, because it was a place of public accommodation covered under Title III, the PGA Tour had to provide some form of reasonable accommodation to Martin. The court again found that allowing Martin to use a cart would merely provide him with access and not fundamentally alter the game of golf, especially when walking is not a requirement specifically found in the official rules of golf.

The PGA would still not give up and appealed to the Supreme Court (*PGA Tour, Inc. v. Martin*, 2001). Substantially agreeing with every decision of the earlier courts, the Supreme Court also found that modifying the rules to provide Martin with a cart during competition would not fundamentally alter the PGA's tournaments. Because the walking rule is not an essential aspect of the game of golf, and because Martin did not gain any advantage over other golfers by using a cart, his use of the cart was a reasonable modification of PGA golf.

Even after this decision, many in the sports world believed that this decision would cause courts to intervene in their sports, forcing them to modify their rules in bizarre ways to accommodate people with disabilities. Some speculated that sport leagues would have to allow for wheelchair basketball players or prosthetic tennis rackets, but none of this has occurred. Instead, the ADA will force professional sport organizations to modify what they do only when such modifications will not fundamentally alter the nature of their competition.

Keep in mind that even Casey Martin had to prove that he was an otherwise qualified individual with a disability. He had to demonstrate that he could still compete at the highest level of golf even though he had a disability. The ADA would not allow for him to show that he could compete only at the highest level if he was given an accommodation. The ADA cannot force sport leagues to find ways to make people with disabilities into high-quality competitors. Instead, it provides high-quality competitors who happen to have disabilities with the same chance to participate as anyone else.

Sexual Harassment

sexual harassment—
A type of lawsuit that involves claims of conduct that is sexual in nature and creates a hostile or abusive work environment.

An issue that is closely associated to gender discrimination is **sexual harassment.**

Points regarding sexual harassment derived from EEOC guidelines and the courts are as follows. Sexual harassment (a) consists of unwelcome sexual advances, (b) is not desired by the employee (victim), (c) creates a hostile or abusive work environment, and (d) can arise from either verbal or physical conduct.

Sexual harassment therefore is conduct that is sexual in nature and can occur with any combination of gender (including same gender). It is conduct that is not consensual between both parties, meaning that one party does not want, or agree to, the sexual conduct. Physical conduct may first come to mind, but verbal conduct can amount to sexual harassment as well. The determination of a hostile and abusive work environment is the central issue in many sexual harassment claims. A hostile and abusive work environment in one in which someone is so affected by the sexual conduct and finds it so offensive or intimidating that it negatively affects his or her job performance. It also means that the working environment becomes filled with intimidation, ridicule, and insult.

In addition to determining sexual harassment by the finding of a hostile work environment, the courts have also used another context. Sexual harassment has also been classified as *quid pro quo* (Latin for "something in exchange for something else"). This type of sexual harassment occurs when sexual favors are demanded in return for things like raises, promotions, a better office, and better opportunities. If a lawsuit for sexual harassment is made, the facts of the case are reviewed in light of these legal considerations.

Sexual harassment litigation often arises after an employee has been fired, quits, or claims that she has been constructively discharged from her job. Constructive discharge occurs when an employee claims she can no longer work at a place of business because the work situation is intolerable. Sexual harassment can occur as a result of interactions with co-workers, supervisors, and nonemployees of the same or opposite gender. Sexual harassment is a critically important issue for sport managers from both an ethical and a legal standpoint. Guidance on sexual harassment comes primarily from Title VII of the Civil Rights Act as amended in 1972, the EEOC, and court decisions. Some sport organizations have staff attorneys who use bulletins, online sources, and short courses to explain to managers the important points regarding sexual harassment. Sport managers should educate themselves about sexual harassment using a valid and reliable source. There should be zero tolerance for abusive and objectionable behavior in the sport organization.

The key for the sport manager is to avoid sexual harassment lawsuits in the first place. This means having a plan in place and promoting a work environment where all employees are treated with dignity and respect and one where everyone knows that sexual harassment will not be tolerated. Managers should also take every sexual harassment claim seriously and initiate the proper agency protocol for handling the situation. Think about the following scenario:

Allie, just out of university, takes a job working for a minor league baseball organization. Soon after she starts her job, her immediate supervisor, Bob, begins asking her out on dates. He does this repeatedly and she refuses every time. Bob then makes harassing remarks and touches her inappropriately. He also tells Allie that if she sleeps with him, he will give her easy tasks and look the other way if she wants to go home early some days. If not, he tells her that she will be spending a lot of time cleaning toilets. Allie is disgusted and speaks to the upper-level manager (Steve) about her situation. She expresses that she is deeply concerned and troubled by her supervisor's abusive comments. Steve tells her that this is baseball, so suck it up and deal with it, and that Bob probably doesn't mean anything by it. Allie leaves his office crying and continues working. Bob hears of her complaint and increases his abusive behavior toward her. He also makes Allie stay late—beyond normal working hours—and do all the "dirty" jobs (e.g., cleaning bathrooms, washing towels, and picking up trash), which eventually comprise more than 90% of her working day. Allie goes to the manager again, complaining of the abusive behavior, and is told that she should just make the best of her situation. Allie cannot take the abuse any longer and decides to quit her job. Jobs are difficult to find and she is now unemployed with a university loan and many bills to pay. Allie hires a lawyer and brings suit against all responsible parties.

What issues do you think the court would rely on to determine whether there was liability on the part of the minor league baseball organization? The scenario certainly raises serious ethical concerns. From a legal standpoint, however, a court would likely consider the following issues in determining whether sexual harassment existed:

- The **quid pro quo** harassment—sexual favors are demanded in exchange for better working conditions.
- Hostile work environment—intimidation and insult alter the work environment.
- The existence of sexual harassment policies and procedures—these should be put in place to promptly correct and prevent any sexually harassing behavior.
- Whether sexual harassment policies and procedures were followed—formal complaints must be taken seriously with remedial action against the supervisor taken as necessary.

quid pro quo—A Latin term used in context with sexual harassment meaning "something for something" whereby sexual favors are requested in exchange for job-related benefits.

An employer might also be liable if managers knew, or should have known, of harassment perpetrated by a co-worker or customer, or if in response to a complaint of sexual harassment, immediate and effective action is not taken to stop the harassment. Protection extends to situations where employees are harassed by supervisors, co-workers, or others of the same gender.

Other issues to consider include knowing who in the chain of command should be legally notified and knowing the proper procedures for interviewing both the victim and the accused. If no one in your agency or organization is responsible for providing guidance on sexual harassment, a competent outside source should be consulted. Remedies available to a claimant of a sexual harassment claim include lost wages (back pay), benefits, punitive damages (if the employer acted with malice or "reckless indifference"), and attorney's fees. The proper handling of sexual harassment claims protects both the manager and the organization from liability and is the right thing to do. Consult the Web for organizations that may help you develop protocols for sexual harassment. Also, see chapter 8 for additonal discussion of sexual harassment in the sport context.

Federal Employment Laws

The health and safety of employees are critical concerns for the sport manager. Sport managers owe an ethical duty to their employees to provide a reasonably safe work environment. Aside from an ethical duty, a legal duty is placed on employers to protect those under their care and at their place of employment. Legislators have stepped in to pass federal and state laws that protect employees from the risk of accidental death, injury, or disease that occurs while on the job.

Occupational Safety and Health Act

Occupational Safety and Health Act—A federal law that provides for the safety and health of employees in the work environment.

The most common and arguably most important law providing for the safety of employees is the **Occupational Safety and Health Act.** This is a federal law, enacted in 1970, with a twofold purpose: (1) to require employers to meet certain specific, federally mandated, safety standards and (2) to impose a general duty on employers to keep their workplace safe. Several enforcement agencies—the Occupational Safety and Health Administration, the National Institute for Occupational Safety and Health, and the Occupational Safety and Health Review Commission—take part in developing and enforcing standards set by this act and have oversight responsibilities for safety and health in the work environment. Table 6.1 provides Web links to these organizations.

There are many health hazards that employees might face in the work environment:

- Sudden cardiac arrest—coaches and sport supervisors
- Heat-related illness—coaches and sport supervisors

Table 6.1   Enforcement Agencies for the Occupational Safety and Health Act

Organization	Purpose	Web site
Occupational Safety and Health Administration (OSHA)	"To assure safe and healthful working conditions for working men and women; by authorizing enforcement of the standards developed under the Act; by assisting and encouraging the States in their efforts to assure safe and healthful working conditions; by providing for research, information, education, and training in the field of occupational safety and health; and for other purposes." (OSH Act of 1970, Public Law 91-596)	www.osha.gov
National Institute for Occupational Safety and Health (NIOSH)	Through the Centers for Disease Control and Prevention, NIOSH provides national and world leadership to prevent work-related illnesses and injuries.	www.cdc.gov/niosh
Occupational Safety and Health Review Commission (OSHRC)	The is an independent federal agency created to decide contests of citations or penalties resulting from OSHA inspections of American workplaces. The review commission, therefore, functions as an administrative court, with established procedures for conducting hearings, receiving evidence, and rendering decisions by its administrative law judges.	www.oshrc.gov

- Carpal tunnel syndrome—office workers
- Heavy equipment–related injury—turf and field maintenance workers
- Blunt trauma—batting coaches
- Chemicals—aquatics personnel
- Blood-borne pathogens—sport and fitness personnel

Blood-borne pathogens (BBPs) pose an especially significant health concern for employees in sport. Fitness personnel, coaches, lifeguards, sport supervisors, athletic trainers, and those who might be required to perform CPR (which would include many in the sport profession) are at risk from BBPs. BBPs are microorganisms in human blood that can cause disease in humans. The BBPs of major concern include, but are not limited to, the hepatitis B virus (HBV) and the human immunodeficiency virus (HIV). A single exposure incident could result in infection, subsequent illness and, in some cases, death (Spengler, Connaughton, & Pittman, 2006). OSHA has created standards for BBPs, the basic components of which are as follows:

1. Employers are responsible for identifying job classifications that entail occupational exposure to BBPs (these include the previously mentioned jobs plus lifeguarding and athletic training).

2. Employers must minimize employee exposure to BBPs through proper planning, education, and record keeping.

3. Employers are required to establish a written exposure control plan that lists the tasks, procedures, and job classifications with which occupational exposure may occur.

4. The employer must provide at no cost to employees appropriate personal protective equipment, such as gloves and pocket face masks.

5. The employer must offer, at its own expense, voluntary HBV vaccinations to all employees who have occupational exposure.

This information can be obtained from various sources and should be implemented in consultation with qualified legal professionals. You can obtain a brochure and fact sheets about BBPs by writing to OSHA Publications, 200 Constitution Avenue, NW, Room N3101, Washington, DC 20210 or by calling 202-219-8148.

OSHA regulations relevant to sport business include:

- Employers with more than 11 employees must keep records of occupational injury and illness for each employee:
  - Employers must report to OSHA the occurrence of any work-related injury or disease.
  - Employers must report to the Department of Labor the occurrence of any work-related accidents resulting in death or any one incident that causes five or more employees to be hospitalized. Employers must submit this report to the Department of Labor within 48 hours or the employer will be fined.
  - Subsequent inspection of premises is mandatory.
- Sport facilities can be inspected by OSHA compliance officers.
- Employees can file complaints about workplace health and safety.
- Employees cannot be fired if they complain or refuse to work in a dangerous area where bodily harm or death may reasonably result.

Employee safety in the sport setting must be approached in a thoughtful and thorough manner. Laws and regulations relevant to employee health and safety must be followed, preferably with the advice and consultation of competent professionals familiar with federal, state, and local requirements.

Fair Labor Standards Act (FLSA)

Fair Labor Standards Act (FLSA)—A federal law that governs child labor practices.

Although it is legal to hire children and youth (minors) to work in the sport industry, an important law called the **Fair Labor Standards Act (FLSA)** regulates child labor practices. The FLSA was enacted to protect children from abuses in employment. The primary concerns addressed by the legislation are the hours of work, wages, and labor (employment) conditions of children and youth. Some important provisions include prohibitions against children working under the following conditions:

- After 9 p.m. in the summer
- Before 7 a.m. or after 7 p.m. (except for after 9 pm in the summer)
- More than 3 hours on a school day
- More than 8 hours on a nonschool day
- More than 18 hours during a school week
- More than 40 hours during a nonschool week
- For less than minimum wage
- In certain occupations (those with particular health and safety risks)

Family and Medical Leave Act (FMLA)

Sometimes employees have family health issues, either their own or those of a family member, that require them to be absent from work for an extended amount of time. The birth of a child, illness, or the death of a family member might all qualify as legitimate health issues. Under the **Family and Medical Leave Act (FMLA),** organizations are required to provide employees with up to 12 weeks (at any time of the year) of leave to attend to health issues. Although required to provide leave time, the organization is not required to provide paid leave. It is required, however, to continue the worker's health care coverage while on leave. When the worker returns, the employer must allow the employee to resume employment at the same or similar position, unless she is considered a key employee (one whose pay falls within the top 10% of the organization's workforce).

Family and Medical Leave Act (FMLA)— A federal law that requires organizations to provide employees with up to 12 weeks of leave to attend to family health issues.

COBRA

Under the **Consolidated Omnibus Budget Reconciliation Act (COBRA),** employees retain the rights to insurance coverage under their employer's health plan even after their employment has been terminated (either voluntarily or involuntarily). This means that employees can keep their coverage (although they have to pay the premiums) for a certain amount of time after they have left the job. The types of coverage protected include medical, dental, and optical. Former employees who choose to continue coverage may do so for up to 18 months after leaving the job. Former employees with disabilities may continue coverage for up to 29 months. Those who were fired because of gross misconduct are not protected by COBRA.

Consolidated Omnibus Budget Reconciliation Act (COBRA)—A federal law that requires organizations to allow employees to retain their rights to insurance coverage under their employer's health plan for a certain amount of time after they have left the organization.

Health Insurance Portability and Accountability Act (HIPAA)

The **Health Insurance Portability and Accountability Act (HIPAA)** does not require employers to provide insurance coverage but instead provides rules for employers that do choose to provide a health plan for employees. The law says that an employer cannot exclude coverage to employees who have preexisting medical conditions for which medical advice, care, or

Health Insurance Portability and Accountability Act (HIPAA)—A federal law that provides rules for employers who provide health plans for their employees.

treatment was provided within 6 months prior to when coverage would begin. The act also requires employers to do what is reasonably necessary to ensure that employees' health information is not available to those without permission to have it. Some ways in which this can be accomplished include personnel training and information relevant to the communication of privacy issues and information.

Table 6.2 outlines the federal laws discussed in this text.

Table 6.2   Federal Employment Laws

Employment issue	Applicable law
Leave for medical and family reasons	Family and Medical Leave Act (FMLA)
Employee safety and health	Occupational Safety and Health Act
Wages and compensation, child labor	Fair Labor Standards Act (FLSA)
Employee insurance and health plans	Consolidated Omnibus Budget Reconciliation Act (COBRA) and the Health Insurance Portability and Accountability Act (HIPAA)
Discrimination in employment based on race, color, national origin, gender, or religion	Civil Rights Act of 1964
Discrimination in employment based on age	Age Discrimination in Employment Act (ADEA)
Discrimination in employment based on disability	Americans with Disabilities Act (ADA)

Summary

Discrimination can occur in hiring, promoting, and firing employees, so employers should put safeguards in place to eliminate or reduce the likelihood that a person will be discriminated against. Categories of discrimination include race, color and national origin, gender, religion, age, and disability. The ADEA, Title VII of the Civil Rights Act, other state and federal laws, the EEOC, and court decisions all influence issues of discrimination in the workplace. The sport manager should also be familiar with affirmative action, a concept closely associated with discrimination.

Sexual harassment is a violation of Title VII of the Civil Rights Act. Sexual harassment should never be tolerated by a sport organization (or any organization), and policies and procedures must be put in place and implemented to ensure that abuses do not occur. This right allows employees to argue their case and tell their side of the story before being terminated. Finally, the sport manager should be aware of employee health and safety issues and the relevant laws and regulations.

DISCUSSION QUESTIONS

1. Should scholarship athletes be considered employees of a university?

2. Which factors in the "economic reality test" (discussed in *Coleman v. Western Michigan University*, 1983) would you give the most weight?

3. In the sexual harassment scenario in the text, what is your reaction to the situation from both an ethical and legal standpoint? What types of sexual harassment might exist? What are the key issues that you would address from a legal standpoint?

4. Name three organizations from your independent research that provide assistance to employers for personnel issues, including discrimination, sexual harassment, and workplace safety. Briefly describe the services these organizations provide.

5. Describe the potential challenges to an organization in raising the BFOQ defense.

6. What is needed to develop a case for disparate-treatment discrimination? Describe in terms of an employment hypothetical.

7. Describe the potential challenges to raising a disparate-impact claim.

MOOT COURT CASE

Carl was the women's tennis coach at the University of Wewilsu. Carl was considered to be one of the top tennis coaches in the country, having led Wewilsu U. to three national championships in his 10-year tenure at the university. He was well liked and respected by most. Last year, he hired a new assistant tennis coach, Cari Tenpro. Cari was a highly accomplished player who had had an excellent coaching career so far, although she had not been coaching long. She was also one of three assistant coaches, the other two having similar skills but more coaching experience. Veronica, an African American, was the head assistant coach. She had the highest pay of all the assistants and was given the most responsibility. Susan, a Latin American, was the assistant in training and was second to Veronica, with pay slightly less than Veronica's but more than the lowest level. Cari was hired as an assistant in training. After several weeks at her new job, Cari began to notice some seemingly odd behavior from Carl. He would make jokes about women that made her uncomfortable and was insistent on numerous "friendship" hugs. She put up with this, thinking that Carl was just a bit quirky. One day, Carl made a very suspicious comment. He told Cari that she was doing such a great job that she deserved a promotion. He told her that she was both a great colleague and friend and that he was looking forward to more friendship hugs in the future. In fact, he asked whether she would like to come over to his condo that evening to strengthen their friendship. After all, he said, love is part of the score in tennis. Cari was extremely upset but badly needed the job and promotion. She told Carl that she valued their friendship and would take him up on his offer the following week. Carl seemed very excited and promoted Cari immediately to the head assistant position with a pay raise effective immediately. The next day, Carl called Veronica into his office and told her that she would have to either find another job or move back to the assistant in training position. Veronica was furious. Carl told Veronica that Cari was better suited for the head assistant position and that she was a fast learner. He could not give Veronica any more specific reasons. Veronica refused to take the assistant in training position and was fired by Carl. She told Susan what had happened. Susan shared her concern and was angry with Carl as well. The next week, Carl asked Cari over to his place again. Cari made up an excuse but Carl would not accept no for an answer. He told Cari that if she came over to his place that night then they could get to know one another better—which he was certain would lead to a more job perks and pay raises for Cari in the near future. Cari asked, "Do you mean if I sleep with you, you will let me keep my job and get these benefits?" Carl said, "I knew you were a smart one." Cari turned in her resignation that hour, even though she desperately needed the job. She then complained to the athletic director but was told that she should give Carl another chance. Cari was deeply upset and could not face Carl again. Carl was not disciplined. Cari, Veronica, and Susan all brought lawsuits against Carl and the university.

7

Constitutional Law

CHAPTER OBJECTIVES

After reading this chapter, you will know the following:

- How the United States Constitution applies to private and public sport entities
- The free speech and freedom of religion protections provided for by the First Amendment
- How the First Amendment regulates religious prayers and activities in sport settings
- What substantive and procedural due process are and how their requirements apply to sport organizations
- How the Equal Protection Clause of the Constitution affects sport-related affirmative action plans

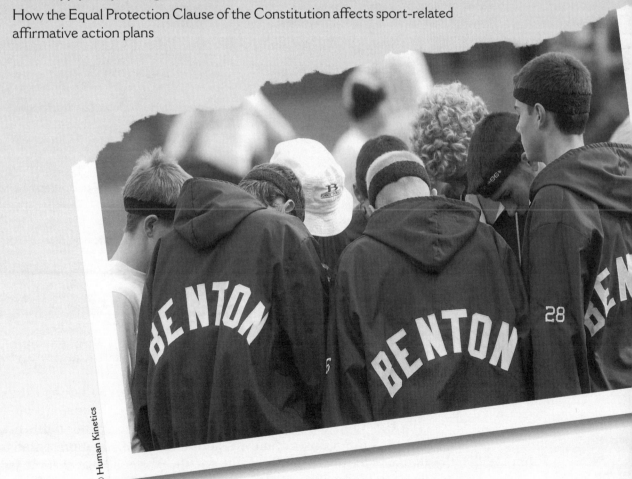

© Human Kinetics

The constitutional rights and amendments that most often apply to the sport industry typically involve issues regarding freedom of speech and religion, due process, equal protection, and the right from unreasonable search and seizure. These rights and protections are found in the First, Fourth, Fifth, and Fourteenth Amendments (see table 7.1). A major portion of this chapter addresses these issues and amendments as they relate to interscholastic and intercollegiate student-athletes. Constitutional law usually is not applicable to professional sports, for two major reasons. One, athletes in professional sports are parties to a collective bargaining agreement. When a players union agrees to a collective bargaining agreement, certain individual rights are relinquished, including freedom of expression. For example, a professional athlete who makes disparaging and insensitive remarks about minority groups may be suspended by the commissioner for his remarks. Second, professional sports leagues are not state actors but rather private entities (Wong, 2002).

Table 7.1   Constitutional Law as It Applies to Sport

Amendment	Protections	Applicability to sport
First	Congress shall make no law respecting an establishment of religion, or prohibiting the free exercise thereof; or abridging the freedom of speech, or of the press; or the right of the people peaceably to assemble, and to petition the Government for a redress of grievances.	• Public school–based prayer • Freedom of expression, such as wearing arm bands • Freedom of association, such as forming leagues and associations (e.g., NCAA, Little League teams)
Fifth	No person shall . . . be deprived of life, liberty or property without due process of law.	• Recruiting rules violations resulting in firing a coach • Failed drug test that causes an athlete to lose a scholarship • Due process clause, which ensures fairness and impartiality before the government denies people of their life, liberty, or property
Fourteenth	No State shall make or enforce any law which shall . . . deny to any person within its jurisdiction the equal protection of the laws.	• No discrimination based on race, gender, or ethnicity • Access of sport administration jobs to minority groups • Affirmative action

The U.S. federal government and all 50 states have separate written constitutions that set forth the basic organization, powers, and limits of their respective governments. Constitutional law is the law as expressed in these constitutions. State constitutions often vary; some are modeled after the U.S. Constitution, and others provide even greater rights to their citizens. The U.S. Constitution was adopted in 1787 by representatives of the 13 newly formed states. Initially, people expressed fear that the federal government might abuse its power. To alleviate such concerns, the first

Congress approved 10 amendments to the U.S. Constitution, commonly known as the Bill of Rights, which were adopted in 1791. The Bill of Rights limits the powers and authority of the federal government and guarantees many civil (individual) rights and protections.

Although the Bill of Rights does not directly apply to the states, the U.S. Supreme Court has held that the Fourteenth Amendment includes many of the principal guarantees of the Bill of Rights, thereby making them applicable to the individual states. So, neither the federal government nor state governments can deprive individuals of those rights and protections. However, the rights provided by the Bill of Rights are not absolute. Many of the rights guaranteed by the Bill of Rights are described in very broad terms. For instance, the Fourth Amendment prohibits unreasonable search and seizures; however, it does not define what an unreasonable search and seizure would entail. Ultimately, the U.S. Supreme Court interprets the Constitution, thereby defining our rights and the government's boundaries.

The majority of the rights and protections afforded by the U.S. Constitution and its amendments only apply to governmental, or state, action. **State action** consists of any action of the federal or state governments or their subdivisions, such as city or county governments or agencies. Only the Thirteenth Amendment, which abolishes slavery, applies to the actions of private individuals. All other protections, regarding individual rights, only apply to governmental, or state, actors.

state action—Any action of the federal or state governments or their subdivisions, such as city or county governments or agencies.

Action taken by private entities may constitute state action if the state exercises coercive power over the challenged private action, has substantially encouraged the action, or was significantly involved in the action (Mann & Roberts, 2007). For example, in *Brentwood Academy v. Tennessee Secondary School Athletic Association* (2001), the U.S. Supreme Court found state action in this athletic association's regulatory activity attributable to the pervasive involvement of state school officials in its structure.

Historically, courts have considered the action of public schools, state universities, or any of their officials to be state action. High school interscholastic athletic associations have also been declared as state actors by most courts. Since the mid-1980s, national organizations that govern university athletics, including the National Collegiate Athletic Association (NCAA), typically have been found not to be state actors (*Arlosroff v. NCAA,* 1984; *NCAA v. Tarkanian,* 1988).

First Amendment

The First Amendment to the U.S. Constitution states that "Congress shall make no law respecting an establishment of religion, or prohibiting the free exercise thereof; or abridging the freedom of speech, or of the press; or the right of the people peaceably to assemble, and to petition the Government for a redress of grievances." The major elements of the First Amendment that often apply to sport include religious issues, predominantly public school–based prayer, freedom of expression, and freedom of association.

Religious Issues

The first part of this Amendment deals with religious freedom and is referred to as the **establishment clause** and the **free exercise clause.** The establishment clause bans the government or its agencies from establishing a state-sponsored religion, promoting (endorsing or aiding) a specific religion, or favoring one religion over another. This is referred to as separation between church and state. The free exercise clause bans the government or its agencies from interfering with anyone's religious belief. In other words, the government cannot interfere with an individual's practice of his or her religious beliefs.

The U.S. Supreme Court has established three tests to determine whether religious practices challenged under the First Amendment are unconstitutional:

- Lemon test—A three-part test used to determine whether a government (religious) practice is constitutional. To be constitutional, (1) the practice must be secular in purpose, (2) the practice's primary effect can neither advance nor inhibit religion, and (3) the practice must avoid excessive entanglement with religion (*Lemon v. Kurtzman,* 1971).

- Endorsement test—Test used to consider whether the government endorses a particular religion or disproves of any religion. The government cannot endorse, favor, or disprove of any religion or practice (*Lynch v. Donnelly,* 1984).

- Coercion test—Test that examines a religious practice to determine whether people are pressured or coerced to participate. The government may not coerce individuals to participate in religion or its exercise (*Lee v. Weisman,* 1992).

Religious practices, such as pregame prayers, have been common at U.S. sporting events for many years. Several recent lawsuits have forced to the courts to determine whether such practices, particularly in public schools, are constitutional. In *Santa Fe Independent School District v. Doe* (2000), Texas high school students held elections to vote on whether a prayer would be said before the start of home football games and, if so, who would deliver the prayer over the public address system. The U.S. Supreme Court agreed with the Fifth Circuit Court of Appeals and held that student-initiated and student-led prayer at public high school football games is unconstitutional.

In *Adler v. Duval County School Board* (2001), the school board's policy that allowed prayer at graduation ceremonies was challenged. The school board's guidelines allowed graduating seniors to decide (1) whether to have a brief opening or closing message at graduation, (2) which student volunteer would give a message, and (3) what the content of the message would be. School officials were not involved in the decision-making process, and the content of the message was solely up to the individual student who would deliver the message. The Eleventh Circuit Court held that the school board's policies regarding student-led prayer were constitutional. The court stated that the school board policy promoted freedom of speech by allowing

establishment clause—A sentence in the First Amendment of the United States Constitution that prohibits the government from establishing a state-sponsored religion, promoting religion, or favoring religion over nonreligion.

free exercise clause—A phrase in the First Amendment to the United States Constitution that prohibits the government from restricting a person's right to exercise his or her religious beliefs.

the volunteer student to speak on any subject of his or her choice, and the message could be religious or secular. The court held that the school board policy was neutral, did not determine the content of the message, and did not establish any religion. This case example demonstrates an issue concerning freedom of religion in a public school that would also likely apply in public interscholastic sport.

Certain religious beliefs may require dress standards that can contradict policies set forth by athletic administrators, as seen in *Menora v. Illinois High School Association* (1982). In this case, an association bylaw prohibited students from wearing any headwear, except a sweatband, while participating in basketball. The bylaw was challenged by a student-athlete who was Jewish. He claimed that the bylaw was unconstitutional because it prohibited Jewish student-athletes from wearing yarmulkes, a requirement of their Jewish faith. Although the court sympathized with the student-athlete, the appeals court affirmed the trial court's decision in favor of the high school association. The appeals court concluded that the plaintiff must decide whether in fact the Jewish faith requirements did not allow his participation in the voluntary sport of basketball and whether his headwear is not appropriate for the sport of basketball.

Freedom of Expression

Also included in the First Amendment is the **free speech clause,** which provides us the right to say what we want without government intervention; however, not all speech is protected. The government may impose restriction on the time, place, and manner in which we express ourselves. Some types of speech, such as obscenity, receive no protection. Most types of speech, however, are protected by the strict or exacting scrutiny standard. These standards require the existence of a compelling government interest to justify restricting speech (Mann & Roberts, 2007; Miller, Cross, & Jentz, 2005). For example, in *Bethel School District v. Fraser* (1986), Matthew Fraser, a high school senior, gave a speech to the student body that was filled with sexual innuendo. The speech created quite an uproar among the students: Some yelled during the speech, whereas others were embarrassed and bewildered. The speech prompted disciplinary action from the school administration, which suspended Fraser from school for 3 days and did not allow him to speak at his graduation ceremony. The U.S. Supreme Court upheld the suspension and found that the school district's policy did not violate the First Amendment. The court stated, "Surely it is a highly appropriate function of public school education to prohibit the use of vulgar and offensive terms in public discourse. The schools, as instruments of the state, may determine that the essential lessons of civil, mature conduct cannot be conveyed in a school that tolerates lewd, indecent, or offensive speech and conduct such as that indulged in by this confused boy. The pervasive sexual innuendo in Fraser's speech was plainly offensive to both teachers and students—indeed to any mature person. We hold that petitioner School District acted entirely within its permissible authority

free speech clause— A clause in the First Amendment to the United States Constitution that protects freedom of speech for all persons.

in imposing sanctions upon Fraser in response to his offensively lewd and indecent speech." Vulgar and offensive trash talking by athletes at a public school sport event may be restricted for similar reasons.

A democratic government cannot survive unless the people can freely express their political views and opinions as well as criticize governmental policies and actions. Freedom of speech, especially political speech, is a very important right, and the courts have traditionally protected this right as much as possible. Symbolic speech, which encompasses nonverbal conduct (articles of clothing, gestures, and other forms of expressive conduct), is also protected under the First Amendment, as shown in the In the Courtroom case below.

In the Courtroom

Tinker v. Des Moines Independent Community School Dist. (1969)

Petitioner John F. Tinker, 15 years old, and petitioner Christopher Eckhardt, 16 years old, attended high schools in Des Moines, Iowa. Petitioner Mary Beth Tinker, John's sister, was a 13-year-old student in junior high school. In December 1965, a group of adults and students in Des Moines held a meeting at the Eckhardt home. The group determined to publicize their objections to the hostilities in Vietnam and their support for a truce by wearing black armbands during the holiday season and by fasting on December 16 and New Year's Eve. Petitioners and their parents had previously engaged in similar activities, and they decided to participate in the program.

The principals of the Des Moines schools became aware of the plan to wear armbands. On December 14, 1965, they met and adopted a policy that any student wearing an armband to school would be asked to remove it, and if he refused he would be suspended until he returned without the armband. Petitioners were aware of the regulation that the school authorities adopted.

On December 16, Mary Beth and Christopher wore black armbands to their schools. John Tinker wore his armband the next day. They were all sent home and suspended from school until they would come back without their armbands. They did not return to school until after the planned time for wearing armbands had expired—that is, until after New Year's Day.

This complaint was filed in the U.S. District Court by petitioners, through their fathers, under section 1983 of Title 42 of the United States Code. It prayed for an injunction restraining the respondent school officials and the respondent members of the board of directors of the school district from disciplining the petitioners, and it sought nominal damages.

An interscholastic athlete who wishes to symbolically express herself by wearing something attached to the traditional uniform (like a sticker or ribbon) may be permitted to do so under the First Amendment but would likely be restricted by league or association rules. Although the *Fraser* and *Tinker* cases are not sport related, these two U.S. Supreme Court landmark cases are frequently cited in legal disputes and cases involving free speech in a public school.

Another form of speech, known as **commercial speech,** can be defined as expression that is related to the economic interests of the speaker and his audience. This would include advertisements for a product or service. Although commercial speech is protected by the First Amendment, it is protected less than political speech. Commercial speech is protected because of the interest such communication has for the advertiser, consumer, and general public. Advertising conveys essential information for the proper and efficient distribution of many resources in our free market system. However, the government may restrict certain types of advertising, for instance, in the interest of protecting the public from being misled by certain advertising practices (Mann & Roberts, 2007; Miller et al., 2005).

The U.S. Supreme Court has made it clear that certain types of speech will not be afforded protection under the First Amendment. For example, defamatory speech, that which disgraces or diminishes a person's reputation by communicating a false statement, is not protected. Speech that violates criminal laws, for example, pornography or threatening speech, is also not protected (Mann & Roberts, 2007; Miller et al., 2005).

commercial speech—An expression related to economic interests of the speaker or the audience. Commercial speech is protected by the First Amendment but is regulated by the government to protect consumers from false or misleading advertisements.

Right of Association

Sport and recreation associations are common, such as Little League Baseball Association, the Amateur Athletic Association, and the National Collegiate Athletic Association (NCAA). Some associations are formed with the purpose of promoting a specific sport or activity by location: for example, "Anytown" Youth Football Association, the Florida Recreation and Parks Association, or the National Intramural and Recreational Sports Association. In addition to promoting sport, some associations protect the interests of athletes and participants. Individuals have the right to form associations, thereby choosing with whom they wish to associate and socialize. This basic right is guaranteed by the First Amendment provided the association does not commit criminal activities or violate an individual's civil rights related to race, gender, age, religion, or national origin.

Other elements of the First Amendment that often involve athletes are **equal protection** and **due process.** Equal protection, contained in the Fourteenth Amendment, guarantees that laws will be applied in an equal and nondiscriminatory manner. Due process rights are contained in both the Fifth and Fourteenth Amendments as well as in many state constitutions. Due process guarantees that a person cannot be deprived of life, liberty, or property without a fair process or hearing.

equal protection—A guarantee that laws will be applied in an equal and nondiscriminatory manner.

due process—A guarantee that an individual cannot be deprived of life, liberty, or property without a fair process or hearing.

Fourteenth Amendment

The Fourteenth Amendment of the United States Constitution provides that "no State shall make or enforce any law which shall . . . deny to any person within its jurisdiction the equal protection of the laws." This sentence is commonly referred to as the Equal Protection Clause (EPC). The EPC, like the Thirteenth, Fourteenth, and Fifteenth Amendments, was enacted at the close of the Civil War and secured free and equal treatment of former slaves.

The EPC has been used to impose a general restraint on governmental inequality based on classifications. The EPC is triggered any time people are classified and treated differently based on classifications. Although there are countless ways in which people can be classified or distinguished, the classifications that receive the most restraint involve immutable characteristics, characteristics with which people are born, such as a race, ethnicity, or gender. A history of discrimination based on race, ethnicity, and gender exists in American sport, so sport managers must be mindful to avoid possible EPC violations. For example, before the civil rights movement, African Americans were not allowed access to university and high school sports teams in many parts of the country. This is no longer the case, but there are still questions concerning the degree of access that African Americans and other minority groups have in seeking sport administration and coaching positions.

Strict Scrutiny

The type of classification assigned to a person affects the way a court scrutinizes the legality of the classification. In this sense, scrutiny means the way a court analyzes whether state action should be condoned or rejected. So how does strict scrutiny work? Think of scrutiny as the degree to which someone analyzes an issue (figure 7.1). For example, teachers scrutinize the work of their students regularly. If a teacher lightly scrutinizes a student's assignment, then that teacher is giving the student leeway in terms of accomplishing the goals set for the assignment. Conversely, if the teacher scrutinizes the assignment strictly, there is little or no room for error. Similarly, courts that use strict scrutiny give the government no room for error in convincing them that the classification is necessary. Thus, strict scrutiny is the most rigorous degree of scrutiny. Once a court decides that strict scrutiny is the appropriate standard, then the court will uphold the state action only if it is necessary to achieve a compelling governmental interest (*Grutter v. Bollinger,* 2003).

Courts use strict scrutiny in EPC cases any time state action uses a suspect classification or a classification linked to a fundamental right (Lockhart, Kamisar, Choper, & Shiffrin, 1991). Classifications based on race or national origin are suspect classifications, so state action that classifies people based on their race or their national origin will be subject to strict scrutiny. For example, state high school athletic associations in the U.S. South once separated African American high schools from white high schools, and the

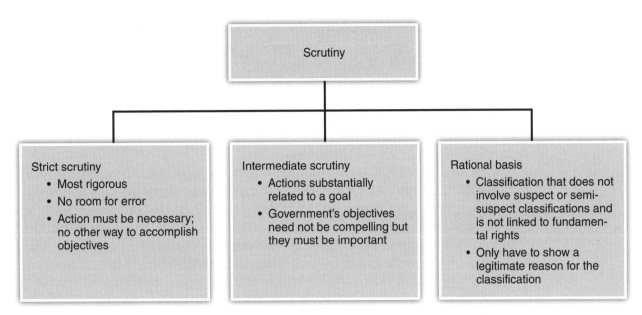

Figure 7.1 Different types of scrutiny used when courts rule on Equal Protection Clause cases.

two types of athletic programs were prohibited from competing against each other. Any state action that separates competitors today based on their race or their national origin will be subject to strict scrutiny.

The other way that strict scrutiny applies concerns a classification that is linked to a fundamental right (Lockhart et al., 1991). If the court concludes that state action has a material impact on a fundamental right or interest, the action must survive strict scrutiny. There are not many fundamental rights. Those rights that have been deemed fundamental by the courts include the right to vote, the right to criminal appeal, and the right to interstate travel. So if a community limited the right to vote to those who have lived in that community for more than 10 years, strict scrutiny would apply. Although time span of residence does not involve a suspect classification per se, the classification is tied to the fundamental right to vote, which is why strict scrutiny is applicable.

As previously stated, when strict scrutiny is applied the court will allow the governmental action to survive only if it is necessary to achieve a compelling governmental interest. To fully grasp the concept of strict scrutiny, we need to understand what courts mean by the words *necessary* and *compelling*. For the purpose of EPC analysis, *necessary* means that there is no other way to accomplish the government's objective. Courts often use the phrase *narrowly tailored* when describing what is intended by *necessary*. This phrase provides a visual example of what the courts expect from governmental action that triggers strict scrutiny. Specifically, a narrowly tailored suit is one that fits tightly; likewise, the means to accomplishing the compelling governmental objective must also fit tightly. That is, in accomplishing the compelling governmental interest, the government must only do what is absolutely necessary. Any unnecessary classification or regulation based on a classification will be found unconstitutional.

The second key term used in strict scrutiny analysis is the word *compelling*. This term means that the objective sought through the state action must compel the court. A court is compelled when the court believes that the action must be taken. This goes beyond the idea that the regulation is important or that it is a good idea. Instead, a high level of justification is needed for the discriminatory classification to survive. As society changes and evolves, so does the law. What a court may find compelling one day may be unthinkable at a later time.

In *Louisiana High School Athletic Ass'n v. St. Augustine High School* (1968), the Fifth Circuit used strict scrutiny in analyzing the need for a segregated high school athletic association. In doing so, the court found no necessity for maintaining a segregated high school athletic system. The court found that the evidence presented in the case supported an inference that race was the basis for the exclusion of St. Augustine (a predominantly African American high school) from the association, and this did not compel the court to allow the association's discriminatory denial of access to the school.

Intermediate Scrutiny

An intermediate level of scrutiny is available to courts to analyze state action that discriminates against people on the basis of gender, illegitimacy, and alienage (Lockhart et al., 1991). Thus far, race and national origin are the only two classifications that courts have deemed suspect. However, courts have recognized that these three groups deserve added equal protection. Although these classes do not rise to the level of suspect, thus resulting in strict scrutiny, they have been labeled as semisuspect by the courts. When the government makes distinctions between people based on semisuspect classifications, then the government's actions are subjected to intermediate scrutiny.

Intermediate scrutiny is not as rigorous as strict scrutiny (Lockhart et al., 1991). For a classification to survive strict scrutiny, the government must show that the classification was substantially related to achieving an important governmental interest. Instead of showing that its actions were necessary, the government need only show that its actions were substantially related to its goal. Thus, the government's actions can survive intermediate scrutiny if there are other, less discriminatory means of accomplishing the government's objectives as long as the means chosen were substantially related to the goal.

Furthermore, the government's goal or objective need not be compelling but it must be important. The difference between *compelling* and *important* can be described as the difference between *must* and *should*. For example, one must eat in order to survive, but one should eat healthily to live longer. Objectives used to justify semisuspect classifications do not have to be so vital that they must be accomplished. Instead, they need only be the type that should be accomplished.

A good example of a court using intermediate scrutiny can be found in *Ludtke vs. Kuhn* (1978). This case involved a challenge against the New York

Yankees' policy of excluding female sport reporters from the baseball team's locker room in a government-owned and -operated stadium. Ludtke, the female reporter challenging the policy, named the mayor of New York, Yankee Stadium, the Yankees, and the commissioner of Major League Baseball in her lawsuit. The defendants argued that the policy was substantially related to the important goals of (1) protecting the privacy of those players who are undressed or who are in various stages of undressing and getting ready to shower; (2) protecting the image of baseball as a family sport; and (3) preserving the traditional notions of decency and propriety (*Ludtke*

© M. David/Icon SMI

Is it legal to exclude female sport reporters from men's locker rooms? Intermediate scrutiny was used to answer such a question in *Ludtke vs. Kuhn.*

v. Kuhn, 1978). The court recognized that fresh-off-the-field interviews are important to the work of sport reporters in that these interviews give a competitive advantage to reporters who have access to the ballplayers at that time. The court also recognized that there were several less sweeping alternatives to simply banning women from the locker rooms. The defendants admitted that players could undress in their cubicles in the clubhouse and could be shielded from the "roving eyes" of any female reporters by a curtain or swinging door on each cubicle. In addition, towels were available to players who wished to maintain privacy after showering or changing out of their uniforms. Based on these findings, the court held that the policy of banning female reporters from the locker rooms at Yankee Stadium was not substantially related to an important governmental interest and therefore did not survive intermediate scrutiny (*Ludtke vs. Kuhn,* 1978).

Rational Basis

The rational basis standard is a type of scrutiny that applies to all classifications not covered by strict or intermediate scrutiny (i.e., all those that do not involve suspect or semisuspect classifications and are not linked to fundamental rights). The courts are charged with ensuring that people are afforded equal protection under the law, so governmental decisions that classify and differently treat groups of people must be scrutinized. However, the standard for all other classifications is much lower in that the government need only show a rational basis for its action. The government only has to show a legitimate reason for the classification proving that the basis for the classification is rationally related to a legitimate governmental interest. The court does not even have to agree with the rational basis asserted by the government as long as the basis is rational. The rational basis standard is the same standard used by courts in evaluating substantive due process claims. It is not the role of the court system to systematically micromanage governmental decisions. Courts only interfere with governmental decisions when the government cannot justify its decision rationally.

Types of Discrimination

de jure discrimination— When the law has a discriminatory purpose.

Two types of discrimination can lead to an EPC challenge. The first is called **de jure discrimination;** roughly translated, this means discrimination by law (Lockhart et al., 1991). De jure discrimination exists any time a law or policy has a discriminatory purpose. For example, a rule that forbids African Americans from competing in high school sports with white athletes would be de jure discrimination because the purpose for the law is discriminatory. The second type of discrimination is called **de facto discrimination.** This type of discrimination exists when the law or policy lacks a discriminatory purpose but has a discriminatory effect (Lockhart et al., 1991). For example, a high school sport association divides up districts in such a manner that the districts divide groups of people based on race. Although there may be no discriminatory purpose behind creating sport districts, challengers may demonstrate that the division results in discrimination.

de facto discrimination— When the law does not appear to have a discriminatory purpose but has a discriminatory effect.

Affirmative Action

Affirmative action is a term given to programs designed to reverse the effects of past and current discrimination. Affirmative action programs often involve hiring or admittance policies that assist people who are members of a group or classification of people who have been discriminated against. The goal of affirmative action is to provide a springboard to those who need assistance because they are disadvantaged in the hiring or admittance process because of their classification. The concept of affirmative action is controversial because discrimination cannot be reversed without treating people differently based on the same criteria on which past discrimination was based (i.e., race, gender, national origin, and alienage). Thus, affirmative action has been labeled by some as reverse discrimination (Cohen & Sterba, 2003). The courts, however, have upheld proper applications of affirmative action under the opinion that such applications result in benign (meaning harmless) discrimination.

The EPC applies to affirmative action programs that have been implemented by state actors. Accordingly, affirmative action plans are subject to the same scrutiny that would be used to analyze other discriminatory programs, rules, or regulations. Any affirmative action plan that uses race or national origin as a criterion for advancement must survive strict scrutiny.

The U.S. Supreme Court has repeatedly held that the goal of reversing past discrimination is a compelling governmental interest. However, affirmative action plans don't always satisfy the necessary requirement of strict scrutiny. Specifically, affirmative action plans must still be narrowly tailored in that they must do only what is necessary, and if less discriminatory means are available, then those means must be used.

Narrowly tailored affirmative action plans are those that are properly administered. Proper administration means employers develop minimum requirements for the position and first obtain a qualified candidacy pool before using race, national origin, or gender as a consideration. Affirmative action plans should not use quotas, and employers or selection committees should not enter a search with the goal of hiring someone based on suspect or semisuspect class status. Hiring or admitting unqualified applicants based on their racial, ethnic, or gender classification is not proper application of affirmative action.

A good example of how to use an affirmative action plan can be found in the case of *Grutter v. Bollinger* (2003). Although this case is not directly related to sport, it provides insight into how courts handle EPC cases that challenge affirmative action programs. The case involved a white law school applicant who accused the University of Michigan School of Law's affirmative action plan of being responsible for the rejection of her application to the school. The applicant filed a lawsuit against the university, alleging that the school's diversity policy violated the Equal Protection Clause. The school's policy required applicants to submit an essay stating how they would benefit the school's policy aimed at developing diversity for its student body. The school evaluated each student to determine how she or he would promote the school's diversity policy. The essay was considered only after it was determined that the applicant satisfied the school's minimum grade point average and LSAT score requirements. The case ultimately reached the U.S. Supreme Court, where Justice Sandra Day O'Connor held that (1) the law school had a compelling interest in attaining a diverse student body and (2) the admissions program was narrowly tailored to serve its compelling interest in obtaining the educational benefits that flow from a diverse student body, and thus the university's policy did not violate the Equal Protection Clause (*Grutter v. Bollinger,* 2003). The court held that the school's policy was narrowly tailored because the school followed proper application of affirmative action. The school did only what was necessary and no more in terms of promoting diversity. The application process consisted of first obtaining a qualified candidacy pool, and only then was race considered.

Affirmative action programs have been used by sport organizations, leagues, teams, and university athletic programs. Affirmative action plans in sport settings are primarily used to promote diversity in coaching hires. The National Football League (NFL) requires each team to interview at least one minority candidate before hiring a head coach. The NFL's rule is controversial because some believe that it promotes needless interviews in situations where it is obvious that a team already has its next coach in mind. Others, however, argue that the rule opens doors that would otherwise remain closed, because it forces teams to consider those who ordinarily would not be considered. The NFL's program doesn't exactly comply with proper administration of affirmative action; the NFL is not subject to constitutional review for its affirmative action program because the league is not a state actor.

Conversely, university athletic associations at state-run schools are vulnerable to EPC review for their hiring practices. Athletic directors at such schools must use care in adopting affirmative action plans for hiring coaches. It is advisable to use *Grutter v. Bollinger* as a roadmap in developing an affirmative action plan: Use race as a consideration, but only do so after establishing a qualified pool of candidates. An athletic program should decide up front what minimum criteria job candidates must possess. Do candidates need head coaching experience? Is a master's degree required? Should the coach have experience in the region or conference in which the athletic program competes? Suspect or semisuspect class status should only be considered after the athletic association's minimum job requirements are satisfied. Affirmative action is used to promote diversity for all suspect and semisuspect classifications, which means that proper administration of affirmative action assists all groups of people who have been subject to past discrimination. These groups include, but are not limited to, African Americans, Hispanics, Asians, and women.

Fifth Amendment

Sometimes the government or state actors restrict persons in their actions, in their professions, or in regard to their possessions. In sport, governmental restrictions can cause a coach to lose his job for violating rules governing recruiting or an athlete to lose a scholarship for failing a drug test. Even when the government is justified in its restrictions, it must still afford those restricted some form of process before the restrictions are enforced.

The rule requiring process from the government can be found in the Due Process Clause (DPC) of the U.S. Constitution. The DPC is found in the Fifth Amendment of the Constitution and provides that "no person shall . . . be deprived of life, liberty or property without due process of law." The Fifth Amendment only applies to federal state actors, but the Fourteenth Amendment extends the DPC to the states. Most state constitutions also include due process guarantees. Due process exists to protect persons from arbitrary, capricious, and unreasonable governmental restriction. In other words, the DPC exists to ensure fairness and impartiality before the government denies people of life, liberty, or property.

Life, Liberty, and Property Interests

To trigger the DPC's application, the government must attempt to deny persons of a life, liberty, or property interest. The government denies people of life interests when it denies people their lives, as in when the government punishes someone for a capital offense, meaning an offense that is punishable by death. This aspect of the DPC is not very applicable to sport. However, life interests can also be restricted when the government incarcerates people for crimes. It is not uncommon to see news stories of sport personalities and athletes who are accused of criminal activities. Before any criminal penalty can be imposed, the government owes the accused due process.

Although life interest is fairly specific, liberty interest is not. Liberty interest includes all privileges recognized as essential to the orderly pursuit of happiness. In sport, the term *liberty interest* is typically used to describe damage to a person's reputation when he is fired from a job. A person who is fired is not deprived of a liberty interest when the employer alleges merely improper or inadequate performance, incompetence, neglect of duty, or malfeasance (*Siegert v. Gilley,* 1991). Likewise, a charge or allegation that merely makes a person less attractive to other employers but does not prevent the person from getting another job does not constitute a liberty deprivation (*Chilingirian v. Boris,* 1989). To activate the DPC, the employer must have made a statement in the course of the employee's discharge that might seriously damage the employee's standing in his profession (*Board of Regents v. Roth,* 1972). In doing so, the employer places a stigma on the employee that damages his career. The stigmatizing statements or charges must be made public, and the employee must claim that the chargers were false (*Codd v. Velger,* 1977). If these requirements are met, the employee is entitled to notice and an opportunity to be heard through a name-clearing hearing. However, the employee must request such a hearing (*Gillum v. City of Kerrville,* 1993). A name-clearing hearing does not have to adhere to any formal procedures to be valid.

A good example can be found in *Ludwig v. Board of Trustees of Ferris State University.* In this case, the coach of men's basketball team at a public university brought a DPC action in state court against the university's board of trustees and various other officials, alleging that the coach was deprived of due process in connection with disciplinary proceedings. One of the coach's claims was that the university deprived him of a liberty interest when school officials made comments in the local newspaper alleging that the coach used racial slurs. Although the court recognized that the coach's reputation had been harmed by the statements made by school officials, the coach had failed to request a name-clearing hearing and this prevented him from successfully prevailing on his DPC claim.

A person's interest in property is the third interest protected by the DPC. Courts have defined *property interest* very broadly in that the term includes all valuable interests that can be possessed outside of oneself, that have exchangeable value, or that add to an individual's wealth or estate (*Board of Regents v. Roth,* 1972). In sport, a property interest can take many different forms, ranging from an owner's interest in a professional franchise to a university athlete's interest in a scholarship. Although the term *property* is broadly defined, courts require that persons actually have an interest in the thing for which they claim they are being deprived. To have a property interest, a person must have more than an abstract need or desire for what she claims. There must be more than a unilateral expectation; instead, there must be a legitimate claim of entitlement (*Board of Regents v. Roth,* 1972).

Price v. Univ. of Alabama (2004) provides a good example of what courts expect of those who allege that the government deprived them of an interest in property. Mike Price was hired as head football coach at the University of Alabama in January 2003. In May 2003, he was fired for alleged inappropriate conduct committed while Price was representing the school at a charity golf event in Florida. Price claimed that the university fired him without any real process or hearing and thus deprived him of a property interest in his employment contract with the university. However, Price and the university had yet to complete the contract, and the university claimed that Price was an at-will employee who could be fired at any time. There is no property interest in at-will employment (*Green v. City of Hamilton Hous Auth.,* 1991). In Alabama, agreements to agree in the future to terms of an employment contract are not contracts (*Price v. Univ. of Alabama,* 2004). The court found that Price did not have a property interest in an enforceable contract with the university simply because the two parties had plans to enter into a contract in the future. Therefore, Price did not have a valid property interest that could be protected by the DPC.

Substantive Due Process

Two types of due process are required under the DPC: substantive due process and procedural due process. Substantive due process concerns the actual rule or regulation in question, that is, the substance of the rule. When a person alleges a violation of substantive due process, that person is challenging the content and application of the rule. The DPC protects persons from unreasonable rules and regulations, and if a rule is unfair or arbitrary in either content or application, then that rule may violate the DPC of the U.S. Constitution.

For example, a university athletic department has a rule that any student-athlete accused by law enforcement officials of using drugs or performance-enhancing substances will be stripped of her scholarship. Dani is a volleyball student at the university and is accused of drug possession after police find drugs in a car in which Dani was a passenger. On notification of the incident, the athletic department suspends Dani's scholarship with no opportunity for appeal. Dani could allege a DPC violation on the basis that the department's substance abuse policy violates substantive due process. Dani must establish that she is being deprived of a life, liberty, or property interest by a state actor. The university is a public university, so she could probably establish state action. The depriving governmental entity is a branch of state government rather than the federal government, so Dani would rely on the Fourteenth Amendment's DPC protection. Furthermore, Dani is being deprived of a property interest through the termination of her university scholarship, something that has real value.

Dani could challenge the rule's content and application to her case on the basis that it is unfair. Dani was accused of possessing drugs merely because she was in a vehicle where drugs were found. It could be later discovered that Dani was walking home from practice when some students she recognized from school offered to give her a ride to her dorm. Dani accepted the ride mere minutes before campus police pulled the car over for a traffic violation. During a legal search, the police found two marijuana cigarettes in the glove compartment of the car. Dani was in the backseat of the car and did not know the cigarettes were in the car. Had the rule not been so strict to include mere accusations of drug abuse, and had Dani been given a chance to defend herself through a hearing, she would have been able to clear her name and keep her scholarship.

The government can survive a substantive due process challenge if it can show a rational basis for the rule or regulation that is being challenged. The rational basis standard is the lowest standard of court scrutiny. Rational basis is also the standard required of the government to overcome equal protection challenges for discriminatory practices that do not affect suspect or semisuspect classifications or involve fundamental rights. The reason that courts have placed such a relaxed standard on the government in substantive due process challenges is that courts do not like to interfere with the rule-making function of the government without good cause.

The United States has three branches of government, and the judicial branch is not the one charged with the responsibility of passing laws and making regulations. Those duties were given by our Constitution to the legislative branch. Furthermore, judges are not always equipped with the expertise to interfere with the decisions of governments and governmental agencies. Let's go back to the hypothetical involving Dani and the drug possession charge. Who is in a better position to make decisions and rules affecting university athletes: athletic directors or judges?

A reviewing court will not strike down the university's substance abuse policy if the university can provide a rational basis for its stringent rule. Dani could argue that the rule is unfair because it allows the university to terminate an athlete's scholarship based on mere accusations and provides no hearing for the athlete. However, the university could argue that the policy is needed because the school has a strong drug culture and student-athletes are the leaders of said drug culture. The university could argue that a strict, no-nonsense drug policy is necessary until the drug culture is curbed and drug abuse is reduced. Does the school's argument provide a rational basis for the rule? Keep in mind that a rational basis is the lowest of standards; the university only has to provide a reason for its policy. The court does not even have to agree with the university's rule. How do you think a court would answer these arguments? Would the court side with Dani or the university?

Procedural Due Process

Procedural due process concerns the procedures used to enforce a rule or regulation. The primary distinction between substantive and procedural due process is that persons alleging violations of procedural due process are not challenging the rule's content, just the way the rule was applied to them. In procedural due process suits, typically a person alleges that he was not given enough process. This brings up a question: Just how much process is due?

The amount of process owed to a person who is about to be deprived of a life, liberty, or property interest varies based on the severity of the violation and the severity of the sanction to be imposed. Two extreme examples demonstrate this concept. The first concerns a parking violation on a university campus. When someone violates a parking ordinance, usually that person is punished by receiving a parking ticket that states the fine imposed and when it is to be paid. The process afforded to someone charged with a traffic violation is called minimum due process.

Minimum due process is the process that is minimally due before someone is deprived of a life, liberty, or property interest (Lockart et al., 1991). Minimum due process includes the following:

- A statement of the specific violation
- Notice of the sanctions that will be imposed
- An opportunity for the accused to comment

Minimum due process should only be used in situations where the offense is minor and the sanction to be imposed is equally minor. A parking ticket typically includes a statement of the violation committed, notice of the fine owed for the offense, and information on what the offender can do to contest the ticket.

The second example includes someone who is being punished for committing multiple murders in a state that has the death penalty. This offense is probably the most severe offense that can be committed in any jurisdiction, and the punishment (either life in prison or the death penalty) is equally severe. For a person charged with committing murder, notice of the violation and the penalty that will be imposed is insufficient; more process is due. Such a person is granted what is called maximum due process.

Maximum due process requires (a) written notice of a hearing, (b) a written statement of the charges, (c) provision of an adversarial hearing (a hearing or trial where both sides can present arguments and have the matter heard by one or more neutral and detached decision makers), (d) a written or audiotaped record of the proceedings, and (e) the right to appeal. In a murder trial, an accused person is afforded all of the aforementioned process. However, maximum due process is required anytime the offense and sanction are severe (Lockart et al., 1991).

The two examples provided, the parking violation and the murder case, are close to extreme cases. Most situations fall somewhere between these extremes. For this reason, the DPC is flexible in its procedural requirements and is dependent on the facts of each case. For example, if a coach is accused of misconduct with an athlete and is likely to be fired, then something akin to maximum due process is probably required. Conversely, if an athlete breaks curfew before a big game and is punished by being made to sit out the first quarter of the game, something closer to minimum due process is in order.

The case of *Jennings v. Wentzville R-IV School Dist.* (2005) provides a good example of the flexibility of due process. In *Jennings,* two students were accused of being intoxicated at a football game and were suspended from school for 10 days. Court in *Jennings* held that school suspensions trigger the DPC because a student's right to education is a property interest. Thus, some form of process was required of the district before it could suspend the students, even if the procedure afforded did not rise to the degree of maximum due process. Courts have consistently held that when students face suspensions of 10 days or less, they are entitled to oral or written notice of the charges against them and, if the students deny the charges, an explanation of the evidence the authorities have and an opportunity to present their side of the story (*Goss v. Lopez,* 1975). There does not need to be a delay between the time notice is given and the time of the hearing.

Summary

The U.S. Constitution's equal protection requirements demand that all persons be treated equally under the law. Anytime the government discriminates between classes of people, it runs the risk of violating the Equal Protection Clause. Courts will review discriminatory cases to determine whether the government's discriminatory policies are justified. If the policy discriminates based on race or national origin, then the government will have the very heavy burden of satisfying the court's strict scrutiny standard. Policies discriminating based on gender will have to overcome intermediate scrutiny, and all other forms of discrimination require a rational basis to survive. Affirmative action is a discriminatory program that is often used by sport organizations. To survive strict scrutiny, an affirmative action program must be narrowly tailored to achieve the compelling interest of reversing the effects of past discrimination.

Due process is an aspect of constitutional law that all sport management professionals will deal with during their careers. Countless situations may arise where a sport manager may either implement process or argue for more process. Whether a sport manager is firing a coach or assistant or sanctioning an athlete for misconduct, some form of process is due. Sport managers must be careful when developing rules and regulations that could restrict someone's life, liberty, or property interests. By understanding what is due in terms of process, sport managers can protect themselves in claims that their actions run afoul of the Constitution.

DISCUSSION QUESTIONS

1. Provide an example of a religious issue in sport. Is the practice constitutional? How can a court decide this?

2. Provide an example of restriction of an athlete's freedom of expression. Is the practice constitutional? How may a court decide?

3. In an equal protection case, when will the court use strict scrutiny? Intermediate scrutiny?

4. How does strict scrutiny work? Intermediate scrutiny? Rational basis?

5. How can a sport organization implement a constitutionally acceptable affirmative action program?

6. What governmental deprivations trigger due process protection?

7. What is substantive due process and how does it differ from procedural due process?

MOOT COURT CASE

Paul was a football player for a public university. He was the first member of his family to attend university and was very proud of his athletic scholarship. Paul made decent grades and, unlike most of his teammates, generally stayed out of trouble. In a game against the university's in-state rival, Paul made a fumble that was subsequently returned for a touchdown. The university president was so infuriated by Paul's performance that he terminated Paul's scholarship. To make matters worse, Paul did not find out about the termination of his scholarship until he tried to enroll the following semester. Paul was confused by the president's decision because he did not violate a university rule or policy and was never afforded an opportunity to challenge the president's ruling. Paul sues the university, claiming that his constitutional rights were violated.

Gender Equity

CHAPTER OBJECTIVES

After reading this chapter, you will know the following:

- The various federal gender equity laws and how they apply to sport
- The history of Title IX, how it has been interpreted, and how it is applied today
- The definition of sexual harassment and how it is regulated in sport
- The various types of employment discrimination laws

© Human Kinetics

Perhaps no area of sport law is more controversial than the laws concerning gender equity. These laws were created to combat discrimination in all areas of education. Title IX has been used to focus on athletics at the high school and university level, because the government and the courts have found athletics to be a valuable part of the educational mission of high schools and universities.

Athletic administrators are often caught in the difficult situation of deciding how to properly and fairly allocate resources within their athletic programs. This includes the allocation of scholarship funds, roster spots, travel, equipment, and supplies and the provision of facilities and practice space. These decisions often come down to finances. Because football and men's basketball are the primary, if not the only, revenue-producing sports in many athletic programs, it becomes difficult for an athletic administrator to balance a budget while also providing opportunities to female athletes.

This chapter explores federal gender equity laws and their impact on athletics. It discusses the legal framework of gender equity and the historical development and modification of this framework. The analysis begins with the federal laws, regulations, and guidelines that make up gender equity law. The focus then shifts to areas of athletics that are subject to gender equity laws, including participation, scheduling, and facilities. This chapter also focuses on conduct within athletics that can be actionable under gender equity laws, including harassment and employment discrimination.

Title IX

In the late 1960s and early 1970s, very few athletes at the high school or university level were female. Those women who participated received little support from athletic department budgets. With the enactment of Title IX, women began to see exponential gains in athletic participation at the high school and university levels.

The legislative impetus for Title IX was the Civil Rights Act of 1964. Its framework, which forced schools and employers to honor the civil rights of minority students and employees, also forced schools and employers to recognize the rights of women. Title IX of the Education Amendments of 1972 (20 U.S.C. § 1681, et seq., 2008) provides the following:

> No person in the United States shall, on the basis of sex, be excluded from participation in, be denied the benefits of, or be subjected to discrimination under any education program or activity receiving Federal financial assistance.

Simply stated, Title IX prohibits programs that receive federal funding from excluding individuals from participating in the programs or denying individuals access to the benefits that the programs might provide. The focus of Title IX is to prohibit discrimination against the underrepresented sex, which historically has been women.

Although the law's prohibition of discrimination seems clear, many questions remain. Title IX says nothing about athletics; instead, its focus is on educational programs. However, courts quickly understood that athletic participation is a benefit within an overall educational program. As a result, the focus of Title IX litigation has been athletic departments and organizations.

There has been confusion over what programs or activities receive federal financial assistance and, therefore, come under Title IX. At first, courts determined that the law applied only to programs receiving federal funding. Therefore, athletic departments were not covered unless it was clear that the department itself directly received federal funding. In fact, in 1984 the U.S. Supreme Court found that only the specific department receiving federal funding should be required to comply with Title IX (*Grove City College et al. v. Bell,* 1984).

In the case of *Grove City College,* a private liberal arts college refused to agree to Title IX's nondiscrimination provisions as required by the Department of Education. As a result, the Department of Education pulled grant and loan money for students. The school sued so that it could get the funding back. The Supreme Court agreed that the Department of Education could pull the funding because the school did not comply with Title IX, but the Court limited its decision to the specific programs at the school that received federal financial assistance.

The results of this case were staggering. Because most universities have separate financial aid offices that provide student financial aid, athletic departments could avoid review under Title IX because the athletic departments themselves did not receive direct federal financial aid. However, 3 years later, Congress passed the Civil Rights Restoration Act, overturning the Supreme Court and making clear that as long as any part of a program or activity receives federal financial assistance, Title IX applies (20 U.S.C. § 1687, 2008). As a result, because virtually every American university and high school receives some form of federal funding, Title IX will apply to all schools.

Although Title IX applies to virtually every school, it does not apply directly to every athletic organization. For instance, the Supreme Court has held that the National Collegiate Athletic Association (NCAA) is not subject to Title IX because the organization does not directly receive federal funds (*NCAA v. Smith,* 1999). Renee Smith sued the NCAA because its rules barred her from participating in volleyball at one institution after she had already graduated from another institution. The Supreme Court found that the NCAA only indirectly received federal funds from the dues paid by its member schools and that this was not enough to force the NCAA to be subject to Title IX. Regardless, the NCAA has voluntarily agreed to work toward compliance with the law and has been at the forefront of providing equitable opportunities for women.

There was also early confusion over who could bring a lawsuit to push for equitable opportunities under the law. Title IX does not provide any specific way for an individual to sue to enforce the law. However, in 1979, the Supreme Court held that there is an implied private right of action under

Title IX (*Cannon v. Univ. of Chicago,* 1979). In *Cannon,* a female student who was denied admission to a medical school sued the school for violating Title IX. The Supreme Court found that an individual can sue under Title IX even though this right is not spelled out in the language of the statute itself. After this case, private individuals, from students to coaches, could sue arguing that a school or program violated Title IX.

For many years it was unclear what a successful plaintiff could receive if she won a Title IX lawsuit. The law provides that federal funding can be pulled from any school that violates Title IX (20 U.S.C. §1682, 2008), but this punishment has never been imposed. In 1992, the Supreme Court ruled that monetary damages could be available to successful individuals in lawsuits alleging intentional violations of Title IX (*Franklin v. Gwinnett County Public Schools,* 1992).

equal opportunity—
A standard set out in the regulations that enforce Title IX. It refers to the responsibility of a program to provide equivalent athletic opportunities for both sexes.

The regulation and enforcement of the law were left to the then Department of Health, Education and Welfare, which is now the Office for Civil Rights (OCR) within the Department of Education. In 1975, the department passed regulations that spelled out how the law affects athletics. The regulations initially focused on **equal opportunity** (34 C.F.R. 106.41, 2008). They began by repeating Title IX's prohibition of discrimination more specifically within any high school, intercollegiate, club, or intramural athletic program. The regulations mandated that high school and university athletic programs must provide equal opportunity for members of both sexes within several program areas, including provision of equipment and supplies, scheduling of games and practices, provision of locker rooms, and practice and competitive facilities (34 C.F.R. 106.41(c)(2-10)). Next, the interests and abilities of both genders and the selection of sports for both must be effectively accommodated (34 C.F.R. 106.41(c)(1)). The regulations also call for equivalency in the administration of financial assistance (34 C.F.R. 106.37(c), 2008). Although meant to explain in more depth the requirements and enforcement of Title IX, the regulations did not accomplish this goal because they did not provide any way for a school to measure whether it was in compliance with Title IX.

policy interpretation—An interpretation provided by the Department of Education in 1979 setting forth ways in a which a school can assess whether it complies with Title IX and the regulations implementing Title IX.

effective accommodation—
Under the third part of the three-part test provided in the policy interpretation, a program must measure whether it effectively accommodates the interests and abilities of the particular gender in order to provide equal athletic opportunities for both sexes.

Once the regulations were in place, advocates began to sue athletic programs that they perceived were not providing equal opportunities to female athletes. In 1979, the government attempted to provide further clarification with its **policy interpretation** (44 F.R. 239, 1979). The interpretation was designed specifically for university athletics but applies equally to high school, club, and intramural athletic programs. The interpretation is divided into three areas.

- Part 1 deals with financial assistance and requires that such assistance be allocated equally to male and female athletic participants.

- Part 2 deals with equality in the other program areas provided in the regulations, such as facilities and equipment.

- Part 3 deals with **effective accommodation** of the interests and abilities of both sexes in order to provide equal athletic opportunity for members of both sexes. This is the area that has seen the most litigation.

The interpretation is not law, but courts have repeatedly deferred to it because it is the interpretation of the law provided by the federal agency responsible for enforcing Title IX.

Female athletes have always been and continue to be the underrepresented sex, but they have made exponential gains in participation, even though their participation still is not equal to male athletes. For instance, at the high school level, according to the National Federation of State High School Athletic Associations (NFHS), during the 2005-2006 season, 2,953,355 girls participated in high school sports, an all-time record. At the same time 4,206,549 boys participated, the second highest total for boys and the highest level since the late 1970s (NFHS, 2006). At the university level, during the 2005-2006 season, 168,583 women and 224,926 men participated in athletics (NCAA, n.d.). Women thus represent approximately 43% of university athletes and an average of 55.8% of undergraduates (Women's Sports Foundation, 2007). These numbers show that girls and women still do not participate at levels equal to boys and men and are underrepresented in athletics. As a result, the specific enforcement mechanisms applied by the OCR and the courts focus on bringing female athletes up to a level of participation equal to that of male athletes.

Since these regulations were put in place, gender equity disputes have focused on the areas that are discussed in the next sections of this chapter, including participation issues, such as the **three-part test,** separate teams, and claims by athletes from discontinued male teams; scheduling of sports and facilities for each sex; harassment of students by coaches or other athletes; employment discrimination; and federal reporting requirements. Sports administrators must be familiar with how the courts have interpreted the law and regulations by using the interpretation. Much of the interpretation has been further clarified by the OCR in the past 2 decades, as discussed later in this chapter.

three-part test—
Three-part analysis set out in the Title IX policy interpretation that measures whether the interests and abilities of both sexes are being equally accommodated by the provision of equal athletic opportunities as provided in the regulations.

Participation

No one can deny that since the implementation of Title IX, and especially since 1979 when the policy interpretation was developed and the *Cannon* case was decided, athletic opportunities for women have increased exponentially. Before the law's passage, approximately 16,000 university female athletes participated on varsity teams (Carpenter & Acosta, 2008). By 2008, there were 9,101 women's university teams. From 1998 to 2008, 2,755 new women's university teams were created. Still, the nature of these increases continues to be debated.

Lawsuits under Title IX are rare occurrences. Although many schools would not be considered in compliance with Title IX for many reasons, this does not automatically mean that student-athletes are looking to sue these schools. A lawsuit usually is not the first thing on the minds of high school and university athletes. Indeed, many female student-athletes appreciate the opportunities they have been given and do not focus their participation in athletics on comparisons to their male counterparts. Still, because the

OCR is understaffed and its role is to enforce the law rather than monitor schools' compliance with the law, most changes are made only when student-athletes raise the issues and a lawsuit starts. Schools must be vigilant in keeping track of participation opportunities by sex not only to make sure they comply with the law but also to be prepared if their best efforts are still met with legal claims by disgruntled student-athletes.

Although some female advocacy groups believe otherwise, most athletic administrators are not solely focused on providing opportunities to men. Lawyers, courts, and even the OCR staff themselves have struggled for years to properly understand, apply, and enforce Title IX. Often, situations arise when well-intentioned athletic administrators make painful budgetary decisions and do not understand their impact on gender equity compliance. The days when there was evidence of pervasive intentional discriminatory conduct by athletic administrators are long gone. Yet, the majority of athletic departments still do not comply with all aspects of the federal gender equity law. The problem is even worse at the high school level, which has not yet been the focus of extensive evaluation or litigation.

Claims brought in connection with presumed participation issues typically focus on the three-part test created in the regulations and policy interpretation used to implement Title IX, separate teams for athletes of separate genders, and claims by athletes from discontinued male teams.

When administrators and managers analyze participation opportunities for athletes, the focus must start with the regulations. As mentioned earlier, the regulations mandate equal athletic opportunity for both sexes and the effective accommodation of the interests and abilities of both sexes. The policy interpretation sets out a three-part analysis, called the three-part test, to assess whether these interests and abilities are being equally accommodated by the provision of equal athletic opportunities (A Policy Interpretation, 1979):

safe harbor—Criteria set out in a statute that if met allows the entity meeting the requirements of the safe harbor to avoid liability under the statute. The first part of the three-part test, dealing with a comparison of enrolled students to participating student-athletes, is often known as a safe harbor because if a school can meet this first part it does not have to meet the other parts of the test and will not be found to have violated Title IX.

1. The first part looks at whether participation opportunities for male and female students are provided in numbers substantially proportionate to the school's undergraduate enrollment.

2. The second test focuses on whether the institution can show a history and continuing practice of program expansion responsive to the developing interests and abilities of the members of the underrepresented sex.

3. The third test looks to whether an institution can demonstrate that the interests and abilities of the members of that sex have been fully and effectively accommodated by the present program. To determine whether these interests have been accommodated, schools must survey their students to determine their interests and abilities.

This analysis begins with a look at whether participation opportunities for male and female students are in proportion to a school's undergraduate enrollment. This first test has often been known as a **safe harbor,** because courts and the OCR have determined that schools that can demonstrate that the numbers of women and men who participate in athletics are proportionate to the numbers of women and men in the student body will have met the requirements of Title IX. In other words, if a school's enrollment is 50% men and 50% women, there should be close to 50% men and women participating in its athletic program.

The second test focuses on whether the school has continuously expanded programs to meet the interests and abilities of women. In the past, many schools complied with Title IX under this test. However, almost 4 decades after the enactment of Title IX, it is hard to believe that schools will still be able to use this test as a defense against a Title IX claim if they have not expanded their athletic programs during this time.

The third test looks to whether a school has fully and effectively met the interests and abilities of female athletes. To determine whether these interests have been accommodated, schools must survey their students to determine their interests and abilities. Courts and commentators do not agree on whether only enrolled students must be surveyed or whether schools must also survey applicants or admitted students. Schools must rely on their attorneys or the advice of experts who are up to date on the law and its impact on athletics.

To better provide athletic programs that comply with the three-part test, athletic administrators and their attorneys (i.e., university general counsels or outside legal representatives) can look to several cases that have interpreted the test (see, for example, the In the Courtroom case below). However, although the law and its regulations have been in place since the early 1970s, the interpretation of this law and its enforcement have developed over time (particularly over the past 2 decades). An administrator or manager must be constantly vigilant to remain up-to-date on new court decisions and governmental interpretations of gender equity laws.

In the Courtroom

Cohen v. Brown University (1992)

Several members of the women's teams at Brown University sued the university for violating Title IX, specifically each part of the three-part test (*Cohen v. Brown University*, 1992).

Virtually all of Brown's women's varsity teams were created between 1971 and 1977. The only women's team created after that time was the winter track team in 1982. In 1991, Brown funded 31 teams, 16 for men and 15 for women. There were 894 athletes on these teams, of which 566 (63.3%) were men and 328 (36.7%) were women. During the same year there were 2,951 men (52.4%) and 2,683 women (47.6%) enrolled in the university. In May 1991, in response to a university directive to cut 5% to 8% from the budget, the school eliminated university funding for men's golf and water polo and women's gymnastics and volleyball. All four teams were able to raise enough of their own funds to continue to compete, and they remained eligible for postseason and championship

» continued

» continued

events. But the teams lost priority in practice times, and the coaches of the women's teams lost their offices and clerical support.

In analyzing the athletic program, the court began by looking at the first part of the three-part test and found it clear that the university was not in compliance. Although 48.2% of enrolled students were female, they represented only 36.6% of the athletes at the school, a 12% difference. For the second part of the test, the court found that Brown failed to show a history of expanding opportunities for women because the bulk of its expansion of female sports ended in 1977. The court also found that because Brown was cutting off varsity opportunities for women, the school was not effectively accommodating the interests and abilities of its female students as required in the third part of the test. The court ordered the university to restore the women's teams with funding, coaching, and other benefits comparable to the men's teams (*Cohen v. Brown University*, 1992). The school appealed to the U.S. Court of Appeals for the First Circuit (*Cohen v. Brown University*, 1993) and the court affirmed the trial court decision.

After more legal maneuvering, the case returned to the First Circuit in 1996 (*Cohen v. Brown University*, 1996). The court found that Brown did not comply with Title IX under the first or second parts of the three-part test. The school attempted to show that female students were not interested in sports and thus the school was in compliance with the third part of the test. But the court, in analyzing the third part of the test, made clear that such stereotypical notions about women's interests and abilities are exactly the type of discrimination Title IX was enacted to combat. The focus of Title IX is on the underrepresented sex, and women have historically been and continue to be underrepresented in high school sports. Focusing on the third part of the three-part test, and pointing specifically to the 1996 clarification, the court noted that when a school cuts a viable women's team, it is not effectively accommodating the interests and abilities of the female students on that team. Therefore, the court again affirmed the prior decisions holding that Brown University discriminated against the female athletes in violation of Title IX.

A 1996 clarification memorandum by the OCR reiterated that the three-part test gives schools three ways to comply with Title IX (OCR, 1996). Under the first part, schools must ensure that the numbers of male and female athletes receiving benefits (e.g., scholarships, tutoring aid, athletic training) from the school are proportional to the school's total numbers of male and female students; however, proportionality is required only if there are enough athletes to make a viable team in a particular sport.

Under the second part, schools must be responsive to projected female interests and the interests of enrolled students. To comply with this part, schools must be able to demonstrate that they continuously expand opportunities in sport in response to women's interests. Cuts to male sports that increase the proportionate participation of women, although allowed under the first part, are not allowed under the second part.

As to the third part, the OCR made clear that a school must effectively accommodate the interests of all admitted and enrolled students. In reviewing a school, the OCR will consider whether there is unmet interest, whether this interest will sustain a viable team, and whether such a team would likely have opportunity to compete in the region where the school is located. Like the second part, schools cannot cut women's teams under this part because the presence of a team is a clear indication of interest and ability in that team.

A case that focused on the three-part test was *Boucher v. Syracuse University* (1998). The case, which involved members of the women's club lacrosse and club softball teams at Syracuse University, focused on the application of the three-part test. In 1971, the university established its women's athletic program with basketball, fencing, swimming, tennis, and volleyball teams. Field hockey replaced fencing in 1972. Women's crew was added in 1977 and indoor and outdoor track in 1981. The OCR performed a Title IX compliance review from 1980 to 1982 and found the school to be in compliance. In 1996 the school added a women's soccer team, and in 1997 it added a women's lacrosse team. During the time of the litigation the school had 10 men's and 11 women's teams, and it planned to start a women's softball team in the 1999-2000 season. All other sports were club sports, meaning that they were funded by funds raised by the student participants.

The student-plaintiffs alleged that the university was in violation of Title IX because it did not provide effective accommodation of their interests and abilities. The plaintiffs claimed that because they were members of successful club teams, the university should recognize their participation as the interest and ability necessary to warrant varsity status and raise them to the varsity level with all of the benefits and university funding a varsity team would receive.

Pointing to the policy interpretation, Syracuse argued that it complied with Title IX under part 2—that it had a history and continuing practice of program expansion for women. In reviewing this defense, the court found that although there was a gap from 1982 to 1995, when no new women's teams were added, the number of female varsity athletes still increased during this time, and the addition of new teams since 1995 also demonstrated a history of expanding opportunities for women. The court also noted that although the university did not have a formal policy of monitoring the interests of its students in order to expand athletic opportunities for them, the athletic director informally monitored this interest by reviewing club sport participation and sport-related interests at the national and regional levels. Therefore, the expansion in the 1990s was in direct response to the interests and abilities of female students. As a result, the court found that Syracuse met the second part of the three-part test.

For many, the results of this case were disconcerting. Although the university had begun to expand opportunities for women, this was after a 15-year lapse and did not take into account thriving club sports teams that were clear indications of interest by female students. Many athletic programs have similar patterns of growth, with large gains for women in the 1970s and little gain after 1980. However, this case is clear evidence that courts do not want to impose their judgment over that of athletic administrators. When there is evidence that administrators have made their best efforts to meet the interests of female students, courts typically will allow the administrators to meet these interests in the manner they see fit.

Separate Teams

contact sport exception— Argument that contact sports such as football should not be taken into account in regard to a school's compliance with Title IX. Courts have consistently held that there is no such exception from the statute.

Although many advocates have argued that one way to ensure equity in participation is to have teams made up of both sexes, the regulations do allow for separate teams. Specifically, schools may sponsor separate teams for members of each sex when the selection of team members is based on athletic skills or the activity involved is a contact sport (34 C.F.R. 106.41(b), 2008). This language has led to what some call the **contact sport exception,** an argument that contact sports such as football should not be taken into account in regard to a school's compliance with Title IX. However, although this language allows for separate teams, courts have consistently found that there is no contact sport exception, and so football and other contact sports must be counted when evaluating a school's compliance with Title IX.

This is where many schools run into problems. No other sport can compare to a football team's roster size. Therefore, no other sport will receive benefits, from scholarship aid to facilities, that can compare to the benefits received by a football team. At the same time, because of revenues associated with larger crowds and bowl games at the highest level of football, no sport produces as much revenue for an athletic department as football. Still, universities must include the football team in any calculations involving the three-part test or other parts of Title IX. As a result, the actual number of teams at a school can often be misleading if one of those teams is a football team. If a school has 12 male teams and 12 female teams, an outside observer may believe that the school is in compliance. However, the football team may be equivalent to four or five female teams, so there still may be problems.

Another interesting situation is when an athlete is allowed to participate on a team of another gender. For example, Heather Mercer was an all-state kicker in high school and tried out for the Duke University football team. In her first year she practiced with the team but did not play in a game until an annual intrasquad game, where she kicked the winning field goal. After that game she was featured on ESPN and the coach told her she had made the team. The next year she again did not participate in any games, but she was listed on the team roster and practiced with the team. However, during that year she faced different forms of discrimination including offensive comments from the coach. At the beginning of the next season she was dropped from the team.

Schools with large football rosters still must comply with all aspects of Title IX. The number of football players must be factored into Title IX compliance.

© Human Kinetics

Mercer sued, arguing that the decision to cut her from the team was discriminatory because other less qualified walk-ons were kept on the team (*Mercer v. Duke University,* 1999). Relying on the contact sport exception, the district court dismissed her claim. The appellate court reviewed the language of the regulations and, pointing to the regulations' overall prohibition against discrimination in all circumstances, found that once an institution allows a member of one sex to try out for a team operated for the other sex, even in a contact sport, the institution cannot discriminate against that individual. Subsequently, a jury awarded Mercer $1 in compensatory damages, $2 million in punitive damages, and attorney's fees. The university then appealed, and the court vacated the punitive damage award, finding that punitive damages are not available for private actions to enforce Title IX (*Mercer v. Duke University,* 2002).

What did Heather Mercer get as a result of winning her case? Not much. She received $1 in damages from the university, and she was reimbursed for the costs of her attorneys. The university was not forced to reinstate her on the team, and even if the court had ordered the school to place her on the team, the remedy would have been insufficient because she had graduated by the time the litigation ended in 2005.

Although the court made clear that there is no specific contact sport exception as previously understood, the result of the case means that allowing female athletes to try out for men's teams is very risky, because then it will be difficult to cut these athletes from the team for any reason. Instead, universities are better served by keeping separate teams as allowed under the regulations.

Cutting Teams

Since the 1970s, a consistent criticism of the application of federal gender equity laws is that they have resulted in the cutting of many male teams, especially at the university level. In the 1980s and 1990s, many schools decided that in order to come into compliance with Title IX, they had to eliminate men's swimming, golf, and wrestling teams. Much of the focus of this litigation has been on the proportionality test contained in the first part of the three-part test. Advocates for men's sports have claimed that this test has forced schools to cut male teams or that schools that seemingly do not provide proportionate opportunities actually do. One problem is that the OCR has never set a ratio that can be seen as proportionate. Therefore, schools do not know whether a 10% difference between the percentage of enrolled female students and the percentage of female students who participate in athletics is enough to satisfy the test. Courts are left to interpret the facts case by case.

In 1993, the University of Illinois decided to cut men's swimming and fencing, and men's and women's diving. The decision was made mainly in response to a large athletic budget deficit. However, since 1982 the OCR had determined that the university was not in compliance with Title IX. In 1993, although women made up 44% of the student body, they represented only 23.4% of the school's athletes. Therefore, even with the cuts, the percentage of women participating was still substantially lower than the percentage of men participating and the percentage of women enrolled. Members of the men's swimming team claimed that the decision to cut the team was illegal because the regulations and policy interpretation violated Title IX and the three-part test mandated a quota system where schools had to constantly push for numerical equality in athletics. The court disagreed, finding not only that it had to defer to the agency rules but that the university's decision to cut the men's teams was specifically an effort to comply with the law, and so the male athletes' claims were dismissed (*Kelly v. Board of Trustees,* 1994).

Of course this is not the end of the story. Male athletes continued to sue universities when their teams were cut. In fact, in 2001, the Secretary of Education's own Commission on Opportunity in Athletics argued that the proportionality test in part 1 of the three-part test has caused schools to cut men's teams. However, the OCR disagreed, pointing out that although men's teams could be cut in order to come into compliance with the law, not only is this method of compliance disfavored, it is also contrary to the spirit of the law in providing opportunities for all (OCR, 2003). Predictably, the lawsuits by male athletes and advocacy groups over these cuts have continued.

In another case, former members of the disbanded male tennis, wrestling, and soccer teams at Miami University of Ohio sued the school, claiming that by cutting their teams the university violated Title IX's prohibitions against eliminating programs on the basis of sex (*Miami Univ. Wrestling Club v. Miami Univ.,* 2002). The school had worked hard to come into compliance, but by

1997, although female students were 55% of enrollment, they represented only 47% of athletes participating in sports. Under the first prong of the three-part test. the university interpreted that this disparity would not be seen as providing proportional opportunities to both sexes. The university also knew that there were unmet interests for women in equestrian, crew, golf, lacrosse, and water polo. After conducting a fiscal analysis, the university administrators realized that they could not afford to add all of these new teams. Therefore, the administrators determined that the only way the university could come into compliance with Title IX was by cutting four men's teams. Reviewing the situation, the court noted that the policy interpretation recognizes that Title IX can lead to difficult choices because universities do not have unlimited funds. Dismissing the male athletes' claims, the court found that gender equity laws provide only members of the underrepresented sex with rights; they do not provide males, part of the overrepresented sex, with any such protection. Therefore, cutting men's opportunities was a reasonable way for the university to comply with Title IX.

This has not satisfied male athletes who have lost their opportunity to participate or advocacy groups such as the College Sports Council, which posits that cutting men's teams is also a form of prohibited discrimination. In answer to this, Congress asked the U.S. General Accounting Office (GAO) to research why universities had cut men's teams. The 2001 report found that from the 1981-1982 to 1998-1999 seasons, opportunities for women increased from 90,000 to 163,000 and women gained 3,784 teams (GAO, 2001). At the same time, male opportunities stayed at a higher level as male participants increased from 220,000 to 232,000 and men gained 36 teams (GAO, 2001). Overall, 386 male teams were cut whereas 150 female teams were cut. When the majority of women's teams were added, there were no cuts in male teams; instead, these schools relied on revenue from other sports or outside sources to fund these new teams. The report found that teams were added in response to female students' interests in particular sports and in order to meet gender equity requirements, whereas men's teams were cut for several reasons, including lack of student interest, budget concerns, and the need to comply with gender equity laws. The report found that for the majority of schools, female participation increases were not at the expense of men's teams.

In 2007, the GAO (which had since been renamed the Government Accountability Office, still GAO) released another report finding that both men's and women's participation in intercollegiate athletics increased from 1991 to 2005. However, whereas men's participation increased 21% over this time and women's participation increased 63%, men's overall numbers in university athletics were still higher than women's (GAO, 2007). Overall participation in most male sports still increased during this time, except in wrestling, which had significant declines in participation.

Advocates for men's sports continue to disagree with the GAO reports and with the use of Title IX, blaming the law and particularly the three-part test for the cuts in their sports. In 2004, the National Wrestling Coaches Association (NWCA) sued the Department of Education trying to get the department to rescind the three-part test, claiming that its misapplication had caused the illegal cuts in men's teams (*National Wrestling Coaches Assoc. v. Department of Educ.*, 2004). The NWCA argued that the GAO report showed that the teams were cut as a result of the application of the three-part test. The court disagreed, finding instead that the report was inconclusive as to the primary reason for these cuts and that many schools had decided to cut male teams as a result of their own budgetary decisions.

Athletic administrators are faced with many difficult choices. Even non-revenue-producing sports can cost a lot of money to maintain. Although it is nice to believe that a school can continue to add women's teams in some effort to rightfully provide opportunities for women, this often is unrealistic because of the financial costs involved. Therefore, honest and fair-minded athletic and university administrators must make difficult decisions and often have to cut men's teams to comply with the law. The following example provides some perspective.

Many schools are faced with cutting men's teams in order to comply with Title IX.

© Icon SMI

If a school has an 80% representation of male athletes among all of its athletic programs, whereas females represent 80% of all enrolled students (but only 20% of the school's athletes), the school does not have to cut male opportunities to comply with the law unless it follows part 1 of the three-part test. If it follows part 1, the school will have to work hard to ensure that the level of female participation in sports approaches 80%—the number of female enrolled students. However, the university does have options, because it can comply with Title IX under the second part of the test by showing a history of program expansion for female students, or it can follow the third part and comply by demonstrating that it is meeting the interests and abilities of its students.

Although schools can cut male teams and opportunities to come into compliance with Title IX, the reverse is not true. In the early 1980s, the OCR conducted a compliance review at Colorado State University (CSU), finding that opportunities for men and women were not proportional to enrollment. During the 3 years reviewed, the differences between women enrolled and women athletes were 7.5%, 12.5%, and 12.7%. In 1992, CSU announced that it was cutting the varsity women's fast-pitch softball team and men's baseball. Similar to the male athletes mentioned previously, the women sued, claiming that the school violated Title IX when it cut the women's team (*Roberts v. Colorado State Board of Agriculture,* 1993). At the time the disparity between enrolled and participating women was 10.5%, and the court found that this percentage was insufficient even though it was a lesser disparity than before the teams were cut. Turning to the second part of the three-part test, the school also could not show any history and continuing expansion of opportunities for female athletes. As to the third part of the test, the fact that CSU was cutting a softball team that played a competitive schedule and had interested and able participants was evidence that the school was not meeting the interests and abilities of the underrepresented sex. Therefore, the court ordered the school to reinstate the team and to provide it with the benefits associated with varsity status.

The *Roberts* court acknowledged that faced with budgetary constraints, most schools will not be able to comply with Title IX by continuing to expand opportunities for female athletes. In addition, schools cannot claim that cutting large men's teams, such as lacrosse with a 40-man roster, somehow results in expanded opportunities for women. Although the percentages of women participating may increase as a result of cuts in men's teams, such cuts do not add any opportunities for women.

So what can a university do? Faced with financial difficulties and compliance with federal law, a university can cut a men's team to meet the first part of the three-part test. This is not preferred or favored, but it is one way for a university to meet its obligations. A university cannot cut women's teams at the same time even if these cuts would alleviate financial concerns. However, things are not this cut and dried: Creative budgetary planning and support of viable athletic programs can allow a university to avoid cutting opportunities for anyone. A university has many options when it comes to complying with Title IX, and administrators who complain that their only options are to cut opportunities may not be running efficient and financially solvent athletic departments in the first place.

Interest Surveys and Recent Guidance

Schools have always been able to survey students to determine whether the school is meeting the third part of the test by fully and effectively accommodating the interests and abilities of the underrepresented sex. Perhaps in further response to the Title IX Commission, in 2005, the OCR issued another clarification (OCR, 2005). According to this clarification, of 130 institutions the OCR investigated from 1992 to 2002, two thirds complied with the third part of the test. The clarification provides a Web-based prototype survey that schools can use, which is based on surveys that schools have used in the past, and a user's guide (available at www.ed.gov/about/offices/list/ocr/docs/title9guidanceadditional.pdf). A school that uses this survey can be found to be in compliance with the third test unless enough female students at the school have enough interest in a sport to sustain a team, if they have sufficient ability to play the sport, and if they likely will find other teams in the school's region with which to compete.

Many female advocates and the NCAA criticized the clarification because it allows a school to interpret nonresponse as a lack of interest. However, although this is allowed, the clarification also states that a school must receive a high level of responses (approaching 85%), the survey must be conducted periodically, and schools cannot use the survey results to eliminate teams. Most important, if a school finds that it has sufficient unmet interest and ability to sustain a team and has reasonable expectations of intercollegiate competition in that sport within the school's competitive region, the school is obligated to create a varsity team or elevate a club or intramural sport.

Although this clarification is not a rewrite of the interpretation, some believe that the clarification changes the way in which schools can and will comply with the three-part test. The NCAA's Executive Committee passed a resolution urging the Department of Education to rescind the clarification on the grounds that it is inconsistent with the 1996 and 2003 clarifications and basic principles of Title IX (NCAA Executive Committee, 2005). Others claimed that counting nonresponse as lack of interest and limiting the survey to enrolled and admitted students violates gender equity law. The Department of Education responded quickly, stating that the third prong remained the same and did not change a school's obligation to comply with the law.

Facilities and Scheduling

As mentioned earlier, the regulations enforcing Title IX discuss other program areas. Although these program areas have not been the subject of extensive litigation at the university level, two areas have been the subject of litigation at the high school level: the scheduling of games and practices and the provision of locker rooms and practice and competitive facilities. For these program areas, the policy interpretation sets out a complicated scheme of enforcement.

The governing principle of the policy interpretation is that male and female athletes should receive equivalent treatment, benefits, and opportunities. The interpretation created a four-part analysis of these program areas:

1. Assessment of benefits and treatment
2. Analysis of nondiscriminatory factors
3. Additional factors to analyze factors from the regulations
4. Overall determination of compliance

The first step is the assessment. This assessment compares the benefits and treatment given to both sexes to see whether they are comparable. For example, if both male and female soccer teams participate in the same season, they are comparable in the assessment of the scheduling program area.

Second, there can be differences in the provision of these program areas if the differences in what is provided to male and female athletes are attributable to nondiscriminatory factors. Therefore, because of the nature of football, schools can have football programs for male athletes that provide more roster spots, larger practice facilities, and other unique benefits, as long as the overall athletic program benefits provided to both male and female athletes are equivalent.

Third, the interpretation provides additional factors that must be analyzed to assess compliance with the 10 factors provided in the regulations. For example, the regulations provide that athletic programs must provide equal opportunity in scheduling of games and practice times for male and female athletes (34 C.F.R. 106.41(c)(3), 2008). The interpretation then explains that in order to assess whether the scheduling of male and female sports is equal, one must look at the number of competitive events per sport, the number and length of practice opportunities, the time of day competitive events are scheduled, and the opportunity to engage in preseason and postseason competition (A Policy Interpretation, 1979).

Fourth, an overall determination of compliance is made. If the school has policies related to these program areas that are discriminatory, the school will not be in compliance with Title IX. If there are significant disparities in the provision of benefits to members of opposite sexes, for instance, if all male teams have better practice facilities than women and women do not have an advantage over men in any other benefits provided to them, the school will not be in compliance. Finally, if there is one benefit provided to male athletes that in itself is substantial, for instance, if male athletes received significantly higher levels of financial aid, it may be enough to deny equal opportunity to female athletes.

This complicated area of the law can best be understood by looking at a sample case. In *McCormick v. School District of Mamoroneck* (2004), two Olympic-level female soccer players sued several New York school districts because girls' soccer was scheduled in the spring and boys' soccer in the fall. The districts put girls' soccer in the spring in response to a survey showing that the majority of female soccer players preferred to play in the spring, and this allowed girls' field hockey, a highly popular sport, to be scheduled in the fall. However, because girls' soccer was scheduled in the spring, girls could not participate in the regional and state soccer championships, which took place in the fall. In addition, university coaches recruit female soccer players in the fall season, and so girls who played in the spring may have missed out on scholarship opportunities.

In reviewing the girls' claim, the court focused on the fact that girls who participated in soccer could not participate in postseason competition, a specific factor provided in the policy interpretation to assess compliance. The district argued that it would be costly to move girls' soccer because there were not enough coaches or enough field space and that it would negatively affect other female sports. The court found this to be unpersuasive and found that this one disparity was enough to show that the scheduling of girls' soccer in the spring was a violation of Title IX. As a result, even though the majority of the girls preferred the scheduling of soccer as it was, the school districts had to change the schedule and move soccer to the fall season with boys' soccer.

When dealing with program areas such as scheduling, athletic administrators cannot rely on what they perceive as serving the interests of the majority. Instead, they must consider the effect of the schedule on participants of both sexes and make sure that the schedule is set to provide equivalent benefits to each sex.

The issue is the same in relation to practice and competitive facilities. The policy interpretation sets out other factors that must be analyzed, including the quality and availability of the facilities, exclusivity of use of the facilities, availability and quality of locker rooms, and maintenance and preparation of these facilities. Schools have encountered problems when the facilities used by their teams are not comparable.

High school girls and boys in Minnesota have historically participated in the state hockey tournament in different facilities. The girls' tournament began in a 3,400-seat facility, but because the seating was insufficient for attendance, the tournament moved to the State Fair Coliseum, which seats 5,200. The boys' tournament is held at the XCEL Energy Center, the home of the NHL's Minnesota Wild, which seats 17,000. The OCR began to review the tournament in 2000. The Minnesota State High School League asked for bids to host the girls' tournament, but the professional sports facility was not interested. The league told the OCR that it was moving the girls' tournament to the brand-new Ridder Arena on the campus of the University of Minnesota, a newer facility than the XCEL Center, but Ridder only seats 2,700. The OCR approved of the move. The 2002 girls' tournament drew 15,551 fans whereas the boys' tournament drew 120,000 fans. In reviewing the organization of the state hockey tournaments, the court noted that differences in the provision of competitive facilities are allowed only if these differences do not limit the potential for women's athletic events to increase in spectator appeal (*Mason v. Minnesota State High School League,* 2004). The court found that restricting the girls to a smaller facility could restrict the growth of the girls' hockey tournament and necessarily restricts the spectators, who can add to the success of the tournament.

At the university level, with the possible exception of some successful women's basketball teams, female athletes are often forced to practice or play in facilities that are not comparable to those available to male athletes. Even if men and women are in the same facilities, male athletes often have the better time slots for practice (morning or afternoon) and competition (weekends or prime time on weekdays); female athletes often suffer through early-morning practices and play in the middle of the week when spectators cannot easily support them. It will not be surprising if female university athletes eventually claim that their practice and game schedules and the facilities they use for practice and games are not comparable to those of men. Sports administrators must ensure that female athletes are given equal priority in scheduling games and practices and are allowed to play in facilities that are comparable to those of male athletes. Administrators who cannot ensure equity in these areas must increase benefits to female athletes in other areas, such as providing better equipment and supplies or better locker rooms, to offset this disparity.

Similar problems have been seen at the high school level when comparing girls' softball with boys' baseball teams. In one case, high school boys' baseball was provided with an electronic scoreboard, batting cage, concession stands, lighting for night games, and quality bleachers. Girls' softball received none of these benefits and played before smaller crowds because of dilapidated bleachers. In another high school, the boys played on baseball fields on campus that had all of the same amenities just listed, including a large storage area for their equipment. The girls were forced to play at public fields designed for boys' softball that contained a single small shed for their equipment. In both situations, the court found that the disparities in facilities and scheduling were violations of Title IX (*Daniels v. School Board of Brevard County,* 1997; *Landow v. School Board of Brevard County,* 2000).

The school board argued that it provided equal funding to each team so it could not be responsible for these inequities. Each team raised its own funds through a booster club, and the boys' teams were able to raise more funds for their facilities. However, equality in funding is also a responsibility of the athletic administration, and so it was the board's responsibility to put a system in place that ensured equal opportunity in the athletic facilities for baseball and softball. The board even attempted to remedy the problem by taking away some of the benefits provided to the boys; for instance, by taking away the scoreboard for baseball. However, although cutting men's teams can bring a school into compliance with the effective accommodation requirements of the three-part test, imposing disadvantages on boys without improving benefits provided to girls does nothing to lead to equality.

Someday universities will face similar scrutiny. The focus could be university basketball programs, where men typically play in better facilities with higher seating capacities than do women. Universities may claim that they cannot bear the cost to provide similar opportunities for female basketball players, but financial considerations such as this are not legitimate excuses for otherwise discriminatory behavior. Intent to discriminate is not the issue: The law makes clear that the assessment is of the program factor, such as scheduling or the facility. There is no requirement that the reasons for inequalities (e.g., women are forced to play in an inferior facility or under a worse schedule) constitute some form of intentional discrimination. The differences may be enough to show that the school or university is in violation of Title IX.

Schools cannot hide the details about what is provided to their male or female athletes. The *Equity in Athletics Disclosure Act of 1998* (Pub. Law. 105-244, 1998) requires that all universities that receive federal student aid and have intercollegiate athletic programs prepare reports that track this financial aid, athletic revenues, and other resources. These reports are provided to the public on the Office of Postsecondary Education's Web site at http://ope.ed.gov/athletics/. The purpose of this reporting is to provide students and their parents more information about the schools these students may attend.

Schools must also be very careful dealing with coaches or other employees who complain about differences in treatment between male and female sports. In 2005, the Supreme Court recognized that it is illegal for schools to retaliate against a coach or other employee who complains of inequalities that may be violations of Title IX (*Jackson v. Birmingham Board of Educ.,* 2005). In this case, the coach of the girls' basketball team complained that his team was not given adequate funding or access to practice facilities and equipment compared with the boys' team. He never claimed that anyone discriminated against him. He was soon fired as coach but kept his job as a physical education teacher. Although Title IX does not provide a way for a coach to sue unless he is the subject of discrimination, the Court found that retaliation against a coach who complains of inequalities in an athletic program is also a form of discrimination.

Most Title IX issues are brought forth because of individuals who complain about inequalities, like this coach. Athletes, especially at the high school level, may not notice the differences between girls' and boys' sports or may simply accept that things have always been one way. These students may not realize that "the way things have always been" is still illegal.

Sexual Harassment

Another area of concern relates to conduct that athletes face that may cause them serious harm and discomfort and that may affect the nature of their participation. Many athletes have faced **sexual harassment** by coaches or players. This not only has harmed them physically and emotionally but also has ruined any chance they have to participate in athletics (see chapter 6 for a discussion of sexual harassment in the employment context). Unfortunately, it was not until 1992 that the courts clearly showed that sexual harassment by coaches was barred under Title IX.

sexual harassment— Unwelcome conduct of a sexual nature. This conduct is a form of sexual discrimination that is prohibited under Title IX.

Christine Franklin was a high school student subject to continued harassment from a coach who was also her teacher. The coach asked her about her sex life, asked whether she would sleep with older men, and forcibly kissed her in the school parking lot. After she complained, the school investigated the coach but did not dismiss him. In fact, the school discouraged her from pressing charges until the coach resigned at the end of the year. She complained to the OCR, which found that the school had allowed her to be subject to sexual harassment but agreed to let the school remedy the situation by putting together a grievance procedure to deal with similar situations in the future. Finding that this did nothing to help her, Franklin sued. The Supreme Court found that Title IX places a duty on schools to stop teachers and coaches from discriminating against students in any school activities (*Franklin v. Gwinnett County Public Schools,* 1992). In addition, because sexual harassment is a form of discrimination, it is also barred. Because of this case, all victims of sexual harassment or other intentionally discriminatory conduct under Title IX can sue for monetary damages.

The OCR attempted to clarify the requirements that schools must follow with its 1997 and 2000 *Sexual Harassment Guidance.* A student can always sue the coach or teacher who harassed her or him. However, the real issue in athletics is determining when a school can be liable for the harassing conduct of its teachers and coaches. The reason is that the school typically will have more financial resources than an individual coach or teacher. Therefore, a plaintiff will most likely attempt to sue the school in order to receive a higher level of potential damages. Because sexual harassment is a form of prohibited sex discrimination under Title IX, schools must have procedures in place to assist students who face such conduct. The procedures must cover both male and female students who participate in any sport or other extracurricular activity no matter whether the activity takes place at school or off campus. A school may be liable for damages for the harassing conduct of a coach who tells a player that she must submit to the coach's advances to make the team **(quid pro quo sexual harassment).** A school might also be liable if the coach's overall conduct is so severe, as in *Franklin,* that it constitutes **hostile environment sexual harassment,** which is harassment that interferes with the athlete's ability to perform. Factors used to determine whether there is a hostile environment include the degree to which the conduct affects one or more students; the type, frequency, and duration of the conduct; the identity of and relationship between parties; the number of individuals involved; the age and sex of alleged harasser; the size of the school or program, location of the incidents, and context; other incidents at the school; and incidents of gender-based nonsexual harassment. Schools have the chance to respond to harassment and fire or discipline a coach, but if they do not take immediate steps to remedy the problem they will be liable under Title IX.

The challenge with sexual harassment cases is that it is often difficult to tell how much harassment is too much such that the school should be liable. The OCR regulations state that harassment must be severe, persistent, and pervasive, and they provide many factors to analyze whether conduct rises to this level. However, each situation is different and although some athletes can laugh or shrug off the advances of their coaches, others will find such conduct to be debilitating. The best policy is for schools to make clear that any conduct that could be interpreted as possibly harassing (such as a male coach hugging female players) will be monitored and should be avoided.

Another issue is that a student may only sue a school for harassment when she or he can also show that a school official in a position of authority knew that something was happening and failed to act (*Gebser v. Lago Vista Independent School District,* 1998). As a result, a student who has been harassed must first notify the proper administrative authorities in the athletic department or at the university or school. According to the courts and the OCR guidance, potential responsibility for sexual harassment begins when school officials first learn of the conduct. If a school administrator knows of the problem and does nothing to remedy the situation, the school itself may be liable for the conduct of these employees. The courts and

quid pro quo sexual harassment— Harassment whereby a coach tells a player that she must submit to the coach's advances to make the team. A school may be liable for damages as a result of the coach's conduct.

hostile environment sexual harassment— Harassment by an employee, student, or third party that is sufficiently severe, persistent, or pervasive to limit a student's ability to participate in or benefit from an educational program, including an athletic program.

deliberate indifference—
Behavior whereby someone in authority knows that sexual harassment has taken place and does not respond to remedy the problem.

regulations have named this type of behavior **deliberate indifference;** however, courts have struggled to define this term.

Students can also sue a school as a result of harassing conduct by classmates or teammates. In one situation, a fifth-grade student kept telling her teacher that a boy was constantly picking on her. Perhaps surprisingly, this fifth-grade boy was constantly making sexual comments to the girl. The teacher supposedly told the principal but neither did anything that stopped the boy's behavior. As a result of this situation, the Supreme Court found for the first time that a student could sue a school as a result of harassment by another student (*Davis v. Monroe County Board of Education,* 1999). The Court found that peer sexual harassment is prohibited under Title IX when the school acts with deliberate indifference and the harassment is so severe and pervasive that it bars the victim's access to an educational opportunity. When the fifth-grade boy's harassment ruined the fifth-grade girl's ability to achieve in the classroom, it was considered severe conduct and prohibited under Title IX.

At the university level, sexually harassing conduct is often even more severe. Since 1995, several female students at the University of Colorado have complained that they were sexually assaulted by football recruits and players. One such student was Lisa Simpson. She alleged that several football recruits and current players sexually assaulted her at a party at her apartment. She reported the incidents to the university, and its Office of Judicial Affairs charged several of the football players with violations of the school's code of conduct. However, even though the district attorney's office charged several of the players with felonies, the school would not pursue sexual assault charges against them and none of the players lost any eligibility to play football. Simpson sued the school under Title IX, claiming that the school allowed a sexually hostile environment to exist on campus that led to her assault. The trial court found that even though the school was aware of earlier incidents, it was not put on notice of the specific type of severe harassment that she faced. This lack of knowledge was not the required deliberate indifference, and it was unclear whether the school could have prevented what happened to Simpson (*Simpson v. University of Colorado,* 2005).

Simpson appealed, and the appellate court focused on whether the university violated Title IX specifically within its official policies. The court discussed a great deal of evidence of sexual harassment involving football players in football programs throughout the country and specifically at Colorado. This harassment often took place during recruiting visits. The court found that the football coach at Colorado knew of these problems but did not supervise the recruiting program to avoid these issues even though he was repeatedly told of the need to do so; the court also found that the coach discouraged women from complaining about sexual harassment, and he always supported players in these situations. After reviewing all of this evidence, the appellate court reversed the trial court and found that the need for more or different training of player hosts within the recruiting program was so obvious, and the inadequacy of the program was so likely to result in

Title IX violations, that the coach was deliberately indifferent to the harassment that Simpson suffered (*Simpson v. University of Colorado,* 2007).

Before the case returned to court to discuss any possible damages for Simpson, the university settled. Still, there are no real winners in this situation. Simpson received $2.85 million from the university but this was 6 years after she was raped. The university spent approximately $3 million on the litigation, and 11 of 12 top university administrators either were fired or left, including the president, two chancellors, and the athletic director. The case is clear evidence that university athletic administrators must supervise their programs at all times and not merely on the practice or playing field. This will protect the university from potential liability, and, more important, it could protect students at the university from potential harassment.

Employment Discrimination

Another important area of gender equity law concerns employment discrimination faced by female employees in athletics. (See chapter 6 for discussion of employment discrimination as it relates to employment law.) In the United States in 1972, 90% of the coaches of women's teams and administrators of women's programs were women. By 2008, only 42.8% of these coaches and 21.3% of these administrators were women. At the same time, only 2% of men's teams were coached by women, 20.6% of all teams had a female head coach, 27.3% of head athletic trainers were female, and 11.3% of sports information directors were female (Carpenter & Acosta, 2008). Overt discrimination against women may not be the only reason for these numbers, but unfortunately the gains women have made in participation in athletics have not been mirrored by gains in employment within university athletics.

Although the focus of employment discrimination litigation in sports has been in intercollegiate athletics, the lack of female representation in employment is not restricted to university sports. In 2008, 34% of the directors and managers and 20% of senior executives in the Major League Baseball central office were women, whereas at the team level 16% of vice presidents and 19% of senior administrators were women (Lapchick & Martin, 2008). In 2007, women held 39% of the professional positions in the National Basketball Association league office. At the same time, there was one female team president in the NBA, and 17% of team vice presidents, 25% of team senior administrative positions, and 41% of team professional administrative positions were women (Lapchick, 2007).

Women who believe that they are being discriminated against because of conduct they are forced to endure while on the job or because of inequities in salary or other work-related benefits can file two possible claims, the first under the Equal Pay Act of 1963 (EPA) (29 U.S.C. §206(d), 2008) and the second under Title VII (42 U.S.C. § 2000e-2, 2008).

The Equal Pay Act prohibits discrimination in wages between employees on the basis of sex for **equal work** on jobs that require equal skill, effort, and responsibility, under similar working conditions. To be considered to

equal work— The concept that individuals of either sex must be paid similar wages for jobs that are substantially equal, although the skill, effort, and responsibility of the jobs need not be identical. However, the jobs must be substantially equal except for the fact that one employee is paid higher wages.

entail equal work, two jobs don't have to require identical skill, effort, and responsibility; instead, the two jobs must be substantially equal except for the fact that one employee is paid more even though he performs what is basically the same job.

Marianne Stanley was a highly successful women's basketball coach at the University of Southern California (USC), a team that had won a national championship. She complained because her salary of $60,000 with a $6,000 housing allowance was much less than the salary of men's basketball coach, George Raveling, who was making between $130,000 and $150,000. After extensive negotiations, Stanley was offered a raise to $96,000, but eventually the university withdrew the offer after she continued to complain that she should be paid as much as Raveling. Stanley sued USC under the EPA, claiming that she was denied equal pay for equal work (*Stanley v. University of Southern California,* 1994).

To start an EPA claim, Stanley had to pick another individual employed by the same employer in a substantially similar job. Obviously, because both Stanley and Raveling were basketball coaches, this choice was simple. The analysis then shifted to the differences between the jobs. Raveling had significant public relations and promotion responsibilities that resulted in 90 times more revenue per year for the men's team compared with the women's team. He was involved in 12 outside speaking engagements, had been a coach for 31 years, had an extensive marketing background, had written two novels, and was a significant public relations representative on behalf of USC. In Stanley's 17 years as coach, her teams were much more successful than Raveling's, but Stanley was not required to engage in the same intense level of promotional and marketing activities. The court noted that these significant job differences resulted in a difference in responsibilities and justified different levels of pay (*Stanley v. University of Southern California,* 1994).

Sports employers may reward employees for greater professional experience and education, as Raveling possessed, without violating the EPA. Employers may also consider an employee's marketplace value and pay a more valuable employee at a higher level. Raveling was a nationally known and renowned coach, and the market for coaches at his level in men's basketball also justified a higher salary for him. The point is that employers can legitimately take these types of considerations into account when assessing salaries. Paying individuals more based on experience, education, and marketplace value will not be found to be discriminatory. What is discriminatory is paying a man more than a woman in a similar job, based simply on the sex of the individual involved.

At USC, the men's team generated higher attendance (men 237,950, women 41,917), more media interest, larger donations (men $98,000, women $828), and substantially more revenue (men $4 million, women $59,918) per year. These team-related factors also justified a higher level of pay for Raveling. Stanley argued that the school did not allocate funds to the women's team, so that they suffered from lower revenue and attendance. The court disagreed, finding that USC made a business decision and could not be responsible for societal discrimination and stereotyped notions of women's sports that cause most people to prefer to watch men's and not women's sports. The court also found that revenue generation is an important factor in determining whether responsibilities and working conditions are substantially equal, and in this case, the differences showed that they were not.

The differences in Raveling's job showed that he had to put in more effort and had a higher level of responsibility than Stanley. In addition, his marketing background and extensive coaching career put him at a higher skill level. Therefore, Raveling and Stanley were not similar and USC was justified in paying Raveling a higher salary.

In 1997, the Equal Employment Opportunity Commission (EEOC), the agency in charge of enforcing employment discrimination law, published a notice related specifically to sex discrimination in the compensation of coaches (U.S. Equal Employment Opportunity Commission, 1997). The notice discussed affirmative defenses available to a school when it has been sued for violating the law. In addition to discussing valid seniority and merit systems, the notice also mentioned several factors other than sex that can justify salary differences. These factors mirrored some of what was discussed in *Stanley,* including production of revenue, marketplace value, experience, and education. These are the exact factors USC used to rebut Stanley's claims. In the end, unless a female coach is hired at the same time as a male coach, both have the same level of experience, and both are given the same responsibilities by the athletic department, it will be very difficult for a female coach to bring a successful EPA claim against a school.

The notice made clear that in addition to making claims under the EPA, coaches may be able to bring a separate claim under Title VII. Title VII prohibits discrimination against any employee based on his or her sex in compensation and other benefits associated with employment. Title VII is different than the EPA because an employee does not have to show that she or he performed equal work; the employee merely has to show some negative job action, such as termination or a reduction in pay, that was taken because of the employee's sex (see table 8.1).

Table 8.1 Statutory Requirements for Title VII and the Equal Pay Act

	Title VII	Equal Pay Act
Prohibitions	Prohibits discrimination against any employee on the basis of sex in compensation and other benefits associated with employment.	Prohibits discrimination in wages between employees on the basis of sex for equal work on jobs that require equal skill, effort, and responsibility, under similar working conditions.
Requirement	Plaintiff merely has to show some negative job action, for example, termination, that was taken on the basis of the employee's sex.	Plaintiff must show equal work, that is, work that is substantially equal except for the fact that one employee is paid more even though he or she performs basically the same job.

An example case involved assistant coach Robin Murphy, who claimed that the University of Cincinnati discriminated against her in violation of Title VII when the head swimming coach fired her after she complained about the way she was treated. She claimed that the head coach did not provide her with enough responsibility or seek her advice in running the team. Although she was fired by the head coach, she could not prove that she was qualified for the job because she would not follow the head coach's instructions and so did not meet his legitimate expectations. Also, she could not show that there was a similarly situated male coach who was treated better. In addition, although she showed that the coach made some rude, off-color comments to her, none of this demonstrated that she was fired because of her gender (*Murphy v. University of Cincinnati*, 2003).

There are several justifications for differences in pay between male and female coaches and other athletic personnel, some of which are illustrated in the case studies in this section. However, this does not mean that women can be paid less merely because they are not men. There must be legitimate differences in the work that men and women perform and the responsibilities they are given in order for there to be differences in pay.

Although an important part of gender equity law, employment discrimination laws have done little to change the landscape of sports and provide more employment opportunities for women. Although professional sports seem to be taking the lead in slowly providing more opportunities for women, university sports are falling short and seem to provide less overall opportunities each year. No gender equity laws mandate equality of opportunity in employment for women, and existing laws have not been successfully used to push for equality for women in this area.

Summary

Sports administrators in high schools, universities, and athletic associations must understand Title IX and its impact on athletics. Because women continue to participate less in athletics than men, any athletic program may be subject to an analysis under the three-part test. Such an analysis would be conducted if female athletes complain that your athletic program discriminates against them in the way in which it provides participation opportunities to men and women.

The law also can be used to review the specific ways in which you run your athletic program, such as scheduling games and practices, building facilities, and providing equipment and supplies. All of these aspects of your program must be at least equitable to both sexes, which demands constant vigilance by administrators, coaches, and athletic departments.

Sport administrators must create environments that protect athletes from possible sexual harassment. Although still underreported by victims, sexual harassment by other players, recruits, coaches, and others remains a serious problem within athletics. By creating programs to address this problem, you will protect yourself and your institution from the liability that may attach to harassment, but more important, you will protect your students or athletes from harassment.

Serious disparities in employment remain, because women still do not have the same opportunities as men in athletics. Unfortunately for women, neither the Equal Pay Act nor Title VII has solved this problem and forced sport organizations to provide more opportunities for women.

DISCUSSION QUESTIONS

1. Does Title IX apply to all universities, schools, and athletic programs?

2. What is the three-part test and how is it used to determine whether a school complies with Title IX?

3. What can a male athlete do if his school discontinues hosting a team in the sport he wants to play?

4. What types of comparisons must an athletic administrator make to determine whether an athletic program provides equal opportunities for boys and girls?

5. What should schools do to manage the risk that they might be sued as a result of sexual harassment of a player by a coach?

6. How could a female head coach successfully argue that she deserves to be paid as much as the male head coach in her sport?

MOOT COURT CASE

SACB University is a small public university with a tradition of having successful teams in men's and women's tennis, men's lacrosse, and women's softball. The university is federally funded and thus subject to the mandates of Title IX. In 2000-2001, SACB had 10,793 students: 4,790 men and 6,003 women. Thus, approximately 55% of the student population was female and 45% male. The percentage of genders in athletics, however, was quite different: 37% of all athletes were female and 63% were male. In the fiscal year 2000-2001, the university was faced with a budget crisis. There were substantial reductions in both state and federal aid to the school, and as a result the university administration advised its various departments that they had to reduce their budgets, including the Department of Athletics, which was instructed to reduce its budget by $500,000. The athletic director was left with some difficult decisions and knew he would be forced to eliminate some programs. In August 2001, he announced that the women's softball and tennis teams and the men's soccer and water polo teams were going to be eliminated beginning with the 2002-2003 school year. The athletic director believed that it was best to eliminate equal numbers of men's and women's teams. The teams that were eliminated included ones that brought the school prestige but also that were expensive to maintain given costs for trainers, travel, equipment, and supplies. At the time of the 2001 cutbacks, SACB had 12 varsity teams (six male and six female). Because of the elimination of the four teams, SACB now had four teams per gender. The athletic director claimed that it was his intent, and the intent of the university, to replace the women's tennis team with a lower-budget women's club tennis team, create a women's club gymnastics team, and reinstate the women's softball program at a time in the future when more money was available to the university. Several of the female athletes who played on the softball and tennis teams brought a lawsuit against the university claiming that the actions of the athletic director and the university violated Title IX.

9

Intellectual Property Law

CHAPTER OBJECTIVES

After reading this chapter, you will know the following:

- The areas of intellectual property law that apply to sport
- The types of trademarks that are used in the sport industry
- Ways that a sport organization can protect itself when its trademarks, copyrights, or patents are used by others who are not authorized to do so
- The value that athletes have in their personal right of publicity

© Greg Crisp / SportsChrome

The success of any sports event often depends on the revenues derived from the event. Although revenues for university and professional sports teams often come from sales of merchandise, tickets, and concessions, some of the revenues come from intangible sources. These revenues include the sale of player or team names and likenesses, sponsorship of events and facilities, sales of merchandise with particular names and logos, or other sources that come under the umbrella of intellectual property law.

In addition, there are differences in the sources of revenue for professional and university sports. In professional sports, teams often make revenue from ticket sales; however, the bulk of their revenue comes from television contracts selling the broadcasts of their games, sales of merchandise with the team name and logo, and sponsorships within their home stadium or arena. University-level sport is similar, although schools may be more dependent on revenues associated with ticket sales. Although universities sell merchandise with the university logo and nickname, this revenue is often for the school and is not given only to the athletic department. In addition, most university teams do not have lucrative television deals of their own and so only make significant revenue from television if they participate in the men's basketball or football championships. While professional teams are individual for-profit businesses that benefit from membership in professional sports leagues whose marketing and media arms make money for all teams, university teams are part of a university and often can only be sustained if the athletic budget allows.

This chapter focuses on intellectual property law, discussing the areas of intellectual property law that are important in sport, such as developing new slogans, selling signage and concession space, and creating marketing plans for events, products, endorsers, or organizations. This chapter focuses on some basic areas of intellectual property law that you need to understand:

- Trademark
- Copyright
- The right of publicity
- Patent

Each area of intellectual property law affects the sports industry in specific ways. Most of these areas are controlled by federal law, so you can use your knowledge about intellectual property law no matter where you work in the United States.

Trademark Law

Perhaps the most valuable asset a sport or recreation organization has is its name, logo, or other defining characteristic that the public can recognize and associate with the organization. Because such defining characteristics can be so valuable, competitors often try to use these "marks" without permission, such as copying them to put on the competitors' own products or events. Event organizers and sport organizations must protect themselves by registering these marks to sell their own products and services. One of the strongest ways to gain this protection is by registering these characteristics as trademarks.

Federal Laws

The Federal Trademark Act of 1946, known as the Lanham Act, governs the law of trademarks and their registration and provides causes of action that protect trademark rights from infringement. The purpose of the Lanham Act is to protect the owner of a mark by preventing others from using the owner's mark without permission or in a way that will cause confusion as to the actual source of the mark.

According to the act, a **trademark** includes "any word, name, symbol, or device, or any combination thereof . . . used by some entity to identify and distinguish the services of one person, including a unique service, from the services of others and to indicate the source of the services, even if that source is unknown" (15 U.S.C. § 1127, 2008). A trademark serves several important functions: It identifies a seller's goods and distinguishes them from those sold by others; it signifies that goods come from one particular source; it indicates that products are of a certain quality; and it advertises, promotes, and assists in selling the particular goods.

Because of these functions, trademarks are known by many different names (see figure 9.1). The strongest marks that an organization can have are **arbitrary or fanciful marks.** These have no direct relationship to the product itself, such as *NIKE* for sports apparel; instead they are inherently distinctive because they indicate the source of the goods rather than describe the goods themselves. **Suggestive marks** may hint at the characteristics of the goods or services but require some imagination to understand the product they stand for. For instance, although some consumers would understand that *Hot Pockets* (a suggestive mark) refers to a warm food item, it takes a bit of imagination to understand that the name stands for a meal wrapped in a flaky crust.

Marks that are merely descriptive only identify a characteristic or quality of a good or service. For example, a golf ball that produces a loud screeching sound when hit is named the Screech Golf Ball, which is a **descriptive mark.** Descriptive marks can only be given trademark protection if they obtain secondary meaning. **Secondary meaning** refers to when a mark has received widespread use and public recognition so that it indicates the source of the good or service instead of the good or service itself. For example, team logos and color schemes, although not inherently distinctive, can obtain secondary meaning once they have been associated with a particular team in the marketplace.

Generic marks do not receive trademark protection because they refer to the name or class of the good or service and are so common that they do not clearly indicate the source of the good or service. Some companies

trademark—Any word, name, symbol, or device that an organization uses to identify and distinguish its services from the services of another organization and to indicate the source of the service.

arbitrary or fanciful marks—Trademarks that are inherently distinctive because they describe the source of a good and not the actual good itself.

suggestive marks—Trademarks that require some creativity to understand the product that they describe.

descriptive mark—Trademark that describes a characteristic or quality of a good or service.

secondary meaning—Meaning assigned to a trademark when it has received widespread use and public recognition so that it indicates the source of the good or service instead of the good or service itself.

generic mark—Marks that are so common they cannot receive federal trademark protection.

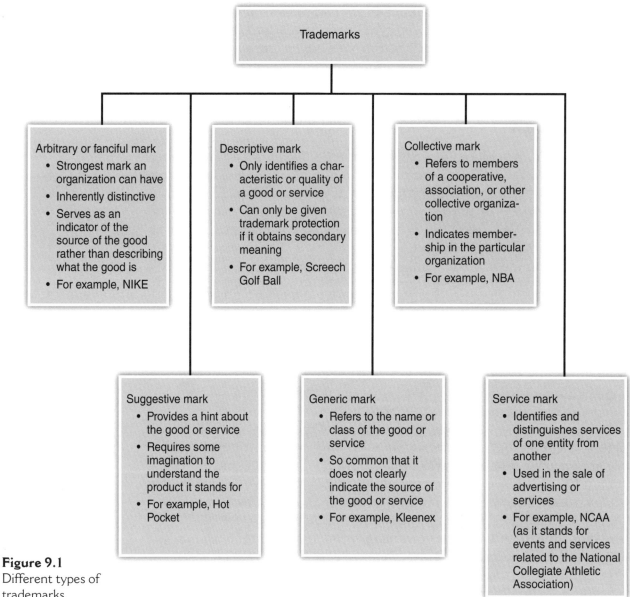

Figure 9.1
Different types of
trademarks.

collective mark—
Trademark used by
the members of a
cooperative, associa-
tion, or other collec-
tive organization to
indicate membership
in that organization.

that create distinctive names or logos eventually lose their trademark rights to some names or logos because they become so well known. The classic examples are *Kleenex* for facial tissue and *JELL-O* for gelatin. When both products were first introduced, their names were merely the company names for the particular brand of facial tissue and gelatin. Now both marks are so generic that people often refer to facial tissue as *Kleenex* and gelatin as *JELL-O* regardless of what particular brand they have purchased.

The Lanham Act also protects collective marks and service marks. A **collective mark** is a trademark used by the members of a cooperative, association, or other collective organization to indicate membership in that organization. Examples of collective marks in sports are widespread, from sports league initials such as *NBA* and *NHL* to college conference names such as *Big Ten* and *SEC*. A **service mark** is used in the sale or advertising of services to identify and distinguish the services of one entity from the services of others. Whereas a trademark identifies the source of a product, a service mark identifies the source and quality of an intangible service. For example, the mark *NCAA*, as it stands for events and services related to the National Collegiate Athletic Association, is a service mark.

service mark—Mark used in the sale of advertising or services to identify and distinguish the services of one entity from the services of others.

To create ownership rights in any of these types of trademarks, the trademark owner must be the first to use the mark in trade (i.e., by selling a product or service that displays the trademark). The owner also must make continuous, uninterrupted use of the mark after this first use on its products or within its services. Once the trademark is used, consumers should be able to identify and distinguish the owner's unique goods or services from those of others in the particular industry. A valid trademark owner may also federally register the mark. However, although federal registration extends rights to the trademark owner to use the mark throughout the United States and provides notice to other users of the mark's validity, registration only extends trademark rights across the United States; it does not necessarily extend internationally. A trademark owner must then reregister the mark every 10 years in order to exclusively use the marks on his or her products and services.

Infringement

One of the main problems a successful sports organization can face is when another organization attempts to use the first organization's marks without its permission in order to capitalize on its success. This can happen in simple ways, such as when fans produce T-shirts or hats with team logos that they are not authorized to use or when students make their own outfits using the school logo to support the team. For example, at Marquette University, student season-ticket holders for the men's basketball team traditionally create T-shirts using the school's logo, the Golden Eagle, and often using the discontinued Warrior logo even though the university still owns the trademark in that logo and has not authorized its use by the students. As with most universities, if the university administration is made aware of this unauthorized use it will vigorously protect its mark by seeking a restraining order against the students or taking other actions to stop the sale of unauthorized products. No matter what the use is, if an individual uses the properly registered trademark of another without the owner's consent, this use may be found to be a form of trademark infringement.

Trademark infringement can cause direct harm to the proper owner of the trademark in several ways. Money that might be spent on products truly produced by the sport organization itself is now spent on the infringing products and so the trademark owner loses revenues. In addition, if the use of the trademark is in a format that the owner would not approve, for instance on lower-quality goods, it can reflect negatively on the quality of officially licensed merchandise. This often happens on college campuses. In the example at Marquette University, students may also use the current Golden

trademark infringement—When a non-trademark owner engages in some unauthorized use of a trademark that is likely to cause consumers to be confused or deceived as to who really owns the trademark.

Eagle logo on low-quality T-shirts. Although the use itself could infringe on the university's trademark rights, even with permission the university may not want to have the logo displayed on low-quality T-shirts when its normal shirts are produced by sport apparel company Champion.

To establish trademark infringement, the trademark owner must first show that he or she has used and registered the mark as required and so has a protectable right in the trademark. Additionally, the owner must demonstrate that the other party's use of the mark is likely to cause confusion or to deceive consumers about who is the true source of the trademark. A court evaluating a claim of trademark infringement will focus on the following factors when evaluating whether consumers would likely be confused by a possible infringing use of a trademark: the strength of the mark, similarity between the marks, evidence of actual confusion, consumer sophistication, quality of the alleged infringer's products, similarity between the products and the ways they are sold, likelihood that the owner will expand the use of his own marks in the future on other products, and whether the alleged infringer acted with good faith.

Individuals and companies are often sued for alleged trademark infringement. For example, in 1979, the Dallas Cowboys Cheerleaders sued Pussycat Cinema, a movie theater that began to show the pornographic movie *Debbie Does Dallas* (*Dallas Cowboys Cheerleaders, Inc. v. Pussycat Cinema, Ltd.,* 1979). The cheerleaders sued, claiming that they had a trademark in their unique uniform and that the advertisements used for the movie showing its star in a uniform similar to the Cowboys cheerleaders' uniform infringed on their trademark. The defendants argued that even though the uniform worn in the movie closely resembled the actual cheerleaders' uniform, the public would not be confused, as required under the federal law. The court disagreed, explaining that the public's mere belief that the true trademark owner must have actually sponsored or approved of the use of the mark within the advertisements was enough to meet the confusion requirement. The court found that the use of a confusing mark in the movie would confuse consumers and injure the plaintiff's business reputation; it therefore affirmed the trial court's grant of an injunction stopping the particular confusing advertising and distribution of the film.

Often the infringement claim deals with the devaluing of the trademark itself. These disputes occur because a sport entity has signed an agreement to provide another entity with a license to produce products including the sport organization's trademark. A **license** is granted by its owner, known as the licensor, to a third party, the licensee, which permits the licensee to associate his or her goods, services, or business with the logos, names, and mascots of the licensor. Granting a license creates a contractual relationship between the licensor and the licensee. The licensor's aim is to gain additional public exposure, expand its business, and generate income by granting permission to the licensee to use its various images. The licensee hopes to increase the public's demand for its business, goods, or services by linking such with a popular local, national, or even international entity. Problems can occur when entities other than the licensee attempt to use the

license—A right granted by an owner, known as the licensor, to a third party, the licensee, which permits the licensee to associate his or her goods, services, or business with the logos, names, and mascots of the licensor. Granting a license creates a contractual relationship between the licensor and the licensee.

licensor's images or when the licensor becomes unhappy with the licensee's use of the granted license. Consider the following case.

Mark Sullivan sold T-shirts and other merchandize with the mark *Boston Marathon*. The Boston Athletic Association (BAA) is a charitable organization that has conducted the Boston Marathon since 1897. BAA registered the name *Boston Marathon* with both the state and federal trademark offices. For several years, the BAA has put together an exposition before the marathon where the organization sells shirts and other official apparel in an effort to defray some of the costs of the race. Although Sullivan originally provided merchandise to BAA, eventually BAA signed an exclusive licensing agreement and gave notice that any use of its trademarks by others would infringe on its rights. Sullivan continued to print shirts including the words *Marathon* and *Boston*. The shirts were of poorer quality than BAA's merchandise.

BAA sued, claiming that Sullivan's use of the marks infringed on BAA's trademark rights (*Boston Athletic Association v. Sullivan,* 1989). In analyzing BAA's complaint, the court focused on whether consumers would be likely to mistake Sullivan's T-shirts for the BAA's. In looking at the eight factors previously mentioned, the courts found that the marks used by Sullivan were identical and were used on the same type of merchandise that BAA produced, that both parties sold and advertised their products in the same venues, that some consumers were confused as to whether Sullivan's shirts were official BAA merchandise, and that Sullivan wanted to realize some profit from his use of marks associated with BAA. On this last factor, it is important to note that although BAA had only recently registered its marks, it had consistently used them on its products and events even before registration. Therefore, the court found that Sullivan clearly infringed on BAA's marks and that his infringement through the sale of inferior products had the potential to negatively affect the perception of the quality of the products produced by BAA.

As this case demonstrates, there are often two issues in a trademark infringement dispute. Initially, the focus will be on determining exactly what trademark rights the owner has. For instance, does a team have a trademark in only the team name, or does the mark extend to merchandise, the team color scheme, and the use of the name in the context of the particular sport? This issue typically will be resolved by determining what was actually registered as the trademark and what forms of the mark have actually been used by the owner.

The focus of an infringement analysis then typically shifts to whether consumers will actually be confused by the use of a mark by another party. It is not enough to simply say that another party used the same words as the owner registered. If that were the case, there could not be a New York Giants in the NFL and a San Francisco Giants in MLB because both teams would not be allowed to share the same name. Instead, one must review the factors previously mentioned to determine whether there is any likely confusion, keeping in mind that courts will typically look for evidence produced by surveys of consumers showing that they were actually confused by the potentially infringing use of the marks.

Still, the trademark laws provide strong protection for sport organizations that continue to find many creative ways to profit from of their own marks, from logo apparel to restaurants named after a particular team. This necessary connection between revenue production and the use of a trademark causes many high-profile professional and college sports teams and leagues to actively seek to stop other organizations from infringing on their trademarks.

Fair Use or Parody

Trademark protection is not absolute and does not bar all possible uses of a trademark by those who do not own the trademark. Section 1115(b)(4) of the Lanham Act provides that where a trademark is used fairly and in good faith only to describe the goods or services involved, there is no trademark infringement. For example, a television station's use of the term *Boston Marathon* to describe the station's unlicensed broadcast of the marathon was not found to be trademark infringement even though another station was exclusively licensed to broadcast the event. The court found that this use was merely descriptive of the event being broadcast and did not create viewer confusion as to who was actually sponsoring the event (*WCVB-TV v. Boston Athletic Association,* 1991).

For the same reason, a parody of a trademark typically will not be held to be infringement. The classic sport case in this regard involved the Major League Baseball Players Association, which sued a parody baseball card maker claiming that the player caricatures on the cards infringed on trademarks that the association owned in player trading cards. The court found that the parody baseball cards did not create confusion regarding the source of the cards, because they were merely meant to amuse the consumer who purchased them (*Cardtoons, L.C. v. Major League Baseball Players Assoc.,* 1996).

Dilution

With the introduction of the Federal Trademark Dilution Act of 1995, trademark owners were given another form of protection (15 U.S.C. § 1125c, 2008). According to this act, **dilution** is the lessening of the capacity of a famous mark to identify and distinguish goods or services, regardless of either the presence or absence of competition between the parties or a likelihood of confusion, mistake, or deception. There are two types of dilution. Blurring occurs when a party uses or modifies a mark in such a way that the use creates the possibility that the original mark will lose its ability to serve as a unique identifier for the trademark owner. Tarnishment occurs where the mark is used in association with unwholesome or shoddy goods and services.

One of the best examples of a dilution claim in the sport industry involved the NBA. In 1999, Untertainment, a record label, planned to release a rap album titled *SDE Sports, Drugs, & Entertainment.* To promote the album, the company made a banner in New York City that included the NBA trade-

dilution—When a famous mark loses its capacity to identify and distinguish goods or services, even if there is no evidence of competition between the parties or there is no likelihood of confusion, mistake, or deception.

mark with the player in the mark holding a gun. The company also sold the advertisement to several magazines. After seeing the advertisement, several individuals contacted the NBA to complain about its participation. In response, NBA Properties, the marketing and licensing arm of the NBA, sued claiming trademark infringement and dilution (*Dream Team Collectibles, Inc. v. NBA Properties, Inc.,* 1997). The court found that the advertisements would create a negative association with the NBA logo; therefore, under the tarnishment theory of dilution, Untertainment was forced to stop using the advertisement.

A dilution claim could be very important to a sport organization that is attempting to protect its trademark rights, specifically because the organization will not need to demonstrate a likelihood of confusion, as is necessary for a trademark infringement claim. The NBA case demonstrates this clearly, because although some consumers were confused about the record label's use of the NBA mark, the typical consumer would not be. Instead, because the offensive use of the mark could damage the NBA because the mark was associated with violence, the NBA needed some other way to protect itself. The dilution claim was this other form of protection. Other trademark owners in sports can similarly protect themselves when their marks are diluted.

Olympic Marks

Perhaps the strongest trademark protection in the United States is provided to the United States Olympic Committee (USOC). Under the Ted Stevens Olympic and Amateur Sports Act, the USOC has the exclusive right to use and license the Olympic marks (including the word *Olympic* and the five-ring Olympic logo) within the United States (36 U.S.C. § 220501, 2008).

San Francisco Arts & Athletics (SFAA) promoted the Gay Olympic Games, to be held in 1982, by using those words on letterhead, merchandise, and various advertisements. After finding out about this use, the USOC contacted the SFAA and requested that it terminate its use of the word *Olympic* in association with the event. When SFAA refused, the USOC sued to enforce its rights under the Stevens Act (*San Francisco Arts & Athletics, Inc. v. USOC,* 1987). In finding that the USOC had the exclusive right to the use of the word *Olympic,* the court determined that there is no requirement that there be a likelihood of confusion, as there would with a normal trademark. Therefore, SFAA's mere use of the word in advertising for its event infringed on the USOC's strong trademark rights.

Even though the USOC's trademark rights are incredibly strong, they are not absolute, and that is why we often see the word *Olympic* used in many ways. The media can still use the word *Olympic* when reporting on Olympic competitions and may include the Olympic marks within newspapers or other media when reporting about the Olympic Games. However, sport event organizers would be wise to not use the word *Olympic* or the Olympic marks in their events, no matter how tame the use may be. The USOC vigorously pursues those who use virtually any form of their protected marks.

Licensing

If you work for a successful sport organization, merchandisers, sponsors, advertisers, and others will want to associate with you so they can take advantage of your success. To ensure that your organization also benefits from the relationship, you may wish to grant these businesses a license so that they can use your organization's trademarks for a fee.

Most professional sports leagues have created licensing programs that allow the league to capitalize on public demand for merchandise and apparel with the logos of the league and its clubs. Each of the four major professional team sports leagues (MLB, NBA, NFL, and NHL) has created separate divisions, often known as properties (e.g., MLB Properties and NFL Properties) that put forth procedures for sponsors, advertisers, and merchandisers to obtain licenses to use league and club trademarks on their products. Typically, the league then divides the revenues created from these licensing agreements among the clubs that make up the league.

The players associations in these leagues (e.g., the National Football League Players Association) have also created licensing divisions to handle licensing for the athletes themselves. These divisions, such as Players, Inc. in the NFL, and the Players Choice Group Licensing Program in the MLB, work with merchandisers, advertisers, and sponsors that are interested in selling products bearing the names and likenesses of current and former players. As do the leagues, these programs typically divide any revenues made between the players who are members of the particular players association.

Some players have even registered trademarks in their own names and likenesses, for example, former Green Bay Packers quarterback Brett Favre. If companies want to sell products bearing his name or image, they must first obtain a license from his representatives.

Licensing is also important at the college level. The NCAA has registered approximately 66 trademarks and service marks that are associated with the organization and in particular with its championships in various sports. The NCAA has approximately 38 merchandise licensees, 10 nonretail licensees, three corporate champions, and six corporate sponsors. These licensees are permitted to use the NCAA's marks on particular licensed products but cannot use the marks to promote their particular brands. Further information on the NCAA's licensing program can be found on the NCAA Web site at www.ncaa.org under the section titled Frequently Asked Questions About Licensing.

Approximately 300 schools have licensing programs for their names and registered trademarks, including team logos and nicknames. The Collegiate Licensing Company (CLC) is the licensing representative for the NCAA. CLC is responsible for administering the licensing program, including processing applications, collecting royalties, enforcing trademarks, and pursuing new market opportunities for the NCAA. CLC's goal is to increase the NCAA's overall merchandise sales through its apparel and nonapparel marketing divisions. The CLC also represents nearly 200 universities, bowl games, and athletic conferences.

Nicknames

Most professional and university sports teams and even some high school sports teams have registered trademarks in their team name. Because the trademark is registered, these teams can sell or license exclusive apparel that includes their trademarked team name. However, some legal problems can develop when dealing with trademarked team names, particularly Native American nicknames.

At the professional level, the focus has been on Native American nicknames that a group may find disparaging. Trademark protection can also be denied if a mark is shown to be immoral, deceptive, scandalous, or disparaging under Section 1052(a) of the Lanham Act. In the late 1990s, several Native Americans petitioned to cancel the trademark registrations for the marks *Washington Redskins* and *Redskins,* which were owned by Pro-Football, Inc., the owners of the NFL's Washington Redskins franchise (*Harjo et al. v. Pro-Football, Inc.,* 1999). The U.S. Patent and Trademark Office initially granted the petition to cancel the marks, finding that they were disparaging to Native Americans. The team sued to avoid the cancellation of the marks and the court reversed, finding that the petitioners did not present sufficient evidence that the marks were disparaging to Native Americans and that the claim was barred by the doctrine of laches. This doctrine holds that when a plaintiff waits too long to sue to protect a trademark, the court can find that this delay would actually harm the defendant and so can rule in the defendant's favor. In this case, because there was a 25-year delay in bringing the suit, the court found that the team would be harmed if the court allowed the Native Americans' claim.

Doug Benc/Getty Images

Sport team nicknames often can be protected under trademark law. However, Native American nicknames, such as the Florida State Seminoles, often face tough opposition.

Many universities, including the University of Wisconsin and the University of Iowa, will not schedule games against schools that use Native American nicknames or mascots. Under a controversial policy introduced by the NCAA in 2006, NCAA schools are prohibited from displaying hostile and abusive racial, ethnic, or national origin mascots, nicknames, or imagery at any of its championships. Institutions that currently use Native American nicknames are required to take reasonable steps to conceal the nicknames or may be prohibited from wearing them altogether. In 2004, the NCAA asked 33 schools to review their use of Native American mascots, and 15 immediately complied.

Several universities contested the NCAA rule and fought to keep their Native American nicknames. A complete list of the schools banned under the policy and current development surrounding their mascot is available on the NCAA's Web site www.ncaa.org under Native American Mascot Policy—Status List. As discussed on this Web site, after an appeal, Florida State University was allowed to continue to use the word *Seminole* because of its close relationship with the Seminole Tribe of Florida. However, the University of North Dakota (UND) lost a similar appeal over its nickname *Fighting Sioux* because it did not have the support of the three recognized Sioux tribes of North Dakota. Unlike many schools, UND sued the NCAA, denying that it has been hostile, abusive, or disrespectful toward Native Americans. In support of UND, the State Board of Higher Education authorized the lawsuit, which was to be paid for by alumni and other donations. In November 2006, UND won a preliminary injunction that barred the NCAA from stopping the university from using the nickname and allowed the university to host an opening round playoff game in the Division II football playoffs. The court specifically found that the school had met its burden of establishing irreparable harm to its reputation if it was characterized as an institution that allows a "hostile and abusive" environment to exist toward Native Americans (*State of North Dakota v. NCAA*, 2006). Soon after, in October 2007, the NCAA and the university settled the dispute. The university now has 3 years to obtain approval from the Sioux tribes for the use of its nickname and related imagery. If UND does not get approval, then the university will transition to a new logo and nickname that do not violate the policy.

Since the NCAA adopted the rule, many other organizations at all levels of sport have begun to review their use of Native American trademarks and nicknames.

Domain Names and the Internet

Use of the Internet to market sports teams, events, and merchandise has increased exponentially since the early 1990s, increasing the need for sport organizations to protect their intellectual property rights on the Internet. In the early 1990s, when teams and other sport organizations began to create Web sites, some organizations found that third parties that were not associated with the organization had already registered the organization's preferred domain name. These parties came to be known as "cybersquatters" because they would acquire domain names and then sit on them, waiting for the actual organization associated with the name to find out. These cybersquatters would then attempt to extort money from the true rights holder to buy back the domain name they had registered. Unfortunately, until very recently this practice was not illegal.

In 1999, Congress finally acted by passing the Anti-cybersquatting Consumer Protection Act (ACPA), which amended the Lanham Act by creating a specific claim against cybersquatters. The act outlaws **cybersquatting,** which is described as the act of registering, with the bad faith intent to profit, a domain name that is confusingly similar to a registered or unregistered mark or dilutes a famous mark. A legitimate trademark owner can sue under the act to stop a cybersquatter, even when the disputed owner of the name cannot be found or cannot be served in the United States.

cybersquatting— Illegal action by which someone registers a domain name that is confusingly similar to a registered or unregistered trademark or dilutes a famous mark. The cybersquatter must intend to profit from this use in bad faith toward the true trademark owner.

A recent case dealing with a claim under the ACPA involved the domain name marchmadness.com, the NCAA, and the Illinois High School Association (IHSA). The NCAA's first use of the phrase "March madness" occurred in 1982 when CBS broadcaster Brent Musberger used it when discussing the NCAA men's basketball tournament; however, the IHSA had begun using the phrase to refer to its boys' basketball tournaments in the 1940s. After some initial litigation concerning who actually owned the phrase, the NCAA and IHSA agreed to work together to protect their rights. They formed the March Madness Athletic Association (MMAA), and each retained a license to use the phrase in connection to advertising their basketball tournaments.

Claiming to be associated with the NCAA, Netfire acquired the domain name marchmadness.com in 1996. MMAA sued, claiming that Netfire was engaging in cybersquatting in violation of the ACPA. The court agreed, finding that Netfire acted with bad faith in order to profit by using the trademarked phrase and that the domain name was identical or confusingly similar to the actual trademark in violation of the ACPA (*March Madness Athletic Association, LLC v. Netfire Inc.*, 2005).

The ACPA is not the only recourse for trademark owners who want to challenge a cybersquatter. The Uniform Dispute Resolution Process (UDRP) is administered by the Internet Corporation for Assigned Names and Numbers (ICANN). Under this process, a trademark owner must allege that its mark is identical or confusingly similar to the mark used by the cybersquatter, who has no legitimate rights or interests in the domain name, and that the cybersquatter registered and used the domain name in bad faith. The World Intellectual Property Organization's (WIPO) Arbitration and Mediation Center, based in Geneva, Switzerland, is authorized to hear disputes under the UDRP process. Information on this organization and particular disputes can be found at www.wipo.int/amc/en/index.html.

The NHL and the owners of the Pittsburgh Penguins franchise, specifically Mario Lemieux, sued a corporation that registered the domain name nhlpenguins.com and linked it to pornographic material while at the same time acting as a true cybersquatter by attempting to sell it back to the true trademark owners (*National Hockey League and Lemieux Group Lp. v. Domain for Sale*, 2001). After the defendants refused to stop using the domain name, the plaintiffs filed a complaint with WIPO's Arbitration and Mediation Center. The center found that the domain name was confusingly similar to the NHL's and Penguins' marks and that it was being used in bad faith to reroute customers to pornographic materials. Therefore, because the defendant was not making any legitimate use of the domain name, the panel ordered that the domain name be transferred to the plaintiffs.

Although organizations can use these processes to challenge unauthorized uses of their trademarks within domain names, often the only thing the organizations get for winning these fights is a difficult-to-enforce decision from the courts or WIPO Arbitration and Mediation Center verifying their rights. It is virtually impossible to try to obtain damages from cybersquatters, especially when they cannot be located because they register domain names around the world. Moreover, the majority of these disputes become one sided because the cybersquatters never even appear in court. To them the benefit is in merely infringing on the domain name for as long as possible, and often the same individuals or entities are repeatedly sued for this type of conduct.

Copyright Law

Sport organizations often want to protect the accounts of their events found in the media through television, media guides, radio broadcasts, newspapers, magazines, and other sources. These forms of expression are protected by **copyright** law. Unlike trademark law, copyright law does not protect intangible ideas; rather, it protects ideas or other items that can be identified on tape, on paper, or on screen.

copyright—A right granted by statute to the author or creator of a literary or artistic production that provides the author with the exclusive right to reproduce, publish, or sell the production.

The federal Copyright Act provides for federal protection and registration of copyrights (17 U.S.C. §§ 101, et seq., 2008). As it explains, copyright protection extends to "original works of authorship fixed in any tangible medium of expression, now known or later developed, from which they can be perceived, reproduced, or otherwise communicated, either directly or with the aid of a machine or device" (§ 102). Copyright protection can be extended to the following "original works of authorship":

- Books and other literary works
- Music and musical works, including any accompanying words
- Dramatic works such as plays, including any accompanying music
- Pantomimes and choreographic works
- Pictorial (photographic), graphic, and sculptural works
- Motion pictures and other audiovisual works
- Sound recordings
- Architectural works (§ 102)

The owner of a copyright has the right to do or authorize others to do the following:

- Reproduce the copyrighted work in copies or phonorecords
- Prepare derivative works based on the copyrighted work
- Distribute copies or phonorecords of the copyrighted work to the public by sale or other transfer of ownership or by rental, lease, or lending
- Perform the copyrighted work publicly, in the case of literary, musical, dramatic, and choreographic works; pantomimes; and motion pictures and other audiovisual works
- Display the copyrighted work publicly, in the case of literary, musical, dramatic, and choreographic works; pantomimes; and pictorial, graphic, or sculptural works, including the individual images of a motion picture or other audiovisual work
- Perform the copyrighted work publicly by means of a digital audio transmission, in the case of sound recordings (§ 106)

Under this federal law, copyright protection begins when a copyrightable work is created, and it extends for the life of the author plus 70 years. The U.S. government also provides a Web site with information for those interested in obtaining copyright protection for their work by registering it at www.copyright.gov. Although registration is not required, it is necessary to register a copyright before bringing a lawsuit against someone for **copyright infringement.**

Businesses often include a copyright policy in their publications and company brochures or even on the company Web site. A good example is the policy for the Lance Armstrong Foundation: Livestrong, a foundation dedicated to helping individuals with cancer. The foundation has a Web site that provides information for individuals interested in the foundation and provides ways for supporters to donate to the foundation. To protect the content of the Web site from being copied by others, the site contains a copyright policy at www.livestrong.org/site/c.khLXK1PxHmF/b.2662415/k.9E1B/Copyright_Policy.htm.

Individuals who duplicate the copyrighted materials of others often are found to have infringed on the rightful owners' copyright. Copyright infringement is an unauthorized use of copyrighted material in a way that violates one of the owner's exclusive rights in the copyright. In most circumstances, copyright infringement is subject to a strict liability standard (the legal principle of strict liability is discussed in chapter 2, and so the owner only needs to show that her protected copyright was copied to sustain her claim. If infringement is found, the copyright owner then has a variety of remedies available, from injunctive relief to the recovery of damages, which could include any profits that the infringer made off of the owner's copyrights, and attorney's fees.

However, beyond clear infringement, some copyright material can be used without the copyright owner's permission. This is known as **fair use.** Copyrights can be used in this way for purposes such as criticism, comment, news reporting, teaching (including multiple copies for classroom use), scholarship, or research (17 U.S.C. § 107, 2008). If an organization attempts to defend its use of a copyright that it does not own by arguing that it was a fair use, the court will consider the purpose and character of the use, including whether it is of a commercial nature or is for nonprofit educational purposes; the nature of the copyrighted work; the amount and substantiality of the portion used in relation to the copyrighted work as a whole; and the effect of the use on the potential market for or value of the copyrighted work.

Copyright issues in sport typically involve one of two areas: (1) who owns the copyright and who can use it in game statistics and accounts and (2) the extent of copyright protection that extends to the Internet.

Game Accounts

With the rise of fantasy sports leagues and other forms of gambling on sports, the statistics produced by athletic participants and the accounts

copyright infringement— Unauthorized use of copyrighted material in a way that violates one of the owners' exclusive rights in the copyright.

fair use—Use of copyright for purposes such as criticism, comment, news reporting, teaching, scholarship, or research.

of the games played themselves continue to grow in value. Media outlets, fantasy leagues, and even the general public want access to these statistics and accounts; but copyright owners, or more specifically, individuals or entities who believe that they are the copyright owner, want to protect their rights to these statistics and accounts and profit from the licensing and distribution of permission to use them.

One of the earliest cases of this type in sport took place in the 1930s and involved the Pittsburgh Pirates. The Pirates played their home games in Forbes Field and sold the exclusive rights to broadcast play-by-play descriptions or accounts of their games to General Mills. NBC then contracted with General Mills to broadcast these play-by-play game accounts over the radio. Another radio station, KQV, also broadcast game accounts provided by its own observers at Pirates games. The Pirates sued to protect their rights in the game broadcasts and stop KQV from its unauthorized broadcast of Pirates games (*Pittsburgh Athletic Co. v. KQV Broadcasting Co.*, 1938). The court found that because the Pirates created the game, controlled the park, and restricted the dissemination of game accounts, the team had a protectable property right in these game accounts. In addition, the team had the right to control the use of this game information for a reasonable time after the games took place. Therefore, KQV violated the Pirates' copyrights by broadcasting their game accounts.

As the law evolved and sports expanded, further considerations came forth. For instance, leagues and teams wanted to know who owned the copyright in the actual broadcast of the game. Keep in mind that copyright protection depends on authorship, that is, there must always be a determination of who actually authored the work in question. However, the Copyright Act also allowed for joint or coauthorship (17 U.S.C. § 201(a), 2008). In the context of sports, this is applicable when teams and leagues (or schools and conferences on the university level, and schools and associations on the high school level) jointly create the broadcasts that are eventually seen. Eventually, a case analyzing whether MLB clubs own exclusive rights to the television broadcasts of their players defined these broadcast rights more clearly.

For years, MLB and its players union argued over who actually owned the right to broadcast the performances of MLB players. In 1982, the union sent letters to each club and to television and cable companies stating that they were broadcasting the players without the players' consent and, therefore, had misappropriated each player's property rights in his performances. In response, the clubs went to court to seek a judicial declaration that they had an exclusive right to broadcast the games and exclusive rights in the telecasts themselves (*Baltimore Orioles, Inc. v. Major League Baseball Players Assoc.*, 1986). The clubs argued that the game telecasts were "works made for hire" as defined under the Copyright Act. Section 201(b) of the act states that if the telecasts are works made for hire, then the clubs that own the broadcasts would be considered to have authored the broadcasts as required for copyright protection. As a result, unless the clubs reached a separate agreement with the players, the clubs would own the right to the copyrights in the game accounts provided in the broadcasts.

To determine whether the clubs owned copyrights under the doctrine of work made for hire, the court began by noting that the different aspects of a game broadcast, such as camera angles, types of shots, the use of instant replays and split screens, and shot selection, all are forms of authorship in the copyrightable telecast that are themselves audiovisual works covered by the Copyright Act. In addition, the players were employees of the clubs, and their employment included playing games before live and remote audiences. Finally, because there was no other formal agreement granting the players a copyright in these game broadcasts, the clubs were found to be the valid owners of the copyright.

As a result of this reasoning and of similar decisions in other courts, clubs and the leagues that they make up can bargain with each other to sell their copyrighted works to television networks. This pooling of rights is discussed further in chapter 10, under a discussion of the exemption of this activity from the antitrust laws as provided in the Sports Broadcasting Act.

Sports employers who hire players and then reach agreements with broadcasters to televise their games usually will be found to own the copyrights in the game broadcasts. Players and their unions can negotiate for these rights within the collective bargaining process; however, typically they instead negotiate for a bigger percentage of the revenues derived from the sale of these broadcasts to the networks. Currently, these values are astronomical (see table 9.1). For instance, the NBA's newly signed contract with ABC, ESPN, and TNT has been valued at $7.6 billion and will run from the 2008-2009 season to the 2015-2016 season.

Another issue related to game broadcasts involves attempts to broadcast games even when leagues have imposed a blackout. Most television contracts with the major professional sports leagues provide that games that are not sold out within a certain number of days or hours are blacked out; that is, they are not broadcast in the team's home region. The reasoning behind these blackout rules is that a blackout in the team's home region will encourage ticket sales and, therefore, encourage sellouts of team home games. If all home games were broadcast regardless of ticket sales in the home region, fans might avoid paying for tickets and merely stay home to watch their team. Of course with something as important as barring local fans from watching their team, litigation has followed these blackout rules. A good example involved the NFL.

The NFL's blackout rule in the mid-1980s provided that games that were not sold out within 72 hours of game time were blacked out and not to be broadcast within a 75-mile (120-kilometer) radius of the home team's playing field. Owners of restaurants within this radius of Busch Stadium (the home at that time of the St. Louis Cardinals) picked up the broadcast of blacked out Cardinals' home games to show in their restaurants. The NFL and the Cardinals sued to stop the restaurant owners from showing the blacked out games, claiming that the broadcasts violated the NFL's and the Cardinals' copyrights (*NFL v. McBee & Bruno's Inc.*, 1986). Although the court recognized an exemption within the Copyright Act allowing for the transmission of copyrighted material in a private home, the satellites used

Table 9.1   Broadcasting Agreements in Sport

Years	Network	Total income	Income per year
National Football League			
2006-2013	ESPN	$8.8 billion	$1.1 billion
2006-2011	NBC	$3.6 billion	$600 million
Major League Baseball			
2008-2013	Fox, Turner	$3 billion	$670 million
2006-2013	ESPN	$2.4 billion	$336 million (both television and radio)
National Basketball Association			
2002-2008	ABC/ESPN, Time Warner	$2.4 billion	$400 million
2002-2008	TNT	$2.19 billion	$365 million
1998-2002	NBC, TNT/TBS	$2.64 billion	$660 million
1994-1998	NBC, TNT	$1.1 billion	$275 million
National Hockey League			
2005-2008	Outdoor Life Network	$207.5 million	$65 million (year 1) $70 million (year 2) $72.5 million (year 3)
2004-2009	NBC	There is no up front money, but there is a revenue-sharing agreement.	
1999-2005	ESPN	$660 million	$120 million
NASCAR			
2007-2014	FOX, TNT, ABC, ESPN	$4.48 billion	$560 million
2001-2006	FOX, Turner, NBC	$2.4 billion	$400 million
NCAA			
2003-2014	CBS	$6 billion	$545 million
1995-2002	CBS (renegotiated)	$1.725 billion	$345 million
1991-1998	CBS	$1 billion	$1.4 million

by the bar owners were not similar to those in a private home and so the exemption did not apply. As a result, the restaurant owners were permanently barred from intercepting the game broadcasts.

Statistics

Other copyright issues have focused on the rights to the actual statistics produced by players and teams. Leagues and clubs often claim that they own the statistics produced within their sports, whereas media outlets and other consumers argue that the statistics should not be subject to copyright protection. One of the seminal decisions in this area concerned the NBA.

Beginning in 1996, Motorola manufactured and marketed the SportsTrax paging device and STATS supplied the game statistics from NBA games transmitted to the pagers. The statistical information was provided by STATS reporters watching the games on television or listening to them on the radio and then keying the statistical information into their personal computers. The NBA sued Motorola, asserting that its activities infringed on the NBA's copyright in its game broadcasts, which the NBA argued were original works of authorship that the league had the exclusive right to republish and sell (*NBA v. Motorola,* 1997). The court determined that the NBA did not hold a copyright to the underlying games themselves because the games are unscripted and the outcome is uncertain so they are not authored as required under the Copyright Act. Even though the broadcasts of the games were subject to copyright protection, the defendants did not infringe on the NBA's copyright in these broadcasts because they only reproduced facts from the broadcasts and not a description of the game itself. According to this decision, sports leagues and teams do not own copyright in game statistics; and newspaper and other media outlets can reproduce statistics in their products. However, a few years later, another decision added confusion to this area of law.

The PGA developed the Real-Time Scoring System (RTSS) to compile tournament scores for PGA events. Under this system, volunteer "walking scorers" would follow each group of golfers on the course and tabulate the scores of each player. "Hole reporters" then relayed this information to a production truck that compiled the scores and transmitted them to electronic leaderboards, distributed along the golf course, as well as to the on-site media center and the Web site pgatour.com. Because the PGA prohibited the use of wireless devices by the press or public during tournaments, the RTSS was the sole source of compiled golf scores for the full list of tournament players. In addition, the PGA required media organizations to agree to other regulations in order to gain access to the media center, including mandated delays before scoring information could be published.

Morris Communications is a media company that publishes print and electronic newspapers and a main competitor with the PGA in the market for real-time golf scores. Morris wanted to continue to sell real-time scores to several Internet publishers, and so it sued the PGA to enjoin it from enforcing these regulations (*Morris Comm. Corp. v. PGA Tour,* 2000). Differentiating this case from the *Motorola* decision, the district court noted that Motorola, one of the defendants in that case, was able to gather its information simply by tuning in to a publicly aired television or radio broadcast that any member of the public could access. However, Morris could only obtain the real-time scores by accessing information gathered throughout the golf course simultaneously and then compiling the information and generating the scores in a private media center through the PGA's system. Therefore, the real-time golf scores are the end-product of a system that the PGA designed for itself. As a result, the court found that Morris was merely attempting to capitalize, not just on the golf scores themselves, but also on the PGA's system for simultaneously gathering and generating the scoring information. On appeal, the court focused on antitrust claims brought by Morris against the PGA and did not address the PGA's property right in the real-time scores (*Morris Comm. Corp. v. PGA Tour,* 2002). The court concluded that the PGA had not illegally monopolized the market for real-time tournament scores and denied Morris' motion for summary judgment.

As a result of these decisions, the NBA was found to have no property rights in any real-time game statistics, whereas the PGA was seemingly found to have a property right in its real-time scores. This is very confusing, and only after you carefully consider the cases can the differences be found.

Initially, the *Motorola* court focused on the fact that the company used its own resources to pay for the collection of the scores. However, Morris Communications merely had a free ride on the collection system that the PGA Tour created and did not invest any resources of its own in the collection of the information. In addition, although NBA game scores are readily available to the public in real time, scores from golf events are not so readily available to the public because the PGA's system does not allow scores to be immediately provided to the public. Of course, unlike the NBA, the PGA also claimed that it had a property interest in both the system it used to acquire real-time scores and the scores themselves and maintained control over the dissemination of these scores by maintaining its system of requiring the media to pay a license fee for access.

The appellate court in *Morris* specifically avoided discussing the potential copyright issues involved, instead focusing on the antitrust issues. The court merely mentioned that the PGA had a property interest in the scores in conjunction with the system it created; the court did not define this interest as a copyright. There is no clear answer, as the Supreme Court has yet to rule on the issue. See the In the Courtroom case that follows for another example of how the courts have dealt with sport statistics as they relate to fantasy baseball games.

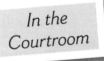

C.B.C. Distribution & Marketing, Inc. v. MLB Advanced Media (2007)

The *C.B.C. Distribution & Marketing, Inc. v. MLB Advanced Media* (2007) case was an important decision concerning sport statistics that involved Major League Baseball and claims by producers of fantasy sports baseball games.

In 1995, the Major League Baseball Players Association granted C.B.C. Distribution & Marketing (CBC) a license to use the names of baseball players and their corresponding statistics in fantasy baseball games. CBC markets, distributes, and sells fantasy sport products, including fantasy baseball games accessible over the Internet. At the time, CBC offered 11 fantasy baseball games, two midseason fantasy baseball games, and one fantasy baseball playoff game. In its games, CBC provided lists of MLB players for selection by participants who pay fees to play and to trade players. Prior to the start of the season, participants form their teams by drafting players. Participant owners then compete against other fantasy owners who have drafted their own teams.

In 2002, the players association granted CBC a renewed license, which gave CBC the rights to use the logo, name, and symbol of the players association (all trademarks) and the names, nicknames, likenesses, signatures, pictures, playing records, and biographical data of each player.

When this renewed license expired in 2005, the players association did not grant CBC another renewed license. Instead, it granted the exclusive right to use the players' names and statistics to MLB Advanced Media (MLBAM). MLB owners formed MLBAM in 2000 to serve as the interactive media and Internet arm of MLB. MLBAM is in charge of running MLB's Internet site, MLB.com. After receiving the license from the players association, MLBAM proposed a license under which CBC could promote fantasy baseball games on MLB.com but could not continue offering its own fantasy baseball products. CBC sued, asking the court to find that it could continue to use the names and statistics related to MLB players without a license from MLBAM.

The focus of the case was on whether CBC's use of the players' information violated their right of publicity or whether any such violation was preempted because the use was protected by the First Amendment. The district court granted summary judgment to CBC, finding that it did not infringe on the players' rights of publicity because it did not use the players' names as symbols of their identity in order to make a profit. The court also found that even if the players' rights of publicity were violated, the First Amendment protected CBC's use of the information and preempted the players' rights.

The U.S. Court of Appeals for the Eighth Circuit affirmed the previous court's finding, although for a different reason. The appellate court found that the use of the players' names was a use of the players' identities, because users would understand that the names in fact referred to particular baseball players. This use was also clearly for profit, because it was the basis of CBC's fantasy sports games. Therefore, this court found that CBC violated the players' rights of publicity. However, the court agreed with the district court and also found that the First Amendment trumped the right to publicity. Specifically, the court found that the information CBC provided was readily available to the public and so was protected by the First Amendment. The court also noted that information about baseball and its players has a public value because baseball has been referred to as the national pastime by many courts. Therefore, because information about baseball is in the public domain, protected by the First Amendment, MLB Advanced Media's claim that the CBC's fantasy sports game violated the players' rights of publicity could not stand. The appellate court affirmed the district court decision and granted summary judgment for CBC.

Right of Publicity

Closely related to copyright and trademark law is the right of publicity. The **right of publicity** has come to signify the right of any person to control the commercial use of his or her identity. This right is not produced under federal law; instead, many states have recognized the right by common law or included it in their state statutes. The right of publicity protects athletes' and celebrities' marketable identities from commercial misappropriation by recognizing their right to control and profit from the use of their names and nicknames, likenesses, portraits, performances (under certain circumstances), biographical facts, symbolic representations, or anything else that evokes this marketable identity. However, this right is not absolute. An athlete cannot use this right to prevent his name or picture from appearing in the newspaper. Newspaper reproductions of this type are protected as free speech under the First Amendment. In addition, although most of the cases protect celebrities (including athletes), the right of publicity extends to everyone.

The phrase was coined in a 1953 case. Haelan Laboratories entered into a contract with baseball players that provided Haelan with the exclusive right to use the players' photographs on baseball cards sold in packets of gum. As part of the agreement, the players agreed not to grant any other gum manufacturer the right to use their pictures. Topps Chewing Gum then entered into a similar agreement with the players, who allowed it to use their pictures on its own cards. Haelan sued Topps, claiming that it illegally induced the players into breaching their contracts with Haelan (*Haelan Laboratories, Inc. v. Topps Chewing Gum, Inc.*, 1953). The case focused on what rights the players had in their own identity and picture and whether these rights were assignable at all. For the first time, the court recognized a property right in the publicity value of an individual's identity, providing the players with a right to grant a company the exclusive right to publish their picture.

Another illustrative case involved boxer Muhammad Ali. In its February 1978 issue, *Playgirl* magazine included a cartoon of a nude black man seated in the corner of a boxing ring, with the caption "Mystery Man" and an accompanying reference to "The Greatest." Ali sued, claiming that the cartoon violated his right of publicity (*Muhammad Ali v. Playgirl, Inc.*, 1978). The court noted that Ali had regularly called himself "The Greatest" and that the media regularly identified him by that moniker. The court also noted that the features in the cartoon man were recognizable as Ali's own features. Therefore, the court concluded that Ali's right of publicity had been violated.

In the *CBC* case discussed earlier, MLB Advanced Media also argued that CBC had violated the players' right of publicity in its litigation against the fantasy sports provider (*C.B.C. Distribution and Marketing, Inc.*, 2006). The court explained that in order to prove a violation of this right, MLB had to show that CBC commercially exploited the players' identities without their consent and in order to gain a commercial advantage. Because it was clear that CBC used the players' identities without their consent, the court focused next on whether CBC did so in order to gain a commercial advantage. There was nothing about CBC's fantasy games demonstrating or implying that the players were associated with or endorsed CBC, and CBC did not use the players in a way to attract business from other fantasy sports providers. Instead, all such leagues use the same player information; therefore, the court found that there was no evidence that CBC used the players' identities to gain a commercial advantage. The court also found that CBC used the players' names only in association with their playing statistics, and not their pictures, personality, or reputation. Finally, the court found that CBC's use of the players' names and records did not dilute the value of each player's identity. In the end, the court held that CBC did not violate the players' right of publicity.

As a result, although all professional athletes do have some recognizable right of publicity in their identity, this right does not extend to the use of their name or career statistics on the Internet. Still, the full extent of the right of publicity within sports remains to be seen. MLB has appealed the *CBC* decision, technology continues to advance, and the numerous fantasy sports and sports gambling sites demonstrate new ways in which information related to professional athletes can be disseminated on the Internet. Presumably, players and leagues will continue to seek to receive revenue associated with the use of player information by these new technologies.

Patent Law

A final area of intellectual property law that affects the sport industry is patent law. (See table 9.2 for a summary of the intellectual property laws discussed in this chapter.) Patent law is designed to advance science and inventions by providing protection to those who create new things. A **patent** is a document provided by the federal government that gives the owner the right to exclude others from reproducing the patented invention for 20

patent—A document provided by the federal government that gives the owner of an invention the right to exclude others from reproducing the patented invention for 20 years.

Table 9.2 Summary of Intellectual Property Laws

Law	Who or what it protects	Sport examples
Trademark law	Any word, name, symbol, or device used to identify and distinguish the services of one person from the services of others and to indicate the source of the services, even if that source is unknown	• Logos • Team names
Copyright law	Literary or artistic productions and the reproduction, publication, or sale of these productions	• Game accounts • Statistics
Right of publicity	The right of any person to control the commercial use of his or her identity	• Baseball cards • T-shirts
Patent law	Inventors of new things that receive federal protection providing the inventor with the right to exclude others from reproducing the invention for 20 years	• Equipment • Apparel design • Games

years. The patent itself specifically describes the invention in great detail. An invention is patentable if it is a "new and useful process, machine, manufacture, or composition of matter, or any new and useful improvement thereof" (Patent Act, 35 U.S.C. § 101, 2008).

A patent can be awarded for any invention that is a new product, process, apparatus, or composition, including living matter. Abstract ideas, laws of nature, literary and artistic works, and inventions that are not considered useful cannot be patented. To obtain a federal patent, the inventor must submit an application to the U.S. Patent and Trademark Office within 1 year of the time the invention will be sold or in public use. The inventor must demonstrate that the invention is new (no one else invented it or applied for a patent for it), useful (it must serve some clear purpose), and nonobvious (an ordinary person would not have found the invention to be obvious in the particular field); however, beyond this the courts have allowed individuals to patent virtually anything (Patent Act, 35 U.S.C. § 102 & § 103).

Sport organizations have patents for everything one can imagine—the equipment used to play the sport (balls, bats, gloves, clubs), designs for the apparel worn (shoes, shirts, jackets, cleats), and even certain games themselves (the Arena Football League owns a patent for that style of football). The patent for Arena Football League–style football, patent number 4,911,443, described as a "football game system and method of play," is registered as follows:

> A new game is disclosed, involving substantially the same rules as American football (e.g., NFL or NCAA) except that kicks or passes into the end zone may be deflected back onto the playing field as a playable ball by a rebounding assembly that surrounds the goalposts. Upon an attempted field goal, an errant kick will result in the ball hitting the rebounding assembly instead of passing between the vertical uprights of the goalpost. The reflected ball can be caught before it hits the ground by only players of the team defending the goal. Once caught, the defending team may advance the ball toward the opposite goal in accordance with the normal rules of American football. If the ball reflected off of the rebounding assembly hits the ground before it is caught by a player of the team defending the goal, the ball is free for players of either team to advance. In order to ensure that an errant kick results in the rebounding of the ball back into the playing field, the rebounding assembly is comprised of resilient material that returns much of the kinetic energy to the ball after it impacts the rebounding assembly. The rebound assembly for playing the game is comprised of a goal post substantially similar to that used in American football, with the exception that the instant goal is provided with a ball rebound net extending outwards from each side of the goal post, along the extremity of the end zone to substantially the entire width of the playing field.

Patents have begun to proliferate in fantasy sports games. One of the most recent such patents is patent number 7,001,279, granted on February 21, 2006, for "systems and methods for providing multiple user support for shared user equipment in a *fantasy* sports contest application":

> This invention provides systems and methods for providing multiple user support for shared user equipment in fantasy sports contest applications. A fantasy sports contest application may allow users to set up unique user accounts, in which user specific information such as, for example, identification information, fantasy sports contest participation information, user preference information, or any other suitable information associated with the user, may be stored. The application may personalize fantasy sports contest information and displays for the user. Local fantasy sports leagues may be created for users of common user equipment so that they may compete against each other.

To find out what patents have been granted in the sports world, anyone can visit the U.S. Patent and Trademark Office Web site at www.uspto.gov/patft/index.html. For example, from the beginning of 2007 until early May 2008, there were 231 sport-related patent applications.

The main purpose of a patent is to give the inventor the right to exclude others from copying an invention for at least 20 years. Theoretically, if the patent is for items of value that can be sold in some market, the inventor will be able to recover any costs of developing the invention and potentially make a profit. Inventors usually market their inventions themselves so that they can make money from them. However, if they are unable to produce and market products using their patent, they sell licenses to others granting them permission to use the patent and sell products themselves.

As with all intellectual property rights, litigation in this area focuses on potential infringement, in this case **patent infringement.** To show patent infringement, an inventor must show that someone else made, used, offered to sell or sold, or imported into the United States their patented material without their permission (Patent Act, 35 U.S.C. § 271, 2008). An inventor can receive damages, attorney's fees, and injunctive relief if he or she succeeds in a claim of patent infringement.

Fantasy Sports Properties, Inc., patented a particular method of playing fantasy football on the Internet—patent number 4,918,603, for a "computerized statistical football game." Fantasy sued Sportsline.com, Yahoo!, Inc., and ESPN, claiming that their computerized fantasy football games infringed on this patent (*Fantasy Sports Properties, Inc. v. Sportsline.com, Inc.*, 2002). A court reviewing a claim of patent infringement first must determine the scope and meaning of the patent claims asserted and then must compare these claims to the alleged infringing product. Here, the court analyzed Fantasy's patent very specifically. Fantasy argued that its patent covered any scoring method awarding any bonus points, whereas the court determined that the patent specifically related to bonus points that can be given in addition to standard points given for a particular play in an actual game, based on the

patent infringement— Action whereby someone other than the patent holder makes, and without permission, uses, sells, offers to sell, or imports patented material.

difficulty of play. Therefore, Yahoo! did not infringe on the patent because its game only awarded miscellaneous points when a kicker scored a touchdown but still valued those points as a regular touchdown with an asterisk. In addition, ESPN's game did not infringe on the patent because its game did not award bonus points beyond the normal points awarded in a football game. However, the court could not determine whether Sportsline.com's software tool awarded bonus points in violation of the patent and so the court remanded that issue to the trial court.

Ambush Marketing

ambush marketing— Practice of creating advertising or promotional campaigns that confuse consumers and misrepresent that a company is an official sponsor of an event.

As a sports administrator, your job is to make sure that your organization can earn money from any sponsorship agreement it enters into. Unfortunately, other companies that have not entered into a written sponsorship agreement may attempt to create some sort of false association with your event or organization in order to profit from the association without paying for a sponsorship. This practice is known as **ambush marketing,** a situation where one company creates advertising or promotional campaigns that confuse consumers and wrongly imply that the company is an official sponsor of an event. This practice harms companies that are official sponsors by weakening their relationship with the event. These types of ambush marketing campaigns are particularly found with large-scale events such as the Super Bowl or Olympics, where companies and organizations pay sponsorship fees in the millions of dollars to be officially recognized as event sponsors. For example, worldwide Olympic sponsors (the highest level of sponsorship) for the 2008 Summer Olympic Games, including Coca-Cola, Samsung, Johnson & Johnson, Kodak, McDonald's, Panasonic, and Visa, paid an estimated $70 million for their sponsorships. Companies that cannot afford to be official sponsors may try to associate with the event in other ways without paying for an official sponsorship.

An interesting example of an ambush marketing campaign occurred in conjunction with the 2002 Winter Olympics in Salt Lake City, Utah. Official sponsor Anheuser-Busch paid approximately $50 million for its sponsorship. This granted the company the license to use the word *Olympic* and the five-ring logo in a marketing campaign running up to the Games. Schirf Brewery, a local brewer in Salt Lake City, attempted to profit by an odd association with the Games by marking its delivery trucks as "Wasutch Beers: The Unofficial Beer. 2002 Winter Games." Because this brewery did not use the word *Olympic* or the logo, neither the USOC nor Anheuser-Busch could sue the company, even though it clearly was attempting to profit from an association with the Winter Games.

Sport organizations and event hosts are reluctant to go after ambush marketers because there is little case law showing that this activity is illegal. In addition, ambush marketing campaigns are often short-lived because companies only put forth an ambush marketing campaign close to the event itself. Sport organizations that do want to take action often focus on trademark or copyright infringement claims against the ambushing company.

Summary

Intellectual property law provides the foundation for the protection of rights that an organization can sell in order to generate revenue. Trademark rights are perhaps most valuable because they allow an organization to generate revenue by licensing the use of its name and logo. Collective marks allow leagues to create new logos and nicknames that represent the entire group of member teams. The law provides specific ways for an organization to stop competitors who try to infringe upon and dilute the organization's marks. With the protection provided by anticybersquatting laws and the Uniform Dispute Resolution Process, organizations can also protect their Web sites and domain names. This is especially important as sport organizations continue to find new ways to sell tickets and merchandise online.

Copyright law provides organizations with ways to protect their rights in television broadcasts, game accounts, media guides, newspapers, and magazines. Still to be decided are the exact rights that a league or team has to protect the statistics produced by players and teams. Although players can control and profit from the use of their identity because of the right of publicity, their playing statistics do not receive similar copyright protection.

Finally, many sport organizations create new and profitable styles of play, equipment, facilities, and products. All of these inventions can be registered as patents, which exclude others from using an invention without permission for 20 years, a long time in which the patent holder can make a profit.

DISCUSSION QUESTIONS

1. Why should sport administrators understand intellectual property law?
2. What types of marks can a sport organization seek legal protection for?
3. Why would a sport organization bring a trademark infringement lawsuit against a competitor?
4. What methods are available for a sport organization to protect its domain name?
5. Why would a sport organization be interested in granting other companies and individuals licenses to use its nickname or logo?
6. How is a copyright different from a trademark?
7. Why is the right of publicity important to a professional athlete?
8. Why are patents such valuable legal rights for an individual to possess?

MOOT COURT CASE

A new professional baseball team was set to be established in southwest Florida, an area once populated by the Native American Seminole tribe. The name chosen for the team was the Florida Redskins. The U.S. Patent and Trademark Office granted permission to the new owners to use this name. The Florida Redskins enjoyed immediate success and popularity in southwest Florida. Native Americans living in Florida, however, were upset with the use of the nickname, which they believed to be disparaging to Native Americans and in violation of the Lanham Act. As a result, a group of Native Americans petitioned to cancel the trademark registrations for the marks *Florida Redskins* and *Redskins,* which were owned by the owners of the MLB's Florida Redskins franchise. The owners immediately brought suit to avoid the cancellation of the marks and to keep the team name.

10

Antitrust Law

CHAPTER OBJECTIVES

After reading this chapter, you will know the following:

- The federal antitrust laws and how they apply to sports
- The types of player restraints that have been reviewed under the antitrust laws
- The types of exemptions from the antitrust laws that apply to professional sports
- The history of team movement and the ways that antitrust laws affect the movement of teams within professional sports
- The specific ways that antitrust laws have been used to regulate college athletics

AP Photo/Ed Andrieski

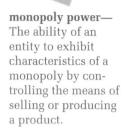

monopoly power—
The ability of an entity to exhibit characteristics of a monopoly by controlling the means of selling or producing a product.

Antitrust laws were implemented to promote competition and efficiency in the marketplace and to protect consumers from the growing **monopoly power** of big business. These laws were designed to maintain a high level of competition among producers, so that consumers would be able to get products at affordable and reasonable prices. In sport, antitrust laws have been used by players, owners, universities, teams, and leagues in an attempt to change conditions that these parties believe have caused them to suffer negative economic consequences. Such negative consequences include lower wages, the inability to relocate a team, unfair competition, and lower television revenues.

The application of antitrust laws in sport is most prominent in professional sports. This chapter discusses the interaction of antitrust laws with professional sport in several areas, including player restraints, franchise relocation, ownership issues, and disputes between leagues. There are several ways professional sports leagues have been found to operate outside of the antitrust laws through various exemptions, and some leagues, such as Major League Soccer, have been created using single-entity structures that provide protection from certain forms of antitrust scrutiny.

Although antitrust has been used to regulate primarily professional sports, amateur sports have not been immune to review under the antitrust laws. In particular, the NCAA has faced numerous challenges under the antitrust laws, typically because individuals claim that NCAA regulations restrain trade.

Before discussing the impact that the antitrust laws have had on the sport industry, the chapter begins by discussing the federal antitrust laws themselves.

interstate commerce—Commerce that takes place between two or more states.

per se rule—Conduct that is inherently anticompetitive, such as price fixing and group boycotts, and so automatically violates the Sherman Antitrust Act.

rule of reason—Rule used by courts in antitrust cases that applies when the conduct is not inherently anticompetitive; under this rule, a court focuses on whether the challenged conduct restrains trade unreasonably.

Federal Antitrust Laws

Federal antitrust laws, particularly the Sherman Antitrust Act, have a substantial impact on sport. This chapter focuses on federal law, but each state has adopted a form of antitrust law that mirrors the federal law. As a result, analysis under the federal law is quite similar to that under state laws. Passed in 1890, the Sherman Antitrust Act includes two major sections. Section 1 states that "every contract, combination in the form of trust or otherwise, or conspiracy in restraint of trade or commerce among the several states or foreign nations, is declared to be illegal" (15 U.S.C. § 1, 2008). To prove a violation of the Sherman Act under section 1, a plaintiff must satisfy three elements. First, the plaintiff must show that there is an agreement between two separate parties. Next, the plaintiff must show that the parties' conduct taken under the agreement unreasonably restrains trade because they are anticompetitive. Finally, the activity must affect **interstate commerce,** that is, commerce that takes place between two or more states.

When a court looks at whether a sport organizations conduct violates section 1, the court will analyze the nature of the conduct under either the **per se rule** or the **rule of reason.** Conduct that is inherently anticompetitive, such as **price fixing** and **group boycotts,** is considered to be illegal per se and automatically violates the Sherman Act. This conduct is so destructive to competition that a plaintiff only has to show that these things happened; the plaintiff does not have to show that he or she was harmed by them.

The rule of reason analysis applies when the conduct is not inherently anticompetitive. Instead, the focus is on whether the challenged conduct unreasonably restrains trade. Under this analysis, a plaintiff must show that there is an agreement among separate entities, that this agreement negatively affects competition in a relevant market, and that the anticompetitive effects of the agreement outweigh any procompetitive effects. A defendant can defend conduct that might otherwise violate the rule of reason by showing that there is a legitimate business reason for the restraining conduct and that the methods used are the least restrictive means.

Section 2 provides that "every person who shall monopolize, or attempt to monopolize or combine or conspire with any other person or persons, to monopolize any part of the trade or commerce among the several states, or with foreign nations, shall be deemed guilty of a felony" (15 U.S.C. § 2, 2008). A **monopoly** is an organization that possesses exclusive control over the means of selling and producing a product. Because a monopoly's control is exclusive, it does not face competition from other organizations that might force it to lower its prices or provide better products to compete in the marketplace. To show a violation of section 2, a plaintiff must show that the organization possesses monopoly market power and has used unacceptable means to acquire or maintain this power.

The other important law dealing with antitrust issues is the Clayton Antitrust Act, passed in 1914 (15 U.S.C. § 15, 2008). This law provides that when a plaintiff proves that there has been a breach of the Sherman Act, the damages that the plaintiff can recover are tripled. For example, in 1984, when Los Angeles Raiders owner Al Davis won his antitrust lawsuit against the NFL, the tripled damages amounted to more than $35 million.

Two other federal antitrust laws, the Sports Broadcasting Act and the Curt Flood Act, are discussed later in the chapter as they specifically relate to professional sports. See table 10.1 for a summary of the antitrust laws discussed in this chapter.

Application to Professional Team Sports

In professional sports, teams have long used different types of restraints to restrict player movement, such as free agent compensation arrangements, option and **reserve clauses,** no tampering rules, and the draft system. Players and their respective players associations repeatedly object to these practices because they limit player salaries and bolster profits for the team. On the other hand, management at both the club and league level views such restraints as necessary to maintain economic viability and competition, and

price fixing—Agreement among members of a group (such as a professional sports league) to set prices at a certain level to avoid competition among group members over prices.

group boycotts—Situation where a league or a group of teams collectively agree not to bargain with a particular group of players, for instance, by setting draft rules that exclude certain players from being drafted.

monopoly—An organization that possesses exclusive control over the means of selling and producing a product.

reserve clause—A clause that used to be contained within every professional baseball player's contract stating that if the player did not automatically sign a new contract with the team for the next season, all of the provisions of his present contract would be automatically renewed.

Table 10.1   Summary of Antitrust Laws

Federal law	What it does	How it applies to sport
Sherman Antitrust Act, Section 1	• Regulates agreements that restrain trade • Focuses on anticompetitive behavior • Regulates only the activities that affect commerce between two or mores states	• Review of ownership rules in professional sports • Review of participation eligibility rules in individual performer sports • Review of salary restrictions in college sports
Sherman Antitrust Act, Section 2	Regulates entities that exhibit some form of monopoly power by possessing exclusive control over the means of selling and producing a product	• Review of franchise relocation rules in professional sports • Review of television contracts in college sports • Review of competition among leagues in professional sports
Clayton Antitrust Act	Allows for damages to be tripled when a court finds that there has been a violation of the Sherman Act	Referred to in all situations where a violation of the Sherman Act is found (e.g., the damages awarded to the Raiders were tripled from $11.5 million to $34.5 million when they proved that the NFL violated the Sherman Act when it tried to stop them from relocating)
Sports Broadcasting Act	• An exemption from the Sherman Act, Section 1 • Allows professional hockey, football, baseball, and basketball to pool and sell their rights in game telecasts	Review of restrictions against individual team television contracts in professional sports
Curt Flood Act	Allows baseball players to sue MLB if they believe that some condition of their employment may violate the antitrust laws	Only applies to potential claims brought by baseball players against MLB

clubs and leagues often are provided with exemptions from the antitrust laws so that these restraints are allowed to continue. What follows is a brief analysis of the impact of the antitrust laws on professional team sports.

Player Restraints

Some of the earliest applications of antitrust law in sport focused on protecting player salaries from illegal restraints or unfair competition. These restraints have taken many forms over the years.

Player Drafts

One restraint that has seen a lot of litigation is the amateur player draft. Each of the major sports leagues uses an annual draft to select and allocate players to its member teams. Each league also sets out specific requirements related to the age of those who can be drafted, their completion or progress in high school or university, and their eligibility to be drafted by a member team.

In the early 1970s, the NBA draft rule only allowed players to be eligible 4 years after they graduated from high school. This did not mean that players had to graduate from university; instead, they were only eligible at a point 4 years past their high school graduation. Spencer Haywood, a talented basketball player playing for the American Basketball Association, wanted to play for the NBA but was barred from the draft because of this rule. He sued, arguing that this player restraint was a group boycott violating the Sherman Act (*Denver Rockets v. All-Pro Mgt., Inc.,* 1971). The court agreed, finding that the NBA draft rule was a group boycott because the NBA conspired to avoid dealing with players who were not 4 years beyond high school graduation, and therefore the NBA was restraining trade in violation of the Sherman Act.

In a similar case 5 years later, James McCoy Smith sued the NFL claiming that its draft system prevented him from negotiating a contract that would reflect the free market value of his services (*Smith v. Pro-Football, Inc.,* 1978). Conducting a rule of reason analysis, the court found that the draft system was an unreasonable restraint of trade. The draft rule forced each seller (the players drafted) to deal with only one team, robbing the player of any bargaining power. The NFL argued that the rule was necessary to achieve competitive balance, to produce better entertainment for the fans, and to create higher salaries for all NFL players. The court found that these justifications had nothing to do with the market for players and held that the rule was an unreasonable restraint of trade.

Even after these decisions, both the NFL and NBA continued to use an amateur draft. Eventually, the NBA modified its draft rules allowing for virtually any athlete to apply for the draft. As a result, even high school players became eligible, and in the 1990s teams began to draft younger and younger players. Recently, as part of its newest collective bargaining agreement, the NBA modified its draft rule again, restricting eligibility to players who are 19 years of age or older. By 1990, the NFL had settled on eligibility rules that permitted a player to enter the draft only three full seasons after that player's high school graduation. Although some speculated that these draft rules would also be found to be a restraint of trade, a recent case against the NFL (see the In the Courtroom case on page 242) seems to show that courts will now uphold draft rules in certain situations.

It seems that leagues can maintain amateur drafts as long as they are created as a part of the collective bargaining process and, most likely, as long as they are included within the collective bargaining agreement. This makes sense because the agreement represents the terms and conditions of employment that have been agreed to by both players (as represented by their union) and management.

Restrictive Free Agency

Over the years several leagues have implemented rules that have restricted the ability of players to move freely to sign contracts with different teams and have forced teams to provide compensation of some form to another team

Clarett v. NFL (2004)

The case of *Clarett v. NFL* (2004) involved Maurice Clarett, who graduated from high school in 2001 as one of the top 100 running back prospects in the United States, receiving *USA Today* high school player of the year and *Parade* All-American honors. He enrolled at The Ohio State University, where he became one of the best university players in the country during his first year. As a freshman, Clarett rushed for 1,237 yards (a school record for a freshman) and scored 18 touchdowns. Ohio State went 14-0 and Clarett scored the winning touchdown against the University of Miami with a 5-yard run in the second overtime in the Fiesta Bowl, winning the 2002 BCS National Championship.

This success did not last. Ohio State suspended Clarett for the 2003 season after he was charged with filing a false police report. He had filed a false claim that more than $10,000 in clothing, CDs, cash, and stereo equipment were stolen from a car he borrowed from a local dealership in September 2003. In addition, the athletic department found that that he had received thousands of dollars in special benefits and repeatedly misled investigators. He later pled guilty to a lesser criminal charge in that incident.

As a result of his suspension from university football, Clarett tried to enter the NFL draft, but he was barred because he was not three full seasons removed from his high school graduation. Since 1990, NFL eligibility rules had permitted a player to enter the draft only three full seasons after that player's high school graduation. Although the eligibility rules do not appear in the text of the collective bargaining agreement, at the time the current agreement went into effect, the rules appeared in the NFL constitution and bylaws, which had last been amended in 1992. The rules are also mentioned in three separate provisions within the agreement.

Clarett sued the NFL, claiming that the eligibility rule was an unreasonable restraint of trade in violation of federal antitrust law. The district court granted summary judgment in favor of Clarett and ordered that he be made eligible for the 2004 draft. The NFL first sought a stay of the district court's order but was denied. The NFL then appealed the district court's decision. Five days before the April 24 draft, the court of appeals issued a stay of the lower court's ruling preventing Clarett and others from being a part of the NFL draft. After the ruling, Clarett filed an emergency appeal with the U.S. Supreme Court, which was denied.

Before the court of appeals, Clarett argued that the NFL clubs are competitors for the labor of professional football players and that the eligibility rules violate the antitrust laws. The court first noted that in order to accommodate the collective bargaining process, certain concerted activity among and between labor and employer has been held to be beyond the reach of the antitrust laws because of the nonstatutory labor exemption. The exemption is a judicially created doctrine that defers to the National Labor Relations Board in determining what specific labor practices are exempt from antitrust scrutiny. Typically, mandatory subjects of bargaining such as wages and working conditions have been protected from antitrust review by the exemption. Therefore, the court noted that NFL teams are permitted to engage in joint conduct with the union with respect to the terms and conditions of players' employment without risking antitrust scrutiny. The court held that the eligibility rules are mandatory bargaining subjects and are protected by the labor exemption. Therefore, Clarett could not contest these rules on antitrust grounds. The Second Circuit Court reversed the district court and remanded the case with instructions to enter judgment for the NFL.

if they sign that team's player. For example, under MLB's reserve system, each player was the property of his team for the extent of his playing career. At the time, each player contract contained a **reserve clause** that stipulated that if the player did not automatically sign a new contract with the team for the next season, all of the provisions of his present contract would be automatically renewed. As a result, each team had the perpetual right to renew each of its own player's contracts. The player could still be traded or fired but this was at the club's option. There was no **free agency,** so players were not allowed to negotiate with other teams for their services. At the same time, league rules prevented teams from negotiating with players on other teams and seeking their services.

Supported by baseball's **antitrust exemption,** the reserve clause remained in force until 1975. In that year, baseball players Andy Messersmith and Dave McNally played without a contract because they could not agree with their clubs on the renewal of their old contracts. At the end of the year, both players declared themselves to be free agents, arguing that the reserve clause only affected them for 1 year after the expiration of their contracts. Their clubs disagreed, arguing that the reserve clause was perpetual and that they were each still under contract. As provided in the **collective bargaining agreement,** the Major League Baseball Players Association filed a grievance on behalf of the players before a designated arbitrator (*Arbitration of Messersmith,* 1975).

Agreeing with the players, the arbitrator interpreted the reserve clause to mean that a player's contract was reserved for a team for only 1 year after his contract had expired. Therefore, Messersmith and McNally were free agents. The owners challenged this decision, but the challenge failed because the court determined that the designated arbitrator was the proper party to interpret the provisions of the players' contracts as dictated in the

reserve clause—A clause that used to be contained within every professional baseball player's contract stating that if the player did not automatically sign a new contract with the team for the next season, all of the provisions of his present contract would be automatically renewed.

free agency—The period of time when a professional athlete is not under contract to any particular team and so is able to freely negotiate with any team.

antitrust exemption—A finding by a court or provision in a statute that exempts a party from review under the antitrust laws.

collective bargaining agreement—A written agreement between employers and employees that provides the exact terms and conditions of the employment relationship between the parties.

collective bargaining agreement. From this time, each subsequent collective bargaining agreement has modified the player contract, providing that the player is bound to the team that drafts him for a defined amount of time before he is eligible to become a free agent.

Rozelle rule—An NFL rule that required a team signing a veteran free agent to provide compensation to the team that was losing the player.

The NFL had a similar rule called the **Rozelle rule.** This rule required a team signing a veteran free agent to provide compensation to the team that was losing the player. The rule effectively stifled competition because teams did not want to pay this compensation, and players were kept on the teams that drafted them and could not reap the benefits of free agency. The Rozelle rule stayed in place until 1975, when several players sued the NFL claiming that the Rozelle rule was an illegal restraint on trade in violation of the Sherman Act (*Mackey v. NFL,* 1976). The court initially determined that as a result of the rule, players were not able to sell their services on an open market and so the salaries they were paid were lower than they would have been in an open market. The league argued that the rule was needed to promote competitive balance. Although the court was sympathetic to this argument and recognized that some restraints on free agency were necessary, it found that the Rozelle rule was too strong of a restraint on competition.

Although each league still maintains some restrictions on free agency, each league also has some form of free agency. At some point during a player's career, the player is free to sign a contract with the team of his choice.

Salary Caps

salary cap—An agreed upon level of revenue that teams must pay out in player salaries for any particular year. The amount is agreed to in negotiations between players and teams and included in the league's collective bargaining agreement.

Salary caps in sports set a limit on the amount of money a team can spend on player salaries (see table 10.2). These caps are set either as per-player limits or as a total limit that a team can pay for its players. In 1983, the NBA became the first league to implement a salary cap, and since then the NFL and NHL have added some form of salary cap. Often the amount of the salary cap is a major issue in negotiations between owners and players over a collective bargaining agreement. The issue is important to many players because they believe that a salary cap will depress their ability to freely negotiate for a maximum salary. MLB players still have not agreed to a salary cap. As

Table 10.2   Recent Salary Caps in Professional Team Sports

Season	NBA	NHL	Season	NFL
2000-2001	$35.5 million	NA	2001	$67.4 million
2001-2002	$42.5 million	NA	2002	$71.1 million
2002-2003	$40.271 million	NA	2003	$75.007 million
2003-2004	$43.84 million	NA	2004	$80.582 million
2004-2005	$43.87 million	Cancelled	2005	$85.5 million
2005-2006	$49.5 million	$39 million	2006	$102 million
2006-2007	$53.135 million	$44 million	2007	$109 million
2007-2008	$55.63 million	$50.3 million	2008	$116 million

NA, not applicable.

a result, teams like the New York Yankees continue to be unrestricted in paying huge salaries to their players, and smaller-market teams that cannot pay these salaries often believe that they cannot compete.

Many players have challenged salary caps. For instance, Leon Wood sued the NBA, claiming that various provisions of the collective bargaining agreement, including the salary cap, violated the Sherman Act (*Wood v. NBA*, 1987). Wood was drafted by the Philadelphia 76ers in 1984 and was offered a 1-year contract for $75,000 under the salary cap. Arguing that he would be forced to sign a contract under his actual market value, Wood sued to stop the NBA's use of its salary cap. The court rejected Wood's claim because it found that the salary cap was created within the collective bargaining agreement as a normal part of the negotiation process between management and labor.

Although many forms of player restraints, including salary caps and player drafts, have been upheld by the courts, the restrictive player restraints of years past are now long gone and all players can become free agents at some point in their careers.

Exemptions

Exemptions from the antitrust laws typically provide a league, club, or other entity with immunity from scrutiny for conduct that might otherwise be found to be illegal. The most well-known exemption in sports is enjoyed by Major League Baseball.

exemptions—Findings by a court or provisions of statutes that exempt a party from review under a particular regulation or statute. Exemptions allow the party to avoid a lawsuit as a result of its actions that otherwise could be found to have violated the regulation or statute.

Baseball

Since 1922, players have not been able to sue MLB claiming that the league's policies violate the antitrust laws, even though such suits are possible in other professional sports leagues. By 1913, the National and American Leagues were well established, but they faced competition from the newly formed Federal League. Both the National and American Leagues offered Federal League owners considerable amounts of money to disband the new league. They also offered Federal League owners the right to purchase franchises in the National and American Leagues. The Baltimore club of the Federal League sued, claiming that this conduct violated the Sherman Act. Baltimore argued that the Federal League was destroyed by a conspiracy between the National and American Leagues. In a landmark decision, Justice Holmes stated that the antitrust laws did not apply to baseball because baseball was an "exhibition" and "not subject to commerce" (*Federal Baseball Club v. National League*, 1922).

Because of this case, players have been unable to sue MLB under the Sherman Act. This judicially recognized exemption has continued for decades, but not without challenge. In 1953, several players sued baseball, claiming that the standard reserve clause in their contracts violated the antitrust laws. As explained earlier, under the reserve system teams were allowed to automatically renew a player's contract at the end of each year. This created a continuous cycle that prevented players from marketing their services to other teams. The Supreme Court affirmed its decision in the *Federal Baseball* ruling, upholding the exemption and leaving it to Congress to decide whether antitrust laws should apply to baseball (*Toolson v. New York Yankees,* 1953).

In 1972, baseball player Curt Flood challenged the exemption, arguing that baseball's reserve system violated the Sherman Act, but was unsuccessful (*Flood v. Kuhn,* 1972). Although the Court finally recognized that as a business, baseball did engage in interstate commerce, the Court also noted that Congress had not intervened in 50 years to change the exemption. Therefore, it again left the matter to be changed by Congress.

It was not until 1993 that courts began to be more vocal in their disagreement with baseball's antitrust exemption. Vincent Piazza and Vincent Tirendi formed a limited partnership in order to buy the San Francisco Giants and move the team to Tampa, Florida. When MLB did not approve of the purchase, Piazza and Tirendi sued, claiming that MLB's actions violated the antitrust laws (*Piazza v. Major League Baseball,* 1993). They alleged that MLB monopolized the market for baseball teams and placed restraints on the purchase, sale, and other forms of competition for these teams. The court found that baseball's antitrust exemption did not extend to the purchase of an existing team. Soon after the case, the Giants were sold to a local buyer.

Pursuant to a provision in the 1994 MLB collective bargaining agreement, the players and owners lobbied Congress to modify the baseball exemption. In 1998, Congress passed the Curt Flood Act (15 U.S.C. § 26(b), 2008) in commemoration of Curt Flood. The act allows baseball players to sue MLB if they believe that some condition of their employment may violate the antitrust laws. Other aspects of the business of baseball itself (i.e., ownership, management, relocation) are still protected by the antitrust exemption.

Nonstatutory Labor Exemption

labor exemption—An exemption that provides that when employers and employees have bargained in good faith, one party can not be subject to antitrust claims brought by the other party.

mandatory subject of collective bargaining—Terms of employment such as wages or hours of work that must be agreed to in negotiations between employers and employees.

The U.S. Supreme Court created the nonstatutory **labor exemption** so that when employers and employees have agreed to a collective bargaining agreement in good faith, neither of them can bring an antitrust challenge related to the terms of the agreement. As a result, terms and conditions that normally could be attacked as violations of the antitrust laws (such as salary caps and player restraints) are immune from antitrust scrutiny as long as they were negotiated for within collective bargaining. Although not created for sports, the nonstatutory labor exemption has been discussed in many sport-related cases.

Courts have developed a three-part test for when a league can use the labor exemption as a defense to claims brought by players or unions. Most challenges will be brought against the league, because it is the employer and enforces the terms and conditions of the player's employment contract. To use the labor exemption, a league must show that (1) the restraint of trade affects only the parties to the collective bargaining agreement; (2) the restraint is a **mandatory subject of collective bargaining** (these include wages, hours, and other terms and conditions of employment); and (3) the collective bargaining agreement is the product of arms-length bargaining, meaning that each party has an equally strong position to bargain from.

Although the nonstatutory exemption can allow employers to avoid antitrust liability in a manner similar to the baseball exemption, courts have struggled to understand its application. Two interesting situations developed out of the possible application of the exemption, the first after a player strike and the second in regard to developmental squad players.

In 1987, after the NFL's collective bargaining agreement expired, the league wanted to maintain the status quo on all of the mandatory subjects in the expired agreement, including player salaries. When negotiations between the league and union soured, the players went on strike. The strike ended after 1 month, but the players and owners still could not reach an agreement and the league insisted on implementing the conditions of the expired agreement. The players sued to stop the NFL from implementing the expired agreement and also asked the court to determine whether the labor exemption protected the league's first refusal/compensation policy (*Powell v. NFL,* 1989). The court found that the labor exemption could be invoked even after the collective bargaining agreement expired. Although the union and owners were at impasse at this stage, there was still the possibility that they could reach an agreement in the future. In addition, because the rule at issue was a mandatory subject and because the parties were still negotiating over the terms of the next agreement, the exemption immunized the league's conduct from antitrust review.

How long the nonstatutory labor exemption can apply after the expiration of a collective bargaining agreement is still unclear. The *Powell* court hinted that the union would have to stop serving as the players' representative within negotiations before the exemption would expire. Therefore, it seems that for most conditions of employment related to salaries and free agency, as long as the parties are negotiating or can still negotiate to reach an agreement, the exemption still applies. As a result, management typically can implement policies from the past agreement and maintain the status quo, even though the union disagrees, without violating the antitrust laws.

The second situation that developed out of the possible application of the exemption occurred in the 1990s when the NFL proposed a new plan where up to six first-year free agent players who failed to secure a roster spot with a team could be designated for a development squad. These players could play in regular practices and were to be paid approximately $1,000 per week. The players union rejected this idea, arguing that all players should receive the same benefits and protections. The union and management could not agree, and they reached impasse. Thereafter, the owners unilaterally implemented the developmental squad plan. Predictably, the players sued, claiming that the NFL's imposition of the policy violated the antitrust laws (*Brown v. Pro Football, Inc.,* 1996). In analyzing whether the nonstatutory labor exemption applied, the court noted that the plan was created during collective bargaining and implemented immediately after impasse was reached. It involved a mandatory subject of bargaining that had to be negotiated for, and it concerned only the parties to the agreement. Therefore,

impasse—A situation that occurs when the parties negotiating an agreement have reached a point where no further progress can be made because the sides cannot agree on further changes to the agreement that would advance the negotiations.

similar to the *Powell* decision, the exemption immunized the league from claims that the imposition of the policy violated the Sherman Act.

Broadcasting Exemption

The Sports Broadcasting Act (15 U.S.C. § 1291, et seq., 2008) was enacted in 1961 to allow professional hockey, football, baseball, and basketball to pool and sell their rights in sponsored telecasts of games. Such pooling of rights to be sold to one buyer would in most situations be considered price fixing or monopoly behavior and would violate the antitrust laws. However, the Sports Broadcasting Act provides that the pooling of these television rights is exempt from section 1 of the Sherman Act. The purpose of the Sports Broadcasting Act was to enable clubs to put their separate rights together into one package so that the league can sell the package to one purchaser, such as a television network, in an effort to protect their home game ticket sales and to allow clubs to share television revenues. The focus on "sponsored telecasts" has been interpreted to ensure that free national and local televising of league games continues. As a result, paid broadcasts on cable and league agreements with cable broadcasters have not been covered by this antitrust exemption.

Teams in the NBA have jointly pooled and marketed some of their television rights through the league under the exemption granted by the Sports Broadcasting Act. In the early 1990s, this agreement with the NBA and TNT provided each team with its single largest source of shared league revenues at about $6.8 million (in 2006 it was roughly $15 million). Since about 1982, in an effort to maximize the value of the agreement, the league has also restricted local broadcasts by teams, especially local broadcasts on superstations. Superstations are independent broadcasters that broadcast in their local market and are carried in other parts of the county, like Chicago's WGN and Atlanta's WTBS. Over the years, the NBA has limited the number of games that teams can air on superstations. The limit was 41 games in 1980 and was lowered to 25 in 1985. In 1990, the NBA's Board of Governors decided to change its rule, lowering the amount of games a team could broadcast on a superstation from 25 to 20. At the same time, teams could televise up to half (41) of their regular season games on local television stations located in their home territory. Most teams would do this because they were able to keep 100% of the revenues from these local deals. Games broadcast on a local superstation counted against this 41-game limit.

In 1990, the Chicago Bulls and WGN sued the NBA, claiming that the reduction from 25 to 20 games was a restraint on the team's ability to broadcast its own games and thus violated section 1 of the Sherman Act (*Chicago Professional Sports Limited Partnership v. NBA*, 1991). The NBA argued that its superstation rules were exempt from antitrust scrutiny under the Sports Broadcasting Act. The court disagreed, finding that only agreements sold by the league (and not an individual team) were exempt under the act and that under a rule of reason analysis the policy was an unreasonable restraint. Among other arguments, the NBA argued that the rule was necessary to protect other teams and their local broadcasts; however, the court explained that the antitrust laws protect competition and not individual competitors like the NBA teams, and so this justification was not enough. The U.S. Court of Appeals for the Seventh Circuit agreed, finding that the Bulls and WGN would suffer irreparable harm as a result of the policy and that the NBA's justifications did not outweigh this harm (1992).

League Versus Team

Leagues also have many rules that govern team owners. Leagues argue that the rules they put in place governing ownership are necessary to maintain financial stability, to improve or maintain the league's image, or to protect the product the league is trying to put forth. Most leagues can be considered joint ventures because the teams that make up the league come together in the league entity so that they can undertake certain economic activities together, such as sharing revenues and expenses, negotiating with the players union on terms and conditions of employment, and forming joint broadcasting agreements. The rules that leagues put in place usually are meant to promote the development of the league as a whole.

Some leagues' rules have become the subject of antitrust litigation because of accusations that the rules are too restrictive. Rules preventing franchise relocation have faced the strongest challenges. Leagues create limits on franchise relocation for several reasons but primarily to protect the overall league product and to protect individual owners from losing revenues when a competing team moves into their geographic area. Often teams want to relocate because they seek stronger stadium or arena deals that will provide them with more revenue, and sometimes a new ownership group buys the team and wants to move it to a new city. All owners in a particular league must unanimously agree to allow a member team to relocate. As a result of these rules, in the NFL, for example, no teams were allowed to relocate from 1963 until the 1980s. However, one franchise owner would change these restrictive rules forever.

In 1976, the NFL's owners approved the move of the Los Angeles Rams to Anaheim. The Los Angeles Memorial Coliseum Commission immediately sought to replace the team with a new or existing franchise. At the same time, Al Davis, the owner of the Oakland Raiders, had reached an impasse in negotiations for a new lease with the Oakland Coliseum. As a result, he wanted to relocate to Los Angeles. Rule 4.3 of the NFL's constitution required that if a team wanted to move to the home territory of another team (a 75-mile [120-km] radius surrounding the home team), in this case the Rams, unanimous consent of the owners was required. In 1980, the owners voted unanimously against the move.

As a result of this vote, the coliseum commission sued the NFL, alleging that the franchise relocation rule violated section 1 of the Sherman Act (*Los Angeles Memorial Coliseum Commission v. NFL*, 1984). Analyzing the rule under the rule of reason, the court found that the NFL's rule restricting franchise movement was anticompetitive because it gave each team a virtual monopoly in its home territory, and the league could not show that the Raiders' move would harm the league in any way. Therefore, the Raiders were allowed to move, the team was awarded $11.5 million, and the coliseum commission was awarded $4.6 million (both tripled under the Clayton Act).

Although the case was in the Ninth Circuit and did not affect all jurisdictions throughout the United States, after this decision several leagues realized that they could not stop franchise relocation and modified their rules. In the NFL alone, six teams have moved since 1984 (Colts from Baltimore to Indianapolis; Cardinals from St. Louis to Phoenix; Raiders back to Oakland; Rams from Anaheim to St. Louis; Browns to Baltimore, becoming the Ravens; and the Oilers to Nashville, becoming the Titans). See table 10.3 for a list of additional team relocations.

Table 10.3   Professional Sports Team Relocations Since 1950

Year	Franchise	New location and name
Major League Baseball		
1953	Boston Braves	Milwaukee Braves
1954	St. Louis Browns	Baltimore Orioles
1955	Philadelphia Athletics	Kansas City Athletics
1958	Brooklyn Dodgers	Los Angeles Dodgers
1958	New York Giants	San Francisco Giants
1961	Washington Senators	Minnesota Twins
1966	Los Angeles Angels	California (Anaheim) Angels
1966	Milwaukee Braves	Atlanta Braves
1968	Kansas City Athletics	Oakland Athletics
1970	Seattle Pilots	Milwaukee Brewers
1972	Washington Senators II	Texas Rangers
2005	Montreal Expos	Washington Nationals
National Football League		
1961	Los Angeles Chargers (AFL)	San Diego Chargers
1963	Dallas Texans (AFL)	Kansas City Chiefs
1983	Oakland Raiders	Los Angeles Raiders
1984	Baltimore Colts	Indianapolis Colts
1988	St. Louis Cardinals	Phoenix Cardinals
1995	Los Angeles Raiders	Oakland Raiders
1995	Los Angeles Rams	St. Louis Rams
1997	Cleveland Browns	Baltimore Ravens
1997	Houston Oilers	Tennessee Titans
National Basketball Association		
1951	Tri Cities Hawks	Milwaukee Hawks
1955	Milwaukee Hawks	St. Louis Hawks
1957	Fort Wayne Pistons	Detroit Pistons

In 2001, many small-market MLB teams could not compete with large-market teams that received higher revenues from amenities including club seats and luxury boxes and were thus able to pay higher player salaries. Because some of the smallest-revenue teams could not afford salaries demanded by quality players, MLB voted in favor of contracting from 30 down to 28 teams following the 2002 season. MLB never specified exactly which teams were facing the prospect of **contraction;** however, the Florida Marlins, Tampa Bay Devil Rays, and Minnesota Twins all feared that they would be targeted.

contraction—Measures that would be taken to decrease the size of a professional sports league or organization.

In response, the attorney general of Florida issued civil investigative demands to MLB, Commissioner Bud Selig, and the Devil Rays and Marlins under his statutory authority to investigate possible violations of the antitrust

Year	Franchise	New location and name
1957	Rochester Royals	Cincinnati Royals
1960	Minneapolis Lakers	Los Angeles Lakers
1962	Philadelphia Warriors	San Francisco Warriors
1963	Chicago Bullets	Baltimore Bullets
1963	Syracuse Nationals	Philadelphia 76ers
1968	St. Louis Hawks	Atlanta Hawks
1971	San Diego Rockets	Houston Rockets
1971	San Francisco Warriors	Oakland Warriors
1972	Cincinnati Royals	Kansas City Kings
1973	Baltimore Bullets	Washington Bullets
1973	Dallas Chaparrals	San Antonio Spurs
1978	Buffalo Braves	San Diego Clippers
1979	New Orleans Jazz	Utah Jazz
1984	San Diego Clippers	Los Angeles Clippers
2001	Vancouver Grizzlies	Memphis Grizzlies
2002	Charlotte Hornetts	New Orleans Hornets
2008	Seattle Sonics	Oklahoma City Thunder
National Hockey League		
1976	California Golden Seals (Oakland)	Cleveland Barons
1976	Kansas City Scouts	Colorado Rockies (Denver)
1978	Cleveland Barons	Minnesota North Stars
1980	Atlanta Flames	Calgary Flames
1982	Colorado Rockies	New Jersey Devils
1993	Minnesota North Stars	Dallas Stars
1995	Quebec Nordiques	Colorado Avalanche (Denver)
1996	Winnipeg Jets	Phoenix Coyotes
1997	Hartford Whalers	Carolina Hurricanes

laws. Relying on the long line of earlier cases on the antitrust exemption, the court denied the attorney general's claims because the decision to force particular teams to cease operations (i.e., the decision to contract them) and the structure of the league itself were essential features of the business of baseball and therefore were exempt.

No teams were ever contracted, because MLB and the players union reached an agreement putting off any discussion of contraction until the agreement's expiration in 2006 and contraction was not discussed in the most recent collective bargaining negotiations. It remains to be seen whether MLB will again seek to contract teams that it deems to not be financially viable.

League Versus League

Other litigation has focused on competition between professional sports leagues themselves. A new league usually faces many challenges when it attempts to compete with an established league for players, facilities, or television revenues. As a result of these challenges, the new league may end up suing the established league, claiming that its conduct violates the antitrust laws. The first litigation in this area was the *Federal Baseball* decision that led to MLB's exemption from antitrust laws, as already discussed. Since that time, new leagues have repeatedly sued established leagues under section 2 of the Sherman Act, claiming that the established leagues maintain illegal monopolies over their particular sports and that they use anticompetitive methods to maintain these monopolies. Remember, to sustain a claim under section 2, a plaintiff league must show that the established league has monopoly power in a relevant market and that the established league has engaged in anticompetitive conduct that maintained this monopoly power.

Historically, most professional team sports in the United States have maintained only one viable league. Although there have been many competitors over the years, none have successfully challenged the dominance of the NBA, NFL, NHL, or MLB. Several factors may explain this, including the sports fans' preference for one champion at the highest level of competition in each professional sport. In addition, upstart leagues often quickly fold as a result of financial mismanagement, the inability to generate revenue, or the inability to find suitable facilities to hold their events.

One of the most interesting cases in this area was brought by a competitor to the NFL. From 1983 to 1985, the United States Football League (USFL) played its games in the spring and summer and thus did not compete with the NFL. The USFL debuted with a dozen teams and national television contracts with ABC and ESPN. Eventually the USFL decided to move its season to the fall in direct competition with NFL games but it was unable to secure any national television deals to carry these fall games. In 1984, right before it decided to fold, the USFL sued the NFL, seeking $1.7 billion in damages and claiming that the NFL monopolized professional football and used predatory tactics to limit the ability of the USFL to grow (*USFL v. NFL,* 1988). At the time, the NFL had television deals with all of the major television stations including CBS, ABC, and NBC. In addition, it rotated the Super Bowl among these stations. The USFL claimed that this gave the NFL leverage to ensure that none of these networks would carry USFL games.

Although the jury agreed that the NFL willfully maintained monopoly power in the market for professional football in the United States, its award of $1 to the USFL, even when tripled under the Clayton Act, was no consolation. One of the major reasons that the award was so low was because the jury believed that many of the problems the new league faced were the results of its own management, for instance, deciding to discontinue its spring schedule even though there were national television contracts available for those games. As a result, after three seasons and losses of approximately $200 million, the USFL folded in 1985. In 1990, the USFL was awarded $5.5 million in attorney fees and more than $62,000 in court costs, but by that time the league had long since ceased operations.

Single-Entity Structure

Since the 1970s, some professional sports leagues have attempted to avoid the problems discussed here by claiming that they are single entities. A single entity cannot violate section 1 of the Sherman Act because there is no combination or agreement between two parties, the first element needed for a violation of section 1.

The NFL has used the **single-entity defense** more than any other league. If a league attempts to defend itself against an antitrust claim by using this defense, it must demonstrate that instead of being an organization made up of separate business entities (the teams), it is one business entity itself and the teams merely buy into that entity in some way or another. For instance, in the late 1980s the owner of the New England Patriots attempted to sell a portion of the franchise to the public in order to raise money to pay off debts. He asked the NFL to waive its policy against public ownership so that he could proceed with the sale. The matter was never called for a vote among the owners of all the other teams, because he felt that a vote would have been futile. In 1988, he sold the team for $83.7 million. In 1991, he sued the NFL claiming that the policy against public ownership forced him to sell the team at a fire sale price in order to pay off his debts (*Sullivan v. NFL,* 1994). A jury found that the NFL violated section 1 of the Sherman Act and awarded Sullivan $38 million. This amount was reduced to $17 million, and then because the Clayton Act allows for damages in antitrust cases to be tripled, it was increased to $51 million. The NFL appealed this decision, arguing that its member teams could not conspire with each other in violation of section 1 because they function as a single entity in relation to the public ownership policy. Although the appellate court reversed the verdict because of problems with the admission of evidence before the district court, it found that the single-entity defense did not apply. Specifically, NFL teams compete in many ways on and off the field for fan support,

single-entity defense—A defense to an antitrust claim; a party using this defense must demonstrate that instead of being an organization made up of separate business entities, it is one business entity itself and so it cannot be a combination or conspiracy in restraint of trade as required to violate the antitrust laws.

players, coaches, local broadcast revenues, and ticket sales, and therefore the teams were not acting as a single entity.

In the 1990s, several new professional team sports leagues attempted to structure themselves as single entities, including the American Basketball League (ABL), the Women's National Basketball Association (WNBA), and Major League Soccer (MLS).

Soon after MLS was formed, MLS players contested the league's structure as a single entity. In MLS, the league office owned all player contracts, controlled all player salaries under a salary cap, and mandated transfer fees for player transactions among teams. To ensure that they could contest this conduct, the players refused to create a players union because a union would have had to negotiate with management over terms and conditions of employment for all players. As a result, the league could not argue that its conduct was protected under the labor exemption previously discussed. The players then sued, claiming that the restrictive player restraints embodied in the salary cap and transfer system violated the antitrust laws (*Fraser v. Major League Soccer,* 2000).

MLS openly admitted that it had created this structure in an attempt to keep salaries and other costs down so that the league could develop a strong base of financial viability in its early years of operation. The league office specifically referred to the single-entity structure as a way to avoid antitrust scrutiny, create evenly matched teams, and capitalize on the ability to place local favorites in areas where they could help the team build a fan base. MLS also pointed to other factors showing that the league was a single entity; for example, all players were employees of the league and not a specific team, MLS could place marquee players on certain teams and had to approve of all other player transactions, individual teams did not own their own logos, and profits and losses were shared in a way similar to the operation of a single corporation. The court agreed with MLS, finding that it was a single corporate entity, and therefore it could not violate section 1 of the Sherman Act.

This decision is very important because it implies that new sports leagues that are set up in a way that is substantially similar to MLS will also be single entities protected from antitrust scrutiny. This allows new leagues to keep better control over their costs, especially over player salaries. Several new leagues, including the Major Indoor Lacrosse League, the Women's United Soccer Association, and the Continental Indoor Soccer League, have been formed following this model. As a result, although they may still be subject to review as illegal monopolies under section 2 of the Sherman Act, their single-entity status may protect them from review under other antitrust laws.

Of course, all of this depends on whether the league stays true to its single-entity structure. Even in MLS things can change. In 2003 the players unionized, forming the Major League Soccer Players Union, and by 2004 they had signed a collective bargaining agreement with MLS that will last until 2010. As a result, although the league may be able to use the labor exemption to protect itself from antitrust scrutiny, it should no longer be able to use the single-entity defense to impose whatever terms and conditions of employment on the players that management prefers.

Application to Individual Performer Sports

The application of antitrust laws extends beyond the five major professional sports leagues discussed in the prior section. Professional boxing, tennis, golf, bowling, and automobile racing have all been found to be businesses engaged in interstate commerce. As explained earlier in this chapter, section 1 of the Sherman Act provides that such businesses engaged in interstate commerce can be sued for alleged violations of the antitrust laws.

Governing bodies of individual performer sports, such as the Professional Golf Association (PGA) Tour or the Professional Bowlers Association (PBA), bring together the best athletes at their particular sport and often organize events for these athletes. If an athlete is excluded from membership in these organizations, there are no realistic alternatives for her to make a living playing her sport. The focus of litigation in this area is on whether the necessary restraints on membership are legitimate business activities or suppress competition and violate the antitrust laws. For example, a professional golfer who was denied entrance to PGA Tour events because of repeated poor performance sued the PGA, claiming that the Tour's eligibility rule unreasonably restrained trade in violation of the Sherman Act. Finding that the purpose of the eligibility performance standards was to maintain a high quality of competition and that the rules were reasonably designed to accomplish this purpose, the court found that they were reasonable and did not violate the antitrust laws (*Deesen v. Professional Golfers' Assoc.*, 1966). In general, eligibility restrictions for individual sports leagues or associations have not been found to violate the antitrust laws because they promote the quality of the competition with the particular leagues, ensure uniformity of the rules, and assist in the orderly scheduling of tournaments and other events.

AP Photo/Norwich Bulletin, Khoi Ton

Eligibility restrictions enforced by governing bodies for individual sports may not violate the antitrust laws if the restrictions promote the quality of the competition, ensure uniformity of the rules, and assist in the orderly scheduling of tournaments and other events.

✕ Application to University Sports

University athletics have seen their share of antitrust litigation. These cases predominantly involve the National Collegiate Athletic Association (NCAA).

The NCAA is a membership organization made up of universities that agree to abide by its rules. However, individual universities, players, coaches, and others often disagree with the application or impact of a particular rule and sue the NCAA, claiming that the rule itself violates the Sherman Act. One of goals of the NCAA is to preserve the amateur nature of intercollegiate athletics as a part of the educational process in university and to ensure that its member schools compete on a level playing field. To meet this goal, the NCAA has created extensive rules restricting the nature of participation in intercollegiate athletics. These rules include limits on recruiting, academic eligibility requirements, financial aid standards, agent regulations, amateurism rules, and a myriad of other topics. At the same time, revenues in university athletics have sky rocketed. As these revenues have increased, the NCAA is often faced with criticism that its commitment to amateurism is nothing but a sham and so the rules are illegitimate.

Regardless of these arguments, schools see an incredible financial value in being part of the NCAA and succeeding within intercollegiate athletics. Many see no alternative to membership within the NCAA, and so when NCAA rules negatively affect them, they sue, claiming that the rules violate the antitrust laws. Until the 1980s, the NCAA was able to defend itself from antitrust claims because most courts found that intercollegiate athletics were not commerce as defined by the Sherman Act. In 1984, the Association for Intercollegiate Athletics for Women (AIAW) sued the NCAA, claiming that it unlawfully used its monopoly power in men's university sports to facilitate its entry into women's university sports and force the AIAW out of existence. The court disagreed, finding that schools simply chose to leave the AIAW and join the NCAA because the NCAA provided a superior product (*Association for Intercollegiate Athletics for Women,* 1984). It seemed that the NCAA would continue to avoid antitrust scrutiny, but this was not the case.

✓ In the 1980s, the NCAA's university football television plan set the price for televised Division I games and limited the number of televised games. The College Football Association (CFA) negotiated an independent television contract allowing for more appearances on television for its member schools. In response, the NCAA announced that it would begin to penalize schools that became members of the CFA. The University of Oklahoma and the University of Georgia sued, claiming that the NCAA's television plan violated the Sherman Act (*NCAA v. Board of Regents,* 1984). The Supreme Court agreed, holding that the NCAA's television plan violated the antitrust laws by unreasonably restraining trade and harming consumers by televising fewer football games. The case was the first successful antitrust challenge to the NCAA and its rules. Litigation over NCAA rules only increased in the following years.

Another crucial decision involved NCAA Bylaw 11.02.3, which restricted the earnings of Division I assistant coaches to $16,000. The coaches sued, claiming that the rule was illegal price fixing in violation of the Sherman Act (*Law v. NCAA*, 1998). The NCAA argued that the rule was necessary to help schools keep entry-level coaches, reduce costs to athletic departments, and maintain competitive equity among programs so that no larger school could attract the most talented coaches by paying higher salaries. The U.S. Court of Appeals for the Tenth Circuit disagreed, finding that the rule artificially lowered coaches' salaries and therefore was illegal per se under the Sherman Act. A jury then returned a verdict in favor of the coaches for $22.3 million ($66.9 million if tripled under the Clayton Act). Instead of appealing the decision, the NCAA settled with the coaches by paying $54.5 million.

The NCAA may be subject to scrutiny under the antitrust laws when it acts in a commercial capacity, as it did in *Board of Regents* by restricting the output of television games and in *Law* by restricting coaching salaries. However, rules that are less commercial in nature typically have not been found to violate the antitrust laws. In these types of cases, the NCAA often argues that the particular rules, often dealing with academic eligibility, promote amateur intercollegiate athletic competition. Courts accept the preservation of amateurism as a justification for rules limiting competition among NCAA members for the services of athletes, which reduces the costs of producing university athletics.

Braxton Banks, a fullback at Notre Dame, had a year of university eligibility left when he declared his eligibility for the 1990 NFL draft. After he was not selected in the draft, he attempted to return to university to pursue a graduate degree and still play football. The NCAA's no-draft and no-agent rules barred him from returning to play football at the university level because he had declared himself eligible and signed with an agent. Banks sued, claiming that the NCAA rules violated the antitrust laws (*Banks v. NCAA*, 1992). Agreeing that the rules were necessary to maintain competition among amateur students pursuing their education, the court held that the rules did not violate the Sherman Act.

Most courts would agree that athletic participation is a valuable part of the educational process. Therefore, NCAA rules that promote amateurism for university student-athletes are typically upheld because they promote university sports as part of the educational process for the student.

Summary

The antitrust laws are intended to promote competition and efficiency in the market and to protect consumers from the monopoly power exhibited by some businesses. In sports, these laws have been used by players and players associations to get rid of league rules related to free agency, player drafts, and salary caps that players believe limit their ability to receive high salaries and their freedom to play for the team they choose. However, leagues and teams have been able to defend these restraints on players because much of what the leagues and teams do is shielded from the antitrust laws by various exemptions. In the end, in professional sports, teams and players negotiate over the terms of employment and come to a collective bargaining agreement that includes free agency rules and player salary caps.

Although much of the discussion about antitrust law has focused on professional team sports, individual performer and university sports can also be subject to review under these laws. Whenever one party undertakes some sort of activity to restrict competition and efficiency in the marketplace, it may be subject to review under the antitrust laws.

Sport administrators need to understand the antitrust laws in order to keep their league, association, team, event, or other organization within the law and to protect their organization in the event another individual or group tries to change an agreement because of its potential negative affects on competition.

DISCUSSION QUESTIONS

1. Why should sport administrators understand the impact that the antitrust laws have sport?

2. Why do professional sports leagues find it important to set rules for drafting players?

3. Why do players want to become free agents?

4. Why do some professional sports leagues impose salary caps on their players?

5. Why is Major League Baseball the only professional sports league that has an exemption from the antitrust laws?

6. What is the difference between an antitrust exemption and a labor exemption and how does that affect the way a professional sports league operates?

7. How is the NCAA subject to the antitrust laws?

MOOT COURT CASE

A group of Texas businessmen decided to start a new sports league to compete with the NBA. The league was called the Professional University Players Basketball Association (PUPBA) and enlisted players from 4-year universities who either currently played in the National Basketball Development League (NBDL) or on professional teams in the United States or Europe or were undrafted, talented players who wanted to play in a new league at the next level. Teams would be formed that consisted only of players who had formerly played for a university. The idea was a hit and drew wide-based fan support from those with ties to the universities represented by the various teams. Sixteen teams were formed and play began in 2016. The concept was so appealing that some players left their NBA and European teams to play for this new league. The new league began play in the summer so as not to compete with the NBA and university basketball. The league debuted with national television contracts with CBS and ESPN. Eventually the league decided to extend its season to include both the spring and early summer in direct competition with both NBA regular season games and the NBA finals. Given the NBA's strength and position in the market, however, PUPBA lost its existing television contracts and was unable to secure any new national television deals to carry these spring games. At the time, the NBA had television deals with all of the major television stations including ESPN, TNT, CBS, ABC, and NBC. In addition, it rotated the NBA playoffs among these stations. The PUPBA claimed that this gave the NBA leverage to ensure that none of these networks would carry PUPBA games. The new league experienced extreme financial hardships, and right before it decided to fold, PUPBA sued the NBA seeking $2 billion in damages and claimed that the NBA monopolized professional basketball and used predatory tactics to limit the ability of the PUBPA to grow.

REFERENCES

2008 Green Bay Packers Tickets (n.d.). www. packers.com/tickets/packer_fan_tours.

57A American Jurisprudence § 227, 2005.

57A American Jurisprudence 2nd § 427, 2003.

57A American Jurisprudence 2nd § 429, 2005.

A Policy Interpretation: Title IX and Intercollegiate Athletics, 44 Fed. Reg. 71,413-71,423 (1979).

Access Now et al. v. South Florida Stadium Corp. et al., 161 F.Supp.2d 1357 (S.D. Fla. 2001).

Adler v. Duval County School Board, 250 F.3d 1330 (11th Cir. 2001), *cert. denied*, 534 U.S. 1065 (2001).

Amended and Restated Lease Agreement by and Between Southeast Wisconsin Professional Baseball Park District, and Milwaukee Brewers Baseball Club, Limited Partnership (January 1, 2004).

Amended and Restated Non-Relocation Agreement by and Among Southeast Wisconsin Professional Baseball Park District, State of Wisconsin and Milwaukee Brewers Baseball Club, Limited Partnership (January 1, 2004).

Americans with Disabilities Act of 1990 (ADA), 42 U.S.C. § 12101 et. seq. (2008).

Anderson v. Little League Baseball Inc., 794 F. Supp. 342 (Az. Dist. Ct. 1992).

Anti-cybersquatting Consumer Protection Act, 15 U.S.C. § 1125(d) (2008).

Appenzeller, H. & Seidler, T. L. (1998). Emergency action plan: Expecting the unexpected. In Appenzeller, H. (ed.). *Risk Management in Sport: Issues and Strategies* (pp. 297-309). Durham, NC: Carolina Academic Press.

Arbitration of Messersmith, Grievance No. 75-27, Dec. No. 29 (1975).

Arlosoroff v. NCAA, 746 F.2d 1019 (4th Cir. 1984).

Association for Intercollegiate Athletics for Women, 735 F.2d 577 (D.C. Cir. 1984).

Athletics, 34 C.F.R. 106.41 (2008).

Averill, Jr v. Luttrell, 311 S.W.2d 812 (Tenn. App. 1957).

Avila v. Citrus Community Coll. District, 111 Cal. App. 4th 811, 4 Cal.Rptr.3d 264 (2003).

Baltimore Orioles, Inc. v. Major League Baseball Players Assoc., 805 F.2d 663 (7th Cir. 1986), *cert. denied*, 480 U.S. 941 (1987).

Banks v. NCAA, 977 F.2d 1081 (7th Cir. 1992).

Bethel School District v. Fraser, 478 U.S. 675 (1986).

Board of Regents v. Roth, 408 U.S. 564 (1972). Brentwood Academy v. Tennessee Secondary School Athletic Association, 531 U.S. 288 (2001).

Boston Athletic Association v. Sullivan, 867 F.2d 22 (1st Cir. 1989).

Boucher v. Syracuse University, 1998 WL 167296 (D.C. NY 1998), *motion granted*, 50 Fed. Appx. 643 (4th Cir. 2002).

Brown v. Pro Football, Inc., 116 S.Ct. 2116 (1996).

C.B.C. Distribution & Marketing, Inc., v. MLB Advanced Media, 443 F.Supp. 2d 1077 (E.D. Mo. 2006), *affirmed*, 505 F.3d 818 (8th Cir. 2007).

California State University, Fresno Public Infractions Report. (2003, September 10). NCAA Division I Committee on Infractions. Retrieved September 2, 2008, from http://www2.ncaa.org/portal/media_and_events/press_room/2006/april/20060426_fresnostate_infractions_rls.html.

Cannon v. Univ. of Chicago, 441 U.S. 677 (1979).

Cardtoons, L.C. v. Major League Baseball Players Assoc., 95 F.3d 959 (10th Cir. 1996).

Carpenter, L.J., & Acosta, R.V. (2008). Women in intercollegiate sport: A longitudinal, national study: Twenty nine year update:

1977-2008. http://webpages.charter.net/womeninsport/2008%20Summary%20Final.pdf.

Carper, D.L., Mietus, N.J., & West, B.W. (2000). *Understanding the law* (3rd ed.). Cincinnati, OH: West.

Chicago Professional Sports Limited Partnership v. NBA, 754 F. Supp. 1336 (N. D. Ill. 1991), *aff'd,* 961 F.2d 667 (7th Cir. 1992).

Chicago Professional Sports Limited Partnership v. NBA, 808 F.Supp. 646 (1992).

Chilingirian v. Boris, 882 F.2d 200 (6th Cir. 1989).

Civil Rights Act of 1964, 78 Stat. 253; 42 U.S.C. 2000e.

Civil Rights Restoration Act, 20 USCS § 1687 (2008).

Clarett v. NFL, 306 F. Supp. 2d 379 (S.D.N.Y. 2004), *reversed & remanded,* 369 F.3d 124 (2d Cir. 2004).

Clayton Antitrust Act, 15 U.S.C. § 12-27 (2008).

Clients. (n.d.). *Rosenhaus sports athletes.* www.rosenhaussports.com/athletes.php.

Codd v. Velger, 429 U.S. 624 (1977).

Cohen v. Brown Univ., 101 F.3d 155 (1st Cir. 1996).

Cohen v. Brown Univ., 809 F.Supp. 978 (D. RI 1992), *aff'd,* 991 F.2d 888 (1st Cir. 1993).

Cohen, C., & Sterba, J.P. (2003). *Affirmative action and racial preference.* Oxford, UK: Oxford University Press.

Coleman v. Western Michigan University, 336 N.W.2d 224 (Mich. App. 1983).

Connaughton, D.P., Spengler, J.O. & Bennett, G.B. (2001). Crisis planning and management for physical activity programs. *Journal of Health, Physical Education, Recreation and Dance, 72* (7), 27-29.

Cooper, M.A., Holle, R.L., & Lopez, R.E. (1999). Recommendations for lightning safety. *Journal of American Medical Association, 282*(12), 1132-1133.

Copyright Act, 17 U.S.C. §§ 101, et seq. (2008).

Costa v. Boston Red Sox Baseball, 809 N.E.2d 1090 (2004).

Cotten, D.J., & Cotten, M.B. (2005). *Waivers & releases of liability* (5th ed.). Statesboro, GA: Sport Risk Consulting.

Curt Flood Act, 15 U.S.C. § 26(b) (2008).

Dallas Cowboys Cheerleaders, Inc. v. Pussycat Cinema, Ltd., 604 F.2d 200 (2nd Cir. 1979).

Daniels v. School Board of Brevard County, 985 F.Supp. 1458 (M. Dist. Fla. 1997).

Davis v. Monroe County Board of Education, 526 U.S. 629 (1999).

Davis, T. (2007). United States. In R.C.R. Siekmann, R. Parish, R. Branco Martins, & J.W. Soek (Eds.), *Players' agents worldwide: Legal aspects* (pp. 655-691). The Hague, The Netherlands: T.M.C. Asser Instituut.

Day v. Ouachita Parish School Board et al., 823 So.2d 1039 (La. App. 2 Cir. 2002).

Deesen v. Professional Golfers' Assoc., 358 F.2d 165 (9th Cir. 1966), *cert. denied,* 385 U.S. 846 (1966).

Definitions, 28 C.F.R. §36.104 (2008).

Denver Rockets v. All-Pro Mgt., Inc., 325 F.Supp. 1049 (C.D. Cal. 1971).

Drape, J. (2005, October 30). Increasingly, football's playbooks call for prayer. *NYTimes.com.* www.nytimes.com/2005/10/30/sports/football/30religion.html?pagewanted=1&ei=5090&en=2817f77b92ac81fc&ex=1288324800&partner=rssuserland&emc=rss.

Dream Team Collectibles, Inc. v. NBA Properties, Inc., 958 F.Supp. 1401 (E.D. Mo. 1997).

Equal Pay Act, 29 U.S.C. §206(d) (2008).

Equity in Athletics Disclosure Act, Pub. Law 105-244 (1998).

Fantasy Sports Properties, Inc. v. Sportsline. com, Inc., 287 F.3d 1108 (Fed. Cir. 2002).

Farber, D.C., & Cross, P.A. (Eds.). (2008). *Entertainment industry contracts.* Available on LexisNexis Total Research System, www.lexisnexis.com.

Federal Baseball Club v. National League, 259 U.S. 200 (1922).

Federal Trademark Act, 15 U.S.C. § 1051, et seq. (2008).

Federal Trademark Dilution Act, 15 U.S.C. § 1125(c) (2008).

Feinsand, M., & Madden, B. (2007, November 15). Alex works to stay a Yankee. Deal expected to be reached within 48 hours. *Daily News* (New York), p. 54.

Fidelity Leasing Corp. v. Dun & Bradstreet, Inc., 494 F.Supp. 786 (E.D. Pa. 1980).

Financial Assistance, 34 C.F.R. 106.37(c) (2008).

Flood v. Kuhn, 407 U.S. 258 (1972).

Franklin v. Gwinnett County Public Schools, 503 U.S. 60 (1992).

Fraser v. Major League Soccer, 97 F.Supp.2d 130 (D. Mass. 2000), *aff'd,* 284 F.3d 47 (1st Cir. 2002).

Gebser v. Lago Vista Independent School District, 524 U.S. 274 (1998).

Gillum v. City of Kerrville, 3 F.3d 117 (5th Cir. 1993).

Goss v. Lopez, 419 U.S. 565 (1975).

Green v. City of Hamilton Hous. Auth., 937 F.2d 1561 (11th Cir. 1991).

Green v. Konawa Independent School District, 105 P.3d 840 (Okla. Civ. App. 2005).

Greenberg, M.J. (2008, April-June). College athletics—Chasing the big bucks. *For The Record, 19*(2), 6-10.

Greenberg, M.J., & Gray, J.T. (1998). *Sports law practice.* (2nd ed.). Charlottesville, VA: Lexis Law.

Gregory, W.A. (2001). *The law of agency and partnership.* (3rd ed.). St. Paul, MN: West Group.

Grove City College et al. v. Bell, 465 U.S. 555 (1984).

Grutter v. Bollinger, 539 U.S. 306 (2003).

Hackbart v. Cincinnati Bengals, Inc., 601 F.2d 516 (10th Cir. 1979).

Haelan Laboratories, Inc. v. Topps Chewing Gum, Inc., 202 F.2d 866 (2nd Cir. 1953), *cert. denied,* 346 U.S. 816 (1953).

Harjo et al. v. Pro-Football, Inc., 50 U.S.P.Q.(2d) (BNA) 1705 (1999), *rev'd, summary judgment granted in part, summary judgment denied in part,* 284 F. Supp.2d 96 (D.C. Cir. 2003).

Hilliard & Taylor v. Black, 125 F.Supp.2d 1071 (N.D. Fla. 2000).

Holle, R.L., & Lopez, R.E. (1999, October). Updated recommendations for lightning safety—1998. *Bulletin of the American Meteorological Society, 80*(10), 2035-2041.

Indiana University. (2007, April 20). Employment agreement between the Trustees of Indiana University and Kelvin Sampson.

Jackson v. Birmingham Board of Educ., 544 U.S. 167 (2005).

Jennings v. Wentzville R-IV School Dist., 397 F.3d 1118 (8th Cir. 2005).

Katz, A. (2008, May 13). Mayo denies ex-confidant's claims of gifts, including TV, cash. *ESPN.com.* http://sports.espn.go.com/ncb/news/story?id=3390695.

Keeton, W.P. (1984). *Prosser and Keeton on the law of torts.* St. Paul, MN: West.

Kelly v. Board of Trustees, 35 F.3d 265 (7th Cir. 1994).

Kiely, T.F., & Ottily, B.L. (2006). *Understanding product liability law* (3rd ed.). Newark, NJ: Lexis Nexis.

Landow v. School Board of Brevard County, 132 F.Supp. 2d 958 (M.Dist. Fla. 2000).

Lapchick, R. (2007). *2006-07 racial and gender report card.* Orlando, FL: Devos Sport Business Management Program.

Lapchick, R., & Martin, S. (2008, April 15). *The 2008 racial and gender report card: Major League Baseball.* Orlando, FL: Devos Sport Business Management Program.

Law v. NCAA, 5 F.Supp.2d 921 (D. Kans. 1998).

Leakas v. Columbia Country Club, 831 F.Supp. 1231 (Md. 1993).

Lease Agreement by and Among Green Bay-Brown County Professional Football Stadium District, City of Green Bay, and Green Bay Packers, Inc. (January 1, 2001).

Lee v. Weisman, 505 U.S. 577 (1992).

Lemon v. Kurtzman, 403 U.S. 602 (1971).

Levert v. University of Illinois, 857 So.2d 611 (La.App. 2003).

Lockhart, W.B., Kamisar, Y., Choper, J.H., & Shiffrin, S.H. (1991). *Constitutional rights and liberties* (7th ed.). St. Paul, MN: West.

Los Angeles Memorial Coliseum Commission v. NFL, 726 F.2d 1381 (9th Cir. 1984).

Louisiana High School Athletic Ass'n v. St. Augustine High School, 396 F.2d 224 (1968).

Lowe v. California League of Professional Baseball, 65 Cal.Rptr.2d 105 (Cal. App. 4 Dist. 1997).

Ludtke vs. Kuhn, 461 F.Supp. 86 (S.D.N.Y. 1978).

Ludwig v. Board of Trustees of Ferris State University, 123 F.3d 404 (6th Cir. 1997).

Lynch v. Donnelly, 465 U.S. 668 (1984).

Mackey v. NFL, 543 F.2d 606 (8th Cir. 1976).

Mania v. Kaminski, 412 N.E.2d 651 (Ill. App. 1 1980).

Mann, R.A., & Roberts, B.S. (2007). *Essentials of business law and the legal environment* (9th ed.). Mason, OH: West.

March Madness Athletic Assoc., LLC v. Netfire Inc., 120 Fed. Appx. 540 (5th Cir. 2005).

Martin v. PGA Tour, Inc., 984 F.Supp. 1320 (D. Ore. 1998), *aff'd,* 204 F.3d 994 (9th Cir. 2000), *aff'd,* PGA Tour, Inc. v. Martin, 532 U.S. 661 (2001).

Mason v. Minnesota State High School League, 2004 U.S. Dist. Lexis 13865 (D. Minn. 2004).

McCormick v. School District of Mamoroneck, 370 F.3d 275 (2nd Cir. 2004).

McMillen, J.D. (2007). Game, event, and sponsorship contracts. In D.J. Cotten & J.T. Wolohan (Eds.). *Law for recreation and sports managers* (4th ed., pp. 398-408). Dubuque, IA: Kendall Hunt.

Miller, W.S., & Anderson, P.M. (2001). *Major league leases: An overview of major league facility leases and how they are negotiated.* Mequon, WI: Front Office Publications.

Menora v. Illinois High School Association, 683 F.2d 1030 (7th Cir. 1982).

Mercer v. Duke Univ., 190 F.3d 643 (4th Cir. 1999).

Miami Univ. Wrestling Club v. Miami Univ., 302 F.3d 608 (6th Cir. 2002).

Michigan's Worker's Disability Compensation Act, MCL § 418.161(1)(b), MSA § 17.237(161) (1)(b) (1980).

Miller, R.L., Cross, F.B., & Jentz, G.A. (2005). *Essentials of the legal environment.* Mason, OH: West.

Moore v. University of Notre Dame, 22 F.Supp. 2d 896 (N.D. Ind. 1998).

Morris Comm. Corp. v. PGA Tour, 117 F. Supp.2d 1322 (M. Dist. Fla. 2000).

Morris Comm. Corp. v. PGA Tour, 235 F.Supp.2d 1269 (M. Dist. Fla. 2002).

Muhammad Ali v. Playgirl, Inc., 447 F.Supp. 723 (S.D.N.Y. 1978).

Murphy v. University of Cincinnati, 72 Fed. Appx. 288 (6th Cir. 2003).

Nabozny v. Barnhill, 334 N.E.2d 258 (Ill.App. 1975).

National Basketball Association. (2005, July). *Collective bargaining agreement 2005-2011.*

National Collegiate Athletic Association (n.d.). 2007 Membership Report. http://web1.ncaa. org/web_video/membership_report/index1. html.

National Collegiate Athletic Association. (2001). NCAA guideline 1d: Lightning safety. *2001-2002 NCAA Sports Medicine Handbook,*12-14.

National Collegiate Athletic Association. (2007, July). *2007-2008 NCAA division I manual.* Indianapolis: NCAA.

National Collegiate Athletic Association. (2008, February 8). Notice of allegations to the President of Indiana University, Bloomington. http://assets.espn.go.com/media/pdf/080213/ ncb_noticeofallegations.pdf.

National Collegiate Athletic Association. (NCAA) (2007, August 1). *2007-2008 NCAA Division I manual.* Indianapolis, IN: NCAA.

National Conference of Commissioners on Uniform State Laws (NCCUSL). (2000). Uniform Athlete Agents Act. www.law.upenn.edu/bll/ archives/ulc/uaaa/aaa1130.htm.

National Federation of State High School Associations. (2006, September 18). Participation in high school sports increases again: Confirms NFHS commitment to stronger leadership. www.nfhs.org/web/2006/09/participation_in_high_school_sports_increases_ again_confirms_nf.aspx.

National Hockey League & Lemieux Group Lp. v. Domain for Sale, Case No. D2001-1185 (WIPO Arbitration and Mediation Center, December 6, 2001).

National Letter of Intent. (n.d.). Text of the National Letter of Intent. www.national-letter. org/guidelines/nli_text.php.

National Wrestling Coaches Assoc. v. Department of Educ., 361 U.S. App. D.C. 257 (D.C. 2004).

NBA v. Motorola, 105 F.3d 841 (2nd Cir. 1997).

NCAA Executive Committee. (2005, April). NCAA Executive Committee Resolution. www1.ncaa.org/membership/governance/assoc-wide/executive_committee/ docs/2005/2005-04/s10_titleIX-revised.htm.

NCAA v. Board of Regents, 468 U.S. 85 (1984).

NCAA v. Smith, 525 U.S. 459 (1999).

NCAA v. Tarkanian, 488 U.S. 179 (1988).

Neary v. Northern Pacific Railway, 110 P. 226 (Mont.1910).

NFL Players Association (as amended through March, 2007). *NFLPA regulations governing contract advisors.*

NFL v. McBee & Bruno's Inc., 792 F.2d 726 (8th Cir. 1986).

Nondiscrimination on the Basis of Disability by Public Accommodations and in Commercial Facilities, 28 C.F.R. 36, Subpart A (2008).

O'Brien v. The Ohio State University, 2006 Ohio 4737 (Ct. Claims 2006), *affirmed,* 2007 Ohio 4833 (Ct. App. 2007).

Occupational Health and Safety Act, 29 U.S.C. §651, et. seq. (2008).

Office of Civil Rights. (1996). *Clarification of intercollegiate athletics policy guidance: The three-part test.* Washington, DC: U.S. Department of Education.

Office of Civil Rights. (1997). *Sexual harassment guidance: Harassment of students by school employees, other students or third parties.* Washington, DC: U.S. Department of Education.

Office of Civil Rights. (2001). *Revised Sexual Harassment Guidance: Harassment of Students by School Employees, Other Students, or Third Parties.* Washington, DC: U.S. Department of Education.

Office of Civil Rights. (2003). *Further clarification of intercollegiate athletics policy guidance regarding Title IX compliance.* Washington, DC: U.S. Department of Education.

Office of Civil Rights. (2005). *Additional clarification of intercollegiate athletics policy: Three-part test—Part three.* Washington, DC: U.S. Department of Education.

OSH Act of 1970, Public Law 91-596 (1970).

Owen, D.G., Madden, M.S., & Davis, M.J. (2000). *Madden & Owen on product liability* (3rd ed.). Minneapolis, MN: West.

Patent Act, 35 U.S.C. §1, et seq. (2008).

Piazza v. Major League Baseball, 831 F.Supp. 420 (E.D. Pa. 1993).

Pittsburgh Athletic Co. v. KQV Broadcasting Co., 24 F.Supp. 490 (W.D. Pa. 1938).

Powell v. NFL, 930 F.2d 1293 (9th Cir. 1989).

Price v. Univ. of Alabama, 318 F.Supp.2d 1084 (N.D. Ala. 2004).

Pugmire, L. (2008, May 13). Tito Maddox sees himself in O.J. Mayo saga. *Los Angeles Times.* www.latimes.com/sports/la-sp-maddox13-2008may13,0,3380367,print.story.

Regions Bank & Trust v. Stone County Skilled Nursing Facility, Inc., 49 S.W.3d 107 (Ark. 2001).

Rehabilitation Act of 1973, Pub.L.No. 93-112 (1973).

Rehabilitation Act, Pub.L.No. 93-112 (1973).

Restatement (Second) of Contracts (1990).

Restatement (Second) of Torts (1965).

Restatement (Second) of Torts § 432, 1965.

Restatement (Second) of Torts § 500, 1965.

Restatement (Second) of Torts § 907, Comment a, 1965.

Restatement (Third) of Agency (2008).

Restatement (Third) of Torts Restatement (2005).

Roberts v. Colorado State Board of Agriculture, 998 F.2d 824 (10th Cir. 1993).

Robinson, C., & Cole, J. (2006, September 15). Cash and carry. *Yahoo Sports.* http://sports.yahoo.com/ncaaf/news?slug=ys-bushprobe.

San Francisco Arts & Athletics, Inc. v. USOC, 483 U.S. 522 (1987).

Sanchez v. Hillerich & Bradsby Co., *128 Cal. Rptr. 2d. 529 (1992).*

Santa Fe Independent School District v. Doe, 530 U.S. 290 (2000).

School Employees, Other Students, or Third Parties. Washington, DC: U.S. Department of Education.

Schrotenboer, B. (2006, May 24). College athletes caught in tangled Web: Teams' regulations, free speech at odds over Internet usage. *SignOnSanDiego.com.* www.signonsandiego.com/sports/aztecs/20060524-9999-1s24myspace.html.

Scott Boras. (n.d.). *Wikipedia: The free encyclopedia.* http://en.wikipedia.org/wiki/Scott_Boras.

Secretary of Education's Commission on Opportunity in Athletics. (2001). *Open to all: Title IX at thirty.* Washington, DC: Department of Education.

Separation Agreement Between the Trustees of Indiana University and Kelvin Sampson (2008, February 22).

Sharp, L.A., Moorman, A.M., & Claussen, C.L. (2007). *Sports law: A managerial approach.* Scottsdale, AZ: Holcomb Hathaway.

Sherman Antitrust Act, 15 U.S.C. § 1, et al. (2008).

Siegert v. Gilley, 500 U.S. 226 (1991).

Simpson v. University of Colorado, 372 F.Supp.2d 1229 (D. Co. 2005), *reversed & remanded,* 500 F.3d 1170 (10th Cir. 2007).

Smith v. Pro-Football, Inc., 583 F.2d 1173 (D.C. Cir. 1978).

Spengler, J.O., Connaughton, D.P. & Pittman, A. (2006). *Risk management in sport and recreation.* Champaign, IL: Human Kinetics.

Sports Agent Responsibility and Trust Act, 15 U.S.C. §§ 7801-7807 (2008).

Sports Broadcasting Act, 15 U.S.C. § 1291, et seq. (2008).

Stanley v. University of Southern California, 13 F.3d 1313 (9th Cir. 1994), *motions granted,* 1995 U.S. Dist. LEXIS 5026 (C. Dist. CA 1995).

State of North Dakota v. NCAA, Memorandum Decision and Order, Civil No. 06-C-1333 (November 11, 2006).

Steinberg Moorad & Dunn, Inc. v. Dunn, Case No. CV 01-07009 RSWL, 2002 U.S. Dist. LEXIS 26752 (C.D. Cal. 2002).

Stringer v. Minnesota Vikings Football Club, LLC, 705 N.W.2d 746 (Minn. 2005).

Sullivan v. NFL, 34 F.3d 1091 (1st Cir. 1994), *cert. denied,* 513 U.S. 1190 (1995).

Taylor v. Wake Forest University, 16 N.C. App. 117 (Ct. App. NC 1972).

Ted Stevens Olympic and Amateur Sports Act, 36 U.S.C. § 220501, et seq. (2008).

The Americans with Disabilities Act, 42 U.S.C. §12101, et. seq. (2008).

The Americans with Disabilities Act, 42 U.S.C. §12101, et. seq. (2006).

Tiger Woods tops SI's list of top earners for fifth straight year. (2008, June 5). *Street & Smith's SportsBusinessDaily.* www.SportsBusiness-Daily.com.

Tinker v. Des Moines Independent Community School Dist., 383 F.2d 988, *rev.d* 393 U.S. 503 (1969).

Title IX of the Education Amendments of 1972, 20 U.S.C. §1681, et seq. (2008).

Title VII, 42 U.S.C. §2000e-2 (2008).

Toolson v. New York Yankees, 346 U.S. 356 (1953).

U.S. Department of Justice, Civil Rights Division. (2005, September). *A guide to disability rights laws.* www.usdoj.gov/crt/ada/cguide. htm.

U.S. Equal Employment Opportunity Commission/ (1997, October 29). *Enforcement guidance on sex discrimination in the compensation of sports coaches at educational institutions* (EEOC Notice No. 915.002). Washington DC: EEOC.

U.S. General Accounting Office. (2001, March 8). *Intercollegiate athletics: Four-year colleges' experiences adding and discontinuing teams* (GAO-01-297). Washington, DC: GAO.

U.S. Government Accountability Office. (2007, July). *Intercollegiate athletics: Recent trends in teams and participants in national collegiate athletic association sports* (GAO-07-535). Washington, DC: GAP Report to Congressional Addressees.

Uniform Athlete Agents Act, Wis. Stat. § 440.99, et seq. (2008).

Uniform Commercial Code § 2-313.

Uniform Commercial Code, § 1-101, et seq. (2008).

Uniform Law Commissioners. (n.d.). A few facts about the . . . Uniform Athlete Agents Act. http://nccusl.org/Update/uniformact_factsheets/uniformacts-fs-aaa.asp.

United States v. Walters & Bloom, 913 F.2d 388 (7th Cir. 1990).

USADA v. Landis, Case No: 30 190 00847 06 (September 20, 2007).

USFL v. NFL, 842 F.2d 1335 (2d Cir. 1988).

van der Smissen, B. (2003). Elements of negligence. In D.J. Cotten & J.T. Wolohan (Eds.), *Law for recreation and sport managers* (3rd ed., pp. 56-65). Dubuque, IA: Kendall/ Hunt.

Walsh, K.M., Bennett, B., Cooper, M.A., Holle, R.L., Kithil, R., & Lopez, R.E. (2000). National Athletic Trainers' Association position statement: Lightning safety for athletics and recreation. *Journal of Athletic Training, 35*(4), 471-477.

WCVB-TV v. Boston Athletic Association, 926 F.2d 42 (1st Cir. 1991).

Whitley v. Com., 538 S.E.2d 296 (Va. 2000).

Wolohan (Eds.), *Law for recreation and sports managers* (4th ed., pp. 398-408). Dubuque, IA: Kendall Hunt.

Wolohan, J. (2007). United States. In R.C.R. Siekmann, R. Parish, R. Branco Martins, & J.W. Soek (Eds.), *Players' agents worldwide: Legal aspects* (pp. 637-653). The Hague, The Netherlands: T.M.C. Asser Instituut.

Women's Sports Foundation. (2007, June 5). *Who's playing college sports? Trends in participation.* East Meadow, NY: Women's Sports Foundation.

Wong, G.M. (2002). *Essentials of sports law* (3rd ed.). London: Praeger.

Wong, G.M. (2002). *Essentials of sports law* (3rd ed.). Westport, CT: Greenwood.

Wood v. NBA, 809 F.2d 954 (2d. Cir. 1987).

www.nflplayers.com/images/pdfs/Agents/ NFLPA_Regulations_Contract_Advisors.pdf.

INDEX

Note: The italicized *f* and *t* following page numbers refer to figures and tables, respectively.

ABOUT THE AUTHORS

Courtesy of J.O. Spengler

John O. Spengler, JD, PhD, is an associate professor in the College of Health and Human Performance at the University of Florida at Gainesville. Spengler received his law degree from the University of Toledo in 1992 and his doctorate in sport and recreation administration from Indiana University in 1999. Using his experience and education in both of these fields, Spengler has written, taught, and consulted on all aspects of legal issues in sport and recreation safety, risk management, and recreation and sport. He has published numerous articles in scholarly and practitioner journals and three textbooks on sport and recreation legal issues, including a sport law casebook.

Spengler is a member of the American Alliance for Health, Physical Education, Recreation and Dance (AAHPERD) and serves as chair of the AAHPERD, AAPAR Safety, and Risk Management Council.

In 2002, Spengler became a research fellow for AAHPERD. He was also named Teacher of the Year in 2003 by the College of Health and Human Performance at the University of Florida and was twice recognized in Who's Who Among America's Teachers.

Spengler resides in Gainesville. He enjoys many sports and outdoor activities.

Courtesy of Paul Anderson

Paul M. Anderson, JD, is the associate director of the National Sports Law Institute of Marquette University Law School in Milwaukee, Wisconsin. Anderson is also associate director and professor in the sports law program at Marquette University Law School, the most comprehensive and advanced sport law program in the world. He has taught, written, and consulted on all areas of sport law for the past 15 years.

As part of his role in the National Sports Law Institute, Anderson researches all areas of sport law and coordinates newsletters and annual surveys devoted to developments in the field. He has written numerous books, book chapters, articles, and other publications related to various areas of sport law. In his law practice, Anderson has also represented many clients within the sport industry.

Anderson is the editor of the *Journal of Legal Aspects of Sport* and serves as co-faculty advisor to the *Marquette Sports Law Review*. He is also past chair of the Sports & Entertainment Law section of the State Bar of Wisconsin. Anderson is a member of the Sport and Recreation Law Association, the Sports Lawyers Association, American Bar Association's Forum on the Entertainment and Sports Law Industries, and the International Association of Sports Lawyers.

In 2008, Anderson received the Faculty Advisor of the Year Award from the Marquette Moot Court Association. He also received the President's Award from the Sport and Recreation Law Association in 2005 and was awarded the Sports Law Alumnus of the Year Award from the Sports Law Alumni Association of Marquette University Law School in 2003. In 2002 he received a Leadership Award from the Society for the Study of the Legal Aspects of Sport and Physical Activity.

In his free time, Anderson enjoys reading science fiction, writing, watching and participating in various sports, and walking. He and his wife, Kerri, reside in Milwaukee.

Courtesy of Dan Connaughton

Daniel P. Connaughton, EdD, is an associate professor in the College of Health and Human Performance at the University of Florida at Gainesville, where he conducts research and teaches in the area of sport law and risk management. He has written two sport law textbooks in addition to numerous publications on sport and recreation safety, risk management, and associated legal issues.

With an educational background in exercise and sport sciences, Connaughton also holds advanced degrees in recreational studies (University of Florida), physical education (Bridgewater State College), and sport management (Florida State University). In addition to his educational experiences, Connaughton has held management positions in campus and public recreation departments, aquatic facilities, and health and fitness programs. He is a licensed emergency medical technician and frequently serves as a consultant and expert witness in exercise- and sport-related lawsuits.

Connaughton is a member of the American Alliance for Health, Physical Education, Recreation and Dance (AAHPERD); National Strength and Conditioning Association; American Red Cross; American College of Sports Medicine; and the Sport and Recreation Law Association.

In 2004, he received the Teacher of the Year Award from the University of Florida's College of Health and Human Performance. He was named an AAHPERD research fellow in 2001.

In his free time, Connaughton enjoys cycling, running, and traveling. He resides in Gainesville.

Courtesy of Thomas Baker

Thomas A. Baker III, JD, PhD, is an assistant professor in the department of kinesiology in the College of Education at the University of Georgia, where he conducts research and teaches in the area of sport law. He has written two textbooks on the subject of sport and recreation law and has numerous publications on sport law and risk management.

Baker holds advanced degrees in law (Loyola University), sport management (University of Florida), and communications (University of Southern Mississippi). He also completed a comparative law program at the University of Vienna in Austria.

At the University of Florida, Baker was a Charles W. LaPradd PhD fellow. Baker graduated from his law school with honors and in the top 10 percent of his class, earning the distinction of William L. Crowe, Sr., Scholar.

Baker's legal experience consists of clerking with two federal judges and the Constitutional Defense Department at the Alabama Attorney General's Office and practicing commercial litigation at a civil defense firm in New Orleans, Louisiana. He is a member of the Louisiana Bar Association.

In his free time, Baker enjoys watching sports, attending concerts, exercising, and cooking. He and his wife, Susana, reside in Georgia.